CW01670157

THE watercolour WHEEL BOOK

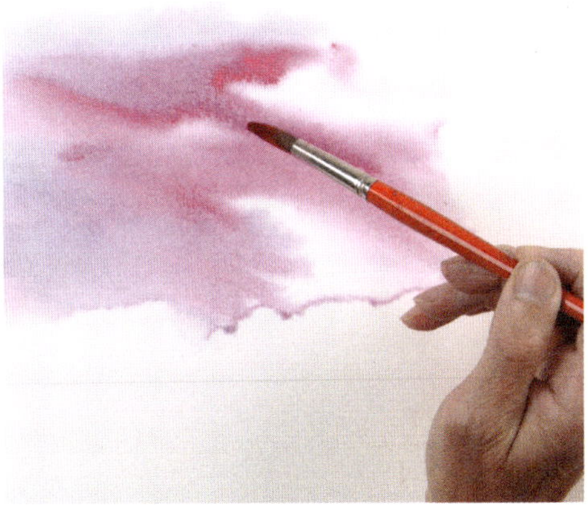

THE watercolour WHEEL BOOK

john barber

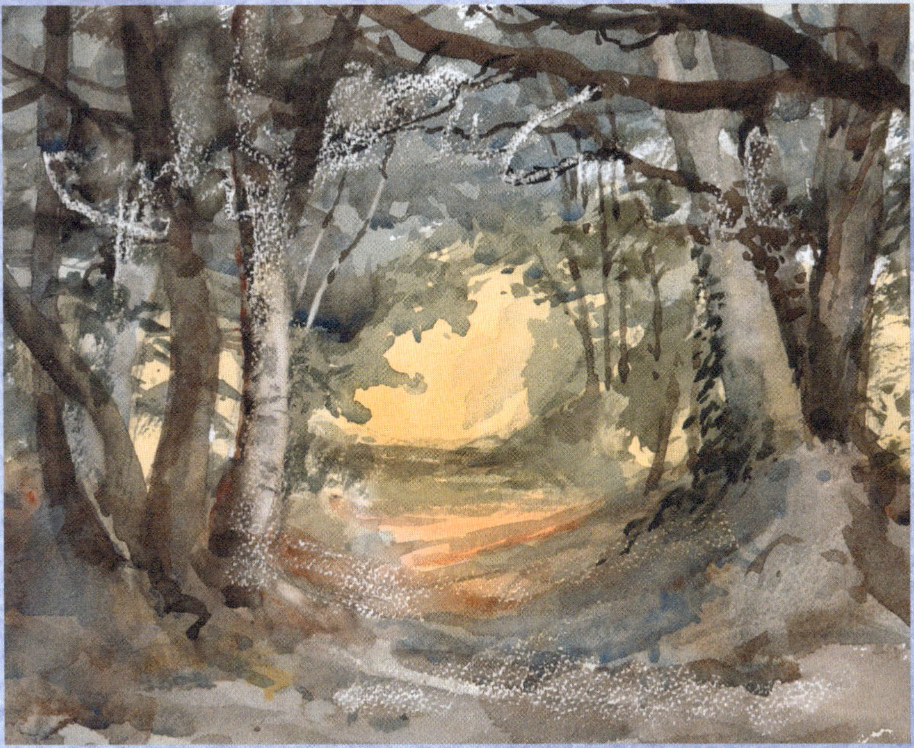

Search Press

First published in Great Britain in 2008 by
Search Press Limited
Wellwood, North Farm Road
Tunbridge Wells, Kent TN2 3DR

Reprinted 2008

Created and conceived by
Axis Publishing Ltd
8c Accommodation Road
London NW11 8ED
www.axispublishing.co.uk

Creative Director: Siân Keogh
Editorial Director: Anne Yelland
Art Director: Sean Keogh
Managing Editor: Conor Kilgallon
Production: Jo Ryan, Cécile Lerbière
Photography: Mike Good, Dave Jordan

ISBN: 978-184448-351-8

Suppliers
If you have difficulty obtaining any of the materials or equipment mentioned in this book, please visit the Search Press website for details of suppliers: www.searchpress.com

Printed and bound in China

contents

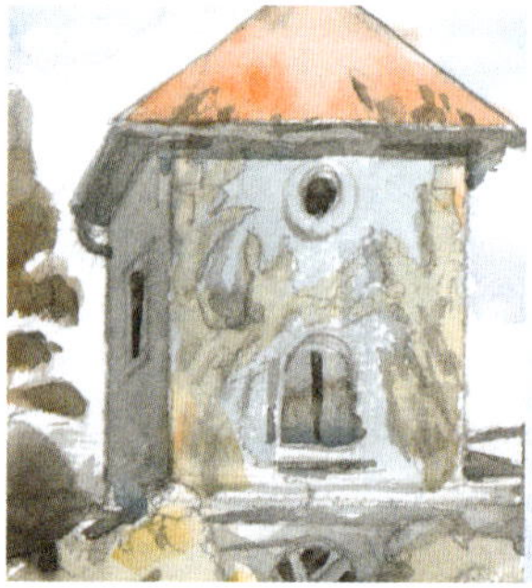

All great art starts with a great sketch. Choose an effective viewing angle then capture the mood of a scene using basic colours.

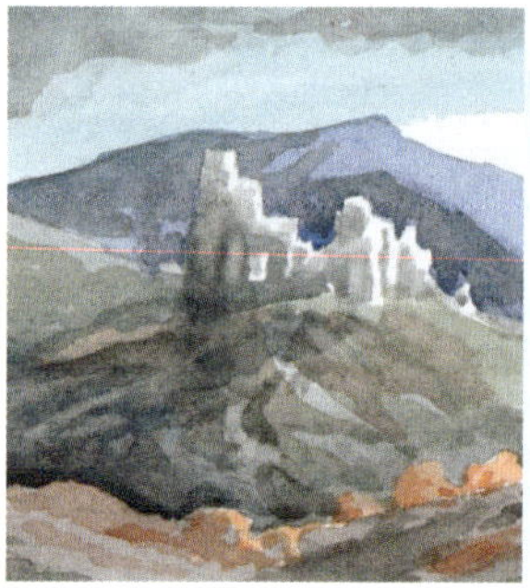

Building up colour is a key technique in watercolour. Lay flat washes to build up tone then create highlight areas.

introduction

Using watersoluble pigments for painting is a prehistoric practice. Ground minerals and soot were mixed to produce the colours seen on cave walls around the world.

But the sophisticated art of China was where painting with pigment and water was brought to perfection. The pigment was usually a block of black or red paint held in a small tray that was then diluted by water on the brush, in a similar way to modern 'pan' watercolours.

classic colour usage

The history of watercolour painting in the West really starts in the 18th century. Watercolour as a medium developed from topographical drawings drawn in monochrome grey or brown ink. The ink was usually sepia or 'bistre,' which was made from beechwood soot ground into powder. From this beginning, artists such as Paul Sandby (1725–1809) emerged, using delicate grey and blue washes to achieve his poetic images. Sandby was influential on Thomas Gainsborough (1727–88), Thomas Girtin (1775–1802), and J.M.W. Turner (1775–1851), the latter using watercolour as a full-colour medium for large works. Turner either borrowed or invented almost every technical trick that we use today, but it is in his sketches that we see the economy of means used to achieve his effects. It was also Turner who developed watercolour painting into a serious competitor to oil painting. His skies and seascapes showed how the whole spectrum of colours could be used in a magical, kaleidoscopic way.

Meanwhile, John Constable (1776–1837) showed how watercolour can describe the weather with small broken washes and swift brush strokes. His colour schemes were much more realistic than had been seen in the earlier monochromes, using broken touches of pure blue and red in his open air sketches. Also at this time, Samuel Palmer (1805–81) was developing his rich stippling method, while Richard Dadd (1819–87) and John Frederick Lewis (1805–76) took meticulous detail to its limits.

In the late 19th century, several American artists came to the fore. James McNeill Whistler (1834–1903) produced minimalist, atmospheric landscapes, while his compatriot John Singer Sargent (1856–1925) painted bold and colourful landscapes, notable for the sweep of the brush strokes and a warm palette. Winslow Homer (1836–1910) is one to study for bold, effective watercolours. Nearer our own time, the Swiss artist Paul Klee (1879–1940) was a great colour theorist – his work provides an excellent guide to colour selection.

understanding colour

What the great artists showed is that successful watercolour painting often depends as much on the effects created by your colour choice as on composition, which is where an understanding of how colour works comes in.

Look at the colour wheel (right) to see how colours are grouped. For each picture you paint, you will need a

THE COLOUR WHEEL

The colour wheel is great reference for artists. The three colours in the centre are the primary colours. Primary colours are the ones that cannot be obtained by mixing other colours together. The middle ring shows the colours that are created when you mix two of the primaries. Red and yellow make orange; blue and yellow make green; blue and red make purple. These are called secondary colours, and show the colours you can expect to create when you mix primary watercolours in your palette. All colours can, in theory, be created by mixing varying amounts of the primaries. The outer ring breaks down the secondary colours further into 12 shades.

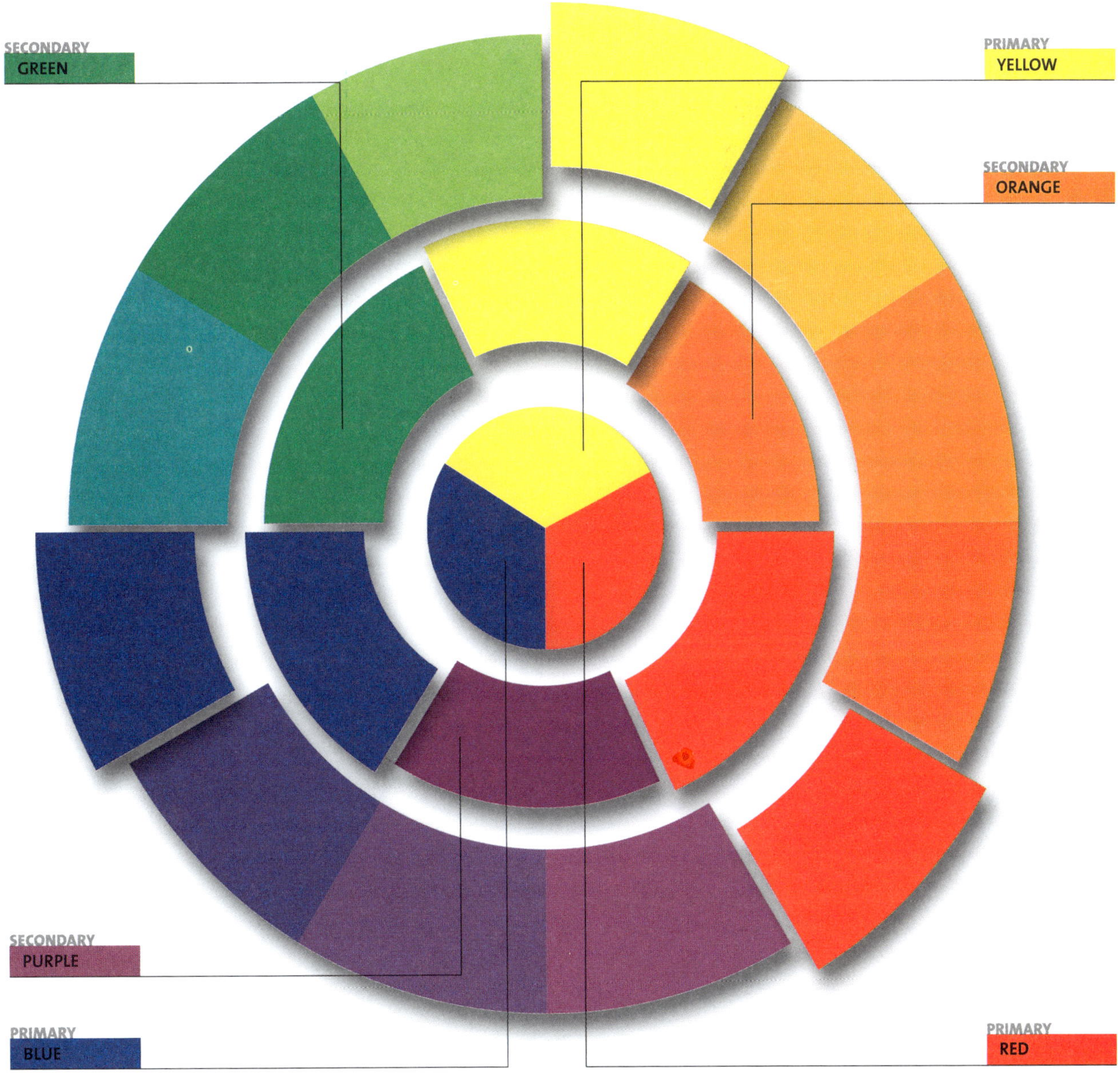
SECONDARY
GREEN
PRIMARY
YELLOW
SECONDARY
ORANGE
SECONDARY
PURPLE
PRIMARY
BLUE
PRIMARY
RED

COMPLEMENTARY COLOUR

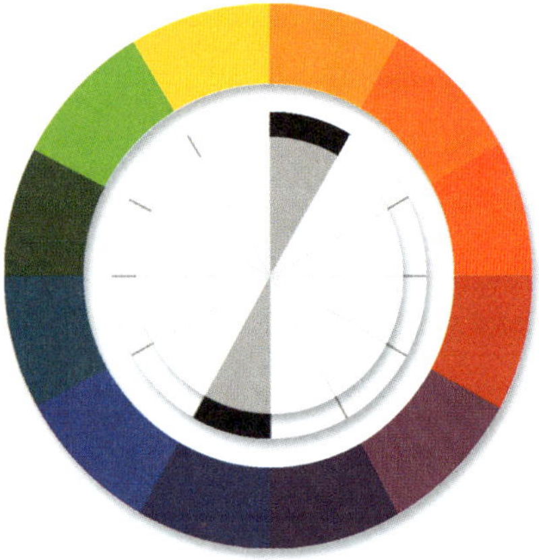

The colours that are opposite each other on the colour wheel are called complementary colours. These work together to create a harmonious reaction. Try using them side-by-side in your work – they will each appear to be stronger by contrast, bouncing off each other.

COLOUR TERMS

HUE

Hue indicates the strength of a colour from full saturation down to white. In practical terms, if you buy any colour labelled 'hue' it means that the colour is less than full strength. This is used as a way of reducing the cost of expensive pigments.

TONE

Tone is the degree of darkness from black to white that creates shade and light. For example, in a black-and-white photograph you can see and understand any object independently of colour, solely by its graduation from light to dark. The word 'shade' is often used instead of 'tone'.

COLOUR

Colour results from the division of light into separate wavelengths, creating the visible spectrum. Our brains interpret each wavelength as a different colour. The colour wheel is an aid that helps us understand how colours are arranged in relation to each other.

TRIADIC COLOUR

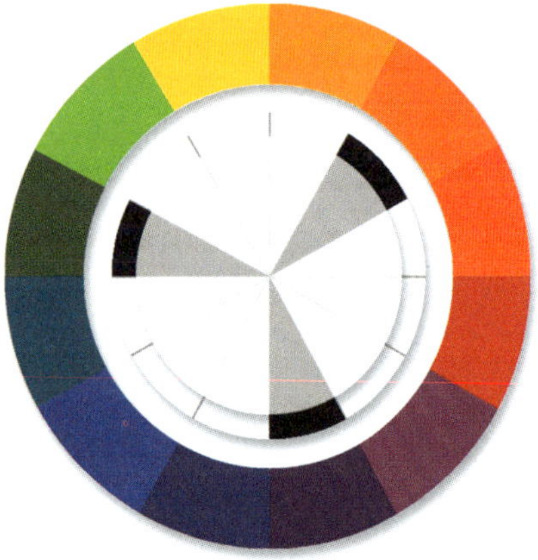

Triadic colour occurs when a 'chord' of three colours is used in combination. A mixture of any two colours of the triad used next to a third, unmixed, colour will give many different effects. A triad of colours from any part of the wheel is the basis for a good colour composition.

SPLIT COMPLEMENTARY COLOUR

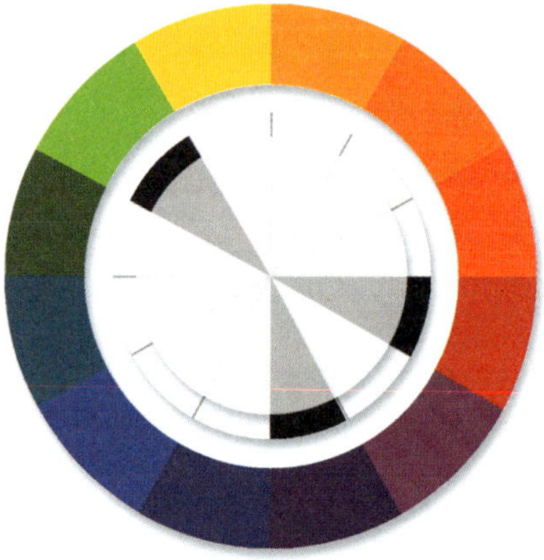

Split complementaries create three colours: the first colour, chosen from any point on the wheel, plus the two colours that come on either side of the first colour's natural complementary colour. These three colours will give plenty of unexpected colour schemes.

watercolour to represent each of the primary colours so that by mixing them, you can obtain all the secondary colours. The primary colours you choose should be determined by the scene you wish to paint. For example, if you are painting cool clear skies and distant hills, choose cobalt blue to represent blue in the colour wheel; permanent rose to represent red; and cadmium lemon to represent yellow. All three colours are cool, enabling you to maintain a consistently cool palette – no clashing 'hot' colours will appear. Likewise, when painting a warm scene, use a warm blue, red, and yellow for your primaries. This idea, along with using complementary colours, which appear opposite each other on the colour wheel and produce harmonious contrasts, will help you keep your colours balanced.

A good exercise is to make your own colour wheels for warm and cool colours. Draw several circles 10cm (4in) in diameter and divide each circle into six pie slices. Paint your three primaries in alternate slices and then mix them: red with yellow for orange, blue with yellow for green, and blue with red for purple. Place these secondary colours in between the primaries and you will see exactly which ones work out well for your picture. Keep this worksheet as a reference palette.

taking style cues

Look at all artists' work, old and new, for ideas and inspiration. Research as many examples as you can, learning each artist's methods and techniques. This does not mean that you should try to produce exact copies of their work, but by your review you will develop your own knowledge and taste.

This book goes hand-in-hand with your own research by providing a wealth of instruction on just what can be achieved with watercolours. Highly accessible, practical, and instructional, what you will gain from it in technical skill will give you the competence that leads to confidence. It is this confidence that will enable you to express your thoughts in paint – it is easy to forget in the struggle to master materials that the real aim of painting is the expression of ourselves. Good technique and practical skill make this expression easier.

INDOOR/OUTDOOR TEST

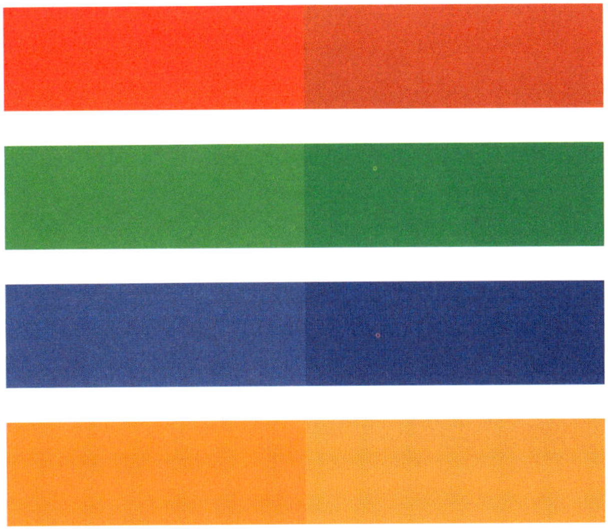

The indoor/outdoor test is designed to show the effect that artificial or subdued lighting has on colours when compared to daylight. If you look at the four strips indoors you can see hardly any difference between the colours on the right compared to the ones on the left. Step out into the daylight and you will be able to see that the right-hand side is noticeably darker. This sort of phenomenon plays an important part in how we perceive colour and all artists have to be aware of it. Although it is never quite as obvious as in the experiment, it does help to explain why art studios are built with high skylights, ideally facing north. For artists whose pictures depend on great colour accuracy, good daylight is an essential need.

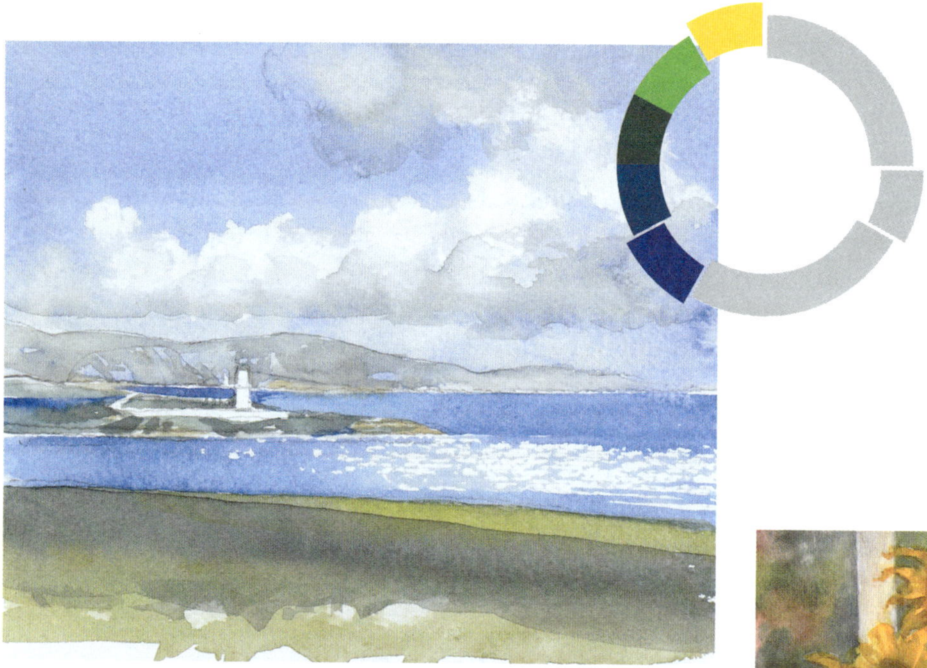

This sketch of the coast of Ireland, with its sparkling waves and fleecy clouds, was painted with a narrow palette of cool blues and greys that suggest pale sunlight and the distance of the coastline. It was created with just three colours – cobalt blue (blue is the coolest colour on the colour wheel), Payne's gray, and yellow. The effect relies on single colour washes and not overpainting the overall light tone or 'high key' colours. In some places, the paper is left untouched to enhance the cool quality of the light.

This is a richly painted still life, with warm oranges, reds, and yellows in the flowers, a wide range of greens in the leaves, and a solid rectangle of deep blue in the watering can. The pink wash over the table and far wall brings in purple shades. The blue colour of the can is taken up into the background leaves to make a soft, turquoise green. This vibrant still life uses most of the colours of the colour wheel to create an overall feeling of warmth.

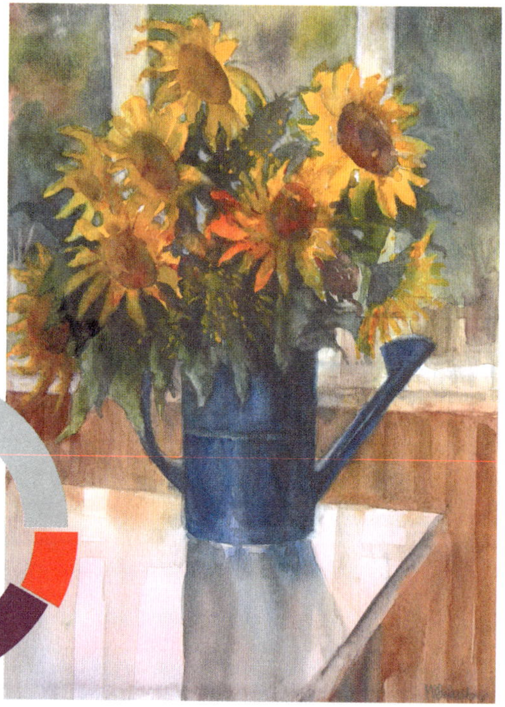

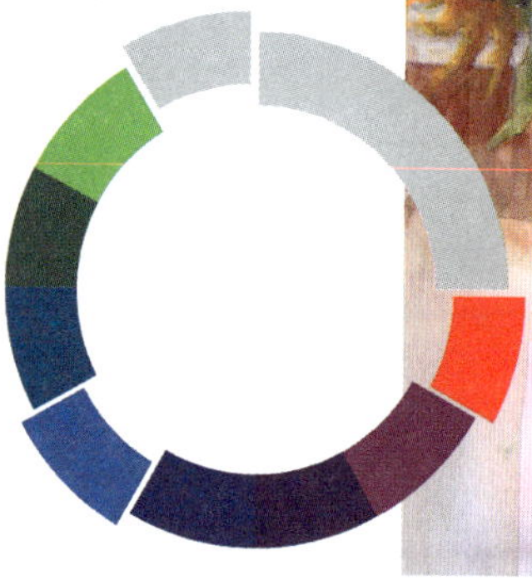

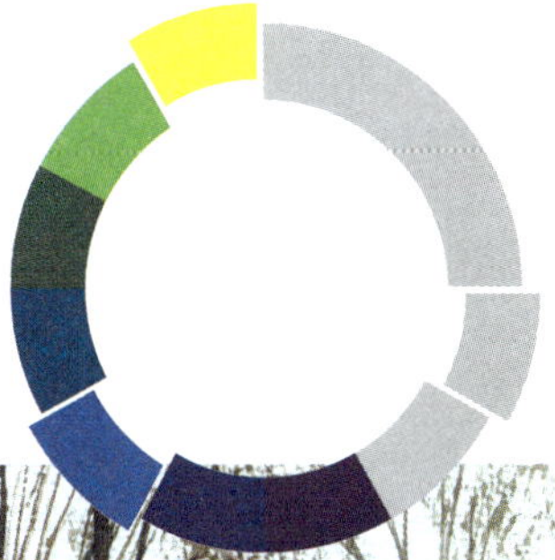

This chilly winter scene is created around four colours – cobalt blue, Hooker's green, Payne's gray, and burnt sienna. The most important element is the cool grey background, which establishes that this is a misty day.

The dark trees make a series of verticals that create the stillness of the scene. The clever use of the burnt sienna makes the other colours look even cooler. This is the complementary blue-orange effect.

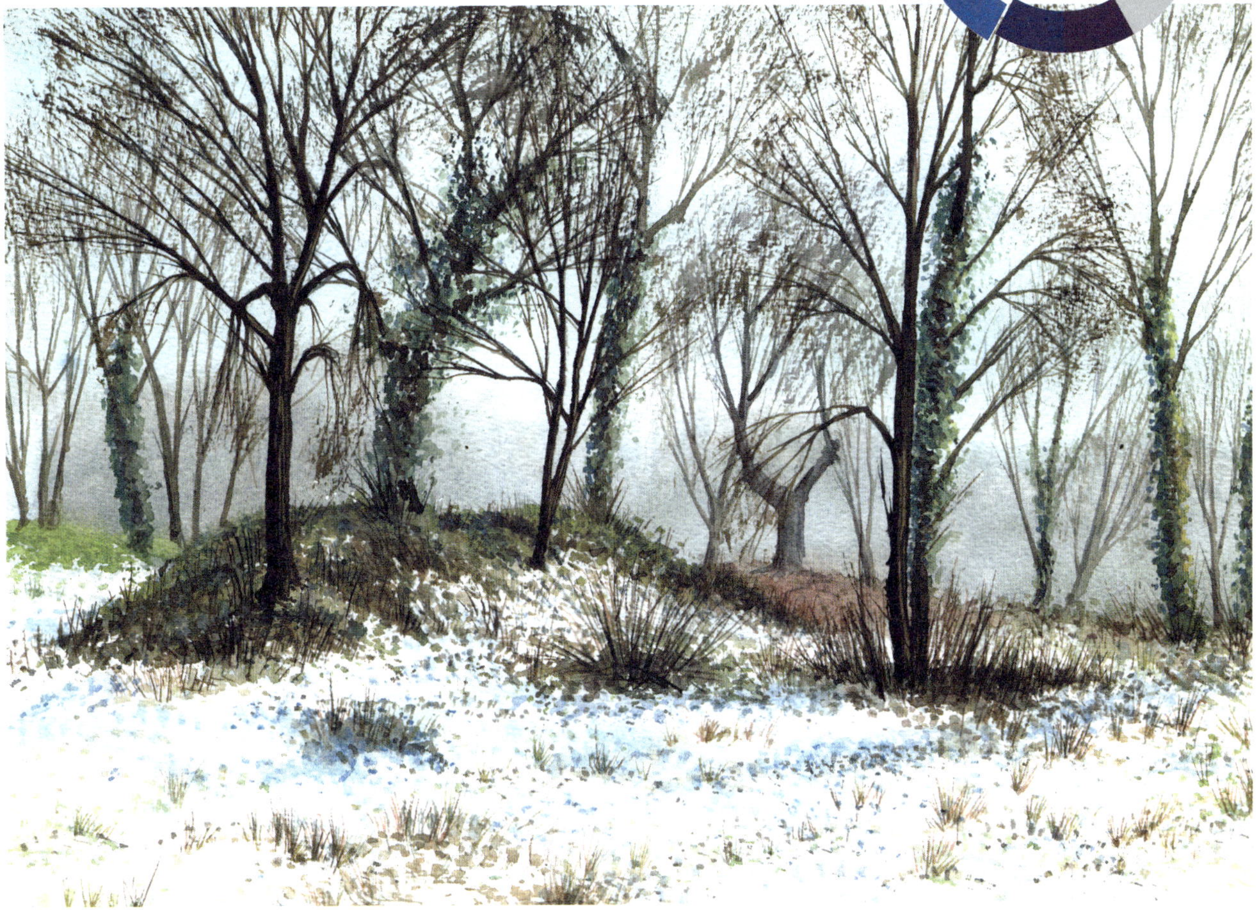

how to use this book

The jacket of this book features a unique colour-mixing wheel that will show you the shade that will result when you mix equal quantities of two colours. The colours have been chosen as the ones that are most useful to watercolour artists. A glance through the projects in this book will give you an indication of the enormous range of colours and tones that can be achieved using these colours. Each project lists the colours you will need and highlights how to mix them to achieve the shades you need.

USING THE COLOUR-MIXING WHEEL

The colour-mixing wheel can be used to help you determine what the result of mixing any two colours from your selection will be. It can also be used if you are unsure of how to achieve a shade you wish to create, from nature for example. Turn the wheel until you find a shade in one of the inner windows you like and read off the two colours you need to mix to achieve it.

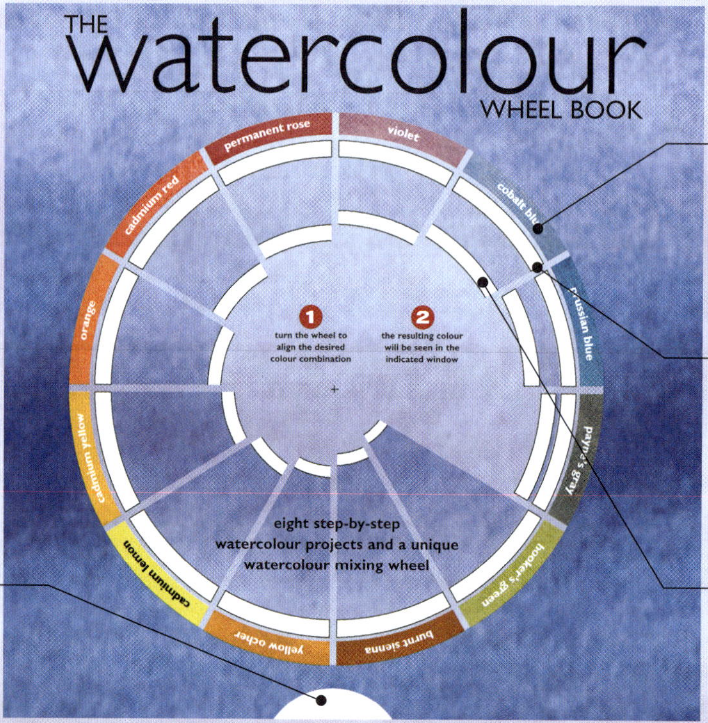

outer colour wheel
The colours on the outer wheel are the standard watercolours that will get you started.

inner colour wheel
Colours on the inner wheel repeat those of the outer wheel.

mixed colour
This window reveals a swatch of the exact result of mixing equal quantities of the colours on the inner and outer wheels.

turn the wheel
The wheel turns so that you can line up the two colours you intend to mix and see the result in the window.

finished painting
The project begins with the completed painting to give a sense of its overall scope and complexity. This is then broken down into several steps, gradually building the work.

picture details
The title of the finished piece of work, together with the artist's name are given. Also included is the size of the work, to give you an indication of scale.

what you will need
All the materials and equipment you will need to complete the project are highlighted at the start so that you can have everything to hand.

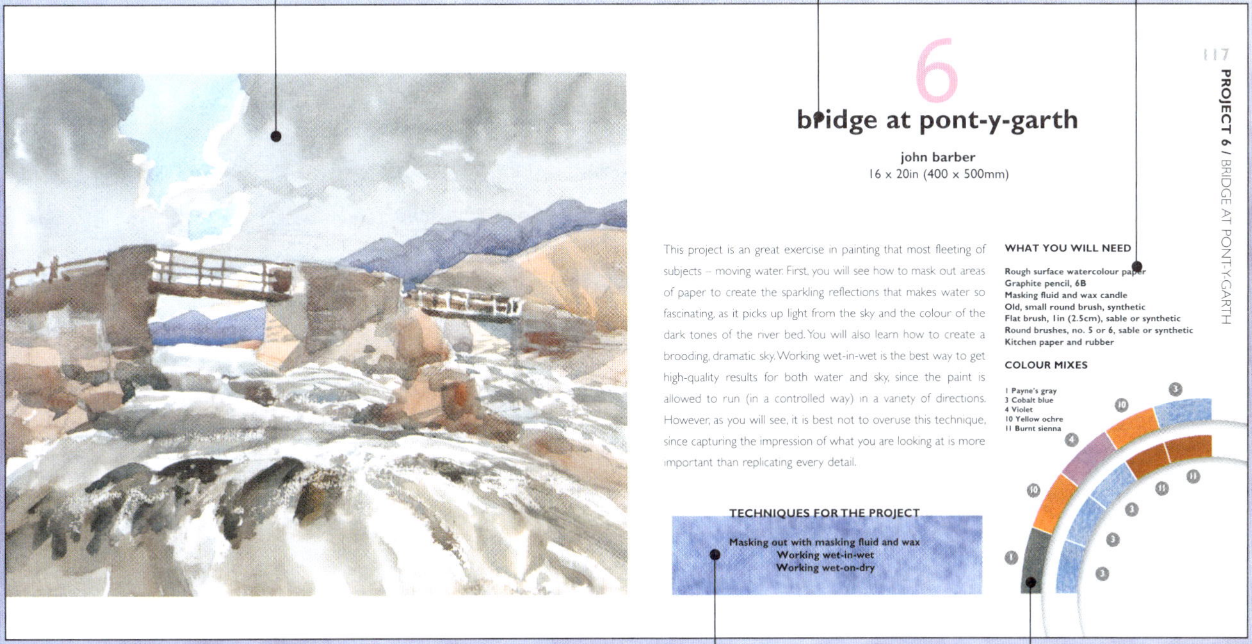

techniques for the project
Different techniques are used in every project to build up your experience and confidence.

colour mixes
The colours used in the project are shown, together with the colours they are mixed with, to create the finished work.

project techniques
Each project begins with an explanation of one of the main techniques that will be used to create the picture, with notes to help you to achieve good results when using it.

detailed working
Close-up photography allows you to see every line and mark the artist makes to build up the practice study.

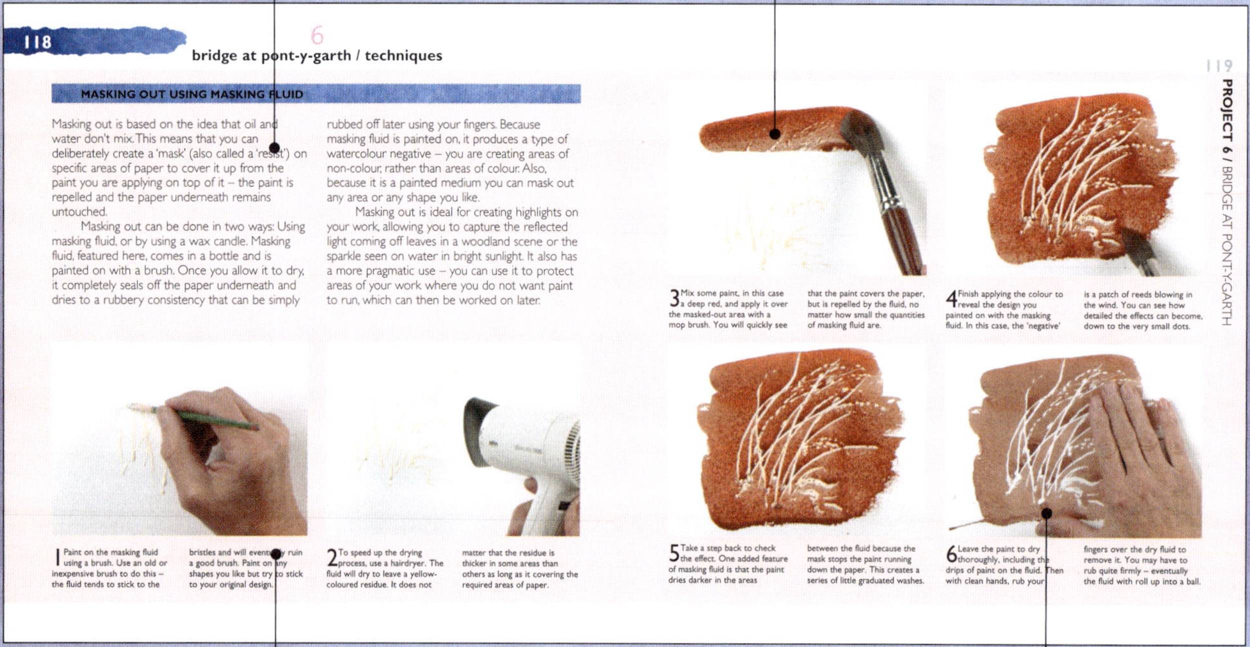
118 6 bridge at pont-y-garth / techniques

119 PROJECT 6 / BRIDGE AT PONT-Y-GARTH

MASKING OUT USING MASKING FLUID

Masking out is based on the idea that oil and water don't mix. This means that you can deliberately create a 'mask' (also called a 'resist') on specific areas of paper to cover it up from the paint you are applying on top of it – the paint is repelled and the paper underneath remains untouched.

Masking out can be done in two ways: Using masking fluid, or by using a wax candle. Masking fluid, featured here, comes in a bottle and is painted on with a brush. Once you allow it to dry, it completely seals off the paper underneath and dries to a rubbery consistency that can be simply rubbed off later using your fingers. Because masking fluid is painted on, it produces a type of watercolour negative – you are creating areas of non-colour, rather than areas of colour. Also, because it is a painted medium you can mask out any area or any shape you like.

Masking out is ideal for creating highlights on your work, allowing you to capture the reflected light coming off leaves in a woodland scene or the sparkle seen on water in bright sunlight. It also has a more pragmatic use – you can use it to protect areas of your work where you do not want paint to run, which can then be worked on later.

1 Paint on the masking fluid using a brush. Use an old or inexpensive brush to do this – the fluid tends to stick to the bristles and will eventually ruin a good brush. Paint on any shapes you like but try to stick to your original design.

2 To speed up the drying process, use a hairdryer. The fluid will dry to leave a yellow-coloured residue. It does not matter that the residue is thicker in some areas than others as long as it covering the required areas of paper.

3 Mix some paint, in this case a deep red, and apply it over the masked-out area with a mop brush. You will quickly see that the paint covers the paper, but is repelled by the fluid, no matter how small the quantities of masking fluid are.

4 Finish applying the colour to reveal the design you painted on with the masking fluid. In this case, the 'negative' is a patch of reeds blowing in the wind. You can see how detailed the effects can become, down to the very small dots.

5 Take a step back to check the effect. One added feature of masking fluid is that the paint dries darker in the areas between the fluid because the mask stops the paint running down the paper. This creates a series of little graduated washes.

6 Leave the paint to dry thoroughly, including the drips of paint on the fluid. Then with clean hands, rub your fingers over the dry fluid to remove it. You may have to rub quite firmly – eventually the fluid with roll up into a ball.

practice sketch
Each techniques spread features a quick step-by-step study enabling you to practice the technique.

finished study
The study builds into a finished sketch. You could practice this several times in different colours before embarking on the project.

step by step
The project is built up in detailed steps right from the first sketched marks to the finished piece of work, enabling you to create a work of your own using these techniques.

pull-out detail
For clarity, some areas of the work are highlighted in greater detail, enabling you to see exactly what shade or effect you are looking for.

artist's advice and tips
A practicing artist offers information and advice based on his experience of materials and equipment and methods of working.

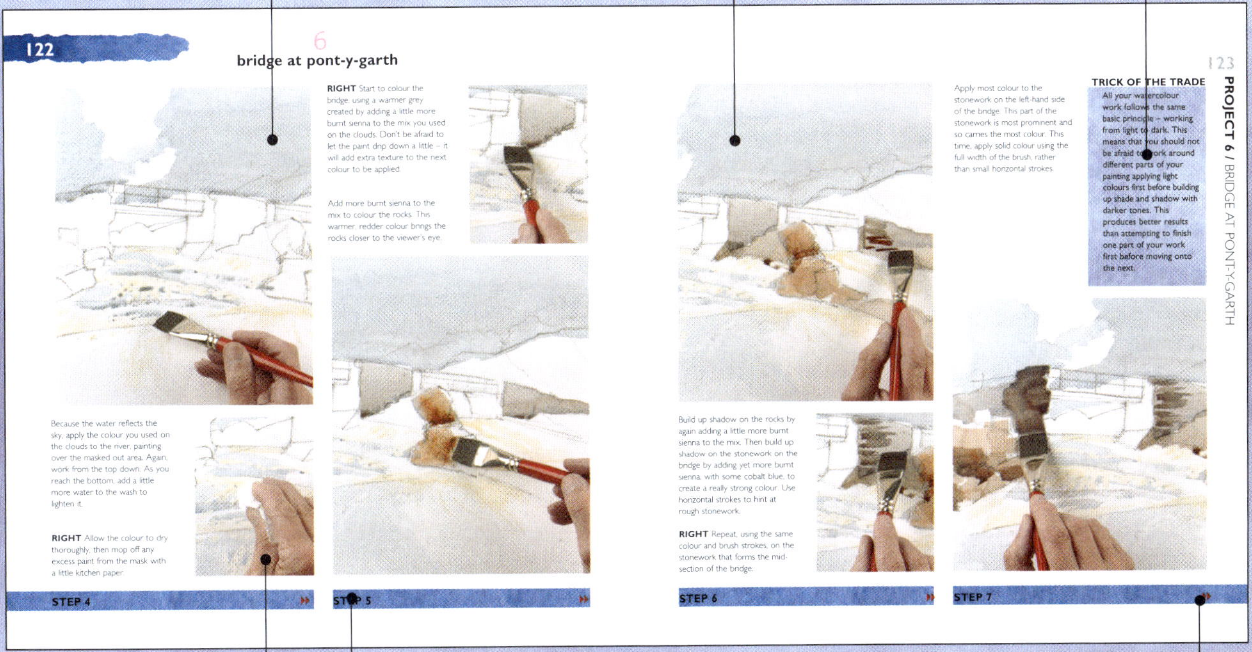
122
6
bridge at pont-y-garth

RIGHT Start to colour the bridge, using a warmer grey created by adding a little more burnt sienna to the mix you used on the clouds. Don't be afraid to let the paint drip down a little – it will add extra texture to the next colour to be applied.

Add more burnt sienna to the mix to colour the rocks. This warmer, redder colour brings the rocks closer to the viewer's eye.

Because the water reflects the sky, apply the colour you used on the clouds to the river, painting over the masked out area. Again, work from the top down. As you reach the bottom, add a little more water to the wash to lighten it.

RIGHT Allow the colour to dry thoroughly, then mop off any excess paint from the mask with a little kitchen paper.

STEP 4

STEP 5

123
PROJECT 6 / BRIDGE AT PONT-Y-GARTH

Apply most colour to the stonework on the left-hand side of the bridge. This part of the stonework is most prominent and so carries the most colour. This time, apply solid colour using the full width of the brush, rather than small horizontal strokes.

TRICK OF THE TRADE
All your watercolour work follows the same basic principle – working from light to dark. This means that you should not be afraid to work around different parts of your painting applying light colours first before building up shade and shadow with darker tones. This produces better results than attempting to finish one part of your work first before moving onto the next.

Build up shadow on the rocks by again adding a little more burnt sienna to the mix. Then build up shadow on the stonework on the bridge by adding yet more burnt sienna, with some cobalt blue, to create a really strong colour. Use horizontal strokes to hint at rough stonework.

RIGHT Repeat, using the same colour and brush strokes, on the stonework that forms the mid-section of the bridge.

STEP 6

STEP 7

detailed practice
Practical photographs of good working practice in using materials as the artist builds up the picture.

clear steps
Each project builds up in numbered steps, with precise details on what to mix, and how to add colour and detail.

guided steps
All the steps are clearly outlined, as the project builds up. Following all the steps results in the finished picture.

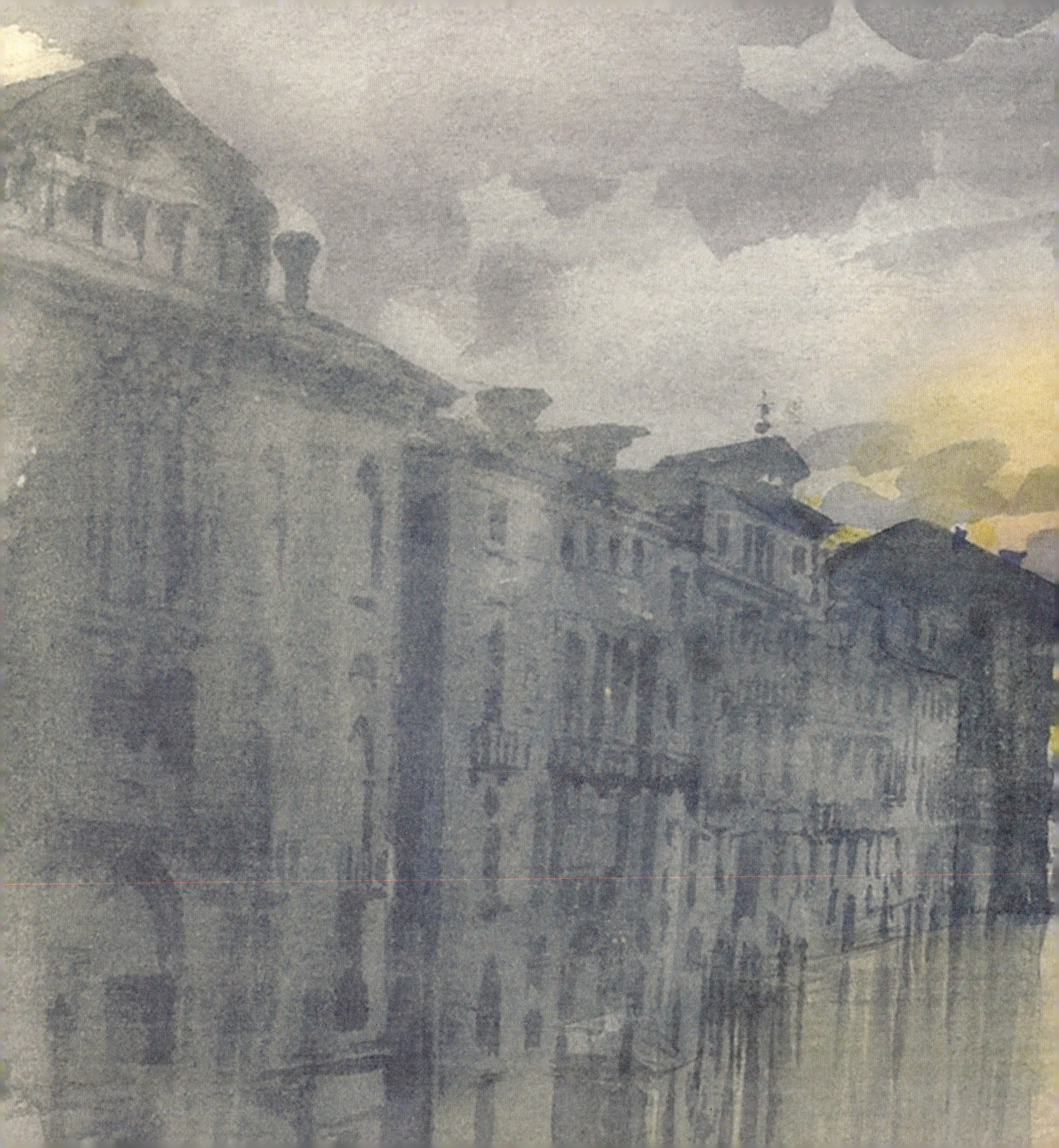

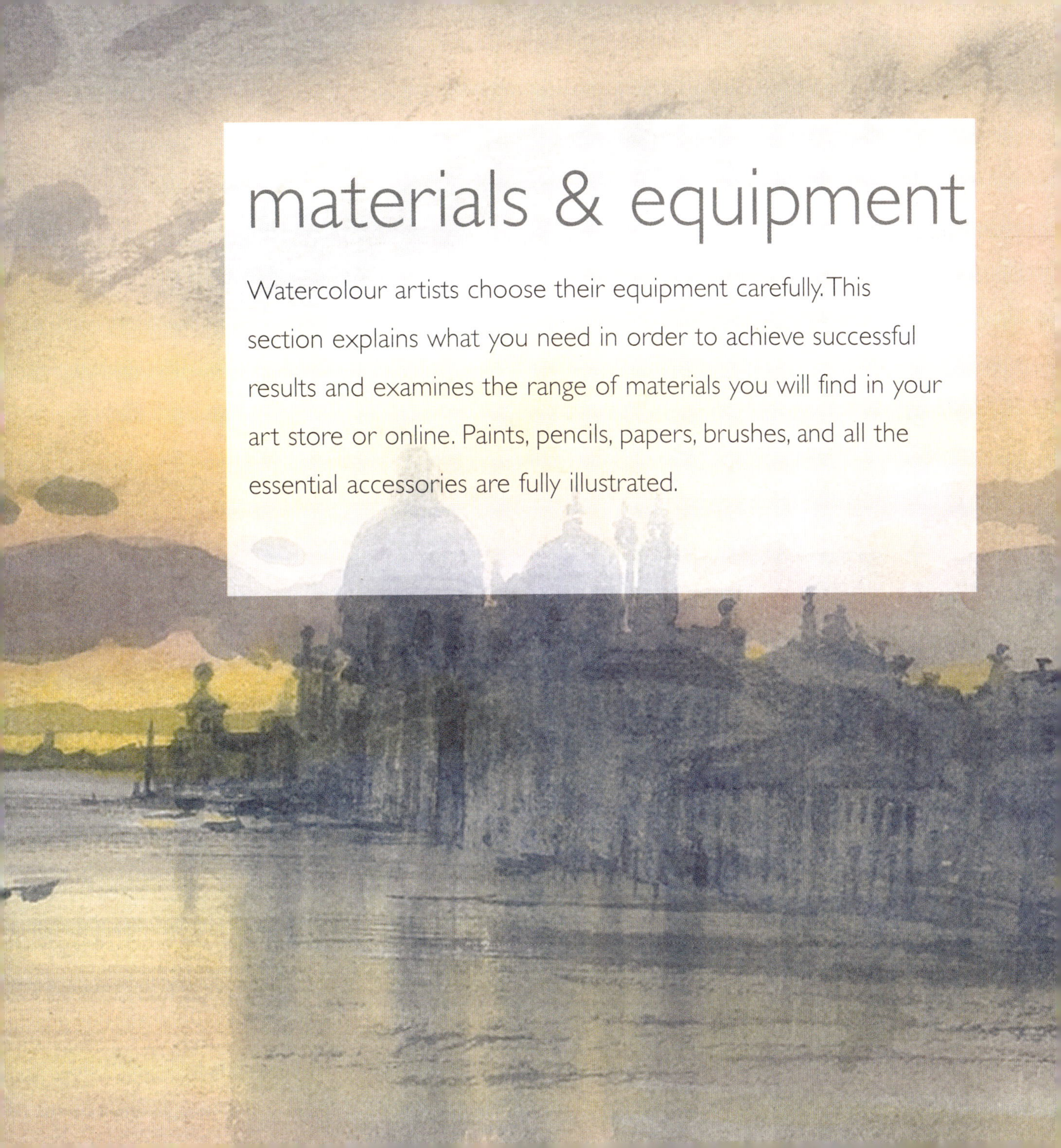

materials & equipment

Watercolour artists choose their equipment carefully. This section explains what you need in order to achieve successful results and examines the range of materials you will find in your art store or online. Paints, pencils, papers, brushes, and all the essential accessories are fully illustrated.

materials and equipment

One of the great attractions of watercolour painting is that the materials required are very simple. Buy a brush, a small selection of colours, and some paper; add water, and you are ready to start. You can work almost anywhere and the results are very durable – the great J.M.W. Turner carried his sketches from France to England rolled up in his pocket. Experimentation is another exciting aspect of this medium, so try different combinations of brushes, paints, and paper – Turner himself sometimes painted on writing paper – to find out which ones best suit your style.

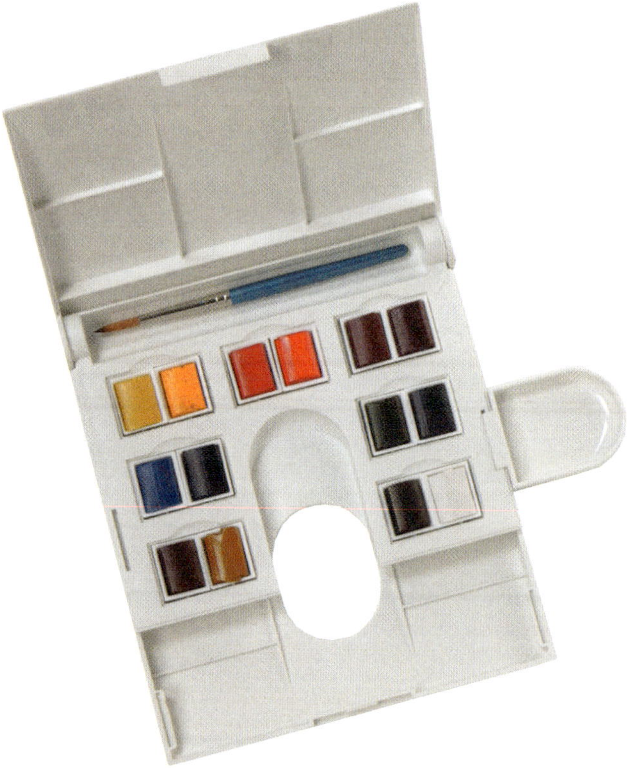

watercolours in 'pans'

Most watercolours are available in 'pans,' which are small plastic trays into which paint has been squeezed and dried. Pans are available as 'half' pans, or larger 'whole' pans. Pan colours quickly dissolve when touched with a wet brush, even when they are many years old. The advantages of pans are that they are dry, making them convenient to handle and transport. Their colour is instantly visible and they can be stored indefinitely. However, they are small, making it difficult to produce large amounts of paint quickly, although this can mostly be overcome by using a wide, flat brush and whole pans.

watercolours in tubes

The paint in tubes is the same as in pans but is mixed with gum arabic and glycerine to make it liquid. In fact, most manufacturers sell the same colour range in both tubes and pans. Tubes give a large amount of colour quickly, which is ideal when you have large areas of paper to cover. Also, if you squeeze out more paint than you need, you can leave it on the palette till the next time you paint. However, you cannot see the true colour of the paint till you open the tube, and you have to remove and replace lids, which can interrupt your work flow.

paint boxes

Most paint manufacturers produce box sets, from pocket-sized versions (see left) to large studio sets containing both pans and tubes. Boxes often work out less expensive than buying colours separately and the selections contained in them are usually sensible. If your favourite colour is missing, you can easily insert it in place of one you would use less often. If you intend to sketch outdoors, look for a box that has a handy thumbhole or a ring underneath.

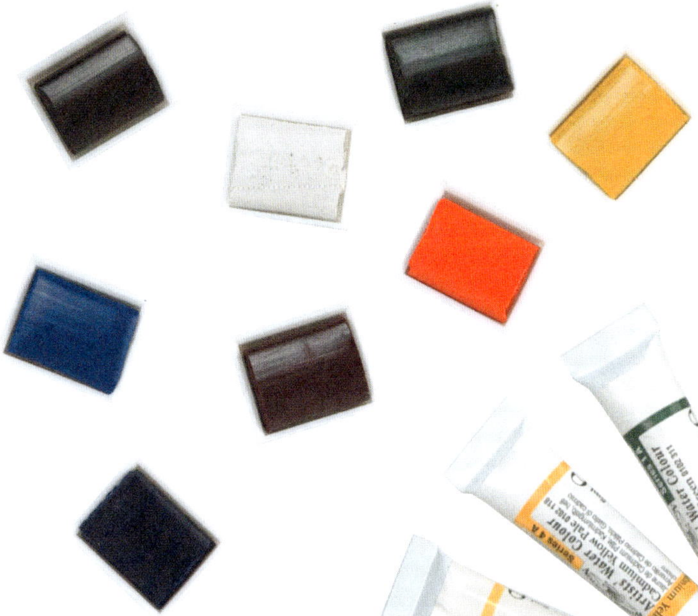

LEFT Colour pans are sometimes loose and move around in their box when the brush is applied to them, or even stick to the hairs and come out entirely. Put a spot of glue or double-sided tape under each pan to keep it fixed in place.

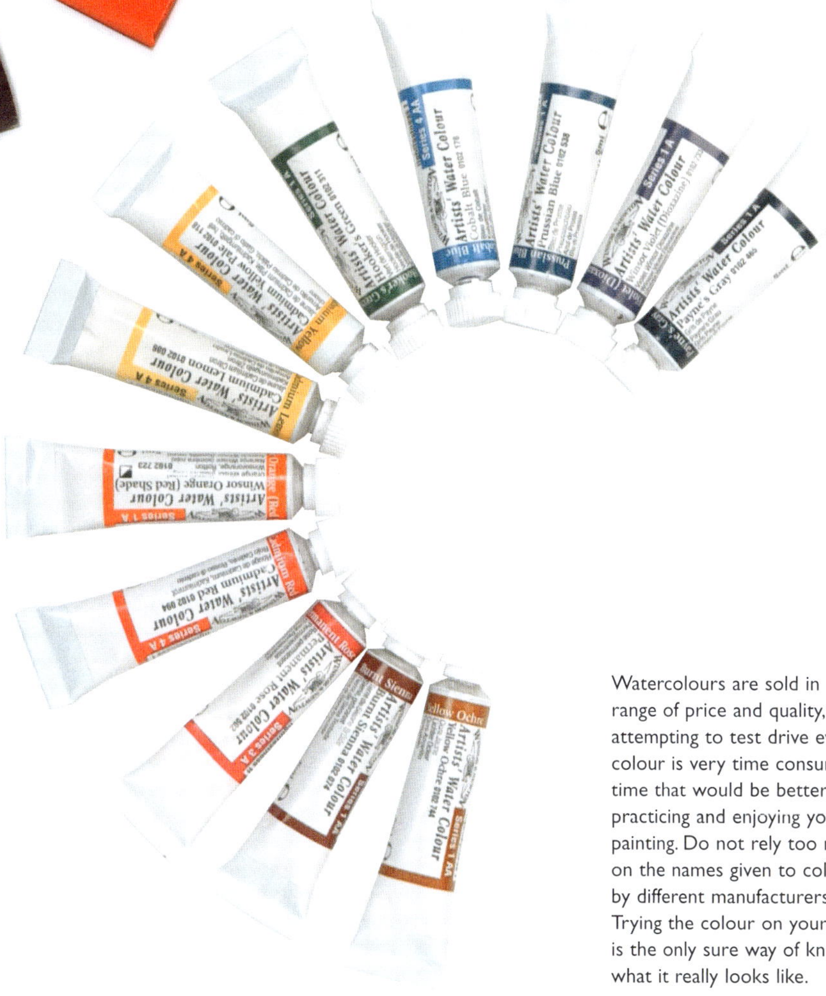

OPPOSITE AND RIGHT Experiment with both pans and tubes to find out which ones best suit your way of working. You may, like many artists, end up using both.

Remember that handling qualities and intensity of colour vary greatly from one manufacturer to the next, so get to know the colours you already have before you rush out to buy new ones. You may find that you are able achieve all the results you want using only half the colours in your first box.

When using your tube colours, do not be mean. Put out plenty of colour so you do not have to keep opening and closing tubes, which can be disrupting.

Watercolours are sold in a wide range of price and quality, so attempting to test drive every colour is very time consuming – time that would be better spent practicing and enjoying your painting. Do not rely too much on the names given to colours by different manufacturers. Trying the colour on your paper is the only sure way of knowing what it really looks like.

SELECTING WATERCOLOUR PAPER

ROUGH SURFACE (R) PAPERS

Rough surface paper, as its name implies, has an uneven texture with many pits and mounds that break up the brush marks. This gives a free, open texture to your work. Rough papers are best for bold, vigourous brush strokes and quick effects.

COLD PRESSED (CP) OR 'NOT' PAPERS

These are smoother papers than rough surface ones, but still have a definite texture that affects the way the brush marks appear. Cold pressed papers are very useful if you want to work freely but then finish in considerable detail.

HOT PRESSED (HP) PAPER

Hot pressed papers are created by crushing the texture of rough paper to produce a smooth surface. These are the papers to use if your work is finely detailed. Botanical drawings, animal illustrations involving fur and feathers, in fact any time fine, continuous brush marks are required, use hot press paper.

STORING WATERCOLOUR PAPER

The best watercolour papers are expensive, so storing them carefully is worthwhile. Keep your papers flat in a dry drawer or cupboard – paper absorbs moisture from the air and this causes buckling. Although this is not a problem if you are going to soak and stretch your paper anyway, it can make small blocks awkward to use. Sketch books are also less likely to buckle if laid flat. Stored properly, good paper can be kept indefinitely.

working with papers

Papers designed to hold watercolours, such as the types listed on the left, generally produce the best results for finished work. They are either machine- or handmade, ranging from 100 percent wood pulp to 100 percent cotton, or usually a mix of the two. Handmade papers are the most expensive, but are rewarding to work on as they have special qualities of texture and handling. These papers are usually only obtainable in large sheets.

However, you are not limited to these alone. In fact, you may find a non-art paper, such as a good-quality white cartridge paper, works well, particularly for studies and sketches. Glossy or semi-glossy papers made for printing, such as those found on the backs of calendars, can produce interesting effects. If you see a surface that you think may take watercolour, try putting a few washes on it – you might just be pleasantly surprised by the results.

paper weights

The thickness of a paper is called its 'weight,' which is measured in 'gsm' (grams per square meter) or 'lbs' (the weight of a 'ream' of 500 sheets). Although paper weight is always less important than the painting surface, there are good reasons why weight does matter. Lighter papers (80–100lbs) should always be 'stretched,' that is, soaked in water before being taped to a board to prevent buckling. Heavier papers (120–300lbs) can be used in small sheets without stretching, although stretching is recommended for all papers intended for serious work.

book sheets or blocks

For outdoor work, you will need a spiral-bound sketch book that will lie flat. Choose one that is around 10 x 15cm (4 x 6in). Alternatively, use 'blocks' of paper, which have glued edges to prevent buckling. Usually these work well, but if too much water is used, the whole block may twist.

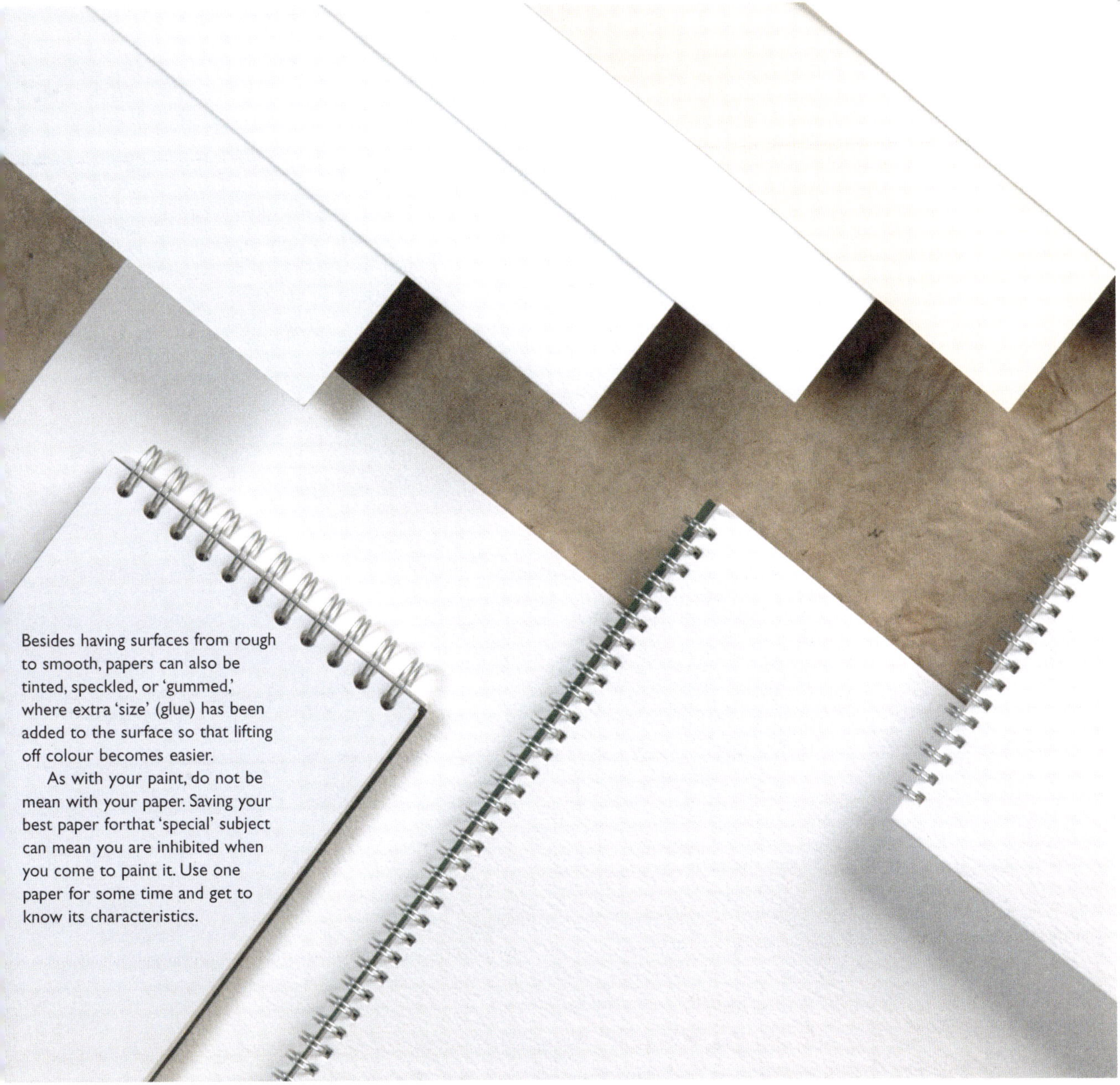

Besides having surfaces from rough to smooth, papers can also be tinted, speckled, or 'gummed,' where extra 'size' (glue) has been added to the surface so that lifting off colour becomes easier.

As with your paint, do not be mean with your paper. Saving your best paper forthat 'special' subject can mean you are inhibited when you come to paint it. Use one paper for some time and get to know its characteristics.

working at an easel

Once you have chosen your paper, you will need something to hold it in place so you can work freely. If you are working indoors at a desk or table, a drawing board or a simple desk easel, such as the one below, work best. Buy one that is fully adjustable so you can work comfortably. You can also use an outdoor sketching easel, with your work held at a slight angle.

For outdoor work, use an outdoor easel. These easels hold the paper at the right height and angle leaving both hands free – one to hold the paints, the other to hold the brush. These easels need to be lightweight so they are easy to transport and there are many excellent metal or fibreglass models available, but visit your art store to do some research before buying one.

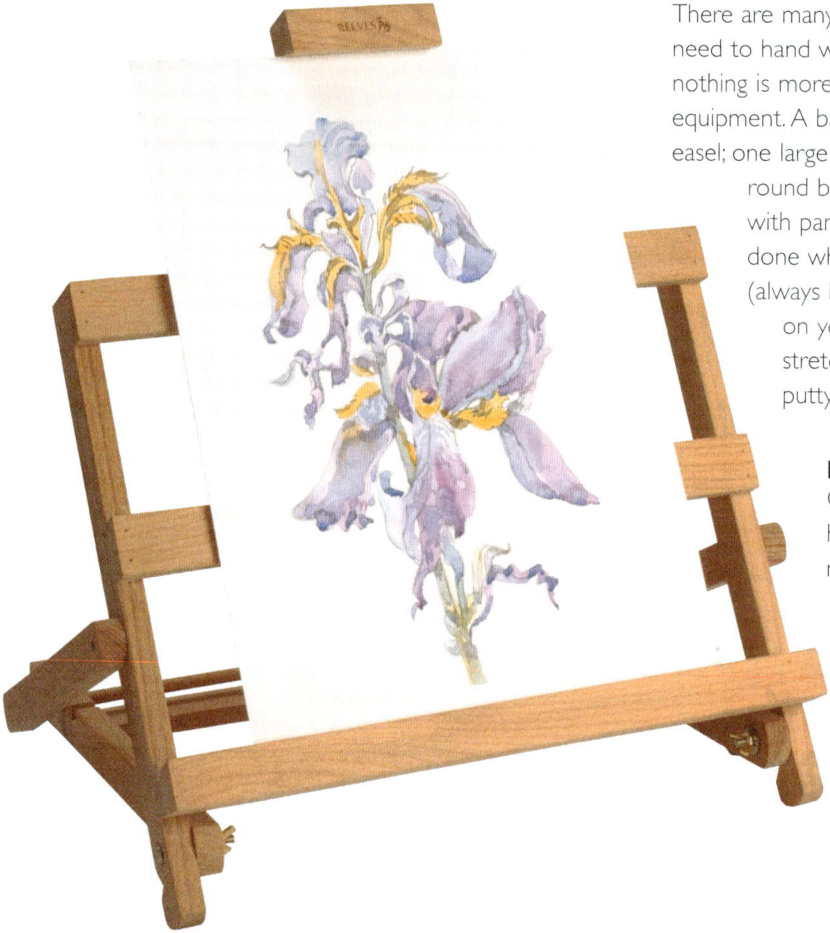

outdoor tips

There are many distractions outdoors, so having what you need to hand will help you concentrate on your subject – nothing is more offputting than having to juggle all your equipment. A basic checklist of materials is: a lightweight easel; one large brush (round or flat) for washes; one round brush for line and detail; a watercolour box with pans and a thumbhole (essential for work done while standing); water in a collapsible pot (always know where your water is, so hang the pot on your easel); watercolour block or paper stretched on a lightweight board; a pencil; a putty rubber; a craft knife or pencil sharpener.

pencils

Graphite pencils are graded from 8H (the hardest) to 8B (the softest). HB is the middle grade. Choose a range of pencils between HB and 6B. If you wish to eliminate all the finished pencil lines on your painting, use the softer grades and

CHOOSING THE EASEL FOR YOU

For indoor work, choose an adjustable drawing board or desk easel (left). You can even prop up the end of a sheet of plywood with a pile of books to create a drawing board. For outdoor work, use an outdoor easel. This needs to be stable and lightweight, and either metal or wood.

do not press hard on the paper. Unfortunately, pencil grades are not consistent across manufacturers, so 4B in one range may be the same as 2B in another; you will have to learn by trial and error.

For black lines, use carbon or charcoal pencils. These are good for dramatic marks that remain in the finished picture and also avoid the grey shine produced by graphite. However, they are harder remove.

Watersoluble pencils can often be used to produce additional emphasis or to disguise hard edges where a wash is not satisfactory. Try them all.

rubbers

There are several materials used for erasing or softening pencil marks, the most useful of which is the putty rubber. This has flat edges and so can be pulled across your whole painting or kneaded into a point for cleaning up small areas. Use a plastic rubber to remove more stubborn marks, but take care not to abrade the paper. Adhesive tack dabbed repeatedly on one spot will gently soften pencil marks without removing them completely. Other rubbers are encased in wood like a pencil and are gritty and abrasive – these work well to lift light spots of paint from areas that will not lift with water.

ABOVE The putty rubber is an indispensable part of an artist's equipment. The large block can be squeezed into any shape to provide just the area you need. Keep your putty rubber clean by keeping it in its original box as the surface will naturally pick up dust. Use it to clean your paper before you start.

BELOW Experiment with the variety of pencils on sale to find the brand you like best. The feel of the pencil on the page is very important, so once you have found a brand you like, stick to it. For watercolour sketching, carefully sharpen your pencils with a craft knife and leave a long lead exposed.

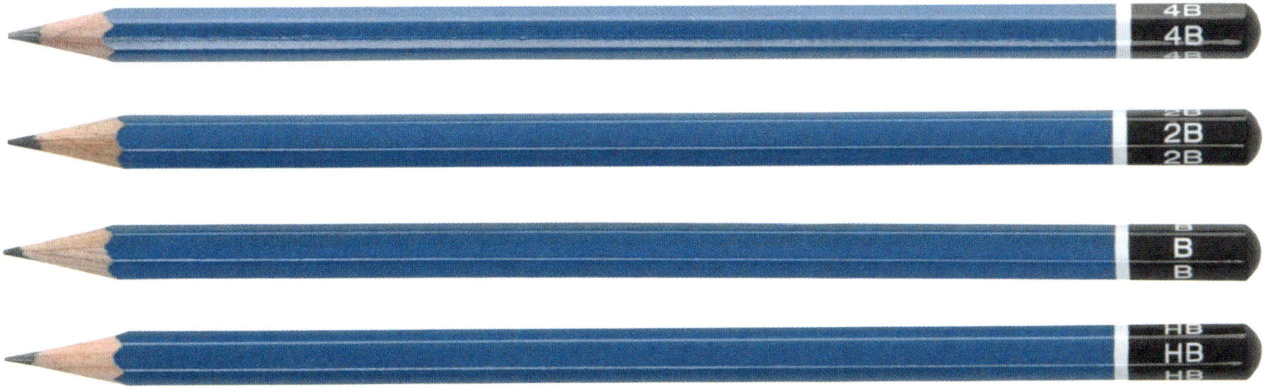

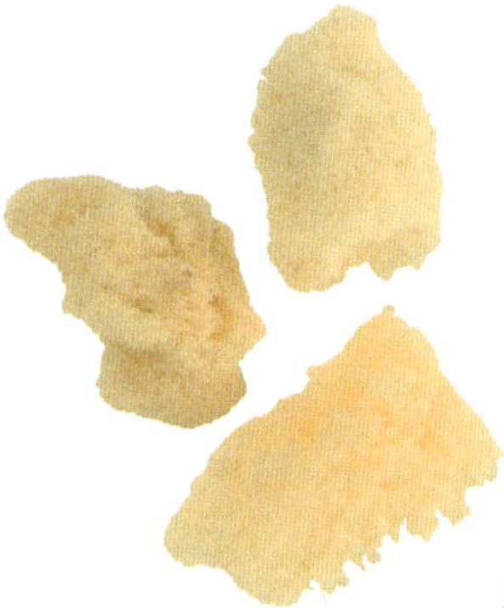

Natural sponges are best for making accidental textures on your work, such as leaves on trees. Larger sponges have coarser textures than smaller ones, so try to have several different sizes to produce several different results.

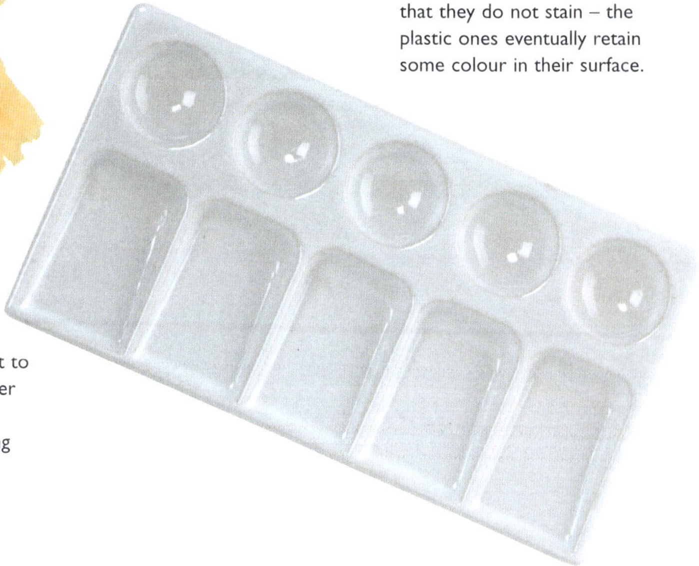

The range of palettes is enormous, both in ceramic and plastic. The ceramic versions are heavier and more prone to breakage but have the advantage that they do not stain – the plastic ones eventually retain some colour in their surface.

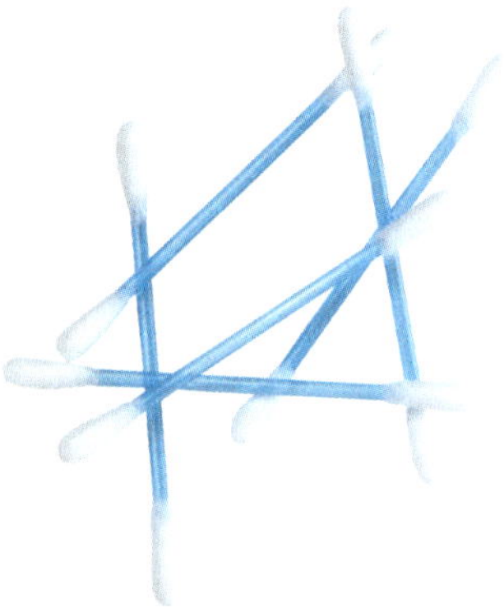

Use cotton buds on wet paint to lift off colour and create lighter spots or highlights. Also use them on larger areas by rolling the bud over the wet wash.

brushes, sponges, and manipulating colour

Over the centuries, almost every kind of hair, bristle, and fibre has been used to make brushes. However, it is generally recognised that the tail hair of the sable (a member of the weasel family) is the best for watercolour brushes. These hairs are fine but tough, designed by nature to stand abrasion on rocks and ice. The Kolinsky variety is regarded as the very best. Unsurprisingly, sable brushes are expensive.

Synthetic fibres are the main alternative to sable and have now reached a very high standard, but there are some important differences. Synthetic fibres (or 'filaments') are made by stretching nylon fibres to breaking point while they are still viscous. This means that the tips of the fibres are the weakest parts, making them inclined to wear out. By contrast, sable is toughest and most resilient at the tip. Also, being hair, it has a scaly surface, which helps the brush to hold more liquid. The advantage of synthetic brushes is their comparatively low price. For this reason, only consider buying two small sable brushes to start.

There are three main types of brush, all named after their shapes – round or pointed (a general-use brush), flat (usually a large brush for washes), and 'mop' (a large, round brush, again for washes). Brush sizes are usually denoted by a measurement or by a number. Large wash brushes, designed to apply lots of colour quickly to paper, are often measured in inches, such as 1/4in or 1in. Smaller brushes are often numbered, with size 14 being among the largest and size 0 among the smallest. A small, flat hog hair brush, more usually associated with oil painting, is handy for scrubbing out colour.

Brushes are not the only way to apply colour to the page. Natural sponge is a great way to create 'accidental' patterns, and is especially useful for creating free, detailed areas of foliage, which could not be created by painting individual leaves. Have a few different sizes ready – larger sponges create different textures than smaller ones.

No colours can be applied without mixing them first with water, and for this you need a palette. These are plastic or ceramic and come in a variety of shapes and sizes – plastic versions are more suitable for transporting because they are light and less breakable. Larger versions are more useful when mixing lots of paint, or when working with other materials, such as large sponges.

As well as applying colour, effects can also be created by 'masking' an area of paper to stop paint reaching it, or removing paint to create highlights. Use masking fluid or a

WHICH BRUSHES TO BUY

Choose two 'round' (or 'pointed') brushes of different sizes that carry lots of colour but which come to a point when loaded. These can be synthetic or sable, according to your budget. You also need two 'flat' brushes for washes, 1/2in and 1in wide, as well as one large, round 'mop' brush with soft bristles. This brush can either be synthetic or made from squirrel hair. A small, flat hog hair brush is handy for scrubbing out colour.

When buying a round brush, ask for a sample, dip it in water and, holding the end of the handle, flick it downward. Discard any brush where the hair does not come to a neat point. Do the same with flat brushes, which should come to a smooth, flat edge. Also take the ferrule in one hand and twist the handle with the other. If you can feel any movement, do not buy the brush.

ANATOMY OF A BRUSH

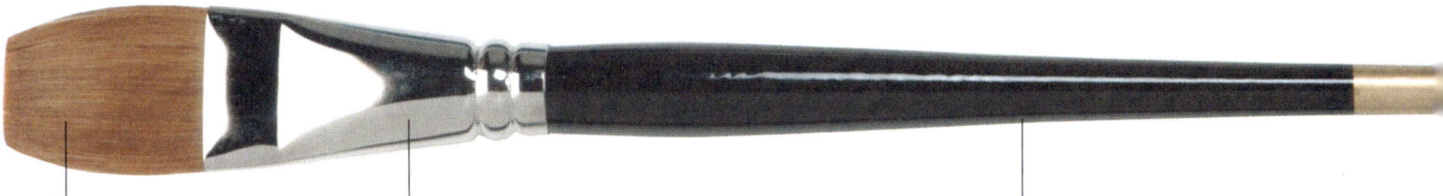

HAIRS
Many kinds of animal hair have been used to make brushes, the best of which is sable. A wide variety of synthetic fibres is also available, which now compare well with sable hairs.

FERRULE
The ferrule is the metal tube that holds the hair and attaches them to the handle. Avoid brushes that have a seam or join on the ferrule – these don't grip the hairs or wood well.

HANDLE
Handles are often made from wood that has been varnished to make it watertight. The brush handle is usually widest at the ferrule, the point at which you usually hold the brush.

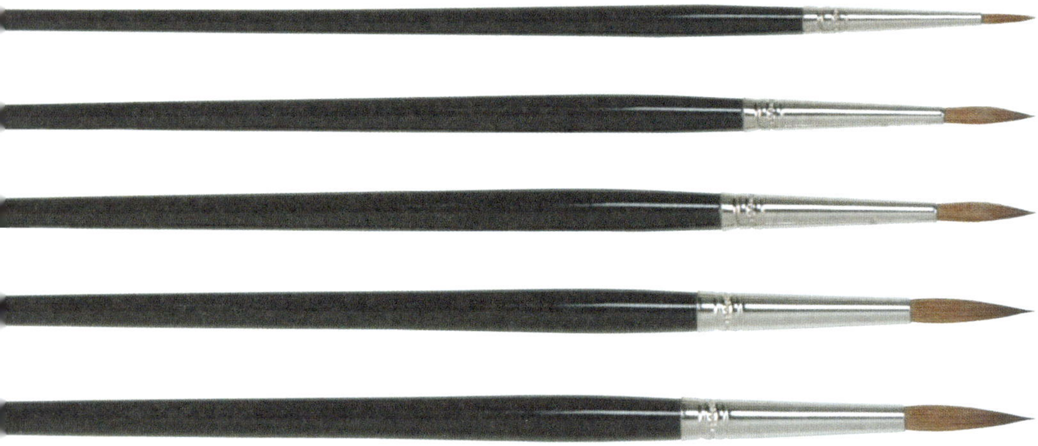

Pointed sables are the finest brushes you can buy. The best ones are assembled by skilled brush makers. Choose two brushes only from this range. The smallest and the largest would be enough.

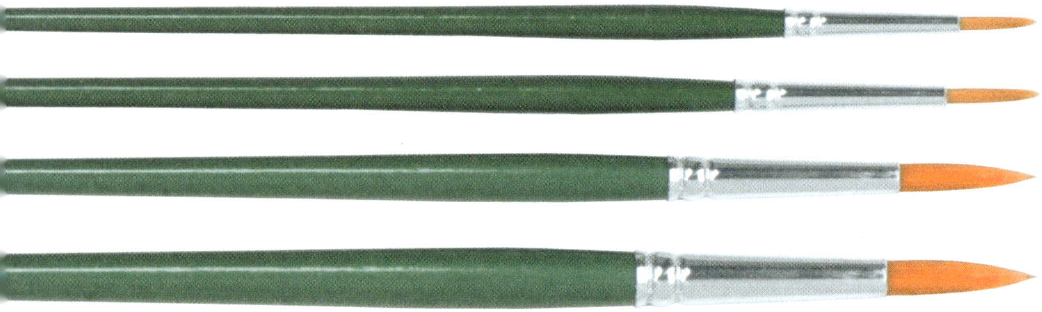

Modern synthetic brushes now almost match the quality of the sables. If you are not using sables, choose two from this range. Again, the smallest and the largest would be enough.

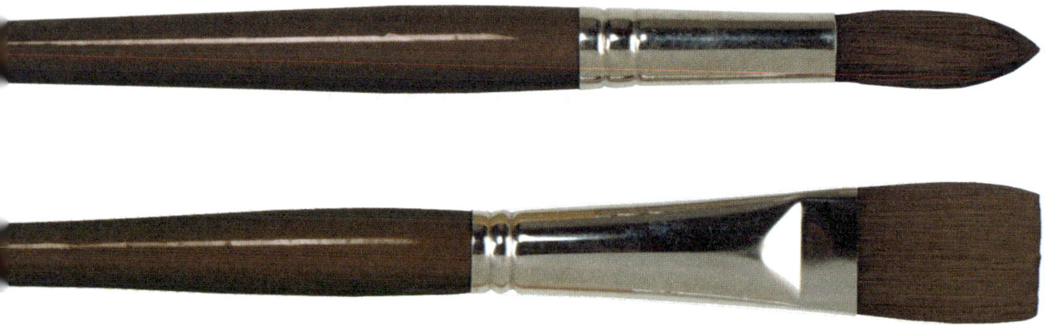

In addition to your choice of two round brushes, select a large, round 'mop' brush (top) and two large, flat brushes (bottom). All are used for washes.

wax candle for masking, and cotton buds for lifting off small areas of paint. For lifting off larger areas, use kitchen tissue. You can also work designs into wet paint using the handle of a brush, but to do this add gum arabic to the paint to slow down the drying process.

other accessories

Before you can start painting, you will need to fix your paper to something solid. A sheet of plywood and some masking tape is ideal for this. When you want to change your colours, you will need to rinse your brush. A simple jam jar filled with water will do, though a collapsible water pot works best outdoors.

Watercolours take time to dry. This can make applying one wash over another very time consuming. Speed up the process with a hairdryer, but be careful not to blow unwanted paint into other areas of your work.

Last, make sure that your workspace is adequately lit. This will not only avoid eyestrain, but allow you to see colours as they really are. Either sit by a window, or use a daylight simulation bulb in a desk lamp – it can be very disheartening to see your work change colour in 'real' light.

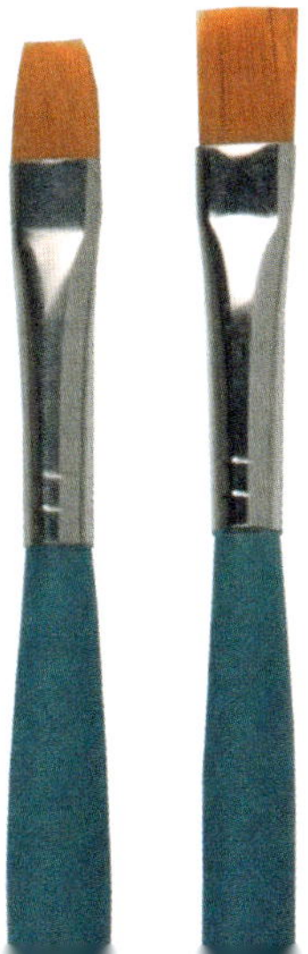

Flat, hog hair brushes like the ones on the left are very useful. These brushes are not used for applying watercolours, but for scrubbing out areas where the paint is too dark. Use a synthetic brush for this purpose.

BRUSH CARE

If you purchase a good range of brushes and take care of them as you use them, they should last a lifetime. In fact, you need to do very little to keep your brushes in good condition.

Always rinse your brushes in plenty of clean water after painting. From time to time, squeeze a little washing up liquid or rub a small amount soft soap onto your fingers and roll the brush between your forefinger and thumb where the hairs meet the ferrule. This is because paint builds up under the ferrule, stopping the hairs returning to their proper shape.

Never leave brushes standing in your water jar with the bristles facing down. This causes the points to curl round and, although they usually straighten after a while, they are difficult to use while the hairs are curved. Do not discard brushes if they lose their point completely – they are often useful as wash brushes.

Take care not to ruffle the hairs when carrying your brushes by using a brush case, which is simply a cylindrical metal tube with a lid, or by securing your brushes with elastic bands to a stiff piece of cardboard.

If the handle of a favourite brush becomes loose, scratch off the varnish and float the brush in water overnight. With luck, the wood will expand and the handle will tighten again. You may have to repeat this as the wood dries. If this does not work, gently hammer the point of a nail in several places round the neck of the ferrule. This pushes a burr of metal into the wooden handle and sometimes cures the movement.

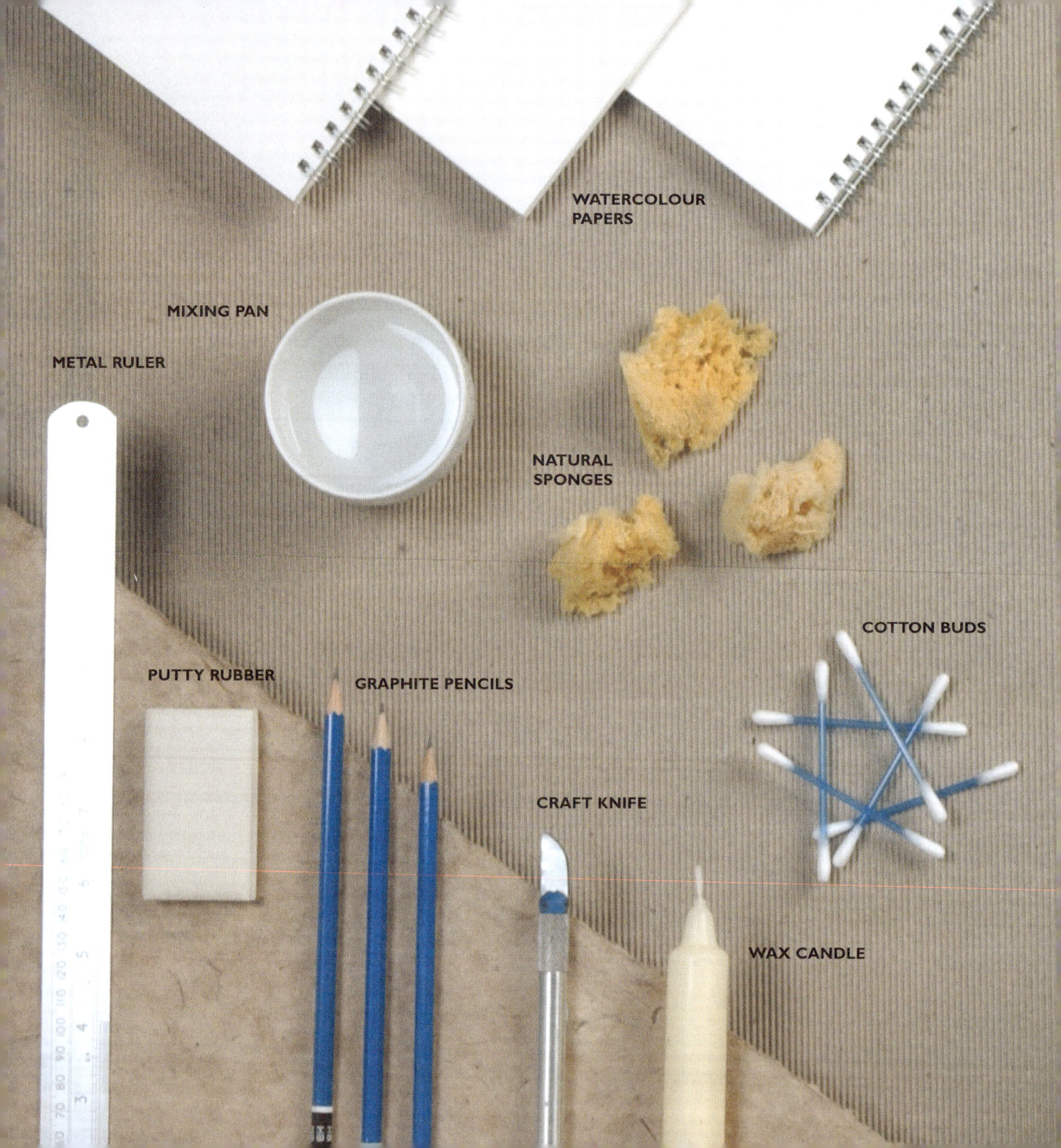
WATERCOLOUR PAPERS
MIXING PAN
METAL RULER
NATURAL SPONGES
COTTON BUDS
PUTTY RUBBER
GRAPHITE PENCILS
CRAFT KNIFE
WAX CANDLE

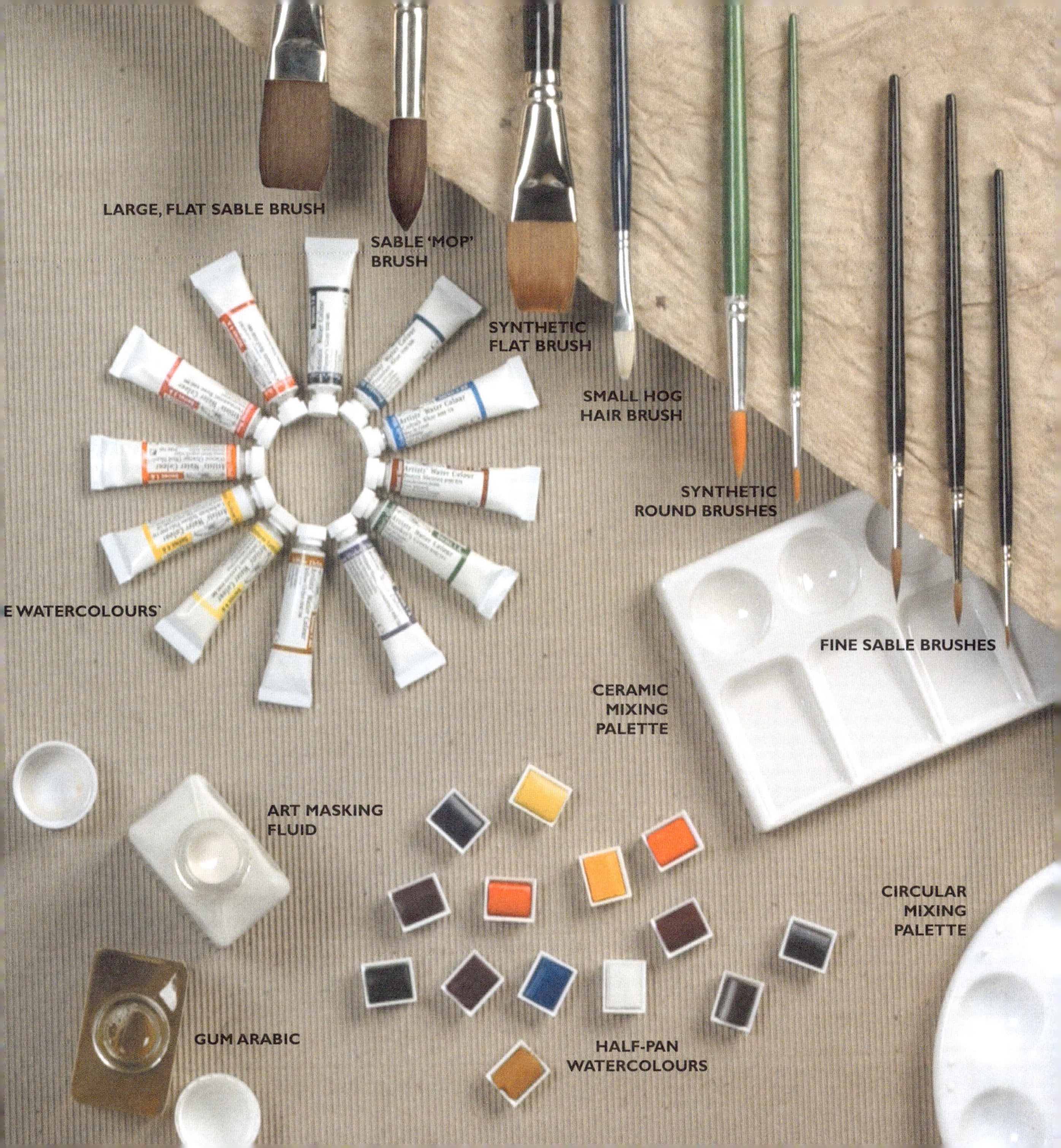
LARGE, FLAT SABLE BRUSH
SABLE 'MOP' BRUSH
SYNTHETIC FLAT BRUSH
SMALL HOG HAIR BRUSH
SYNTHETIC ROUND BRUSHES
E WATERCOLOURS
FINE SABLE BRUSHES
CERAMIC MIXING PALETTE
ART MASKING FLUID
CIRCULAR MIXING PALETTE
GUM ARABIC
HALF-PAN WATERCOLOURS

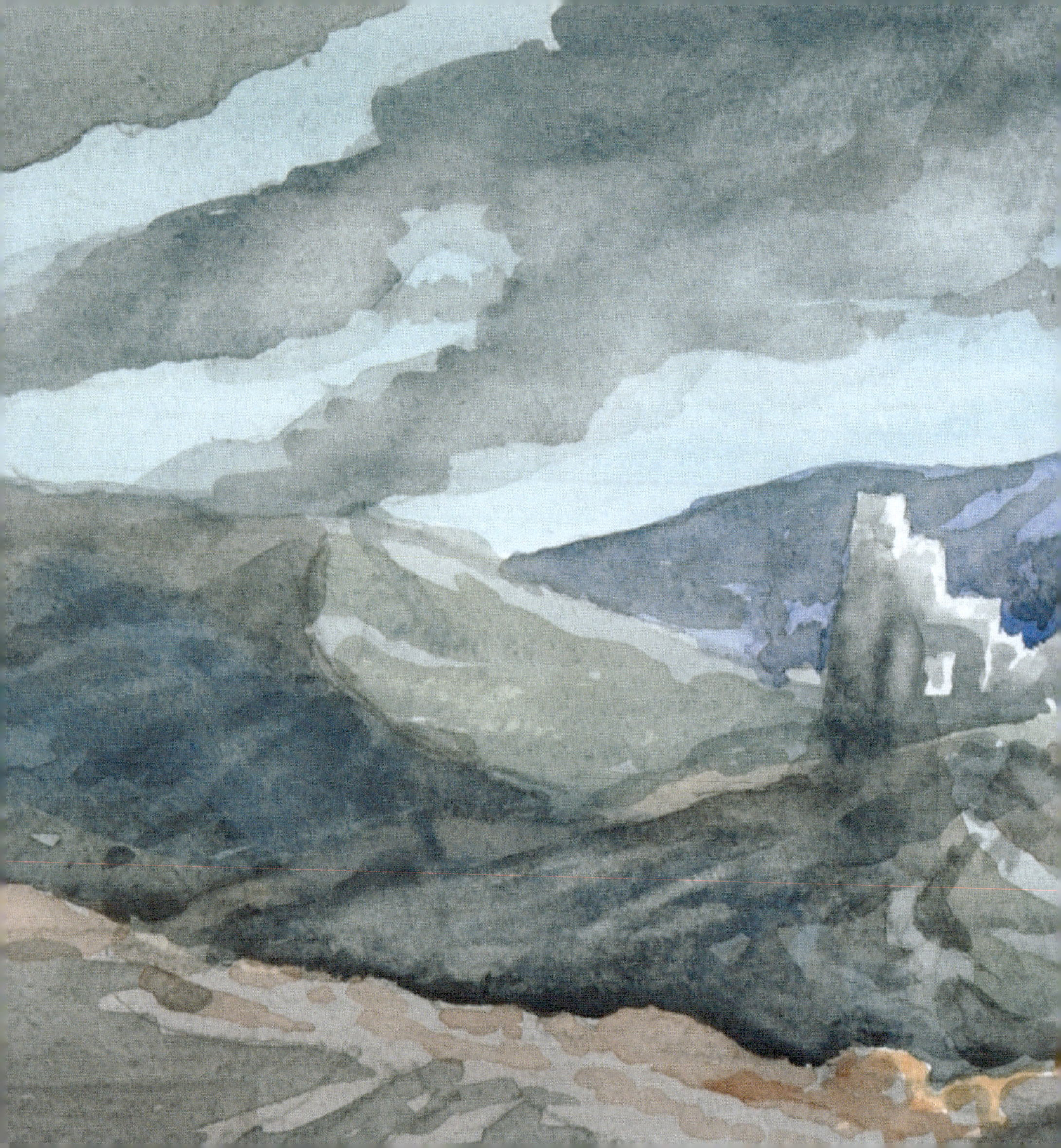

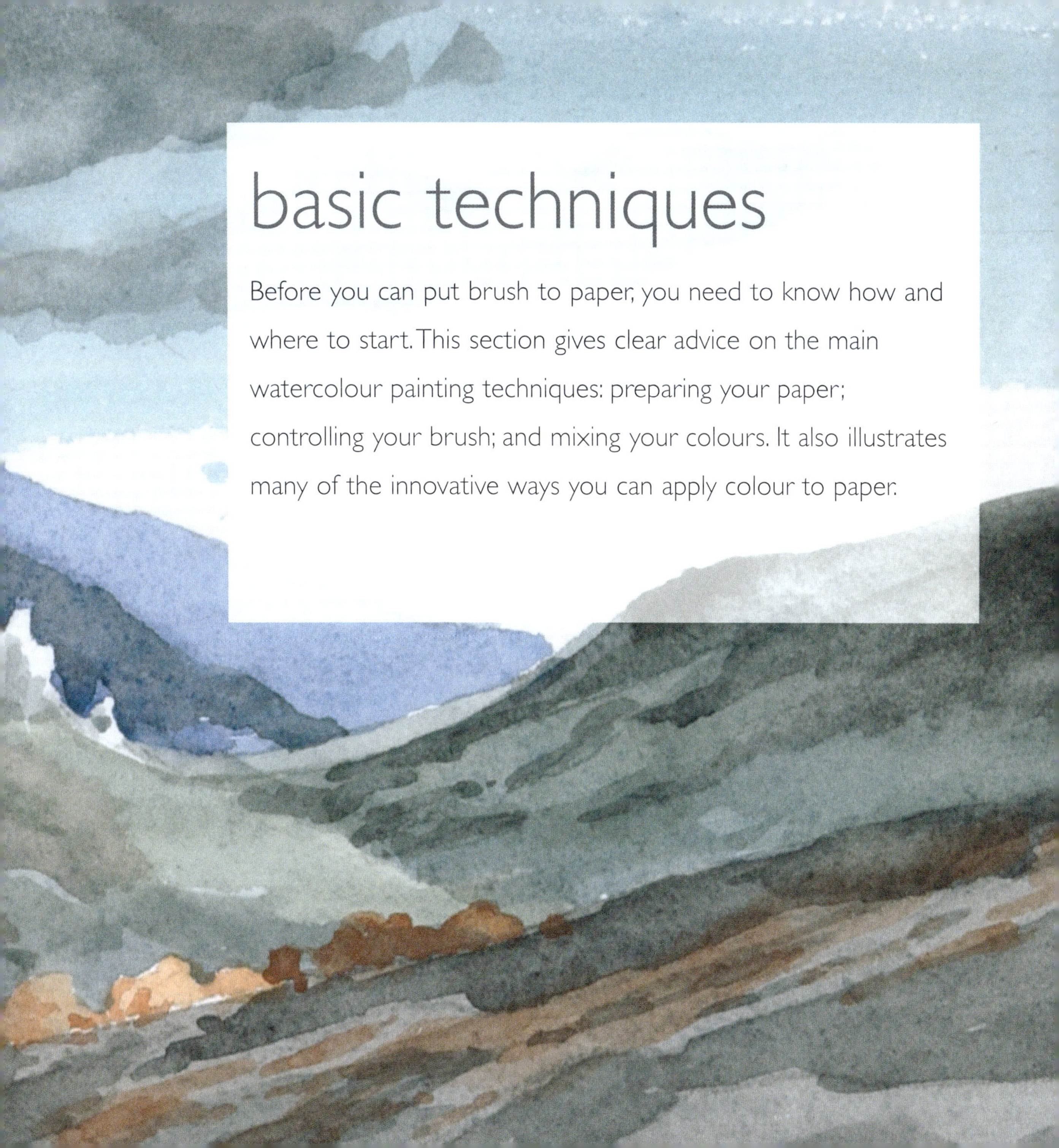

basic techniques

Before you can put brush to paper, you need to know how and where to start. This section gives clear advice on the main watercolour painting techniques: preparing your paper; controlling your brush; and mixing your colours. It also illustrates many of the innovative ways you can apply colour to paper.

basic techniques

Watercolour is one the simplest of the painting media but at the same time, is probably the most subtle and sensitive to personal interpretation. The basic technique of watercolour is the laying of transparent washes on white paper; the white paper represents light and every application of paint gradually darkens the picture. Once the white of the paper glowing through the paint is lost, the watercolour has been overworked. To work well, you need paper that is as white as possible and will stay white over time. The range of papers developed to meet this need is very wide and there are papers to suit every type of painting. Also, laying flat washes is not easy at first but it is a basic technique that can quickly be learned with practice, along with handling the softhaired brushes that work so well with waterbased colours.

For the most part, watercolour papers need to be soaked with water then 'stretched' on board and left to dry (see p. 39). This is your starting point; paper that has

CONTROLLING THE MARKS YOU MAKE

All brushes have their own handling characteristics according to their shape, hair type, and size. As with a tennis racket or golf club, you will need to get to know just what your brushes will, or will not, do. The types illustrated throughout this book may be all you need for your watercolour art, but experiment with different combinations of brushes and papers. With practice, you will develop your own touch.

BELOW The wide, flat brush is used for applying washes, making rectangular marks, and drawing fine lines with its edge. Hold this brush sideways in a pen grip where the handle bulges.

BELOW A good round brush will come to a point when loaded with paint. Hold this brush with an angled pen grip, toward the end of the handle.

BELOW This brush, called a 'rigger,' draws fine lines. The long hairs carry lots of paint – you will surprised at how much. Hold this brush as you would a pen, near the ferrule.

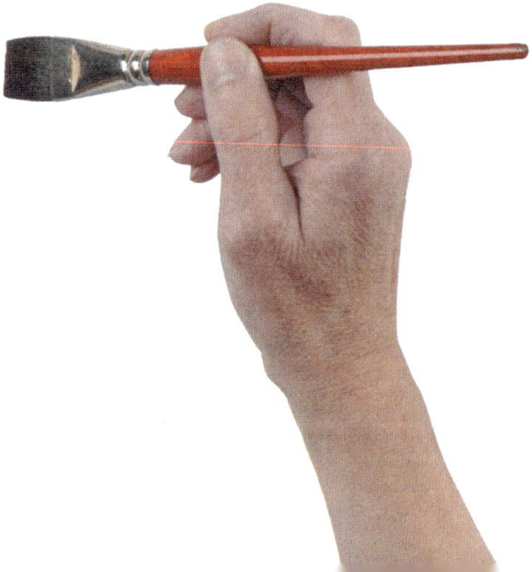

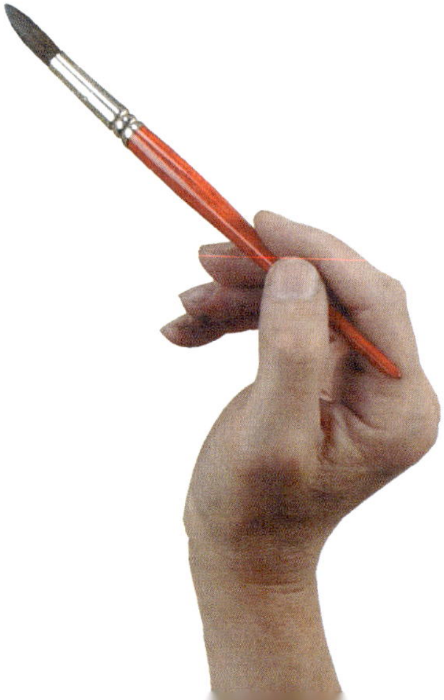

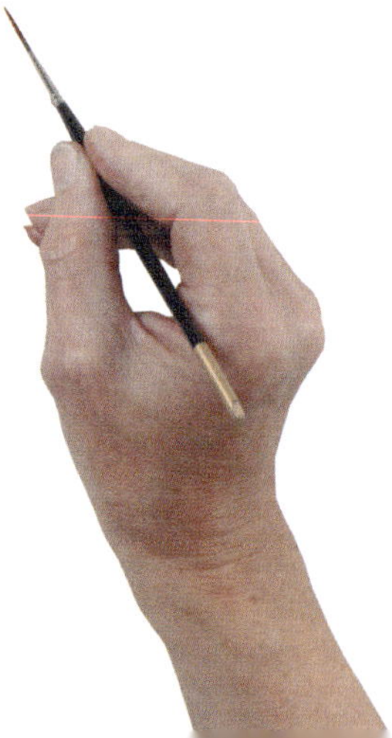

STIPPLING

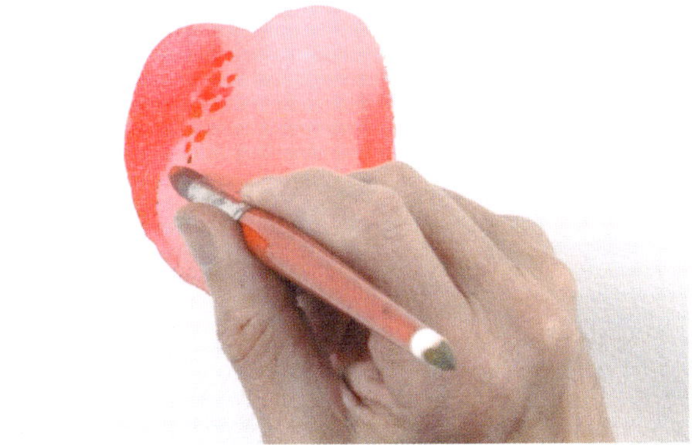

1 Add a base colour of permanent rose to the paper, painting it in the shape of a strawberry. Decide where your light source is, then darken your mix slightly. Start stippling on the shadow side of the fruit, dabbing on spots of colour with the point of the brush.

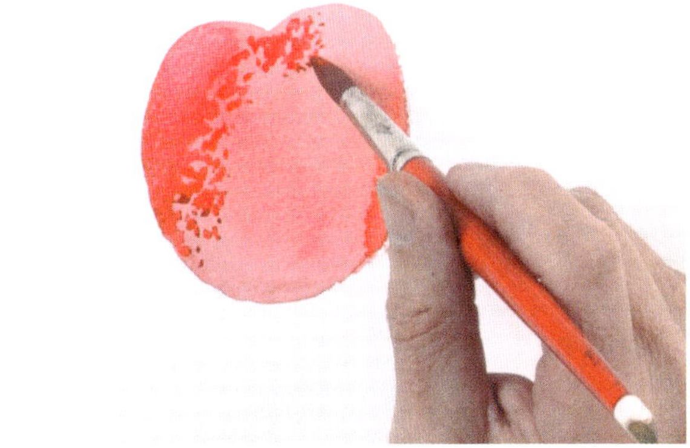

2 Work your way around the side of the fruit toward the top. Stippling works well from dark to light – create darker areas by adding larger dots, closer together. As you work toward the lighter areas, use fewer, smaller dots, farther apart.

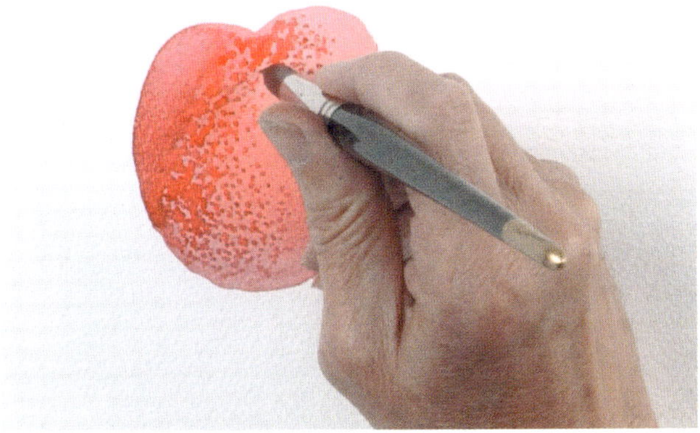

3 Increase the effect by using a smaller-tipped brush to create smaller dots. This adds a fine level of detail to your work and helps you control the tone between light and dark more accurately. It also helps blend the light and dark areas together in the viewer's eye.

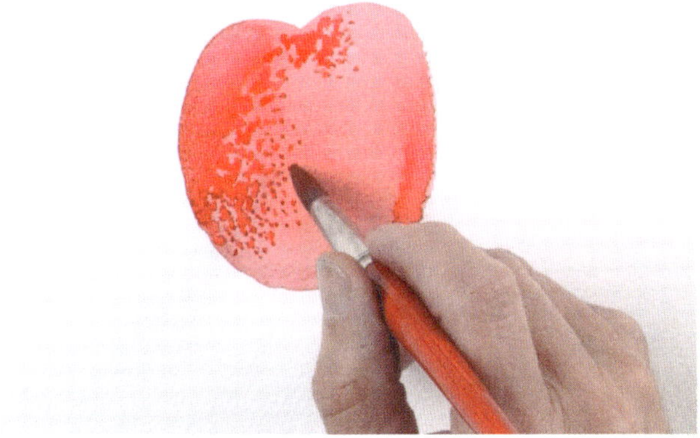

4 You are not limited to using one colour only – stippling can be built up using a spectrum of colours, but bear in mind that the tone of each colour needs to be the same in order for the effect to look smooth. Also, stippling is best suited to small areas – large areas are hard to fill.

not been stretched will buckle when wet paint is applied to it. Not only will you need to control your paint across the paper, but up- and downhill as well – an impossible task and a waste of good paper.

brush control

A basic set of brushes (see pp. 16–29) is all you need to get started. In general, the softer the hairs, the more water the brush will hold, but large, soft brushes are very floppy when wet – although they cover large areas, you will have very little control over shape or drawing. They are good for large, wet-in-wet subjects and free abstracts. The best of the synthetics (or sable and synthetic mixes) have a good spring to them and are very durable. Apply your brushes carefully to the paper until you know how much bounce there is in the hairs. Try using each brush flooded with colour and carry on painting until there is so little paint left on the brush that it hardly marks the paper. In this way, you will learn how each brush performs and you will start to develop your own personal touch.

colour selection

There are hundreds of watercolours available but their basic formula has remained unchanged since the 18th century. Raw pigments are ground very finely and mixed with gum arabic and water to form a stiff paste. After drying, 'pan' colours can be dissolved by applying a wet brush. The more finely the pigment is ground, the more colour comes out. Cheap watercolours often contain too much gum and not enough pigment. The result is that your work becomes sticky and the colour is streaky.

The use of the colours shown on the wheel will cover most of the mixes you will need and the way to get the mixes you want is shown in the projects. This will give you

SPATTERING

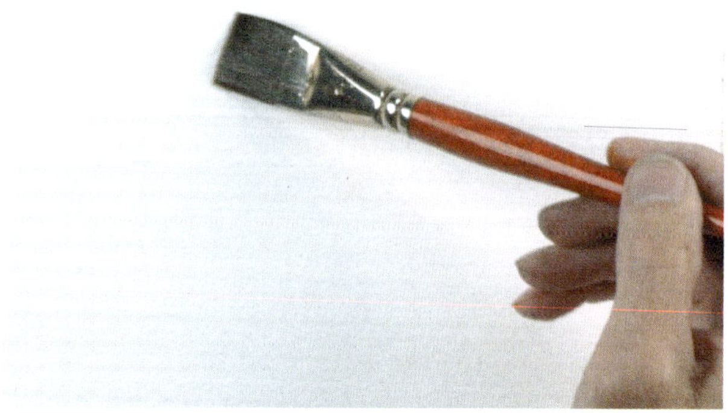

1 First, lay down a wash of clear water across the page with a wide, flat brush. Apply the water by pulling the brush across the paper in horizontal strokes to form bands. This is the technique for applying any flat wash to paper.

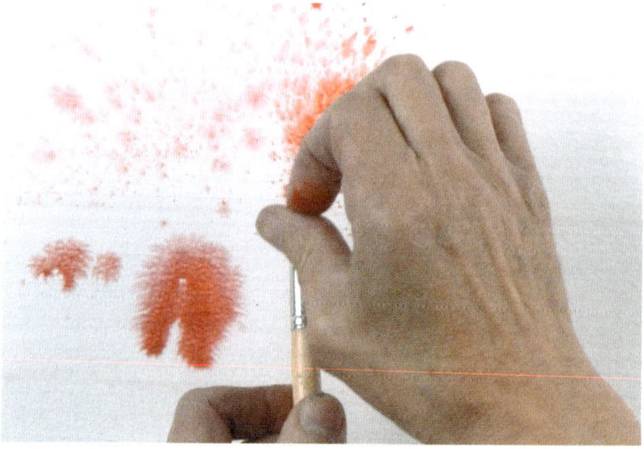

2 Dip a stiff hog hair brush into your paint. Don't mix the paint too thickly, or it will tend to stick to the brush. Then pull your index finger across the hairs. It is important that you only pull your finger toward you – otherwise, you will cover yourself in paint.

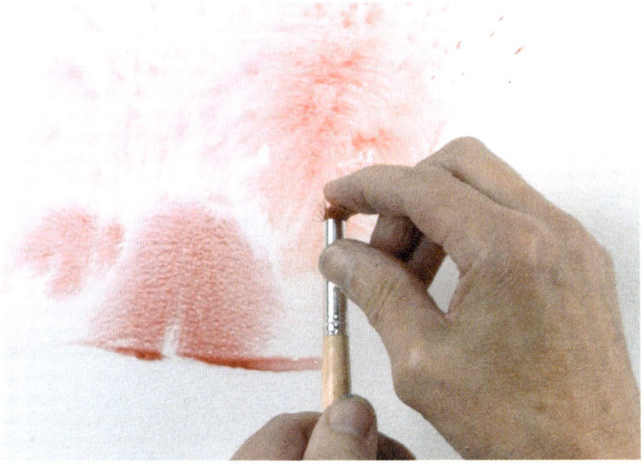

3 This creates an explosion of colour across the page, which expands and merges as it spreads in the water. Repeat the spattering process to increase the effect. The overall result is to liven up an otherwise flat colour with a textured effect.

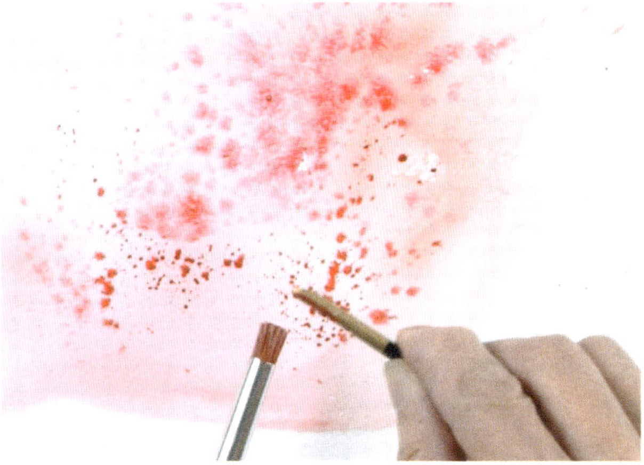

4 As well as using your finger, you can also use the handle of another brush. As before, simply pull the handle toward you to spatter the paint over the paper. Successive applications of spattered paint creates more and more texture on the paper.

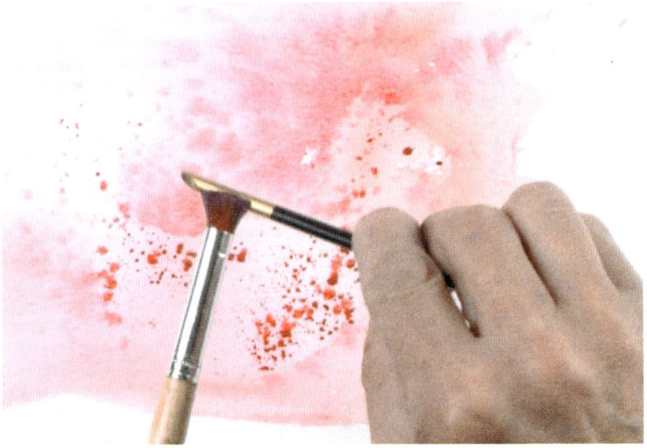

5 You don't have to stick to the same colour all the way through. In fact, you can add almost any colours you like, building them up one after the other. As a guide, though, you should only use colours with the same tonal range – this will give your image a more unified look.

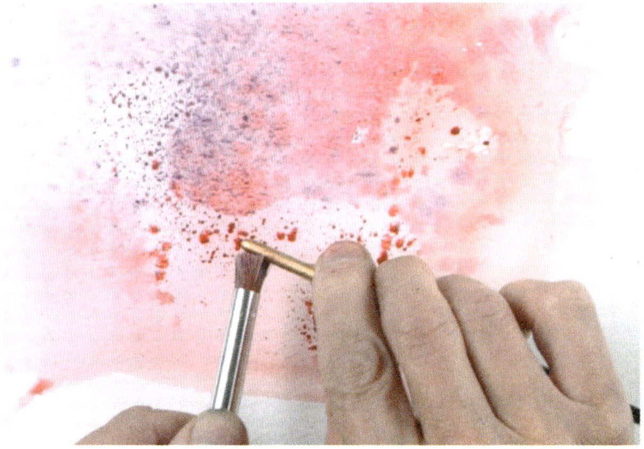

6 Add the last colour, in this case violet, by dipping just a few bristles on the edge of the brush into the paint and carefully spattering it with the handle of the brush. This creates a lighter spray of paint across the page, in contrast to the larger drops underneath.

USING A SYNTHETIC SPONGE

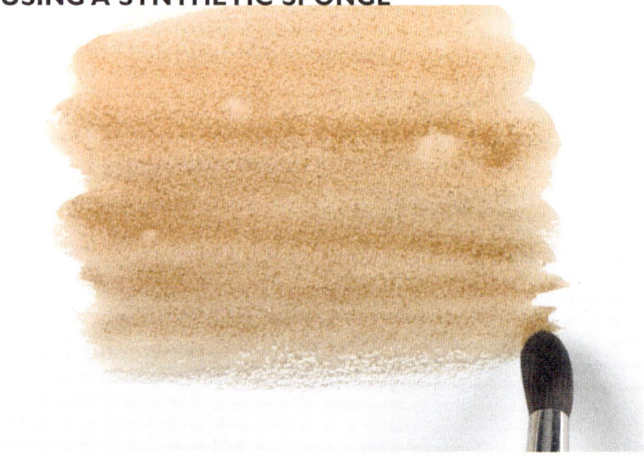

1 Apply a flat wash of colour with the mop brush, pulling it across the paper in horizontal bands. Here, we have used burnt sienna as the wash colour. Pick up any unwanted drips with the point of the brush to create a smooth, flat colour.

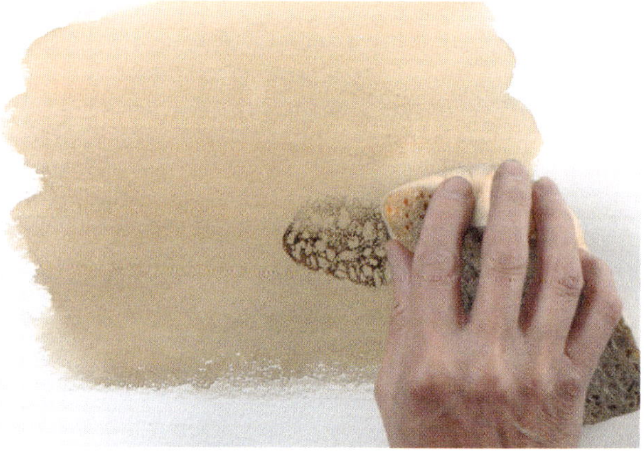

2 Let the paint dry thoroughly. Then make a darker mix of your paint by adding, for example, a little cobalt blue. Dip your synthetic sponge into the mix and start dabbing it onto the wash. The pattern of the sponge is printed onto the paper.

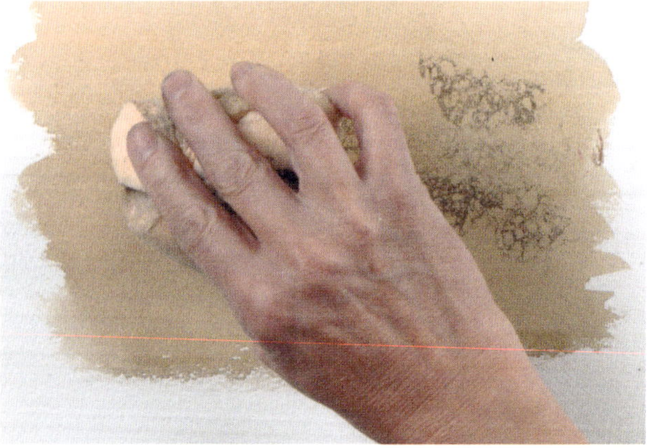

3 Make sure that your mix is quite thick and that the surface of the sponge is not saturated with paint. This will stop the paint running and also stops it smearing as you apply it to the paper, both of which will ruin the patterned effect.

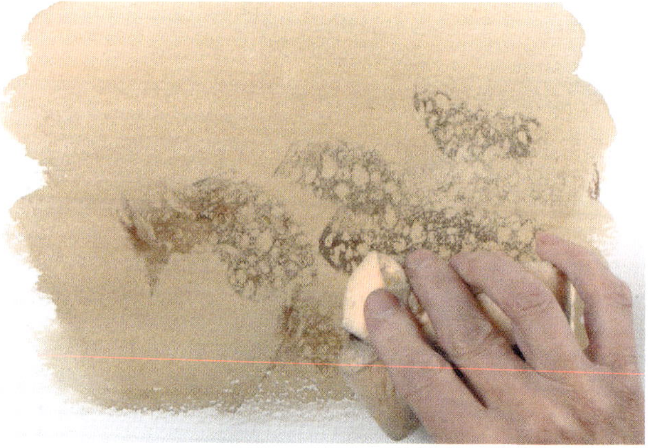

4 Synthetic sponges produce a predictable print across the page. This can be very useful when you need regularity in your work, but for a more random pattern, such as that needed to produce foliage on a tree, use natural sponge – its surface is never regular.

the confidence to know how your mixes are going to turn out – soon you will be able to move on to making your own. Work for some time with a limited palette until you know the results of all the mixes, then start again with another palette of your own choosing. This will help you develop – don't just rely on the same old favourites. You may then to decide to add further colours – ultramarine blue and viridian (a deep strong green) are the ones to choose. Practice playfully with your paints and your brushes, sponges, kitchen roll, pencils and paper before you attempt the projects. This will allow you to do the mechanical things almost automatically.

colour mixing

Getting the colour mix that will give you the finished result you want depends on two things – the amount of colour and the amount of water. Have a clean pan or reservoir in your palette ready for each colour. Put a little clean water in each but not too much – it is easy to add more water to a strong mix but a waste of paint to tint large amounts of water, creating a mix you will never use up. Take your brush, dip it in your water pot then stroke it firmly across your desired watercolour pan. You will need to do this several times until the colour begins to dissolve. If you are using tube colours, squeeze a bit of paint about the size of a pea onto the rim of your pan. Don't forget to replace the lid on the tube.

Put the brush carrying the colour into your wet pan and stir until all the paint is dissolved. In the case of tube colours, check that there are no bits of solid paint sticking to the brush hairs. Test your mix on a piece of scrap paper, or better still, keep a little book for all your test patches and label each mix with its component colours. If the colour is too pale, add more colour to your pan; if it is

USING SEA SALT

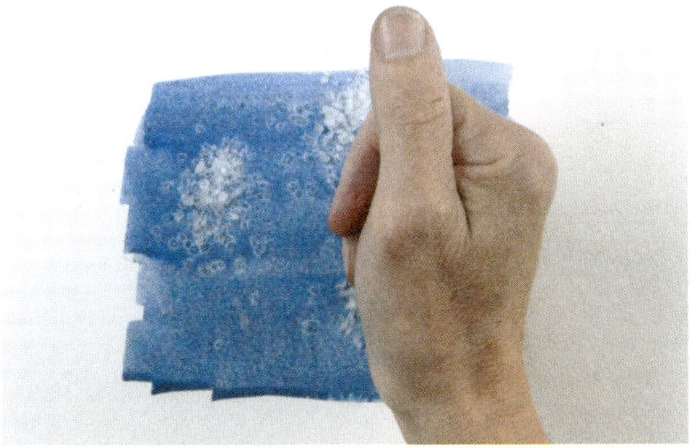

1 Apply a flat wash by painting horizontal bands of colour across the paper. Plan where you want the salt to go before you start, then drop small amounts of it onto the surface of the wet paint. Don't use too much – just enough to cover the paper.

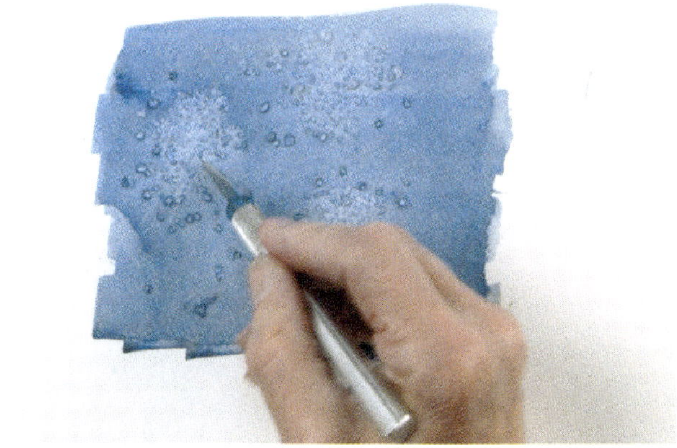

2 Let the paint dry thoroughly then scratch off the salt carefully with the point of craft knife. The salt crystals will absorb the paint as it dries. The paper underneath is left patterned and textured, according to how much salt you use and the proximity of the crystals to each other.

too strong, add more water. Leave your results to dry. The most important thing to notice is that watercolours always dry lighter than the colour of the wet paint would suggest. This is more noticeable in some colours than in others – you will gradually learn how each one behaves.

To mix two colours to make a third, wash your brush, dip it in the clean water again and apply it to the next colour pan. Add this to the colour already in your palette, stir thoroughly, then test it on some scrap paper. In this way, practice colour mixing until you feel that you are in control. Change the water in your pot frequently or have one pot for clean water and one to wash your brushes in. Try to achieve your colours with a mix of only two paints (three at most) – this will keep your washes clean and attractive.

experimentation

Watercolour is the one painting medium where the paint is meant to move about after you have put it on the paper. It does this in unpredictable and beautiful ways. Experiment wholeheartedly and don't be afraid to make a mess. This example shows the rewards of experimentation: Take some Payne's gray and ultramarine and drop each colour separately onto wet paper, leaving a gap in between each colour. Take your drawing board and, holding it at arms length, raise it to shoulder height then bring it down quickly. Repeat this several times until the paint begins to flick off into the air. Lay your paper flat and allow it to dry. The result will be a windswept sky that no brush could paint.

WAX RESIST

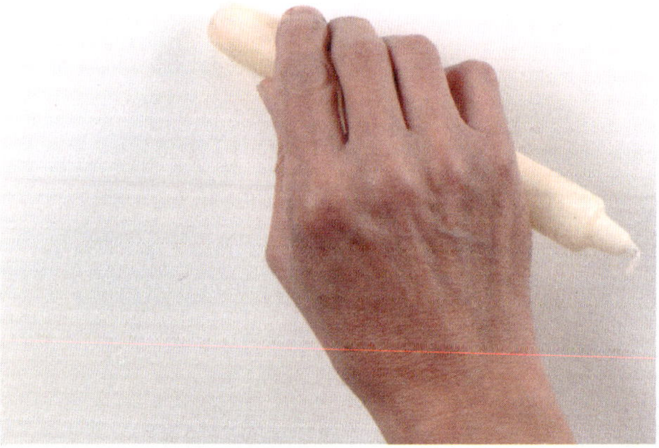

1 Using the end of a standard household candle, scratch the pattern you want to 'resist' the paint onto the paper. You need not press too hard – the rough surface of the watercolour paper will easily remove enough wax to create the effect.

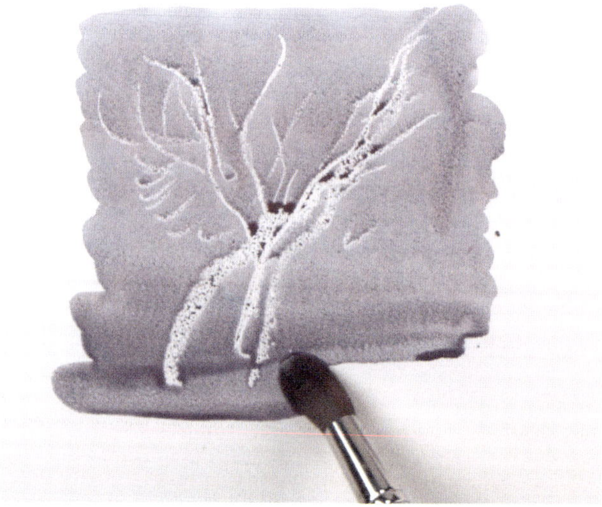

2 Apply a wash of paint over the wax resist. The pattern underneath shows through the paint. Notice how even the thin lines show through and how the paint gathers in the joins between the lines of wax, adding texture to the image.

STRETCHING WATERCOLOUR PAPER

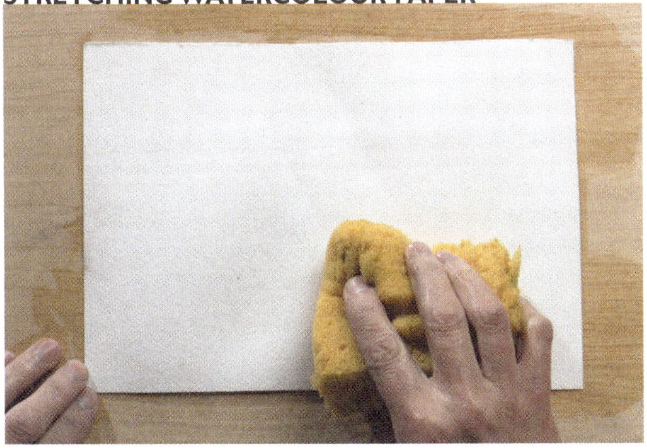

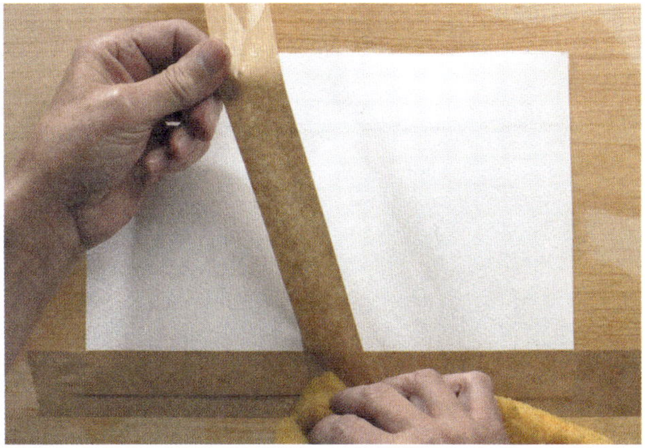

1 Put your watercolour paper on your board. If the paper has a watermark, put this facing upward. Then, with a clean sponge, thoroughly soak the paper in water. Make sure that the water has soaked through to the other side, turning the paper over if necessary.

2 Smooth the wet paper over the board to make sure that no air bubbles are trapped underneath. Then cut, or simply tear, four strips of gummed tape. Wet each strip with the sponge before applying it to the edges of your paper.

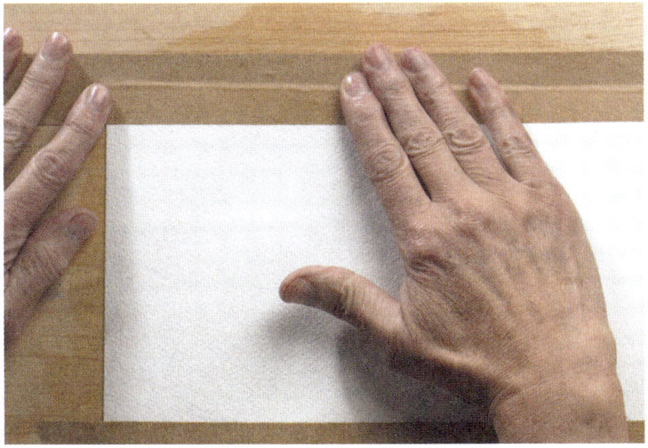

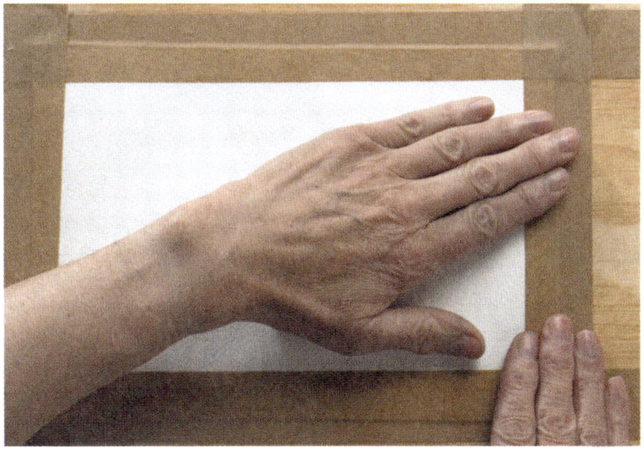

3 Apply the gummed tape with roughly half its width on the board and half its width on the paper. Stick down each edge of the paper to the board, starting with the two longest sides. Try and keep the paper taut to make sure there are no corrugations.

4 Stick down the two shortest sides in the same way, smoothing out the tape with the tips of your fingers. Leave the paper to dry flat at room temperature. Do not leave it next to a heat source or the gummed tape may lift, allowing the paper to buckle.

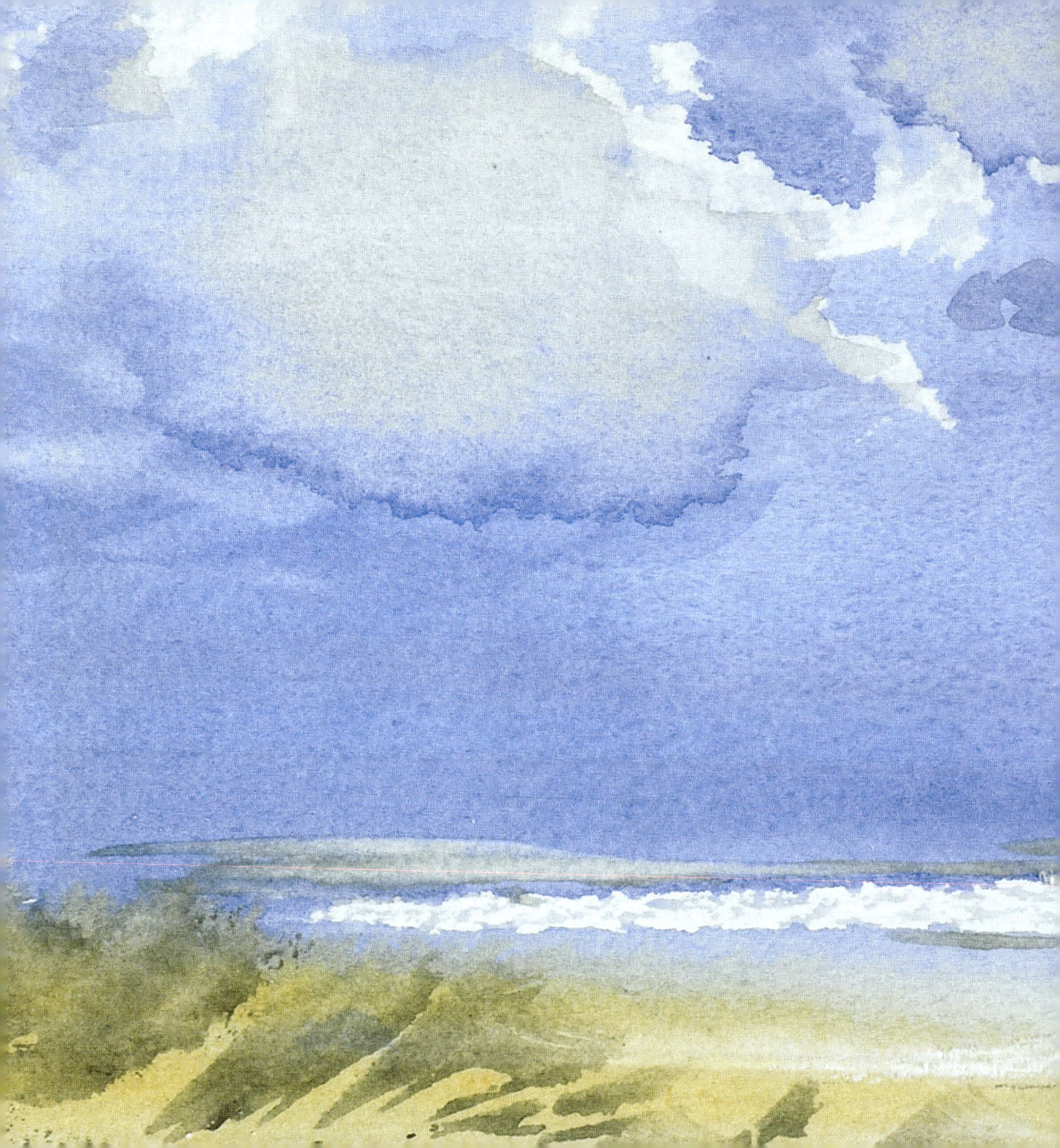

gallery

Watercolour is a wonderfully flexible medium and here you will see many styles and effects. From tight, meticulous draughtsmanship to soft free-flowing washes, each artist has their own vision and approach. Study the paintings carefully – each one can suggest a starting point for your own work.

after the storm

280 x 400mm (11 x 16in)

david evans

The close harmony of the greys and blues perfectly evokes the cool, misty atmosphere on the river Thames in London. This is achieved by the narrow range of cool colours. The vigour of the dry brushwork is helped by the rough surface of the paper.

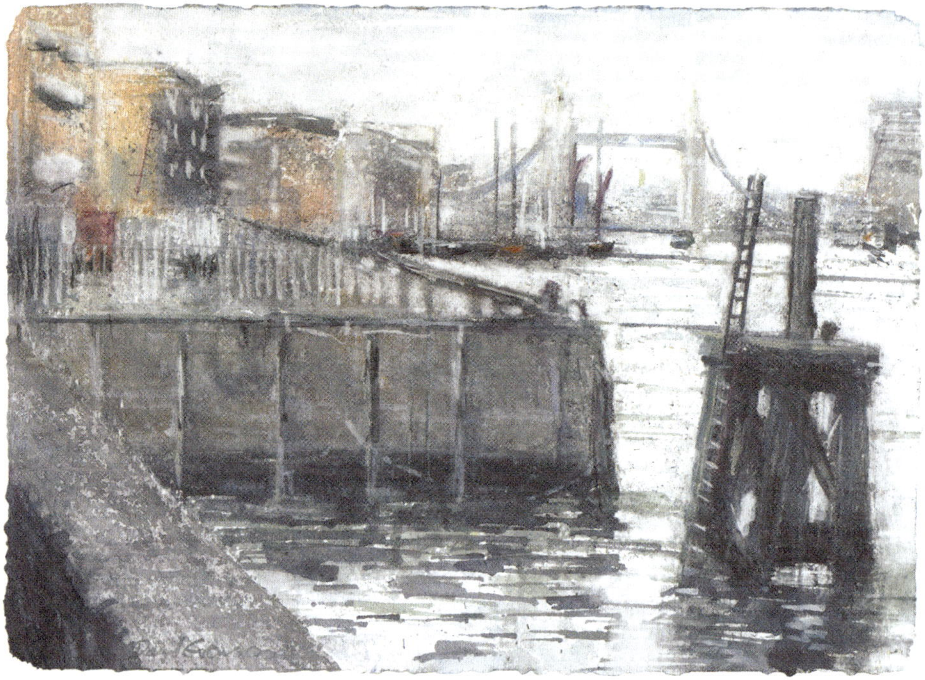

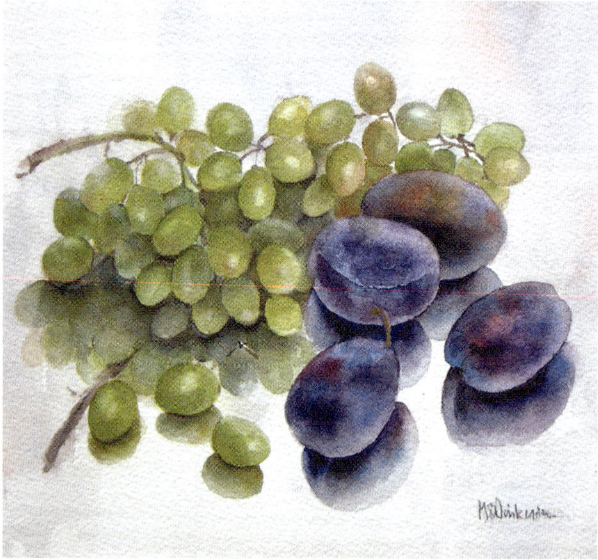

ripe and reflecting

430 x 450mm (17 x 18in)

margaret dinkeldein

Crisp draughtsmanship and good control of tone and reflections make this still life a success. Note how the forms soften as you look deeper into the bunch of grapes. Highlights are lifted out from each of the grapes and the form of the plums is achieved by dropping colour into the wet surface.

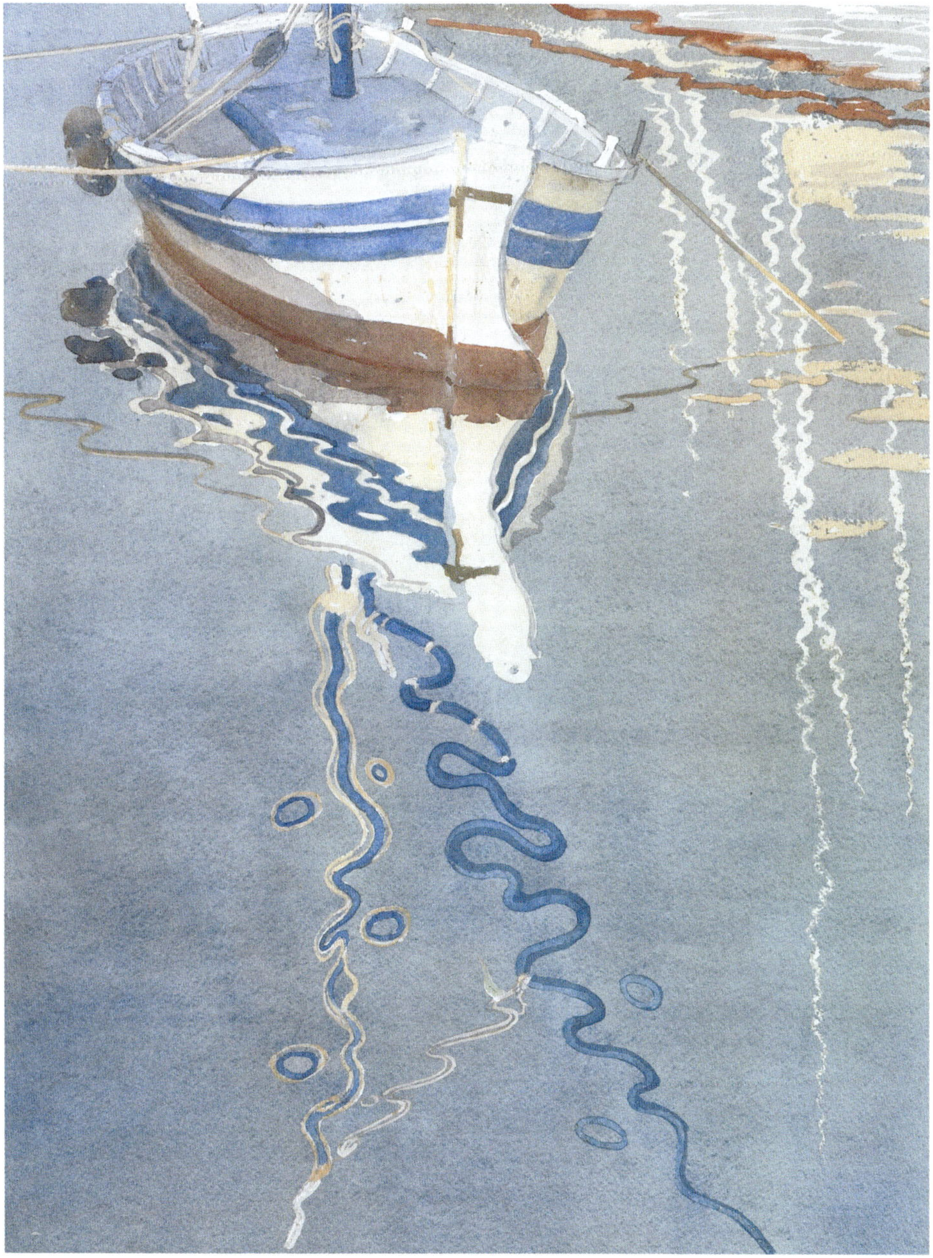

early morning reflections

400 x 300mm (16 x 12in)

pat rae

An almost abstract evocation of a sunlit harbour. The boat and its reflections form a single motif where the clean lines of the boat change almost imperceptibly into the dancing lines of the reflections. The whole image is laid over a beautiful turquoise wash.

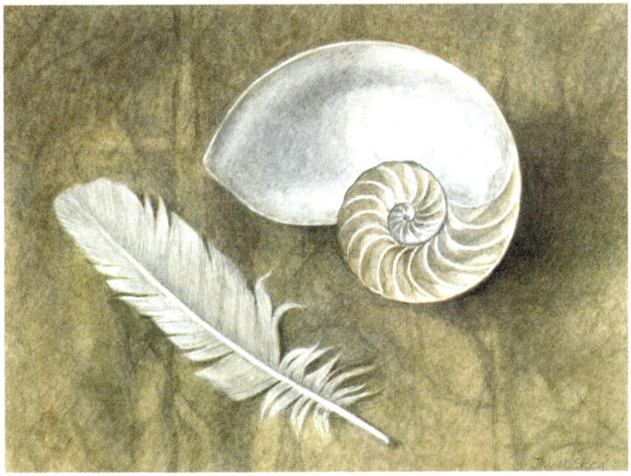

shell and feather

160 x 210mm (6½ x 8½in)

janet skea

The painter of this intensely observed picture uses the most accomplished of techniques to realize the beauty of the shell and feather. Don't miss the importance of the crafted background in presenting the objects. The whole image was created using small brushes.

empty beach

280 x 280mm (11 x 11in)

john barber

The fleeting effect of the light on clouds and waves was achieved with simple washes, a narrow colour range, and economy of brushwork. Rolling kitchen tissue across a wet wash provided the cloud shapes. The dry brush strokes add texture to the foreground.

still life with vegetables

230 x 300mm (9 x 12in)

shirley felts

A group of ordinary vegetables was used as a starting point for this glorious ensemble of rich colour, contrasts, and harmonies glowing out from a somber background. Colours are built up with a combination of soft washes and gentle stippling.

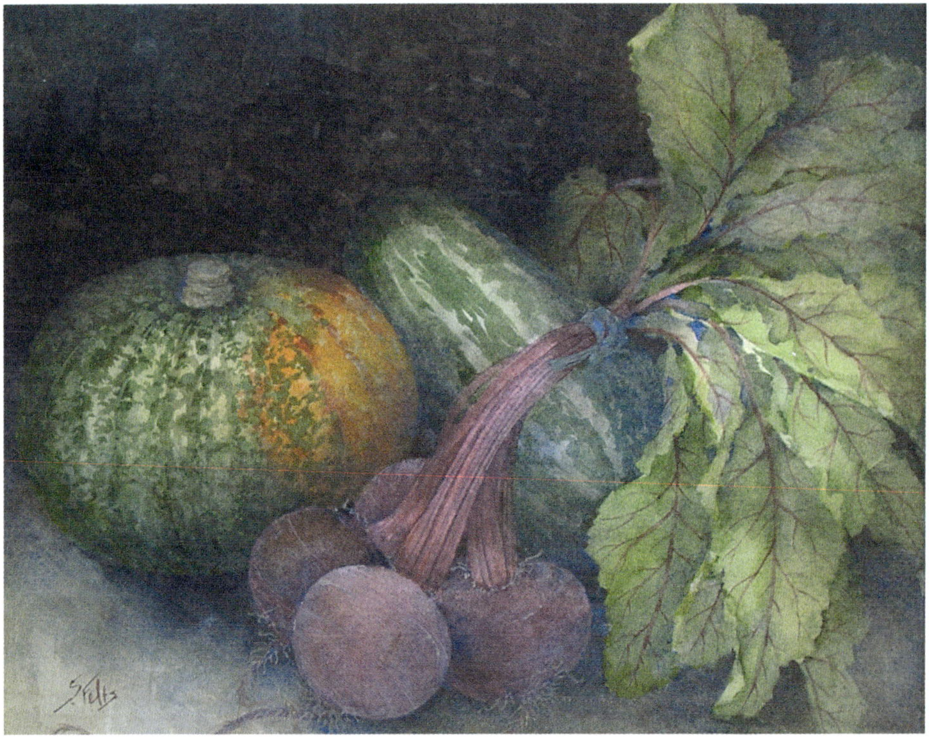

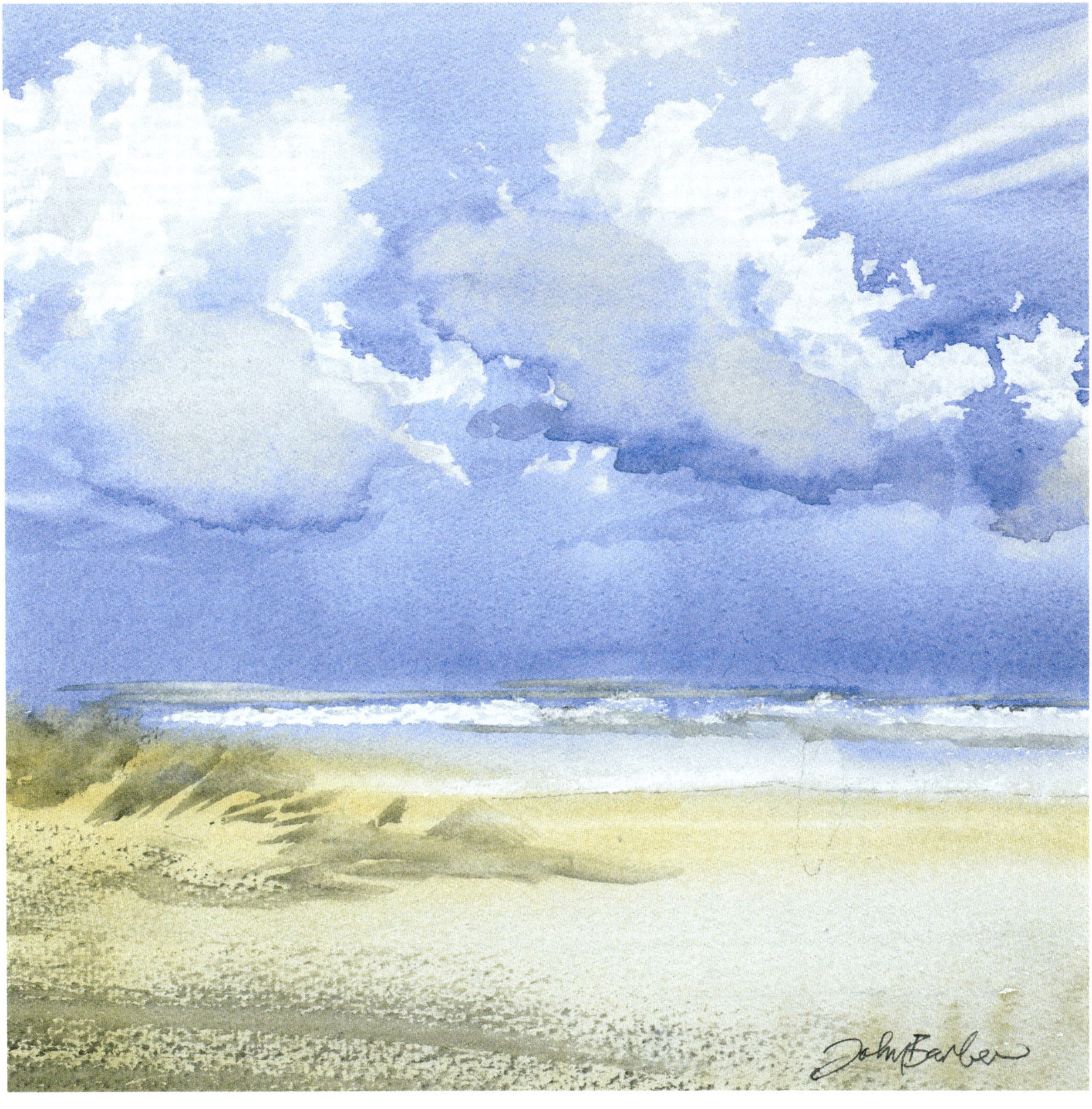
John Barber

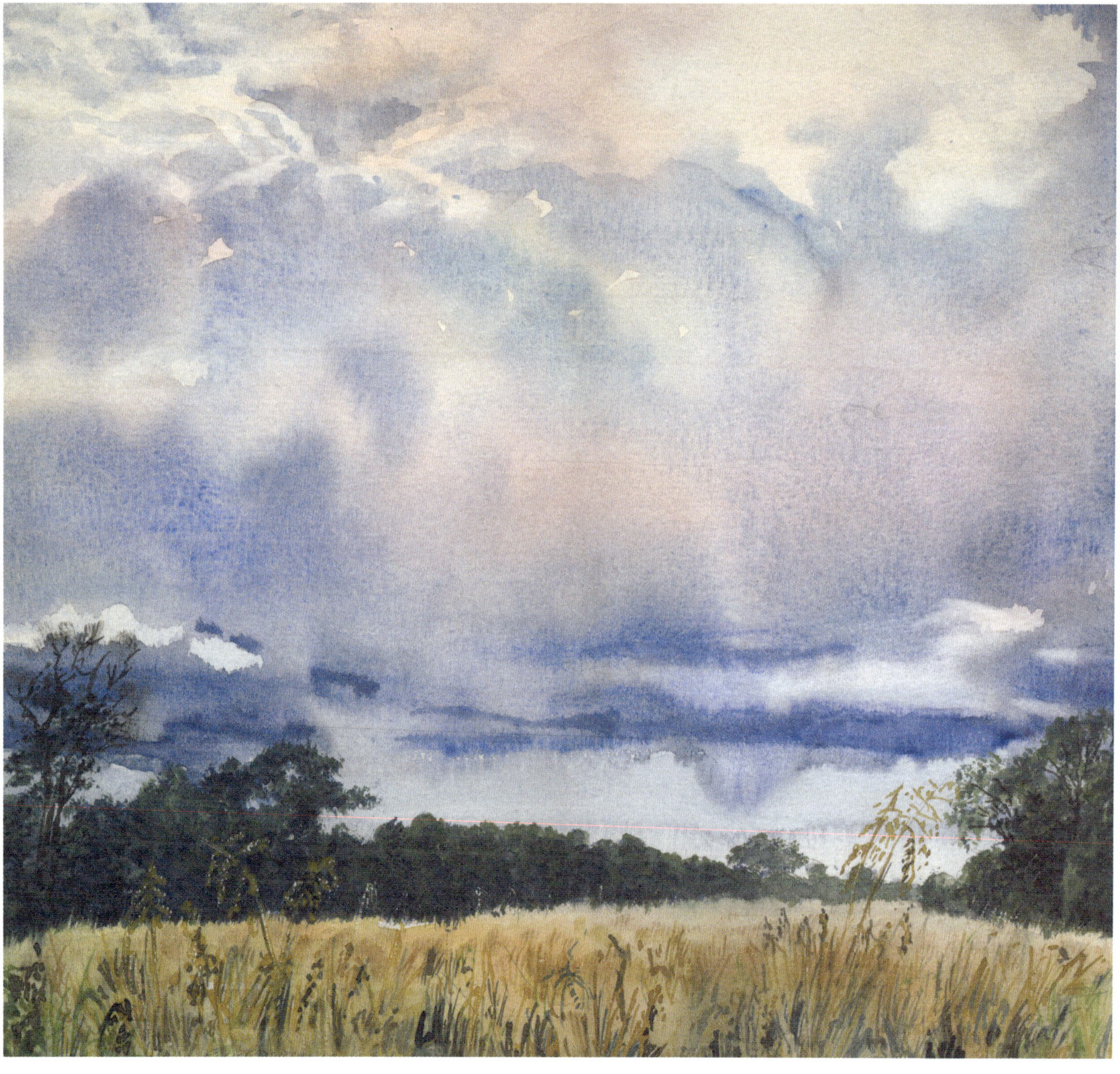

cornfield

300 x 350mm (12 x 14in)

roger hutchins

A wet-in-wet sky with a pink wash floating through the clouds creates what brush marks cannot. The strength of the foreground landscape holds the whole composition together.

sunflowers

580 x 450mm (23 x 18in)

margaret dinkeldein

The riot of golden colour looks casual but is actually carefully painted, with subtle hints of light coming through the petals. The wet-in-wet reflection in the table works beautifully.

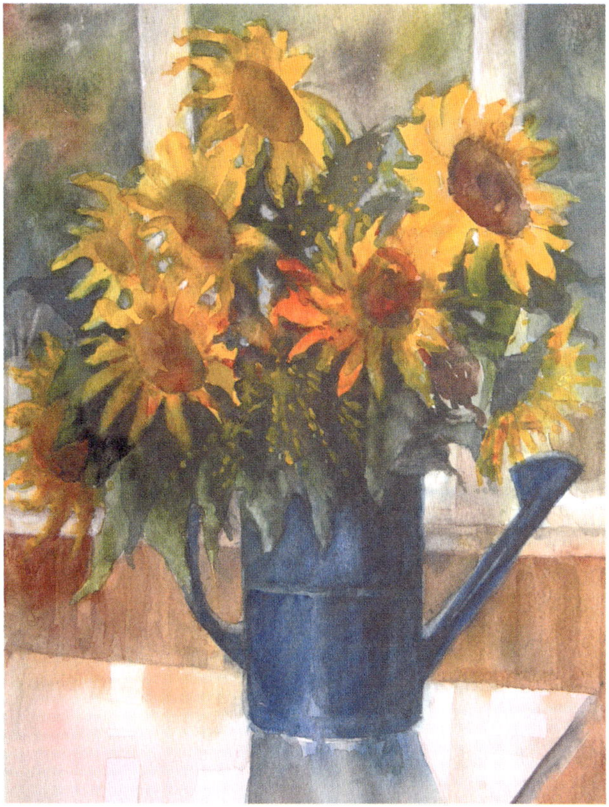

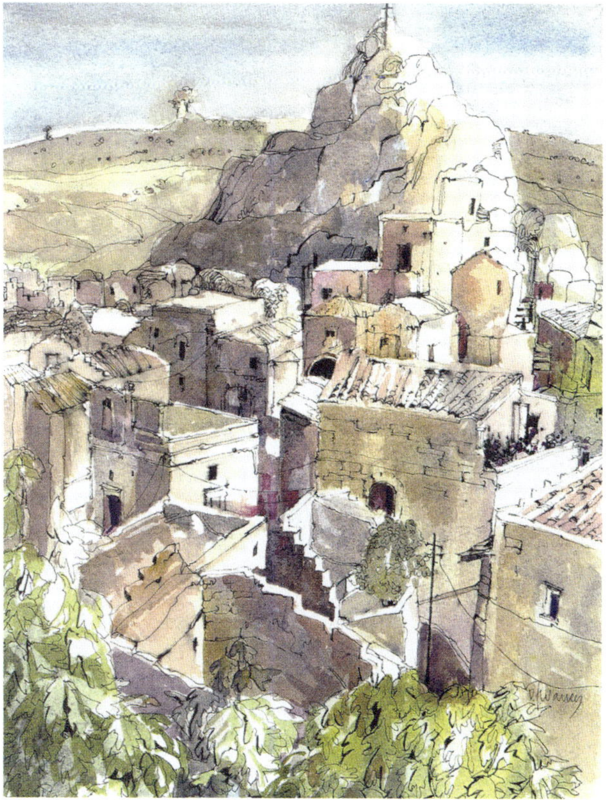

matera

400 x 300mm (16 x 12in)

valerie warren

The broken pen marks cleverly indicate the crumbling old buildings and the washes alternate between pale sunlit shapes and glowing shadows to create an almost three-dimensional effect.

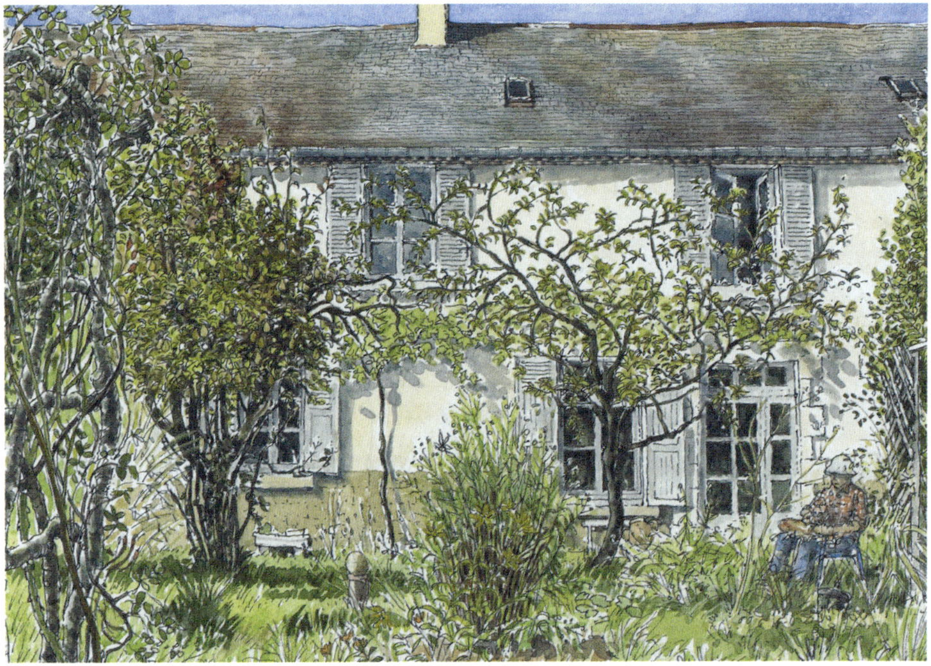

late summer sunshine
240 x 340mm (9 1/2 x 13 1/2 in)
audrey hammond

In this sunlit scene of a French garden, every twig and leaf was lovingly drawn with delicate pen strokes. The meticulous scene was coloured with gentle washes and the delicate shadows establish the dappled sunlight. This is a classic pen-and-wash painting.

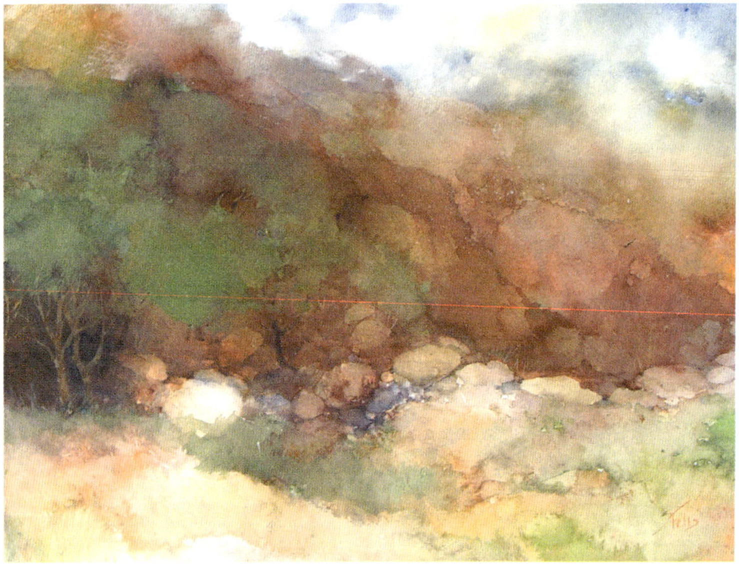

enchanted rock
550 x 750mm (22 x 30 in)
shirley felts

The wet-in-wet technique softly blends the colours so that the edges of forms are rarely defined. The clue that there are trees growing here is in the two tree trunks in the shadows.

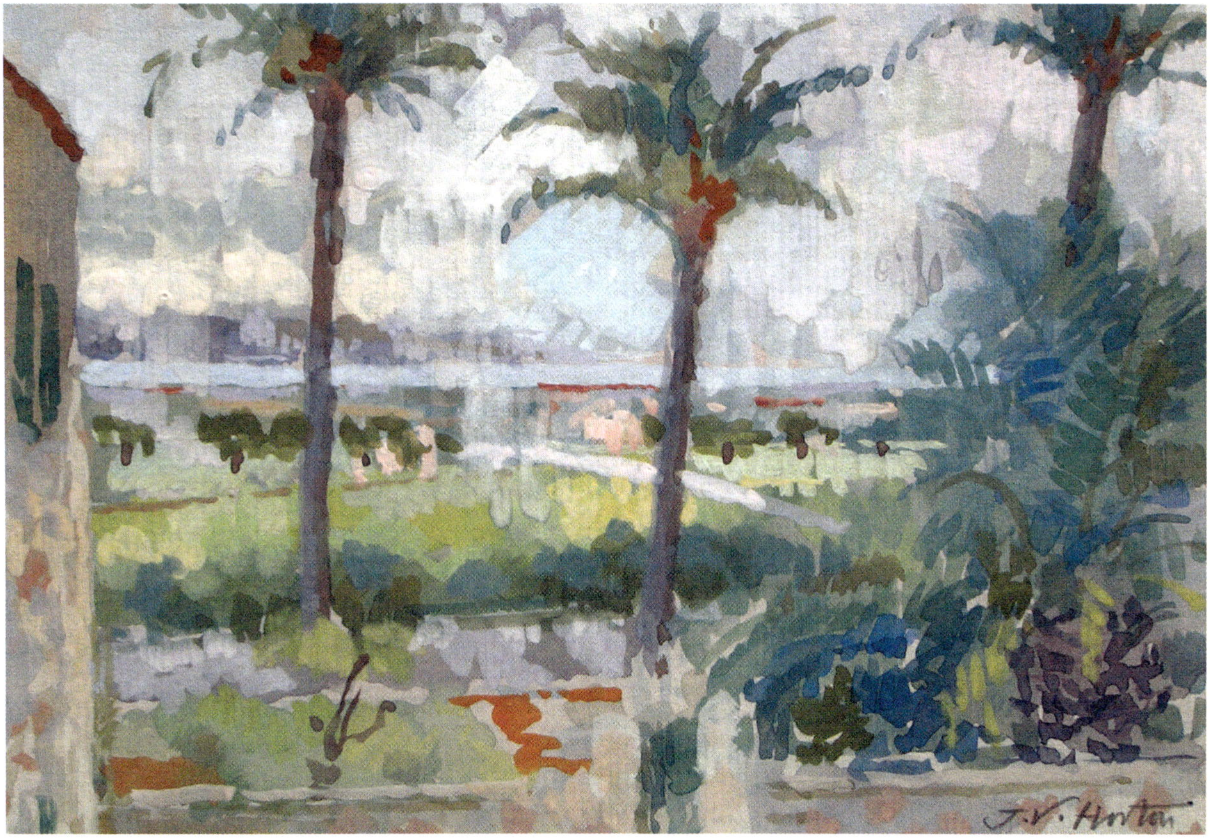

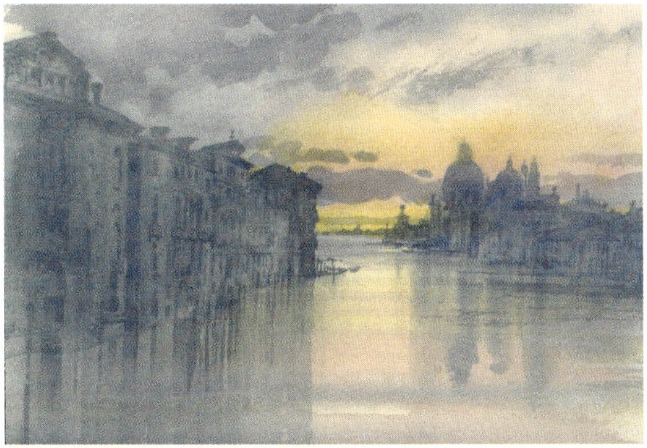

venetian scene
130 x 180mm (5 x 7in)
john barber

This tiny sketchbook watercolour shows how a large area of water can be made to look flat with a few uncluttered washes that reflect the colours of the sky and the buildings.

rainy day at can-xenet
230 x 300mm (9 x 12in)
james horton

A warm palette is used to conjure up a tropical feeling. Vertical brush marks create a bold overall effect; the misty background is also suggested with large brush marks.

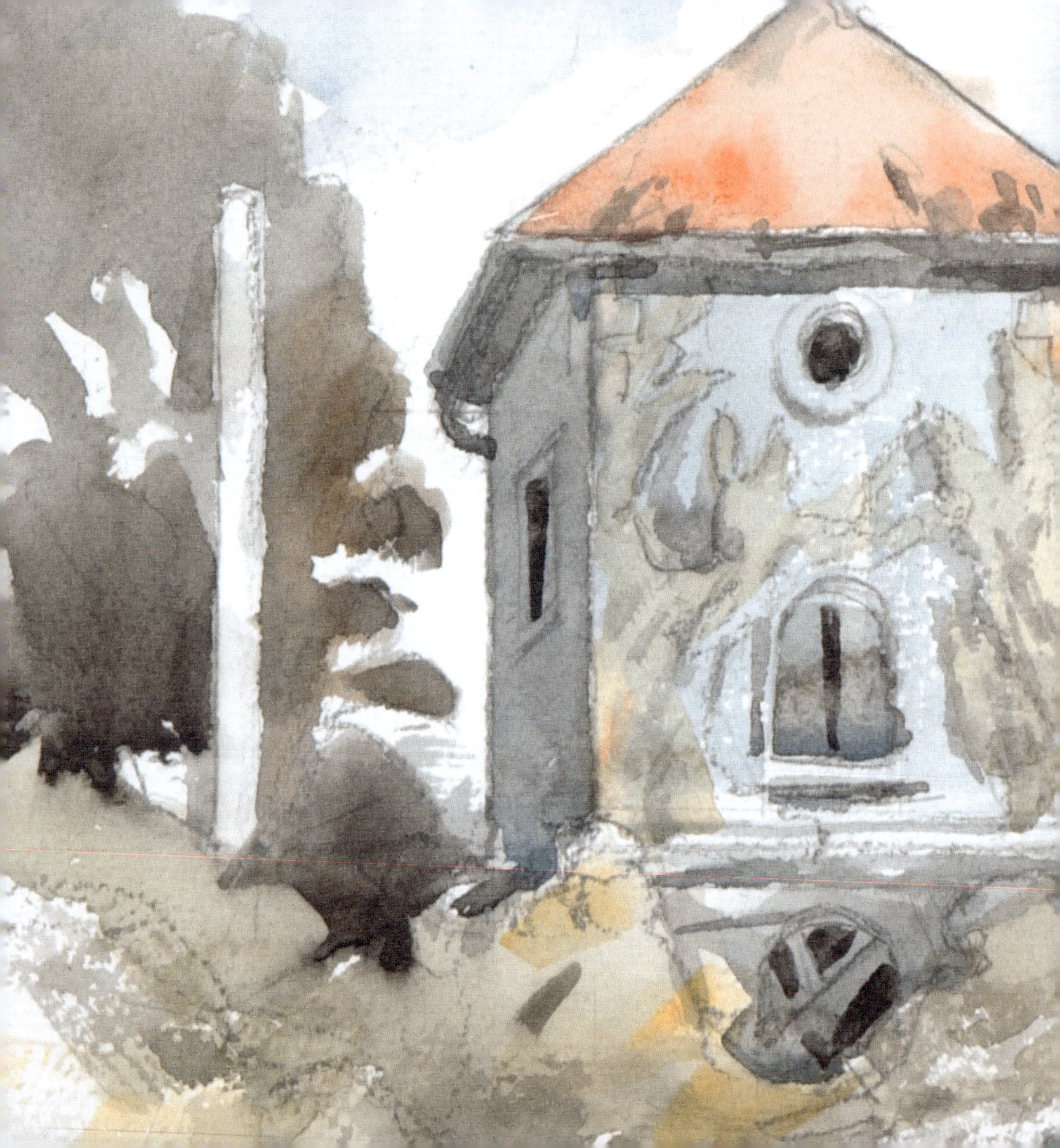

the projects

Being able to capture the essence of a scene is the skill all artists seek to master. These projects take you step-by-step through a wide range of different subjects, from still lifes to distant landscapes, using a range of techniques that will help you develop your talent as an artist.

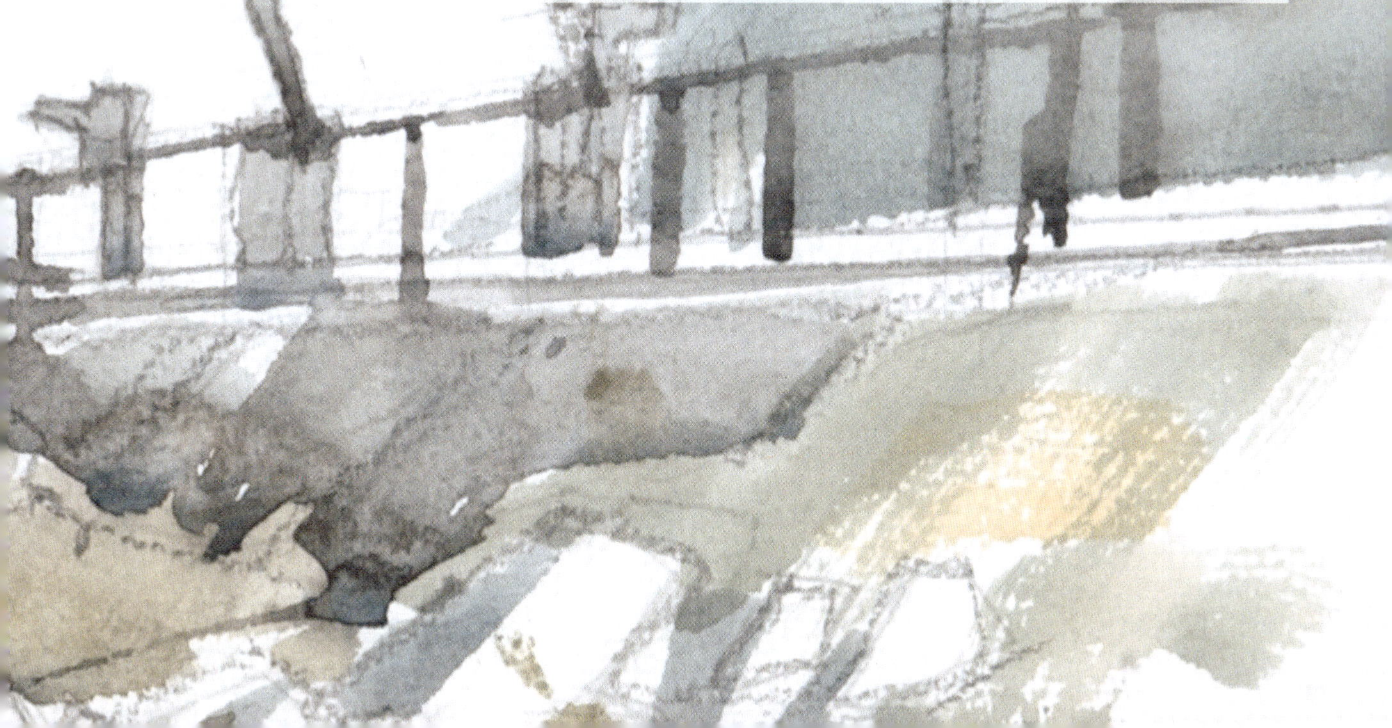

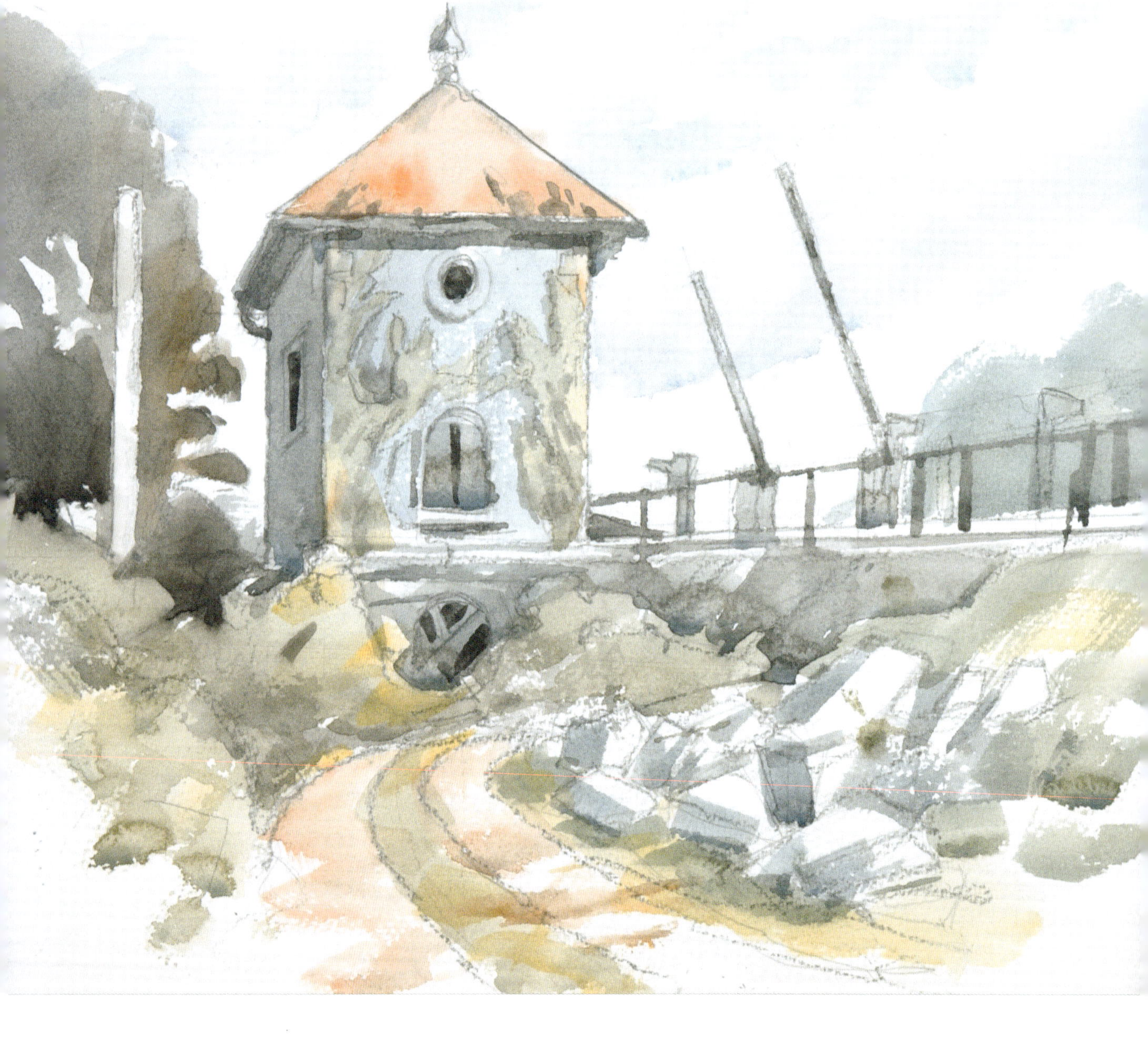

1

signal box

john barber

380 x 500mm (15 x 20in)

The basis for any great painting is a good sketch, which captures the essence of a subject without the fine detail. Sketching is the first skill all artists have to master and this project will show you how to construct an accurate pencil drawing and then lay down basic colours. It will also encourage you to think about how to create a strong impact on the viewer through your choice of angles and eye lines. You will then see how to apply your water-colours to capture the mood generated by your subject, picking out areas of light and shade, contrasts, reflections, and any accent colours and interesting features that will give your work the visual impact it needs to be successful.

TECHNIQUES FOR THE PROJECT

Sketching with a pencil

Laying a flat wash

Working wet-on-dry

WHAT YOU WILL NEED

Rough surface watercolour paper
Graphite pencil, 6B
Flat brush, 2.5cm (1in), sable or synthetic
Round brush, no. 5 or 6, sable or synthetic

COLOUR MIXES

1 Payne's gray
3 Cobalt blue
4 Violet
10 Yellow ochre
12 Hooker's green

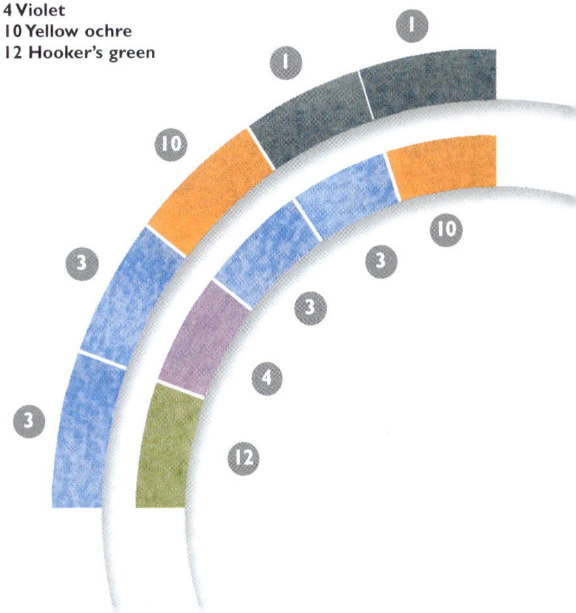

FLAT WASHES AND WORKING WET-ON-DRY

In most contexts, 'flat wash' is the term used to describe paint laid over an area of paper that is too large to be filled by only one brush stroke, making it very useful for skies, mountains, and seascapes. It can also be used more generally to describe any brush stroke that covers any area of paper, no matter how small. Whatever the exact definition, flat washes need to be laid down quickly, particularly if you are using several brush strokes. If you are too slow, or run out or have to mix more paint, the first brush stroke will dry, producing an unwanted hard edge when the next stroke is laid next to it.

Watercolours are inclined to drip and this is very noticeable on all flat washes. These drips can often be turned to your advantage, but if you need a crisp edge, for example, where the sky meets the roofline of a house, you will need to stop them. Do this by tilting your paper, or by picking up the excess paint with the tip of the brush. In any case, make sure you know where your colours are going before you start painting.

Once the flat wash is dry, you can lay new washes on top of it. This is called working wet-on-dry and is a classic way of building up new colours and textures.

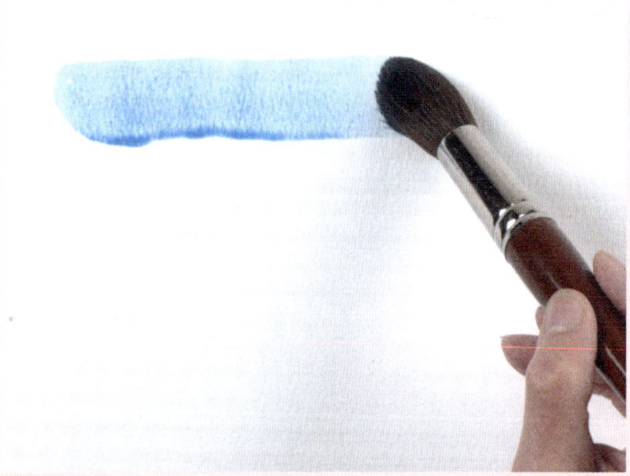

1 Mix lots of colour to avoid running out. Then decide where you are going to apply the wash, and which areas it should not run into. Load your mop brush and start working from the top in horizontal bands across the paper.

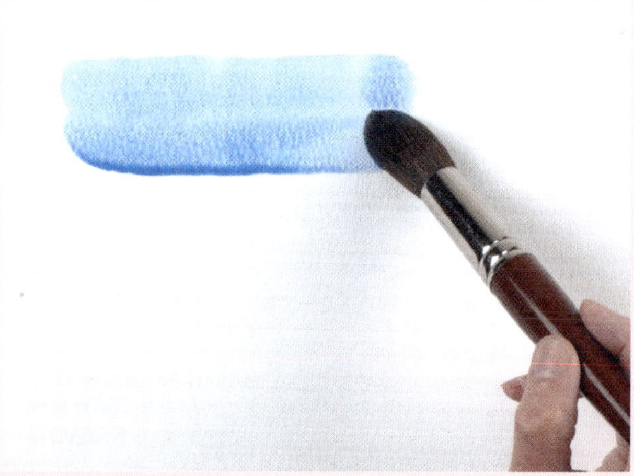

2 As soon as one band is completed, immediately move on to laying down the next, working in the same direction. Make sure that there is no gap of white paper showing through between the bands of colour.

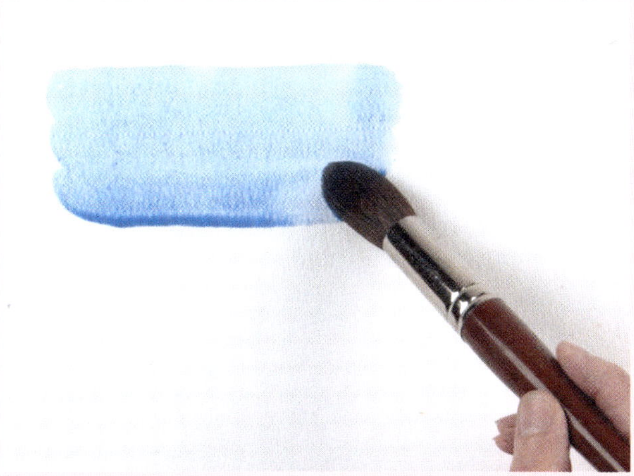

3 Immediately add a third band, working in the same direction as before. Continue working down the paper until the whole area you wish to cover has been filled. Check that all the areas are complete and that there are no white gaps.

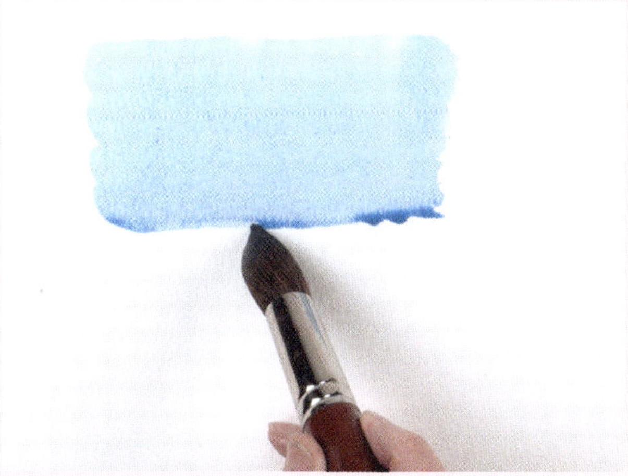

4 To maintain a perfectly even tone on the flat wash, pick up the drips that form along the bottom edge of each band with the tip of the brush. This is especially important on the last band where unwanted dripping paint can run over your work.

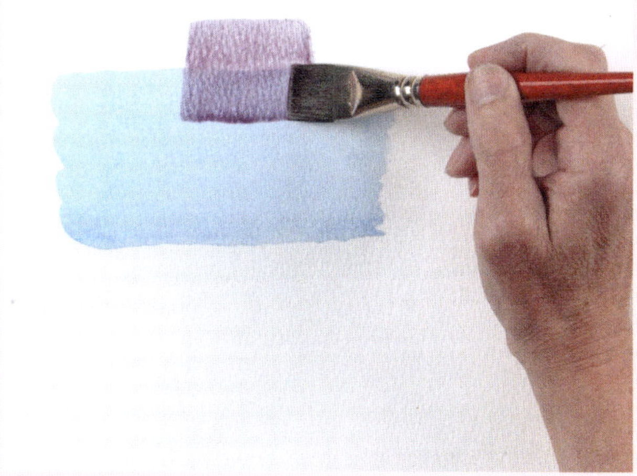

5 Let the bands of paint dry thoroughly. You should now have a flat wash with an even tone and no hard edges. Mix a new colour, and apply this as a flat wash over the edge of the previous wash, in exactly the same way, using the flat brush.

6 You can see how laying down successive flat washes, one on top of the other, builds up new colours and textures on the paper. Applying a new wash over an existing dry one is a key watercolour technique and is called working 'wet-on-dry.'

1

signal box

The first part of creating a good sketch is making sure that you get proportions and perspectives right. This means that you need to take some time to think about the technicalities of what you see. Here, the scene is constructed around the principle of one-point perspective, with the eye- and roof-line all leading to the same point. Use the soft graphite pencil to lightly draw the lines.

REMEMBER

When sketching landscapes, look for simple shapes seen against the sky, which is usually always the lightest part of a painting. This makes the shapes easier to draw accurately. Paint buildings, trees, and hills as darker, flat shapes. The right shape or silhouette will often give enough visual information without the need for further detail.

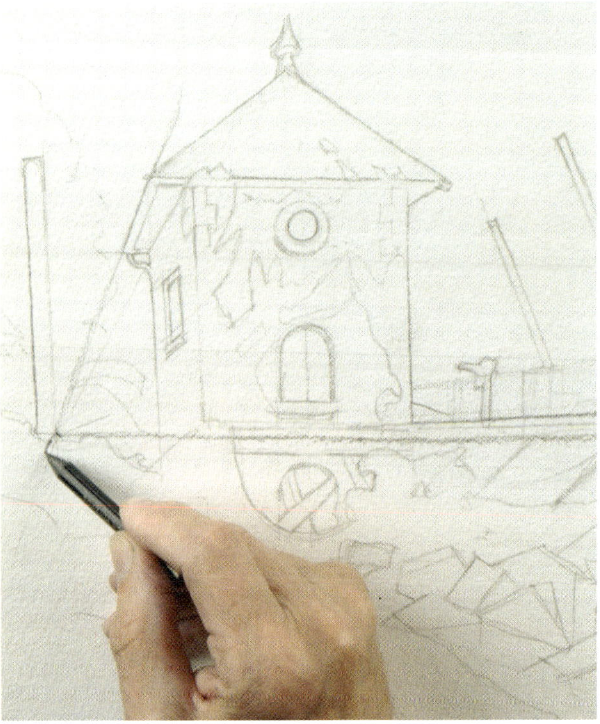

STEP 1

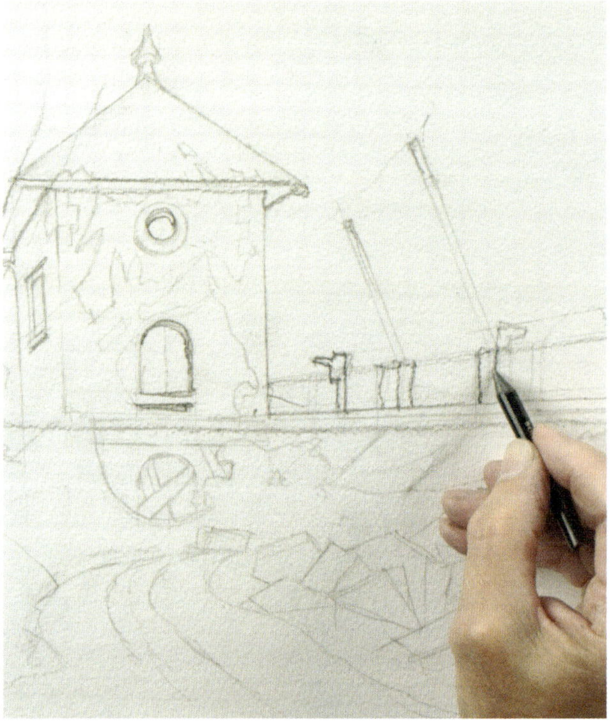

The composition works well because of the low eye-level – the viewer is looking up from below at the scene. Once the light sketch is completed, start to finalise the most prominent lines by working over them again with the pencil.

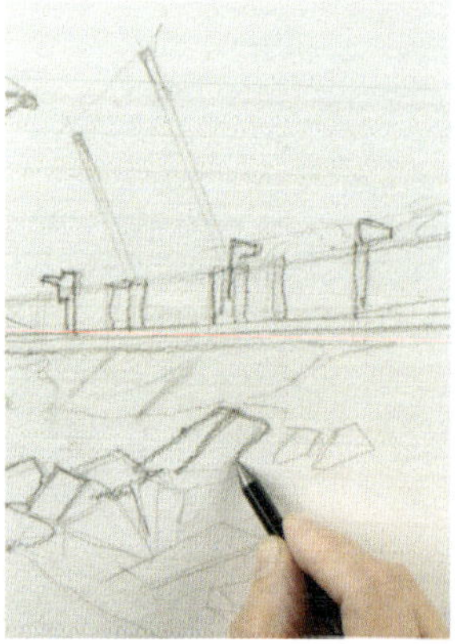

RIGHT Work your way down the sketch to the stones. Try to make sure that your lines highlight the three-dimensional quality of the stones and the random patterns they make.

STEP 2

Once you are satisfied that your perspectives are correct, finalise all the straight lines on the signal box, starting with the pitch of the roof. Even though these are straight lines, work freehand (rather than with a ruler) to create a slightly uneven, tumbledown look.

BE CONFIDENT

Allow your brush to move freely and let accidental marks become part of your painting. Record your first impressions only, stopping the moment the object is recognisable – this will keep your work lively. If it goes adrift, stop sketching and start again. Above all, avoid trying to rescue your sketch by adding detail.

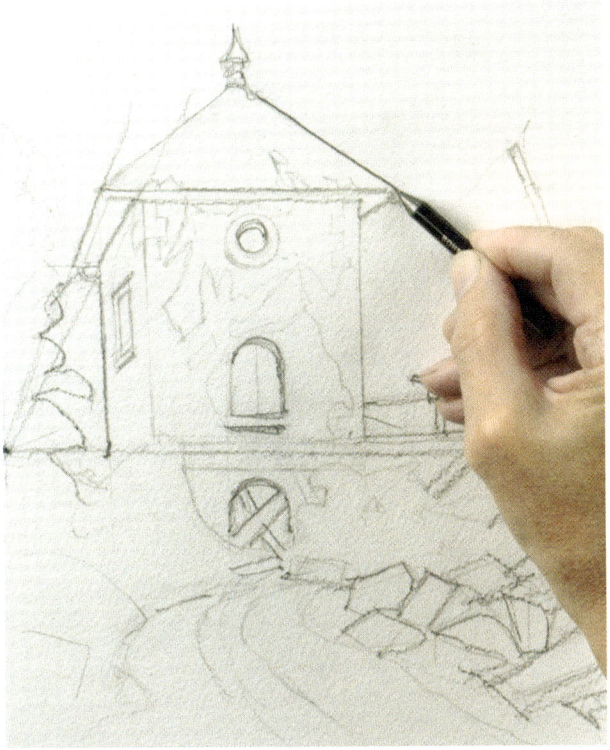

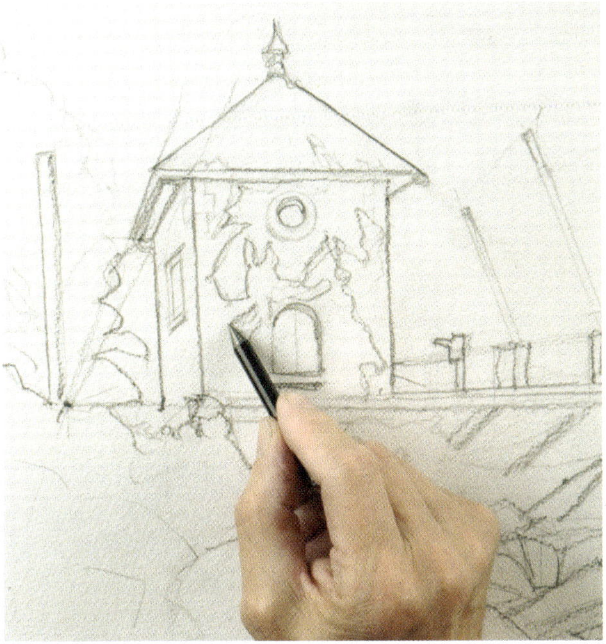

Build up some detail on the front of the signal box. Again, because the building is old, add to the tumbledown look by sketching in lines to indicate foliage growing up the walls.

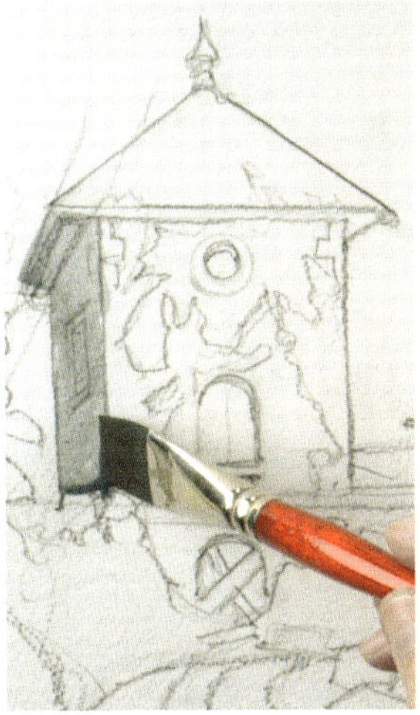

RIGHT Establish where your light source is and work out which parts of the signal box will be in shadow. Here, the side wall of the building, the eaves, the windows, and the doorway all need to carry darker tones than areas of the sketch in light. Use the flat brush to apply a mix of Payne's gray and yellow ochre in these shadow areas.

STEP 3

STEP 4

1

signal box

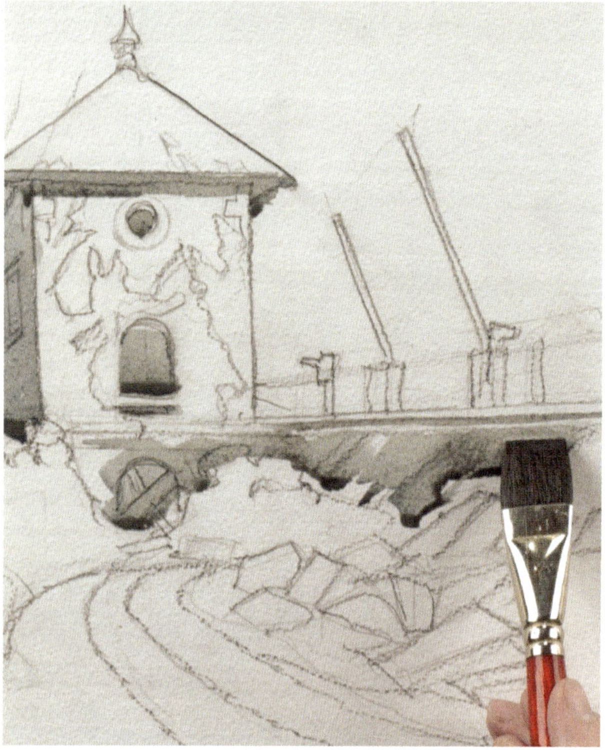

Use the same mix under the eaves, in the windows, and in the doorway, as well as along the railway embankment.

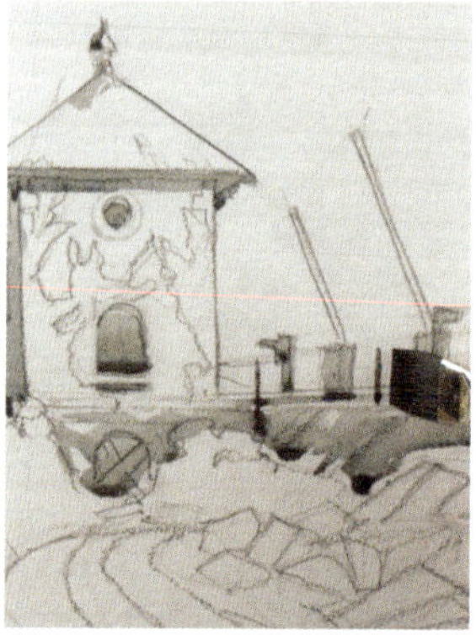

RIGHT Colour the railings next to the railway line, again using the same mix. Create the upright fence posts by simply holding the brush vertically and touching the paper with the edge.

STEP 5

RIGHT Add a little more yellow ochre to the mix and apply it to the tree, which is in the shadow of the signal box. Then mix a light wash of Payne's gray and cobalt blue for the top half of the tree and the ground underneath it. Both these areas are in light.

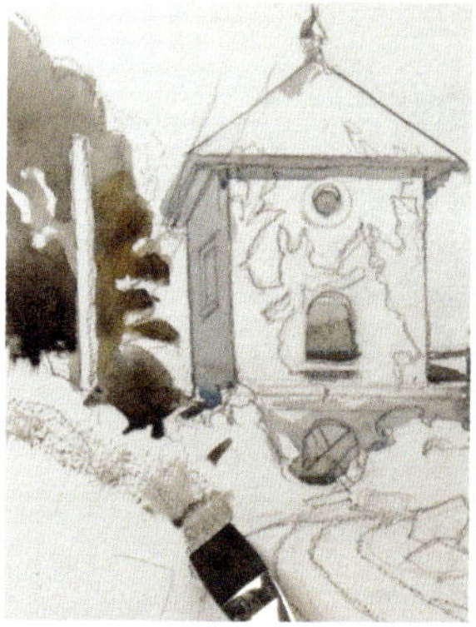

Mix cobalt blue with only a little Payne's gray for shadow on the stones. Also put touches of this mix on the shadow areas of the building.

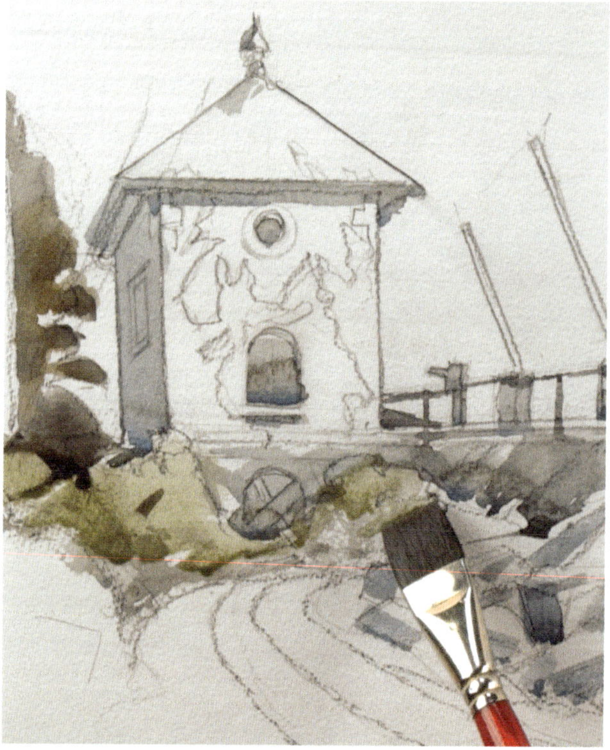

STEP 6

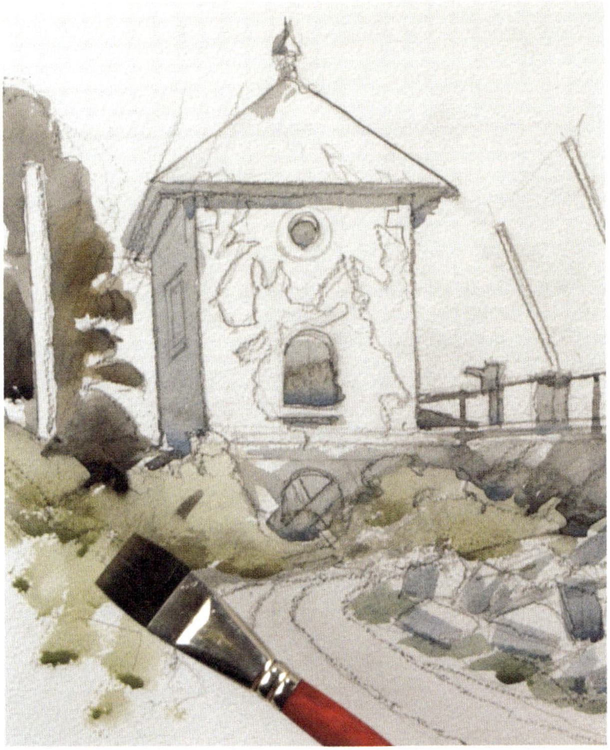

The foliage at the front of the building is a soft green – mix yellow ochre and cobalt blue to create this colour. Since this area is in light, keep the colour light. This mix creates a good contrast with the darker, mostly cooler, tones around it.

TRICK OF THE TRADE

Watercolour washes look much lighter when dry than the wet paint would suggest. Avoid any surprises by testing your colour mixing on a piece of the same paper you are painting on. Do this for each mix and let it dry before applying it to your picture. In this way, you will learn how colours change from wet to dry.

STEP 7

RIGHT The front wall of the signal box is also in light, so use the same grey colour you used on the side wall, but lighten it with a little water. Apply more paint to the areas that will be darkened by the foliage.

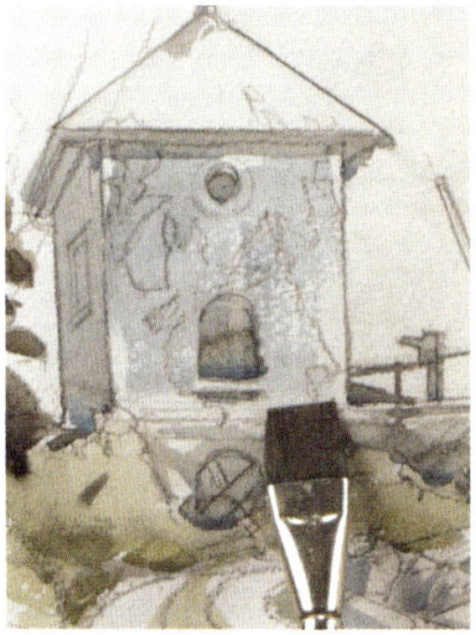

Build up the colour of the foliage by adding a little more yellow ochre to the grey mix, to produce a dark grey-green colour. Apply this with the edge of the brush.

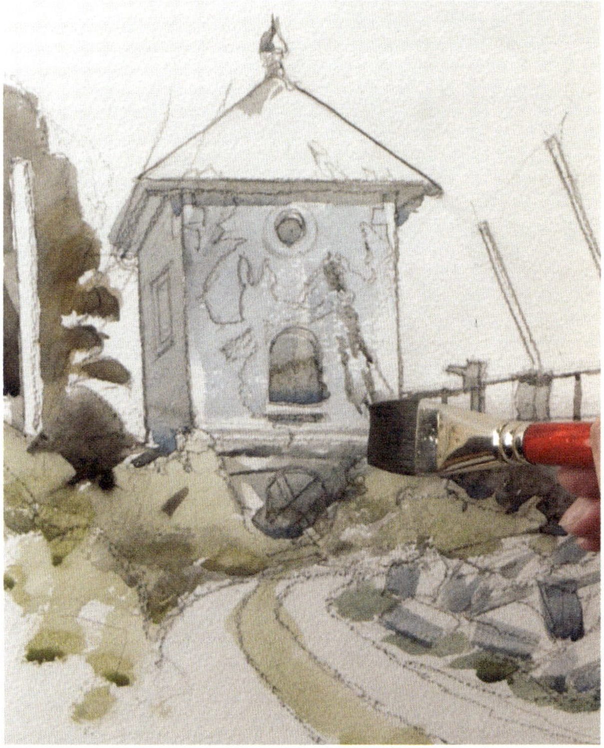

STEP 8

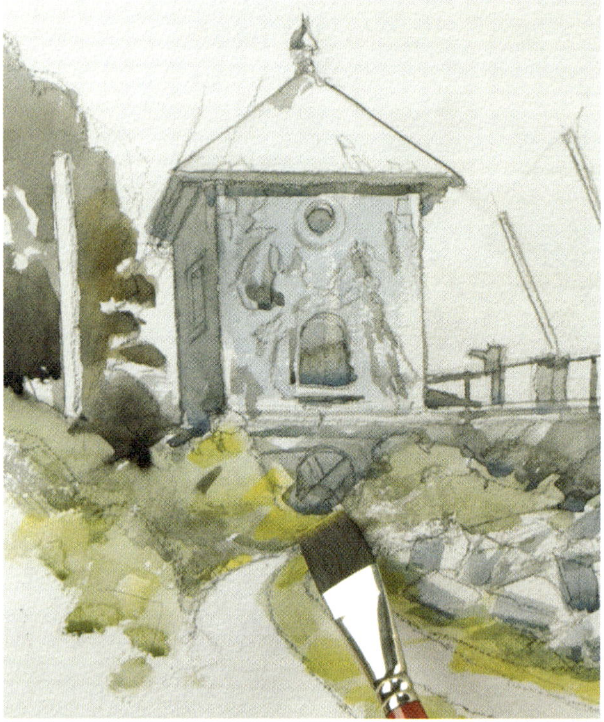

Add a little cadmium yellow to the soft green colour you mixed for the foreground foliage and apply it to the pathway. Also use it to build up texture on the soft green areas.

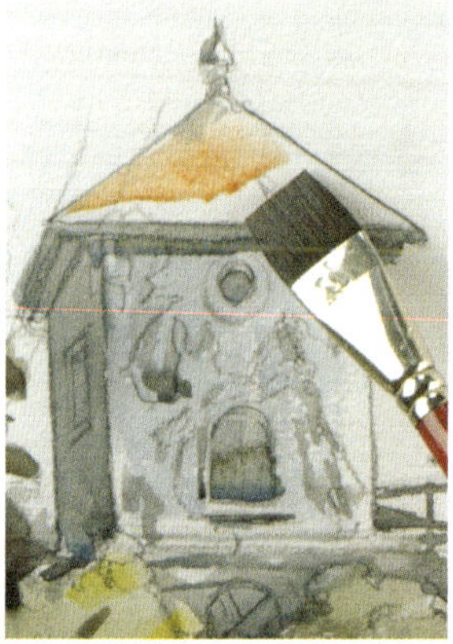

RIGHT Complete the roof by using a light wash of burnt sienna. Not only does this colour indicate terracotta tiles but it immediately warms the scene.

STEP 9

RIGHT While the paint is still wet, add more of the same colour. This deepens the tone and creates extra texture on the roof. Try not to add too much paint – only enough to break up the flat colour of the first wash.

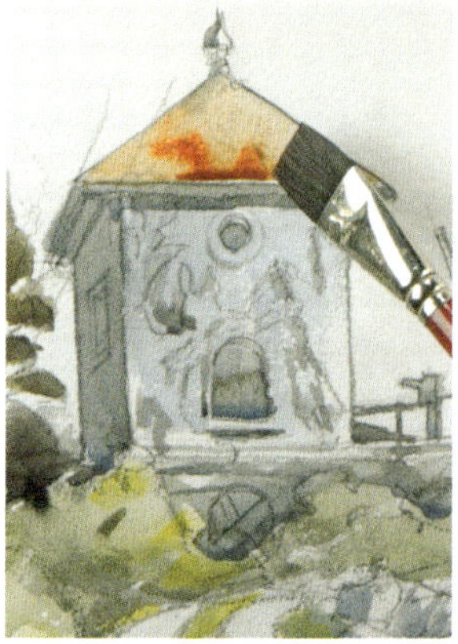

Mix more of the soft green you first used on the foreground foliage and add patches of it to the front of the signal box, running it down over the yellow underneath. This helps 'ground' the building.

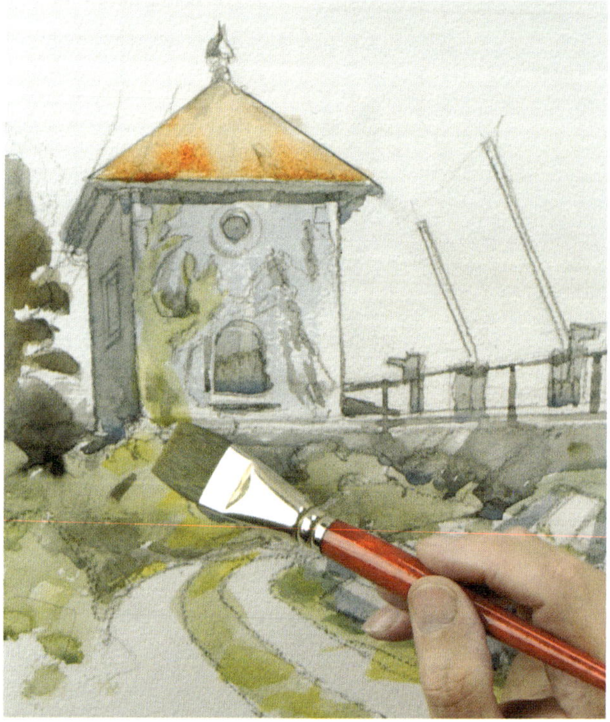

STEP 10

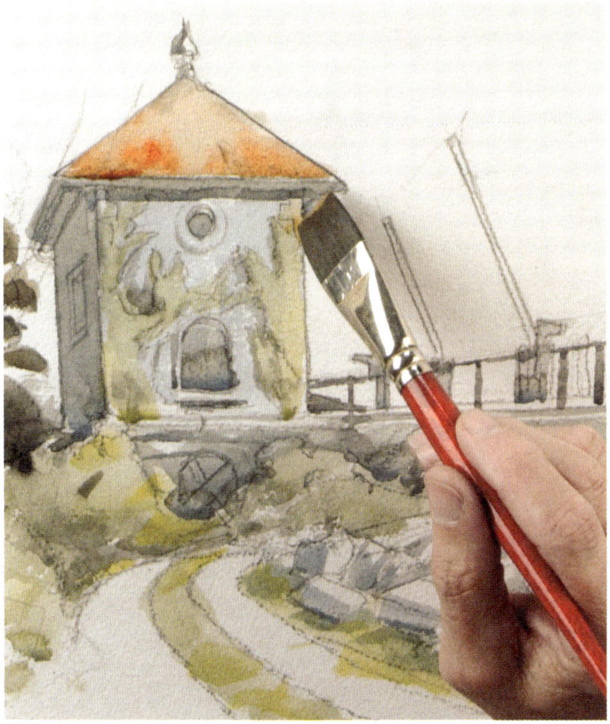

Tie in the colour of the roof to the front of the signal box by adding small dashes of the burnt sienna mix to the foliage on the front of the building. Also add it to the path to create the look of red soil.

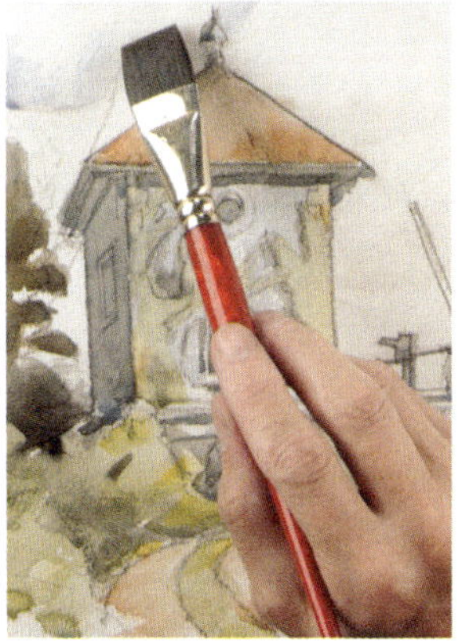

RIGHT For the sky, mix a light wash of cobalt blue and violet and apply a band of colour across the paper, heading toward the vanishing point. Try not to overelaborate here – this is only a sketch.

STEP 11

RIGHT Add a little more violet to the mix, and again work in bands. Leave white areas in between the bands of colour to hint at high, wispy cloud.

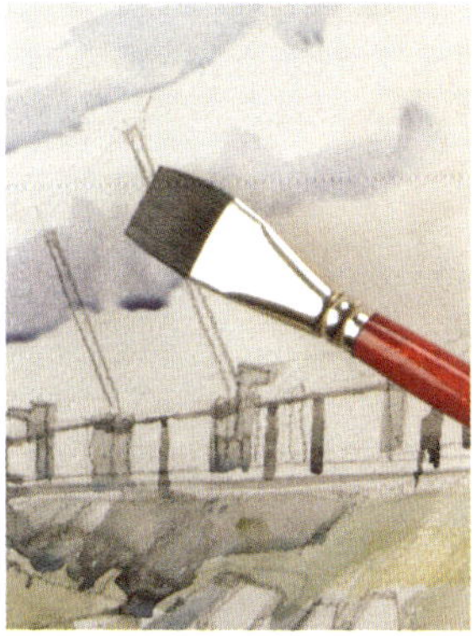

Alternatively, paint a few bands of clean, clear water across the paper. While the paper is still wet, drop a little of the mix onto it. The paint will run in random patterns within each band of water – this is called the wet-in-wet technique.

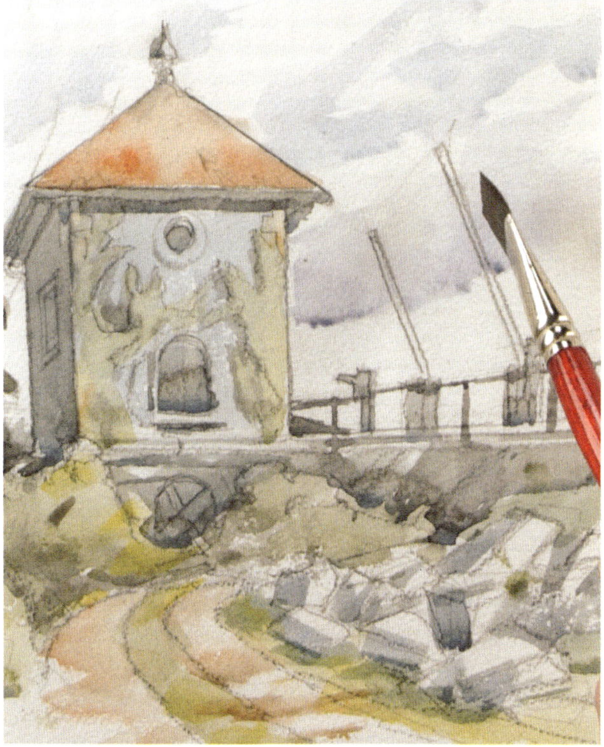

STEP 12

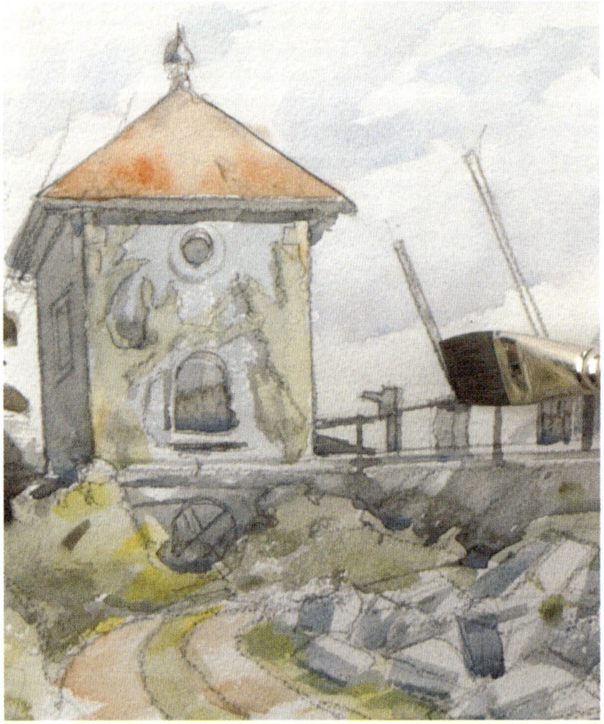

You now have all the main elements of the scene captured on the page. All that remains to do now is to build up a little detail. First, add a light mix of Payne's gray to the barriers.

RIGHT Then build up the shape of the trees beyond the railway line using a mix of cobalt blue, Hooker's green, and yellow ochre. Add a little more colour to the barriers to darken them.

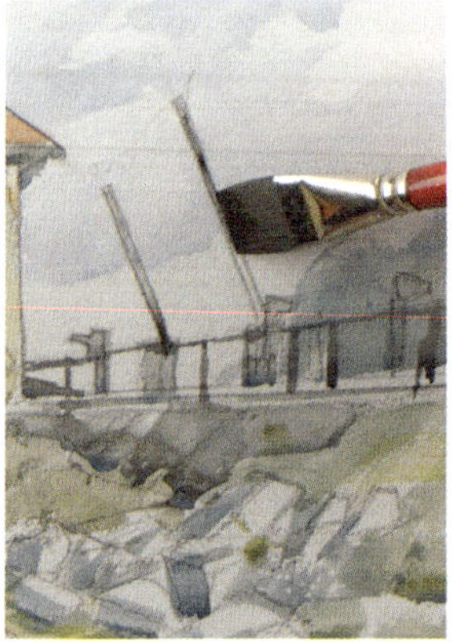

STEP 13

Add in areas of very dark contrast. These are useful for drawing the viewer's eye to detail, but because they are so strong, keep them to a minimum. Start by adding Payne's gray to the foreground shape using only the corner of the brush.

TRICK OF THE TRADE

If a wash dries to a shade much darker than you anticipated, brush over it with clean water and leave it for a few seconds. Press kitchen paper or other absorbent tissue firmly onto the wet area and a little paint will come off. You can repeat this as many times as you need to.

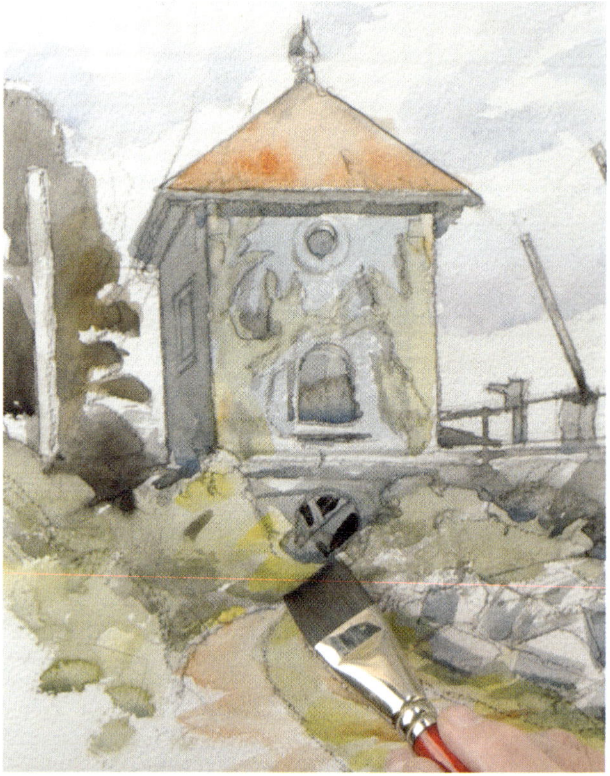

STEP 14

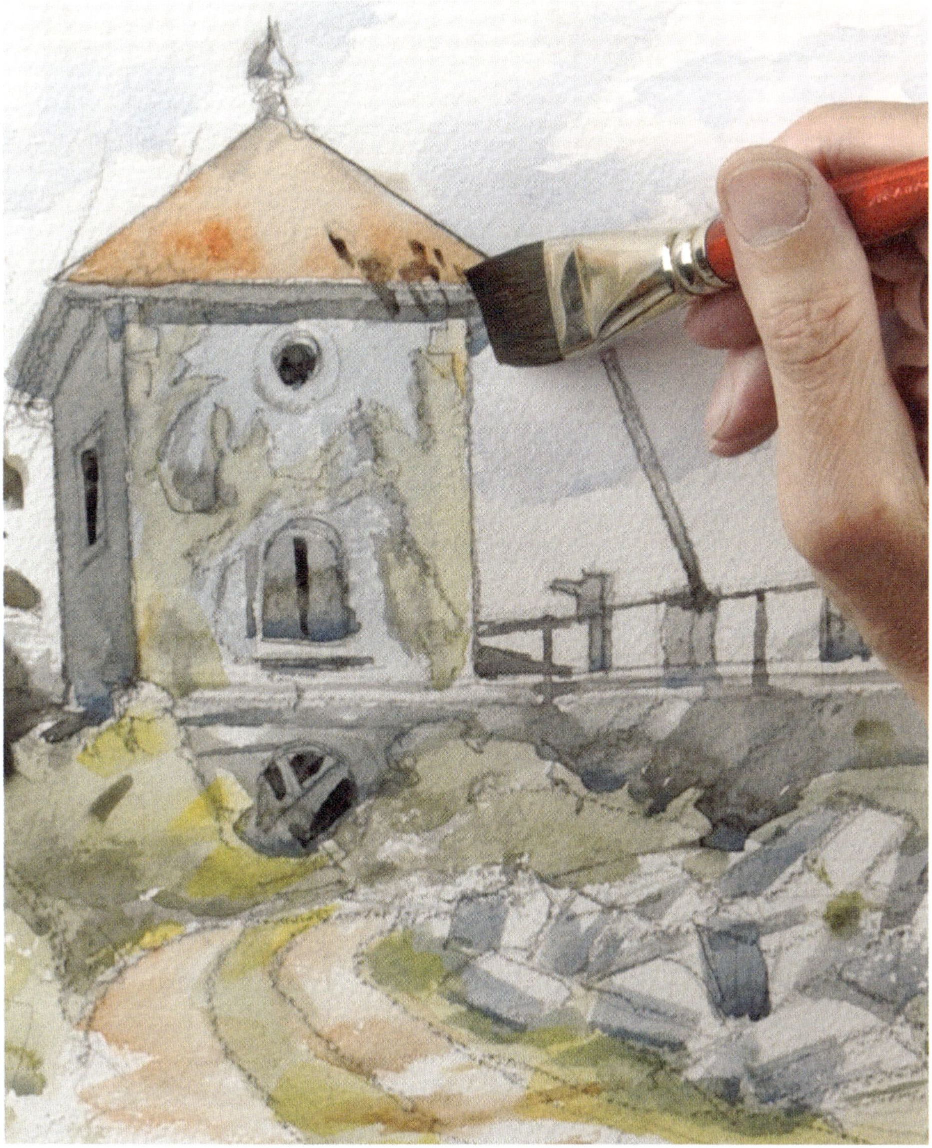

TRICK OF THE TRADE

When painting buildings, try pressing a quilted or textured tissue onto a wet wash that covers a roof or wall. The texture on the tissue will produce light random patterns that suggest tiles or bricks in a much more natural way than drawing detailed lines of bricks. Then give some of these light patches a tiny cast shadow on one edge.

LEFT Add the same colour to the windows and doorway of the signal box. Also add it to the edge of the roof to hint at broken tiles. This is visually more interesting than a perfect roof.

Finish your sketch by adding touches of dark shadow under the eaves, applying the same colour with the round brush.

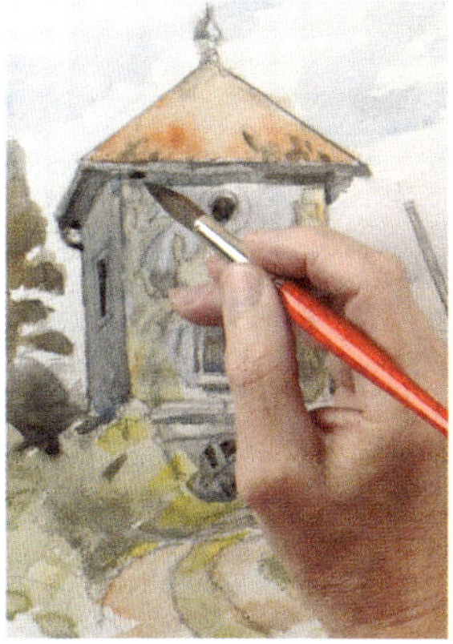

STEP 15

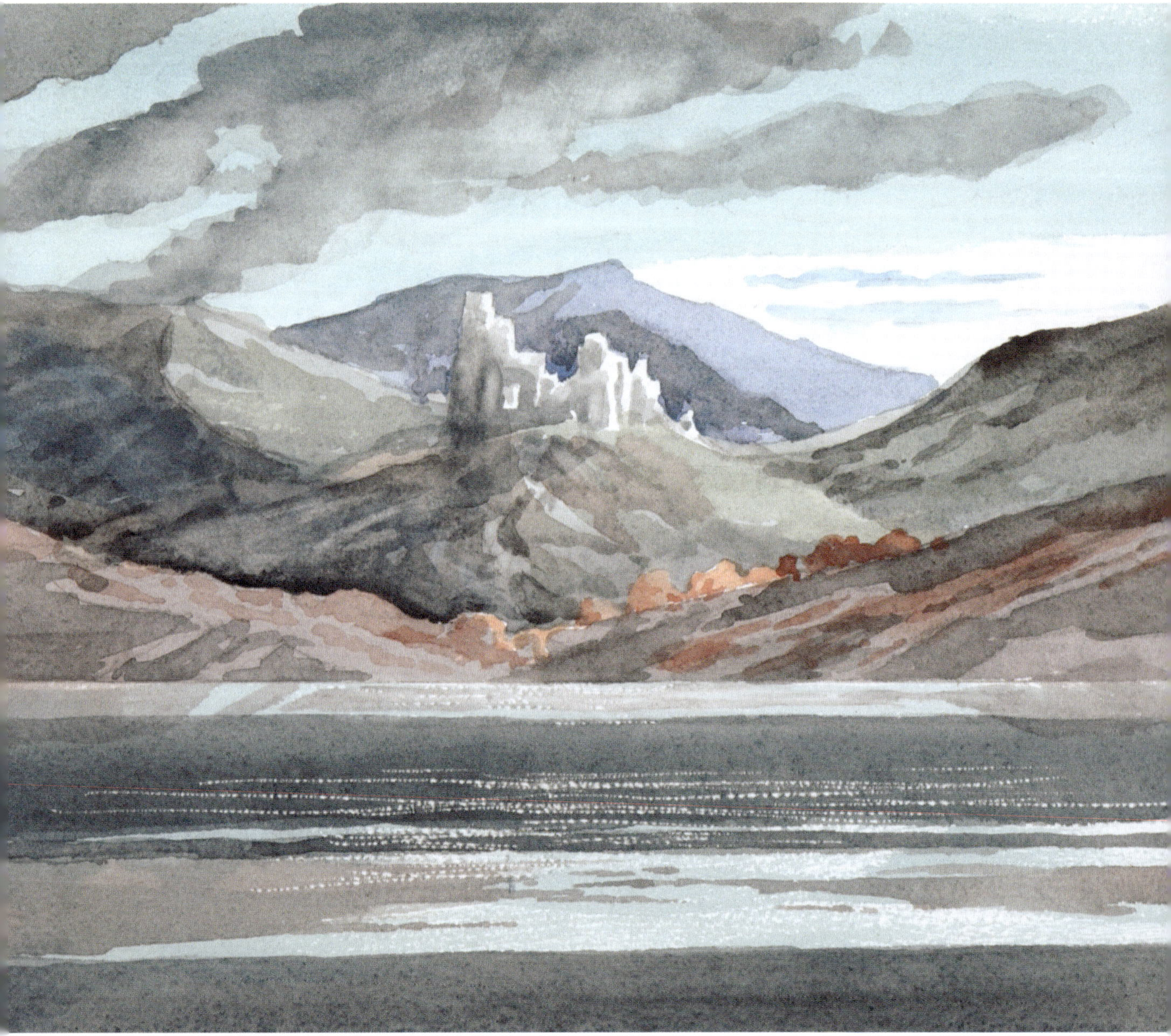

2

castle ruins

john barber
400 x 500mm (16 x 20in)

Building up colours and tying them all together convincingly is a key skill in watercolour painting. In this project, you will see how to do this, using simple flat washes applied to the areas marked out in your pencil sketch. Since watercolours are transparent, you cannot add lighter colours over darker ones – they would be invisible. So this project will show you another key principle in watercolour painting – building up colour by applying darker washes over lighter ones. You will also learn how to create areas of tone and texture within flat washes by lifting off some of the paint, and how to create areas of sparkling, reflected light by scratching off some of the paint to reveal the white paper underneath.

TECHNIQUES FOR THE PROJECT

Laying a flat wash

Lifting off

Scratching off

WHAT YOU WILL NEED

Rough surface watercolour paper
Graphite pencil, 6B
Flat brush, 2.5cm (1in), sable or synthetic
Round brush, no. 5 or 6, sable or synthetic
Kitchen paper
Rubber
Craft knife

COLOUR MIXES

1 Payne's gray
2 Prussian blue
3 Cobalt blue
4 Violet
10 Yellow ochre
11 Burnt sienna
12 Hooker's green

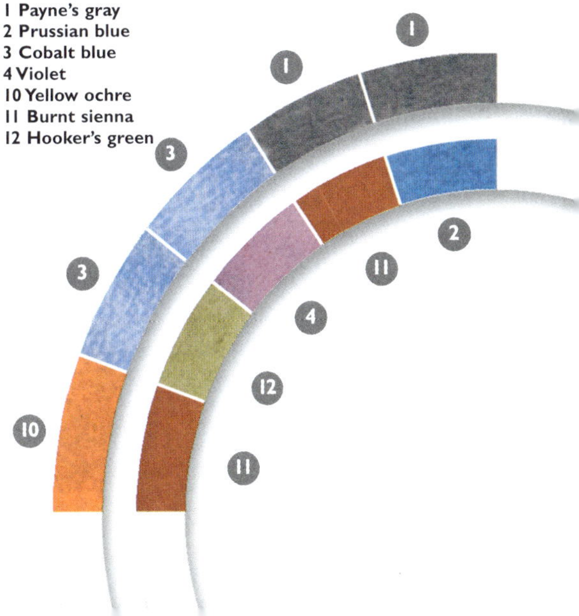

LIFTING OFF

Lifting off is the process of removing dry or wet paint from the paper and can produce some dramatic results.

When used on dry paint, lifting off is often used as a correction technique to soften hard edges between flat washes. This is done by applying a little clean water to the hard edge, then with a soft brush, rubbing the paper gently until both colours start to lift off and blend together. Alternatively, lifting off on dry paint can be used as a technique for creating new shapes and textures that would be difficult to reproduce with brush strokes. In this instance, apply a little clean water with a soft brush to the area to be worked on. Rub the brush over the paint until it starts to lift off. Dab away the wet paint with kitchen paper to reveal the paper underneath. You can also dry your brush and use the bristles to lift off the wet paint. The paper never returns to its original white colour but leaving a hint of the original colour behind works to your advantage. Lifting off in this example is very useful for creating highlights and lightening muddy colours.

Lifting off wet paint is a valuable creative skill in itself. Apply paint to the paper and, before it is dry, dab some of it away with kitchen paper to leave a textured, irregular pattern behind. This technique is great for skies – many complex cloud shapes can be created using this method.

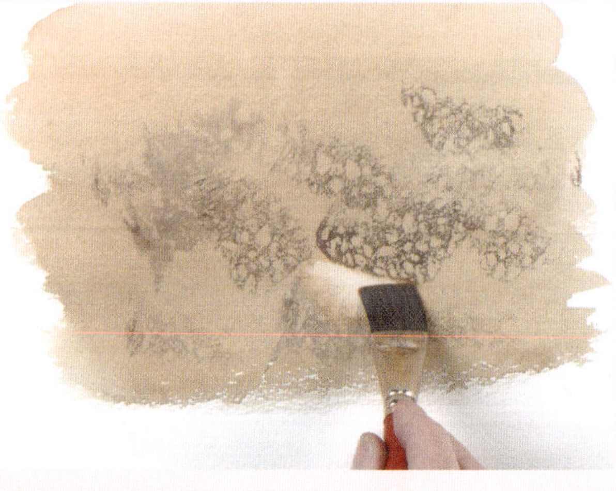

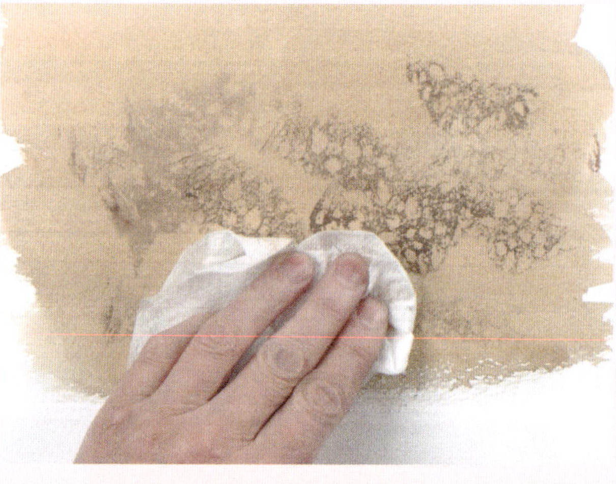

1 Lay down your flat wash and any other techniques you wish to use over the top of it. Then apply a little clean water with the flat brush to the area you wish to work on and rub it over the paint until it starts to lift and the white paper appears.

2 Immediately dab away the excess paint and water with a little kitchen paper. Make sure that your kitchen paper is absorbent and is not the type that leaves fluffy residue behind. Also, remove the kitchen paper quickly – don't press and hold.

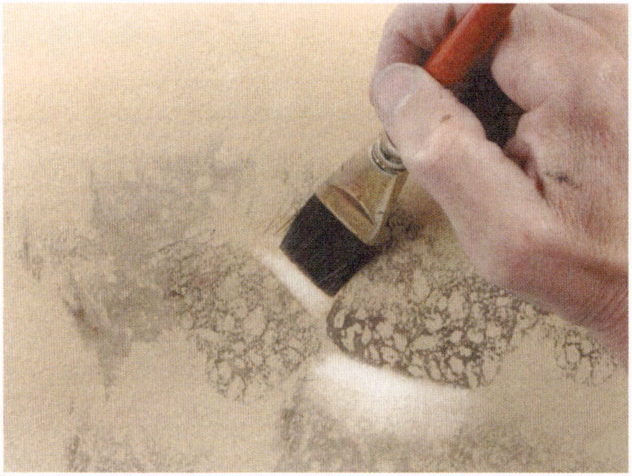

3 By applying just a little water with the brush, you can remove very detailed areas of paint. In this way, you can start to introduce shapes into your compositions that would not be possible using a brush and watercolours alone.

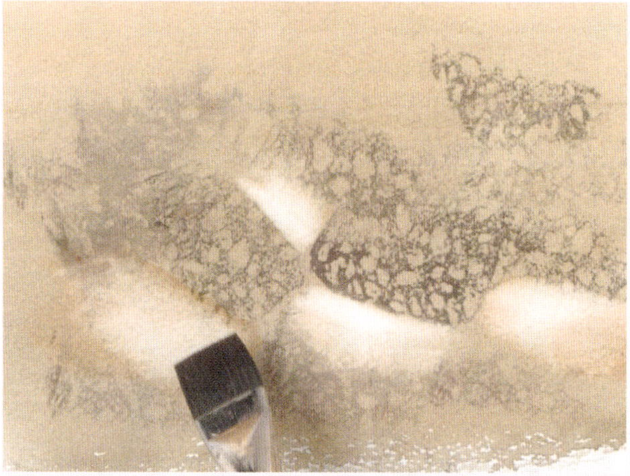

4 In this example, we have added texture and pattern to the paper with a synthetic sponge, which produces a printing effect. You can highlight these shapes by lifting off, leaving white areas of paper that outline the sponge work.

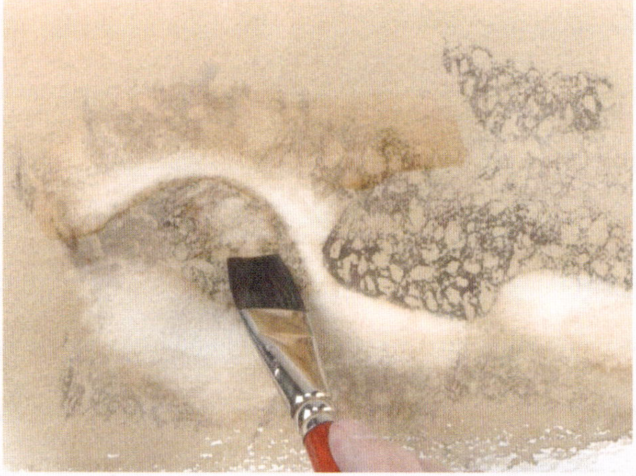

5 In the same way, lifting off can also be used for creating highlights. Lift off a little paint using water applied with a soft brush. Work in a gentle circular motion and dab away the lifted paint with a tissue. This effect gives flat artwork more depth.

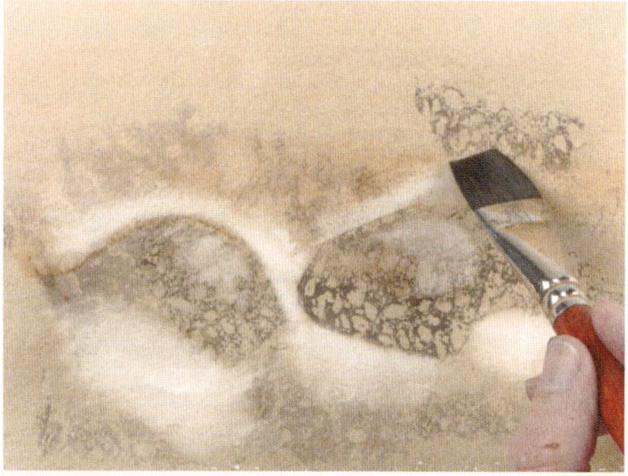

6 Lifting off is very useful for softening hard edges. Apply a little water with the brush to the hard edge and gently rub over it. As the paint lifts off, move it around with the corner of the brush until you achieve the softer edge you want.

2
castle ruins

Start your sketch using the graphite pencil. Tilt the pencil so you are using the side of the lead more than the point. This creates more of a tone than a line – the ruin and the hills do not need to be precisely defined. However, use a ruler for the shore – this works best as a sharp, accurate line. Lastly, draw in the shapes for the clouds. Make sure you plan where they are going to appear – this will help when you come to paint.

REMEMBER

The far edge of any flat surface will appear as a horizontal line, even the base of flowerbed against a strip of grass a few yards away. So make the far side of the lake a ruled straight line. When you put a matte around your picture, this line will be parallel to the bottom edge. If your water line is titled or ragged, it will not look convincing.

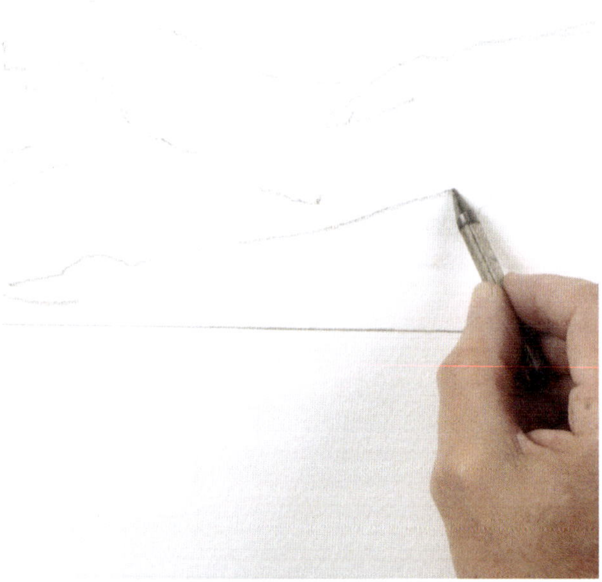

STEP 1

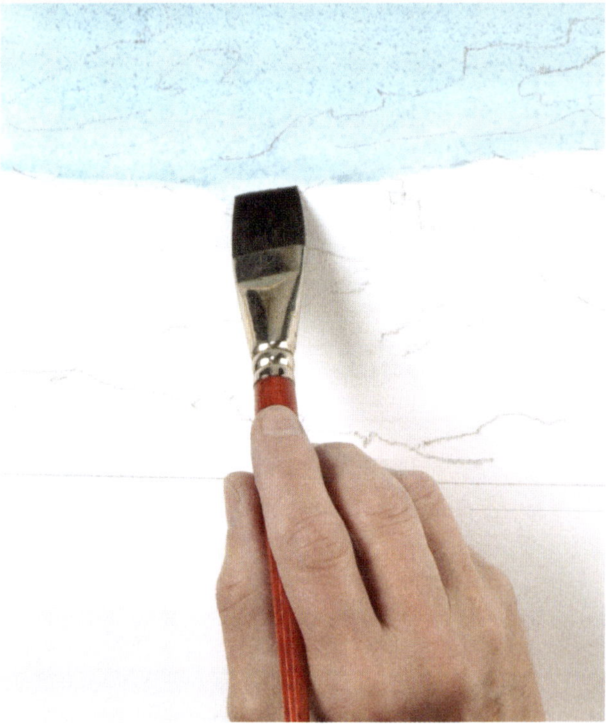

Apply a flat wash of Payne's gray and Prussian blue for the sky, using the flat brush. Work in stripes across the page, starting at the top and working down.

RIGHT Use a touch of cobalt blue for the distant clouds, using the tip of the round brush. Then darken your first mix with more Payne's gray. Apply this to the top cloud, keeping to the lines of your pencil sketch. Add more water to lighten the mix for the right-hand cloud.

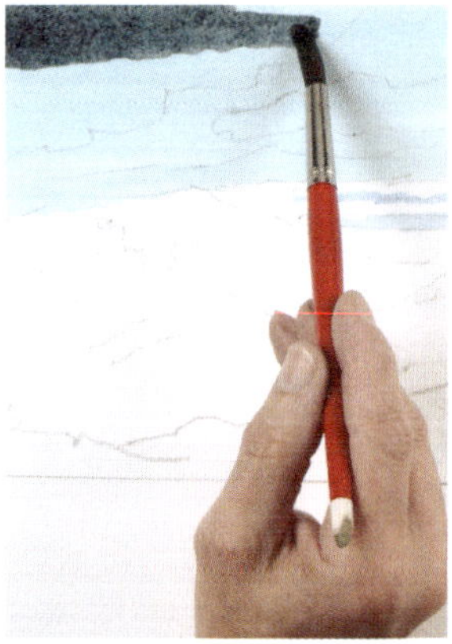

STEP 2

Add a little more water to the same mix and apply this to the hills on either side of the ruin. Lighten the mix for the last time for the ground under the castle – the colour is now faint. As you get toward the bottom edge, add a little more paint to darken the scene as it runs down to the shoreline.

BE CONFIDENT

Pick up your painting and tilt it so that the drips of paint at the bottom of a wash stay in the right place. This will give a dark, crisp edge a more effective contrast with the area next to it. If the paint looks as if it will run down the paper, stand your painting on its side and let the drips run off, or lie it flat until dry.

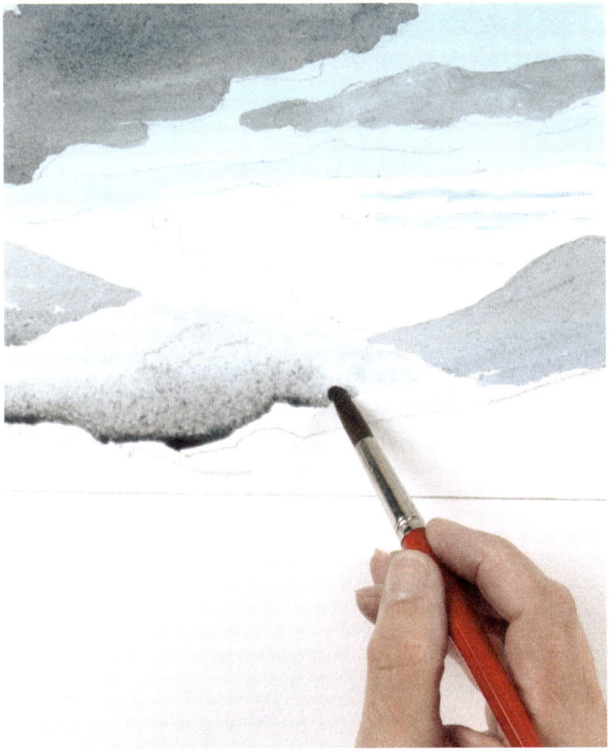

STEP 3

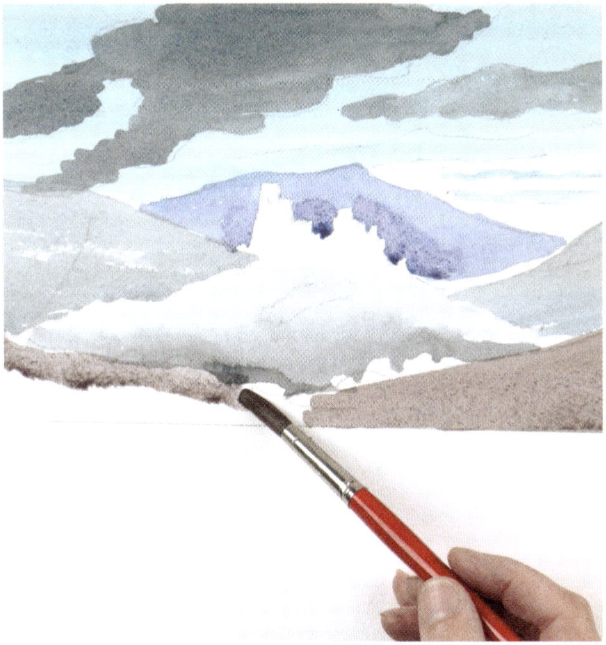

Mix cobalt blue with a little violet for the mountain behind the ruin, leaving a white edge to suggest reflected light and to lead the viewer's eye to the focal point. Darken the mix with more violet and add this behind the ruin to highlight it. Then mix Payne's gray, burnt sienna, and violet and add this to the foreground hills.

RIGHT Apply a flat wash of Prussian blue and a little Payne's gray to the lake by quickly pulling the flat brush over the paper. This leaves some of the white paper showing through and hints at sparkle coming off the water.

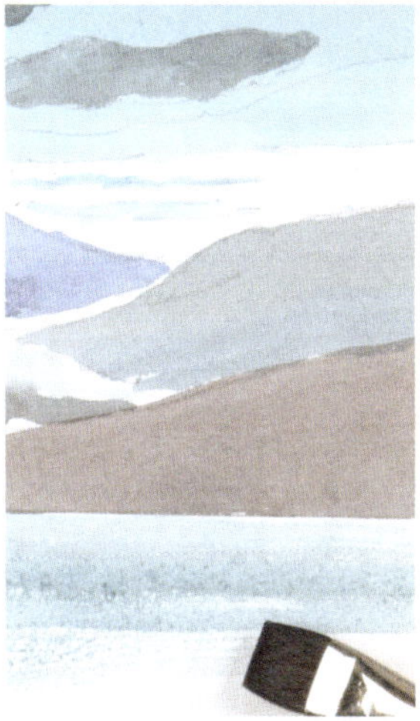

STEP 4

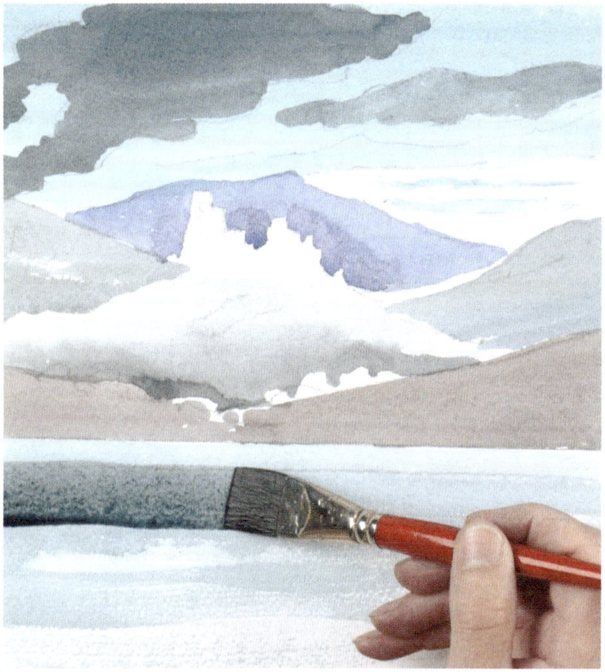

With a pencil, mark horizontal bands across the lake to indicate where the dark reflection of the sky will fall. Add a mix of Payne's gray and Prussian blue in a line right across the paper. Repeat this line twice over, in varying widths.

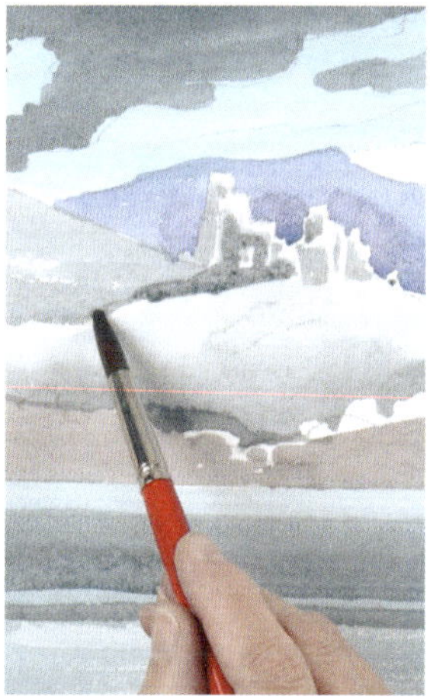

RIGHT Apply the same mix to the ruin with the round brush. Then darken the colour with a little more Payne's gray and add this to the shadow side of the ruin, running it down into the hill. Leave the edges of the ruin white to suggest reflected light.

STEP 5

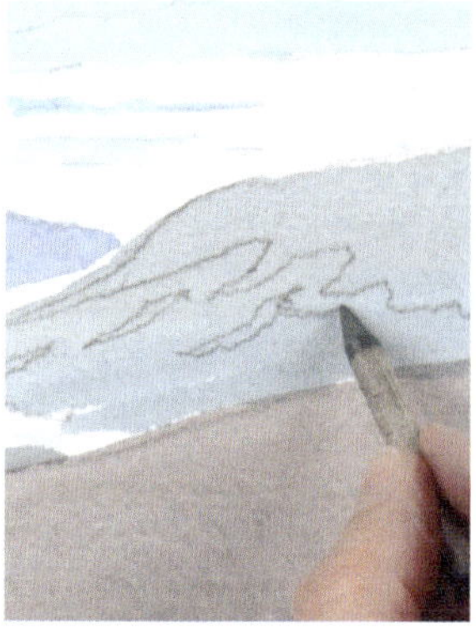

RIGHT Using the pencil, add some outlines to the hill sides. These outlines are useful guides to help you work up areas of texture and shading.

Start applying this texture and shading using a flat wash of Payne's gray on the left-hand hills, as well as smaller areas of colour under the ruin. You don't have to stick precisely to the pencil lines you have just drawn – they are just a useful guide.

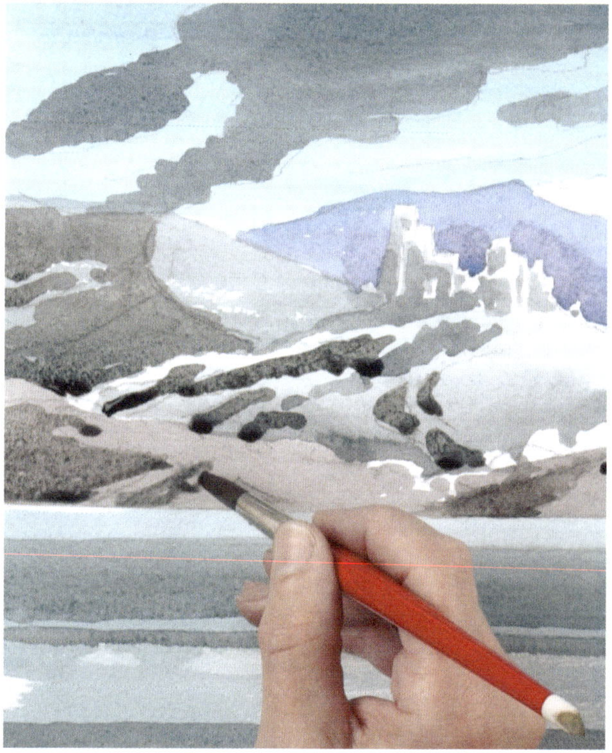

STEP 6

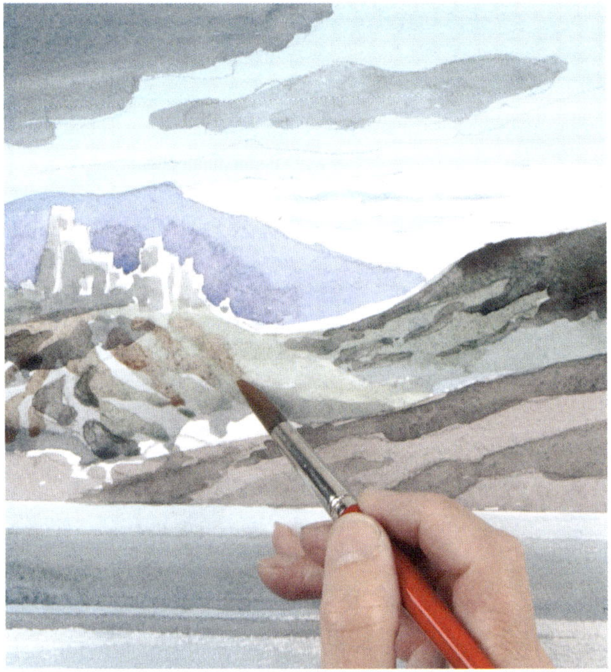

Darken the right-hand hills with Payne's gray – this contrasts well against the sky. Add a muted green wash to the hills to warm them by mixing Hooker's green and cobalt blue. Then add some burnt sienna to the green mix and apply this to the hill on the left, before mixing in some violet for the area under the ruin.

RIGHT Lastly, use Payne's gray for building up shadow on the mountain behind the ruin. This matches the dark colour of the sky behind. Work the colour down to the right.

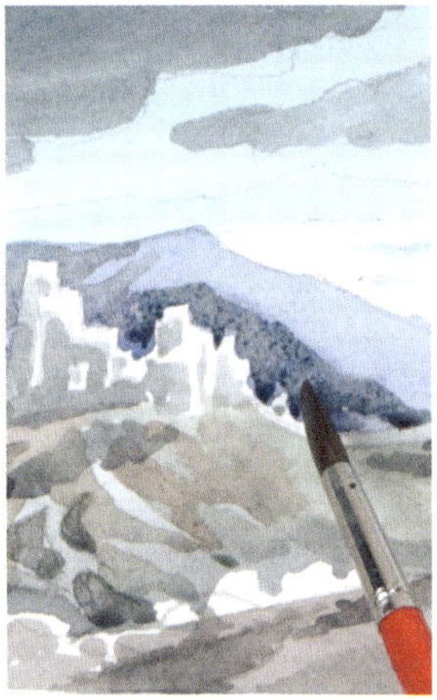

STEP 7

RIGHT Further darken the left-hand hill with a strong mix of Payne's gray. This adds a dramatic area of shading that can be worked into later.

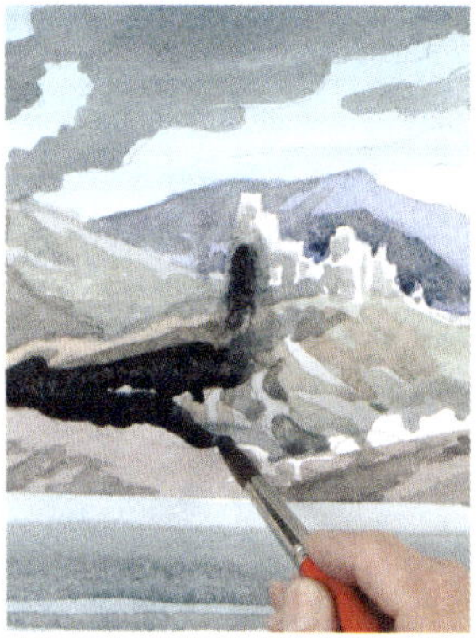

Mix burnt sienna and yellow ochre and apply it to the area above the near hills on the right to add a hint of yellow sunlight.

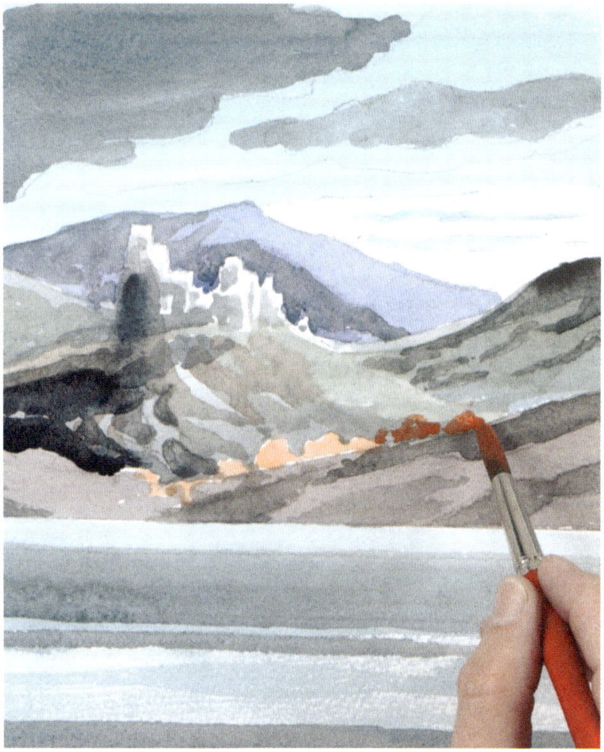

STEP 8

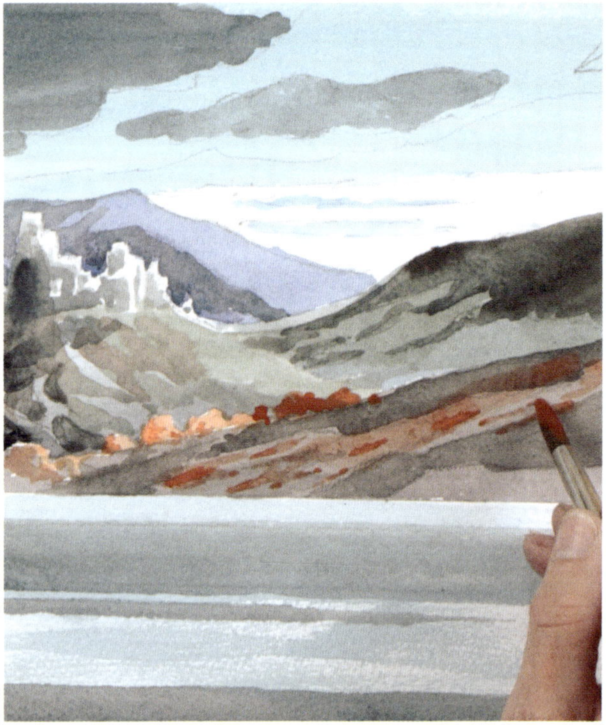

RIGHT Lighten the underside of the clouds by applying clean water and lifting out the wet colour with some kitchen paper. This softens the colour, makes the cloud reflect the colour of the sky, and balances the cloud with the colour of the landscape.

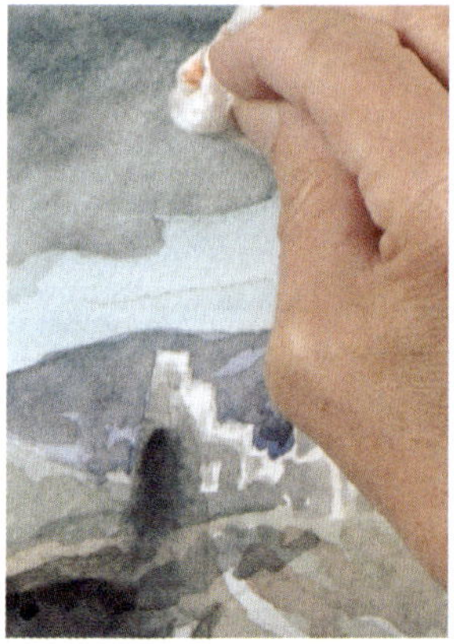

Soften any hard edges on the hills on the right by rubbing a little clean water over the edges between light and dark.

Add a little more burnt sienna to the mix and work it down the light parts of the foreground hill. Apply the colour in touches and run it over parts of the darker washes to help blend it all together.

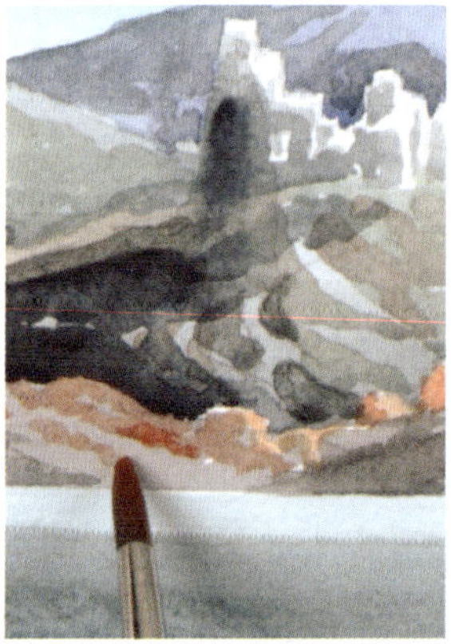

RIGHT Continue adding areas of warm yellow down to the shoreline. By making these lines irregular, you can hint at low-level foliage heading down to the lake.

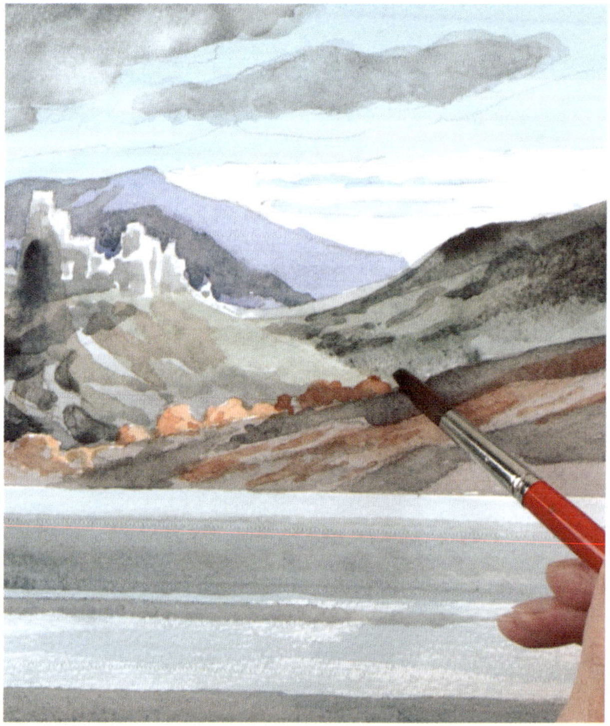

STEP 9

STEP 10

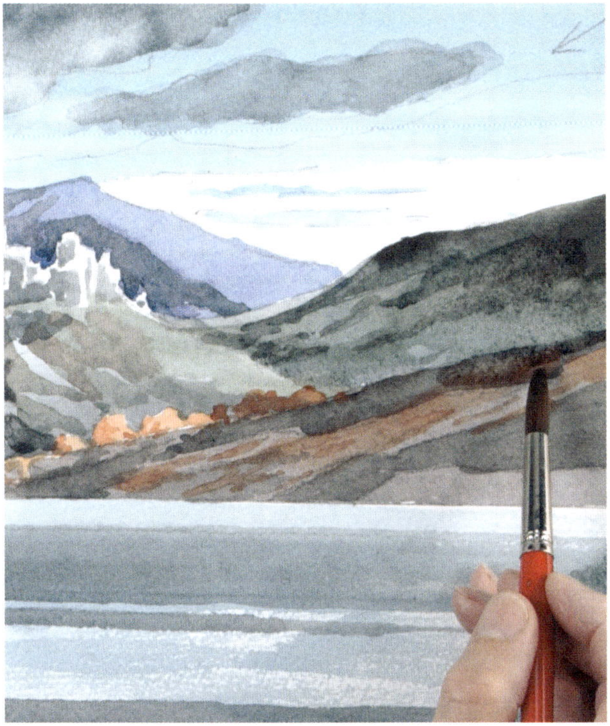

Once some of the paint has lifted off, flatten the brush and, using only the side, gently blend the colours together.

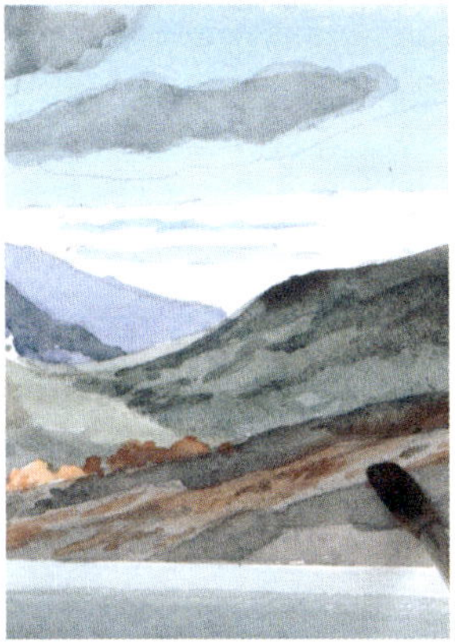

RIGHT Use the colour that comes off on the brush to add extra detail and texture to the hillside. This also helps to blend the colour.

STEP 11

RIGHT Work your way around the hard edges, blending them together. You don't have to do too much of this – just enough to soften and blend the colours together. Then use the colour on the brush to add extra detail to the hillside.

Lift off some of the very dark Payne's gray under the ruin in the same way, using the colour on the brush to slightly darken the white outline of the building.

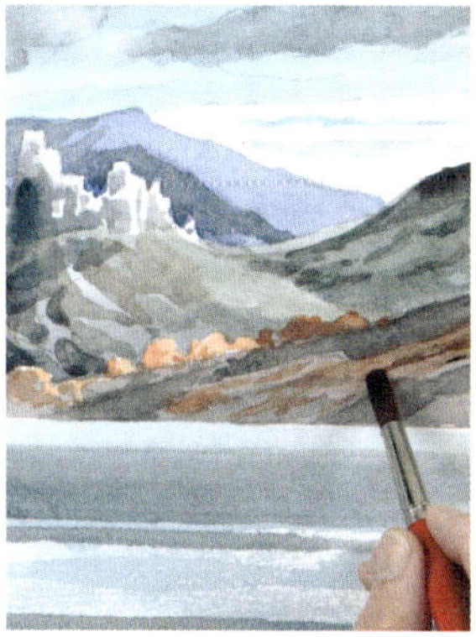

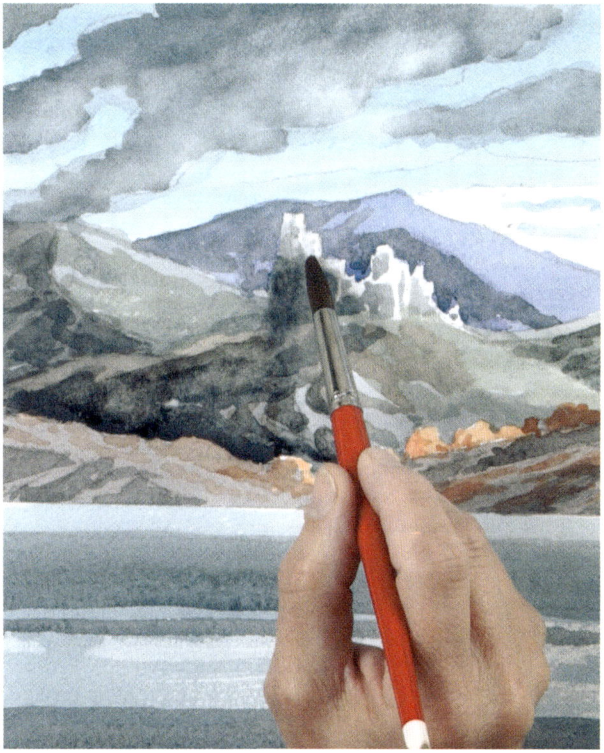

STEP 12

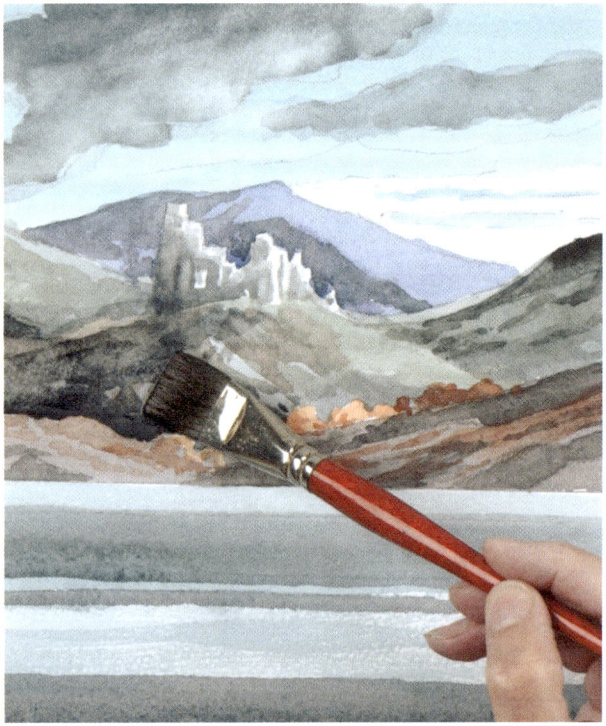

Go back over the dark wash you applied to the lake, to accurately tie it in to the tones of the landscape. Work a strong wash of Payne's gray over the original band of colour. Create textures in the wash by applying a second layer over the wet first layer. This is not easy, but try to work confidently. Do not go back over your work.

TRICK OF THE TRADE

For a stormy sky, apply a dark grey wash over the whole sky area. While the wash is still wet, rub a stiff brush on a bar of soap then swirl it around in the wash to form clouds. Take the brush away and the soap will continue to move the paint around. Then wash your brush thoroughly.

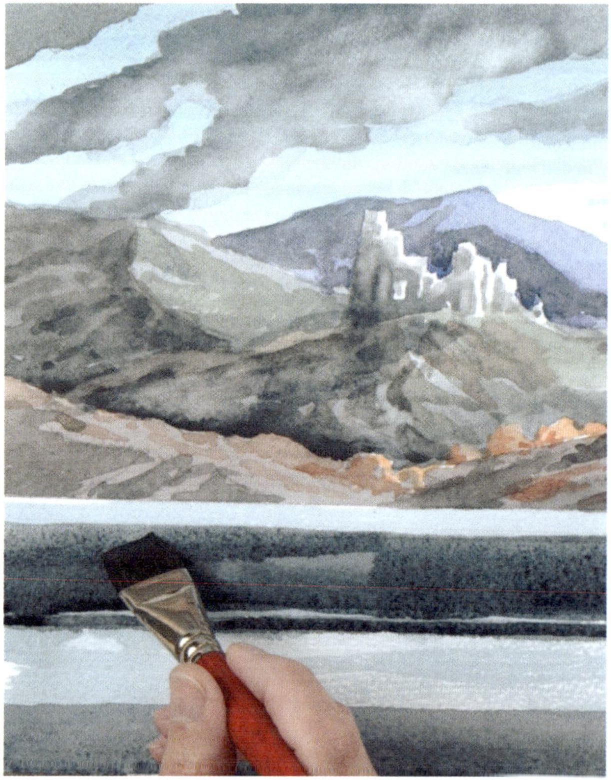

Soften the whole of the dark area to the left of the ruin by applying water with the flat brush and lifting off some of the colour with kitchen paper. This creates effective, textured areas of light within dark.

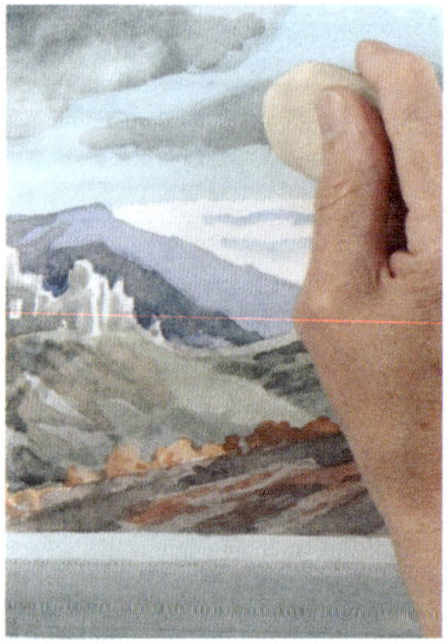

RIGHT Rub out pencil lines where visible. Do this gently so as not to scuff the paper or wear away the paint.

STEP 13

STEP 14

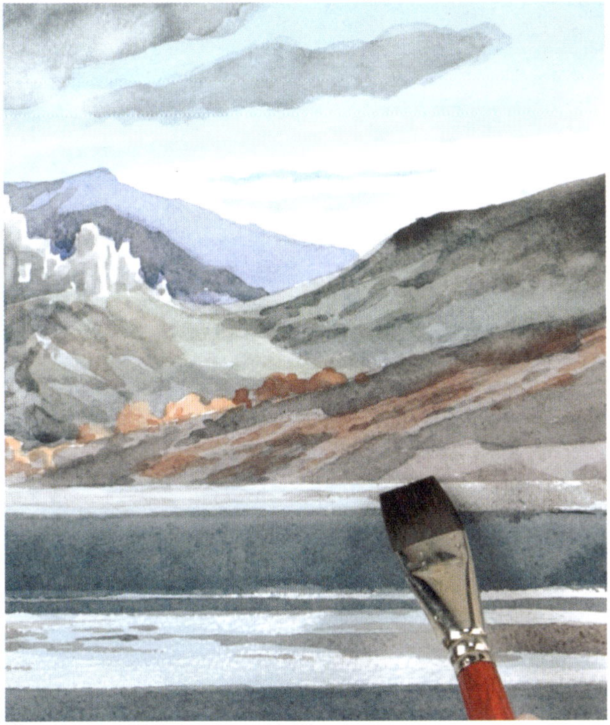

Take a step back from your work and check the overall effect of what you have created. Here, we have worked back over the hills on the left of the ruin with a light mix of cobalt blue. This has cooled this side of the hill, throwing it into a shadow that contrasts more strongly with the green beyond it. Also soften up any further hard edges on the clouds and the hills by applying clean water and lifting off the wet paint with kitchen paper.

TRICK OF THE TRADE

When your picture is finished and completely dry, you can remove any surplus pencil marks by rolling a piece of adhesive tack over the surface. This will not lighten delicate washes in the way that rubbing with an rubber can sometimes do. The early watercolourists used fresh breadcrumbs to do this job.

For a clever piece of detail, add a light mix of Payne's gray to the edge of the lake to hint at the reflection of the ruin. Then lift off some of the colour of the foreground hills and blend it with the water. Keep these as small touches only.

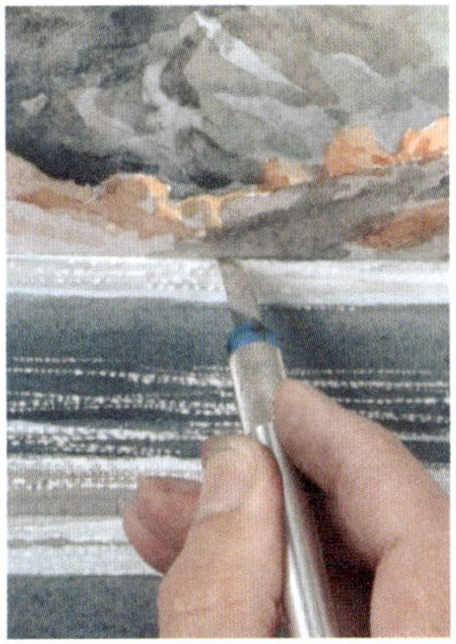

RIGHT With the edge of the craft knife, scratch off some of the colour in the dark areas of the water. This reveals the white paper underneath and adds to the sparkle effect.

STEP 15

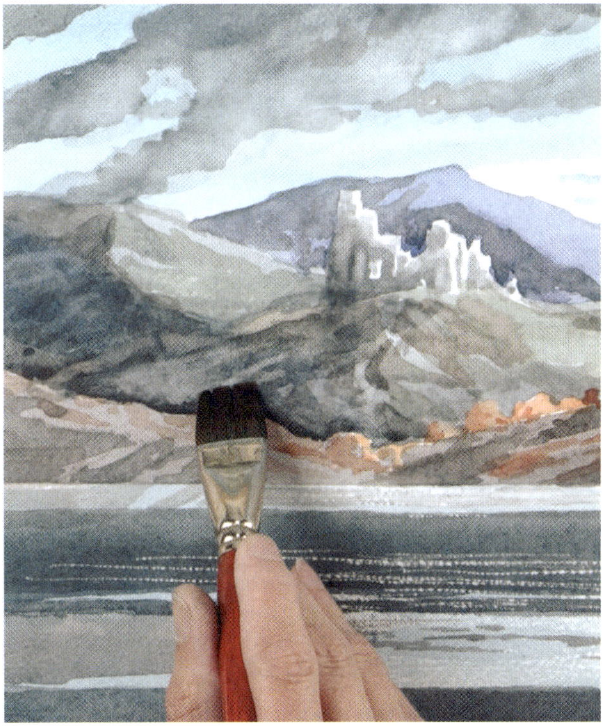

STEP 16

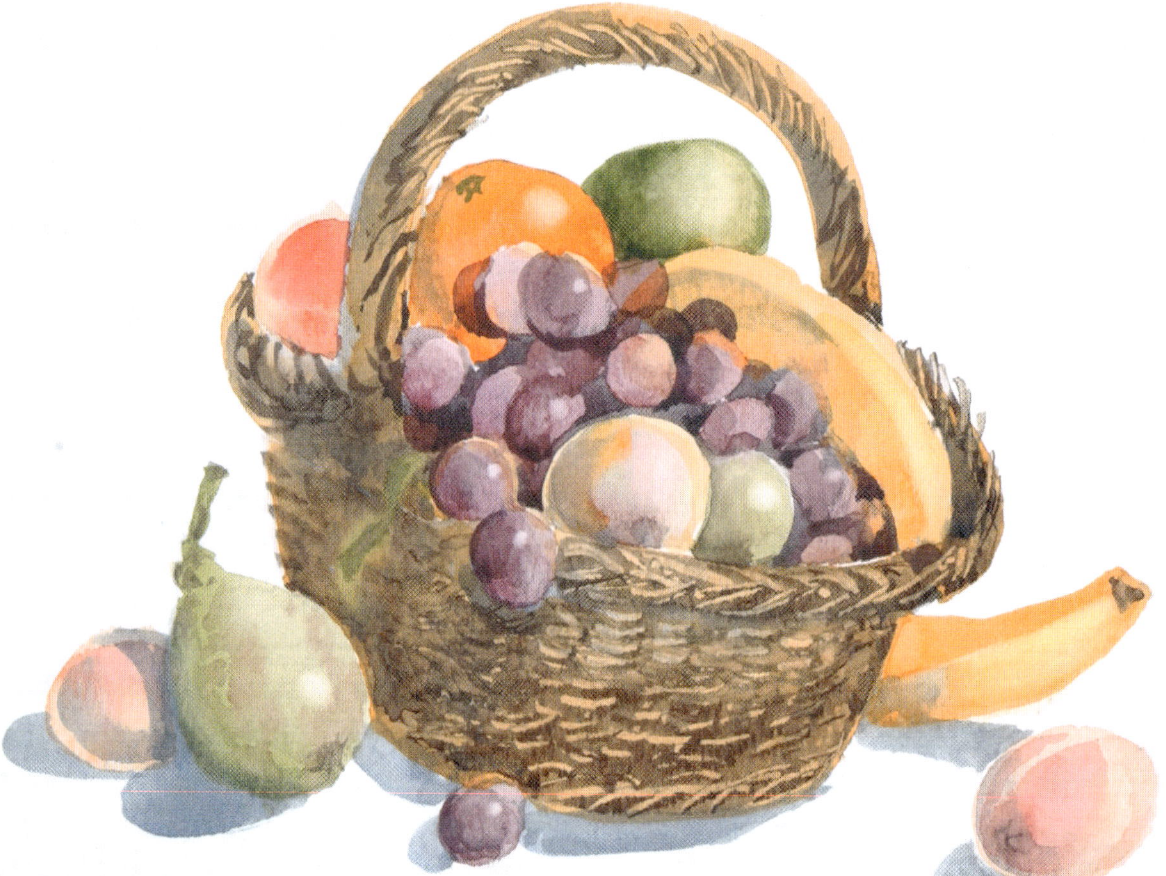

3
still life

john barber
380 x 500mm (15 x 20in)

The great joy of painting still lifes is the high degree of control you can exercise over the composition. The items to be painted, the lighting, the arrangement, the background colours, even the amount of time you spend painting can all be fixed, in stark contrast to trying to capture changing landscapes or moving figures. Because your subject does not move, you can arrange almost anything you like, but it is best if you have a theme running through your work. The theme of this project is fruit, and you will see how to create a visually interesting arrangement, build up precise, detailed colours, develop a balanced range of shadow tones, and use different materials and techniques to make your watercolours effective.

TECHNIQUES FOR THE PROJECT

Using gum arabic

Lifting off

Working wet-in-wet

WHAT YOU WILL NEED

Rough surface watercolour paper
Graphite pencil, 6B
Round brush, no. 5 or 6, sable or synthetic
Flat brush, 2.5cm (1in), sable or synthetic
Fine brush, no. 1 or 2, sable or synthetic
Rubber
Gum arabic
Kitchen paper and craft knife

COLOUR MIXES

1 Payne's gray
3 Cobalt blue
4 Violet
5 Permanent rose
7 Orange
8 Cadmium yellow
11 Burnt sienna
12 Hooker's green

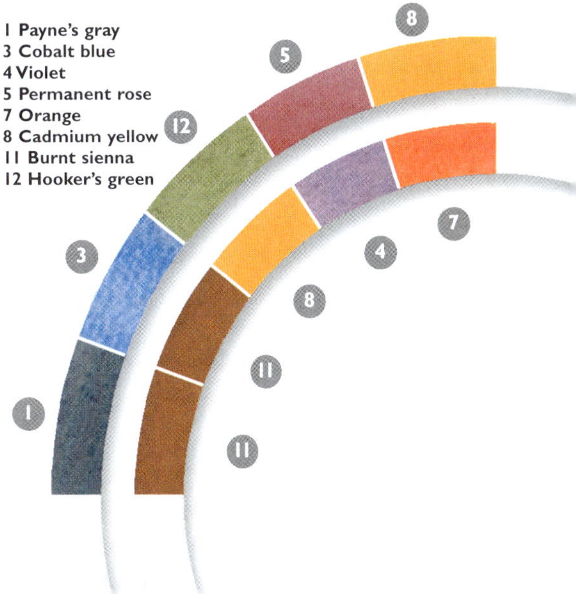

USING GUM ARABIC

Gum arabic is a liquid that can be added to watercolour paints (or to gouache) to help bind the pigment. The result of this is that paint becomes less runny, more controllable, and dries less quickly. This means that you can create different effects in the paint that would not otherwise be possible with standard wet washes.

Gum arabic comes in a bottle and is easy to use. Once you have mixed your paints, add the gum to the mix and stir it in with the brush. Exactly how much gum to use depends on the consistency you want to achieve and the amount of paint you have mixed. This means that you will have to experiment to find the right amount but as a rough guide, three or four drops will be enough to cover an area of a few square inches.

Use your mix of paint and gum arabic to colour very small parts of your work as the gum will stop paint from running from one area to another. You can also create precise highlights and other shapes by working into the paint while it is still wet with the handle of a brush.

You can easily lift off paint and gum arabic using water and kitchen paper, because the gum is water soluble. This is very useful if you need to lighten dark colours.

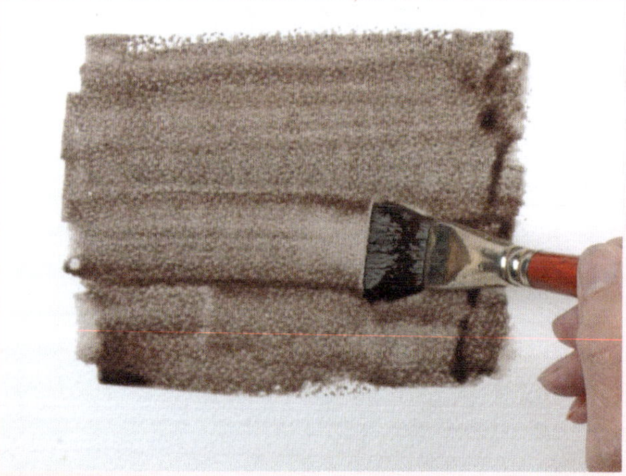

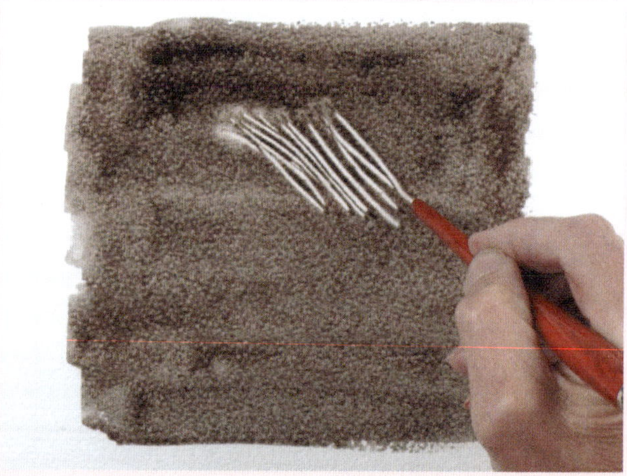

1 Mix your wash in the usual way, making sure you have enough to paint to cover the area you are working on. Add a few drops of gum arabic to the mix and apply your colour to the paper using a flat brush. The paint will be thicker than usual.

2 While the paint is still wet, turn the brush around and, with the point of the handle, start working patterns and shapes onto the paper. The paint comes off very easily, leaving paper that is almost untouched showing through.

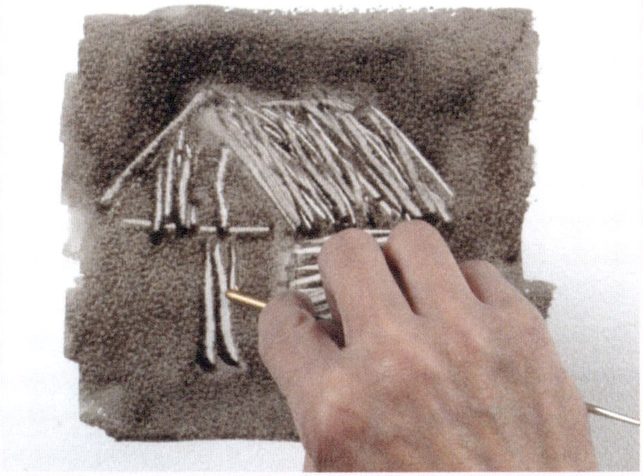

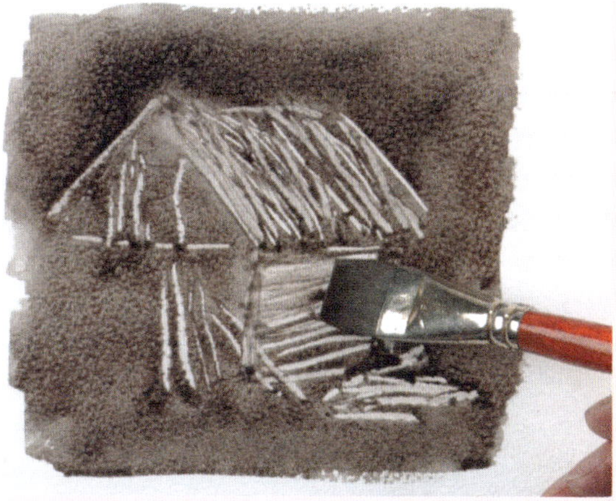

3 You can build up any shape or pattern you like in the paint. Here we have created the rough outline of a wooden shed. However, you can use your paint and gum arabic mix in smaller quantities and create highlights in specific parts of your work.

4 Gum arabic increases the drying time for paint, making it very forgiving to work with. For example, if you find that the shapes you have worked into the paint are too stark, you can gently blend them together using the brush.

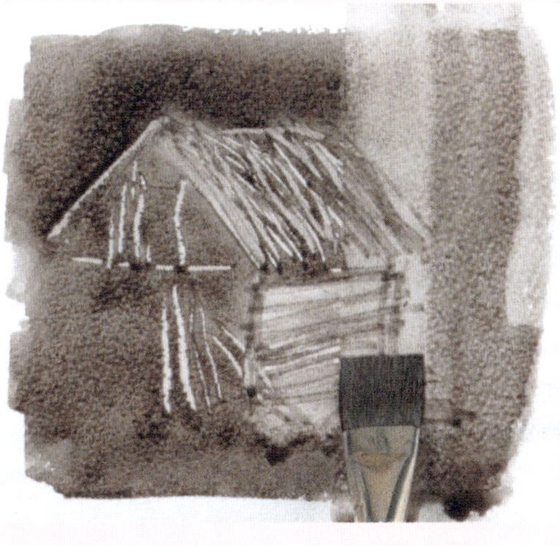

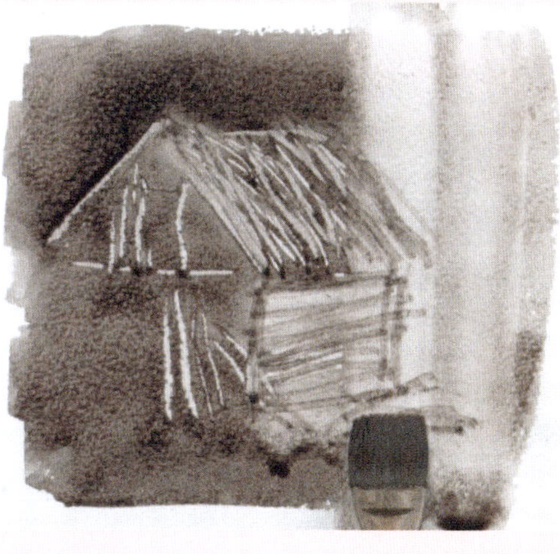

5 Gum arabic is water soluble, so once the paint dries, you can work into it again to lift off paint. This means that you can lighten the colour of the paint if it is too dark. Apply water with a brush and run it over your work to remove the paint.

6 Lift off the paint as necessary to achieve the look you want. It is possible to lift almost all the paint off the paper using a wet brush and kitchen paper to dab away the excess water. Use this property to create lots of different effects.

Sketch in the outline of the basket first, including the sections at the back that will be covered over when you apply the watercolours. Then add in the shapes for the fruit, accurately relating them to one another. This gives the composition a tight, cohesive look, rather than just a collection of random outlines.

REMEMBER

You start composing your picture from the moment you place the first object on the table, so take some time to arrange the objects as an attractive ensemble. When you settle on an arrangement you like, move around and view it from different angles. You may find a better composition or you may discover several other pictures.

STEP 1

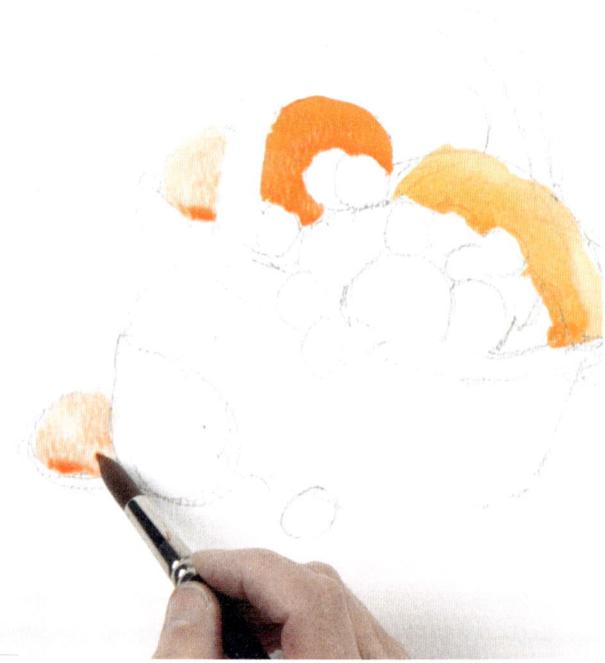

Make a light mix of cadmium yellow and apply it as a flat wash to the banana, using the round brush. Use more paint along the bottom edge, which is in shadow. Add a little orange to the mix and apply this to the orange itself. Then lighten the mix with water and apply it to the red apples.

RIGHT Wet a couple of small areas on the apples and drop in some pure permanent rose, wet in wet. This gives the fruit a ripe look.

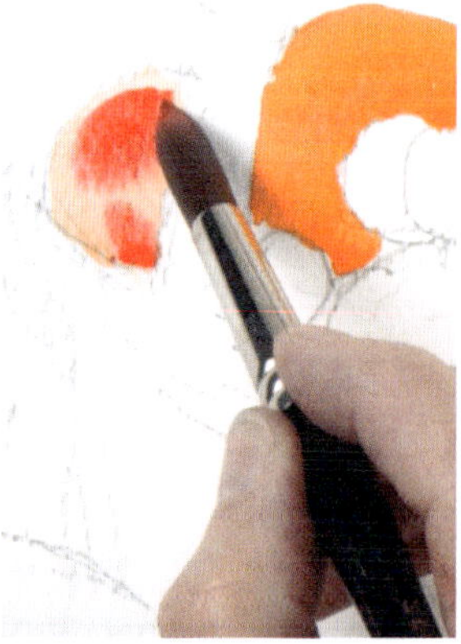

STEP 2

RIGHT Mix permanent rose with a little violet to colour the grapes. Add the colour as a flat wash, being careful not to paint outside the pencil lines – your washes need to be applied accurately in this project.

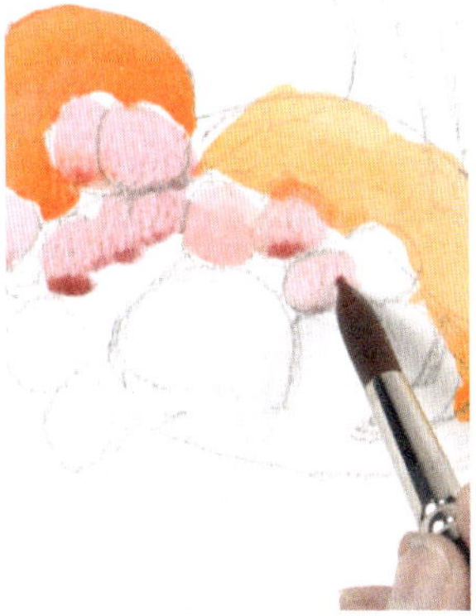

Start to build up shadow on the underside of the grapes, wet-in-wet. Add small areas of clean water to the wash and drop in more of the same mix. You can build up areas of shadow and texture very effectively using this technique.

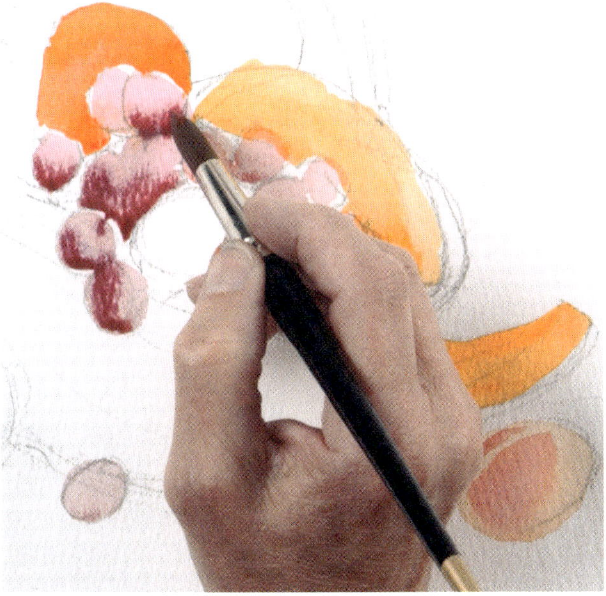

STEP 3

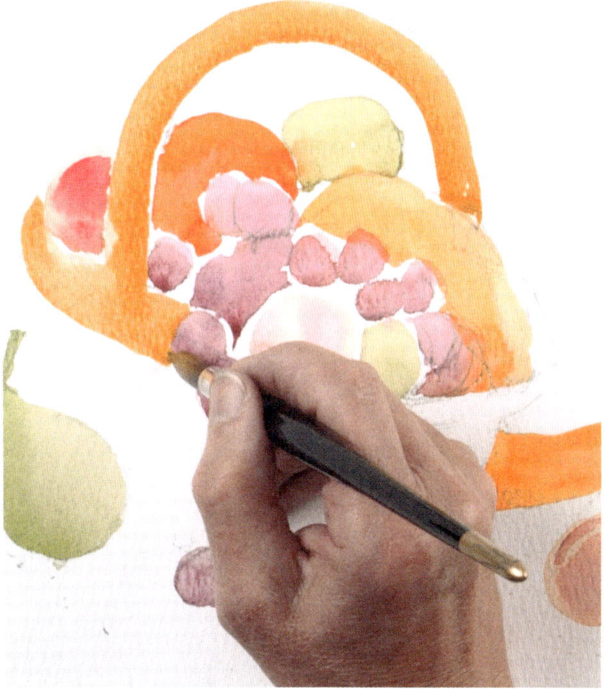

Mix Hooker's green with a touch of cadmium yellow and add it to the apples at the front and back of the basket and to the pear on the table. As before, use the wet-in-wet technique for creating shade on the underside of both pieces of fruit. Once the paint is dry, gently erase any visible pencil lines and add a flat wash of yellow ochre to the whole of the basket, starting with the handle and the rim.

BE CONFIDENT

Try dropping colour into a wet wash and letting it run. This wet-in-wet technique is often a more successful method of applying detailed colour than careful copying of mottling on fruit or leaves. An exciting quality of watercolour is what happens after the colour is on the paper. Be bold and improvise with the marks you have made.

STEP 4

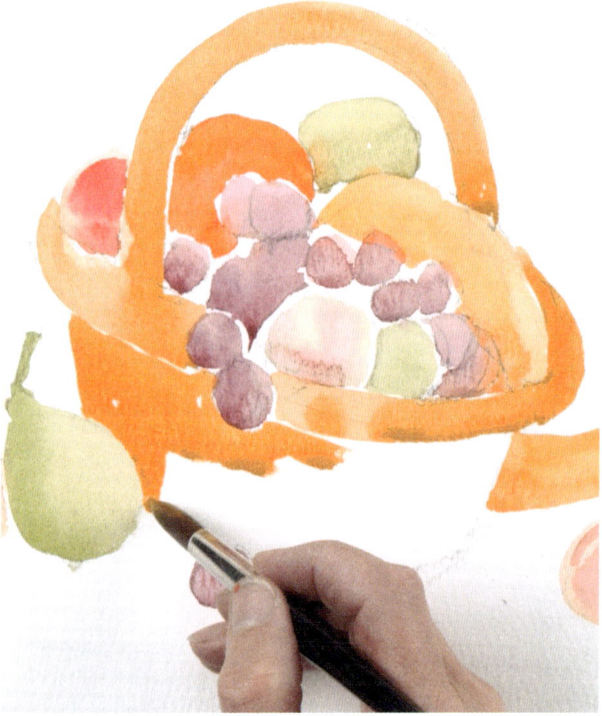

Use this mix to add shadow to the side of the apple at the front of the basket. Make sure that all your shadow areas match up. This means that you must know where the light source is – in this project, the light is coming from the right. However, creating shadows will produce some hard edges, which you will need to soften. This is done by gently rubbing a soft brush loaded with water over the hard edges. As the water starts to lift the paint off, the brush mixes the two colours together slightly, blending one into the other. Don't overdo this or the edges will look smudged.

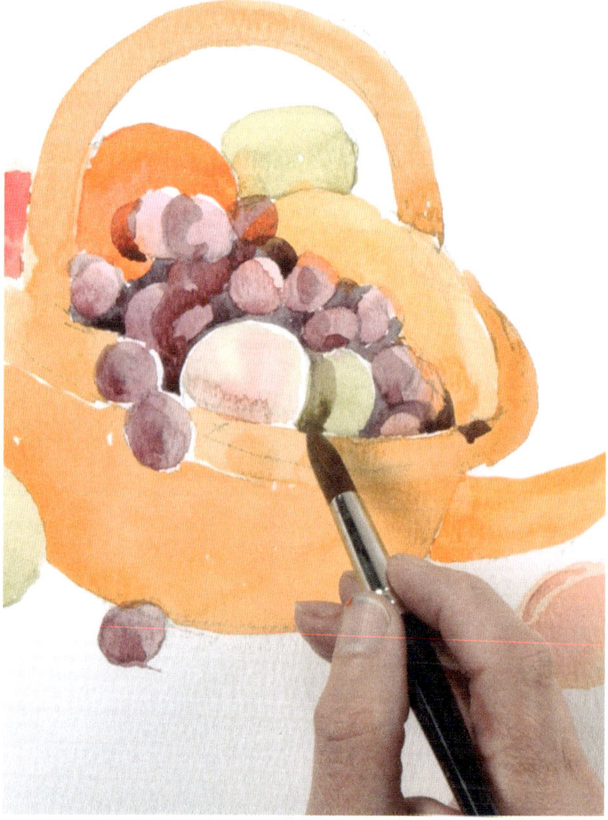

Then add more yellow ochre to the mix to darken it. Apply this darker colour around the handle and the rim to build up texture and shading in these areas. With the same mix, apply a flat wash to the body of the basket.

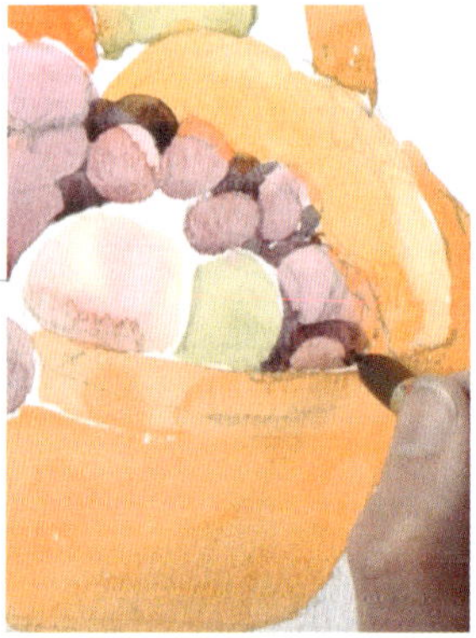

RIGHT Mix permanent rose, violet, and a touch of Payne's gray to build up the shadow areas between the grapes. Use the tip of the brush for accuracy.

STEP 5

STEP 6

RIGHT Add a little permanent rose to the peach at the front of the basket. This adds a little extra shading and texture and emphasizes the ripe look.

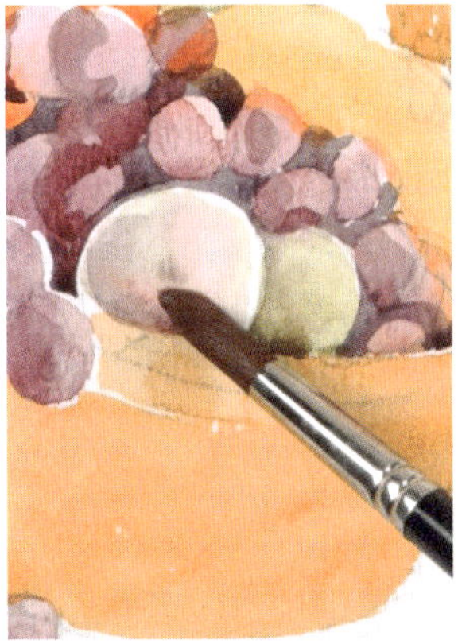

Create some areas of reflected light. Apply clean water along the top edge of the banana in the basket, using the flat brush. Lift off the paint with some kitchen paper. The yellow-white band left behind is an effective highlight. Repeat the process on the other banana.

Using the round brush, build up touches of shadow on each piece of fruit, the basket, and the fruit on the table. First, use a mix of cobalt blue with a little burnt sienna for touches of lilac-grey shading on the handle, the rim, and the left-hand side of the basket. Use this colour for the drop shadow under the fruit on the table. Then wet the pear with a little water and, wet-in-wet, use the tip of the brush to drop some burnt sienna into it to create a speckled effect.

TRICK OF THE TRADE

A wash of burnt sienna and cobalt blue can be mixed to obtain a wide range of cool or warm greys. Choose a grey to suit the tone of your picture and paint the shadow side (and the cast shadow) of each object with this one tint. This will unify your work and show the 3-D effect created by light coming from one source.

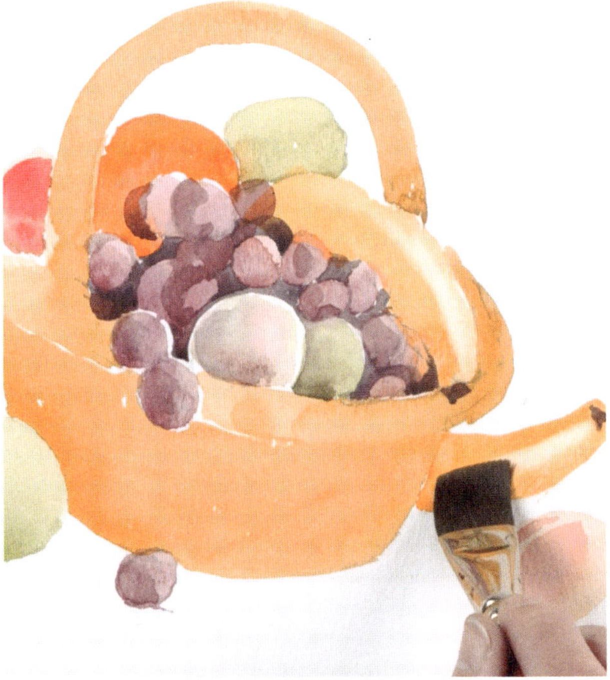

STEP 7

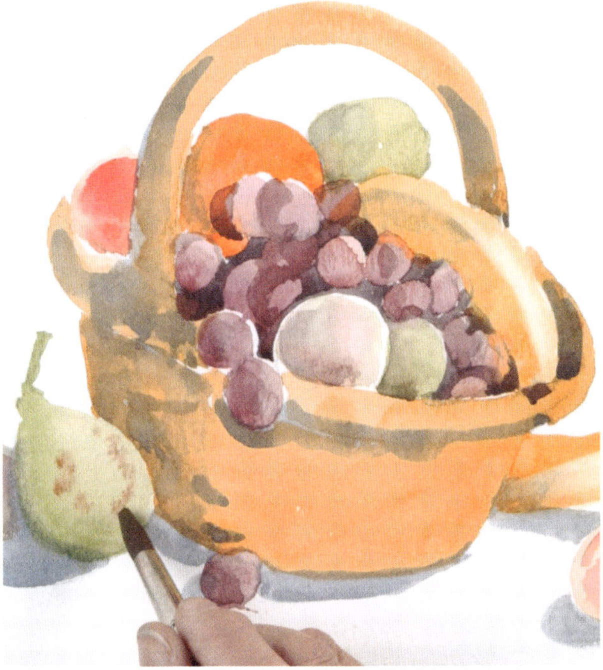

STEP 8

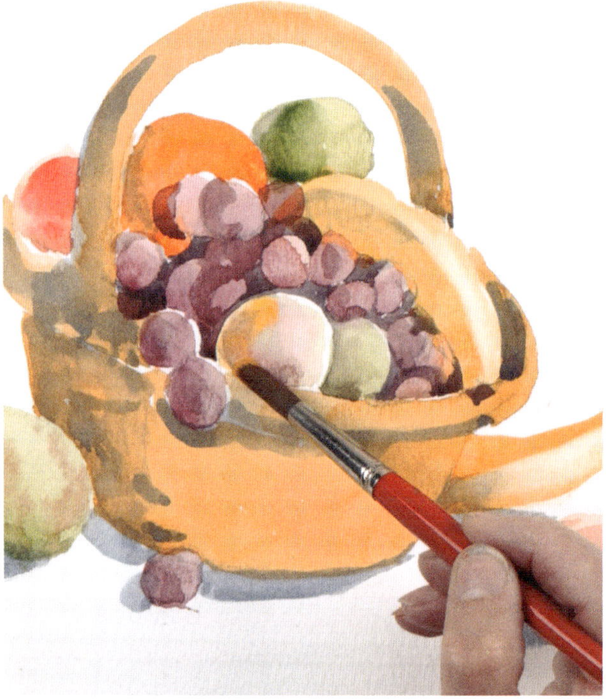

Add shading to the apple at the back of the basket with a stronger mix of Hooker's green and cadmium yellow than you used earlier. Then build up some colour on the peach at the front with a light mix of yellow ochre. Finish off any shading, for example, using permanent rose.

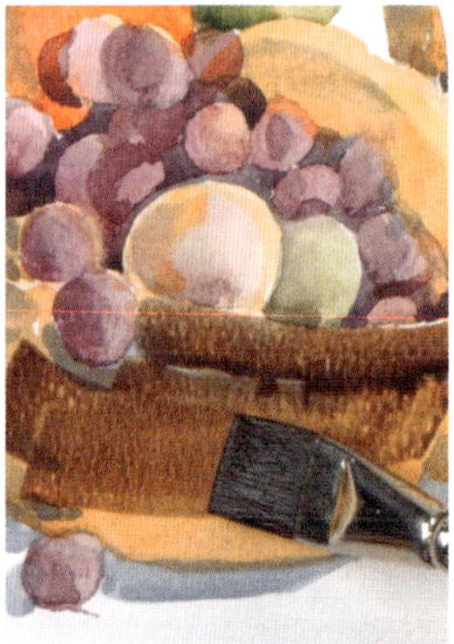

RIGHT Drop some gum arabic into a mix of Payne's gray and burnt sienna. Apply this colour to the rim and front of the basket using the flat brush.

STEP 9

RIGHT Because the gum arabic keeps the paint wet for longer, you can then scratch the pattern of the weave into the paint. Do this with the end of the brush handle and only in areas where light would reflect off the weave.

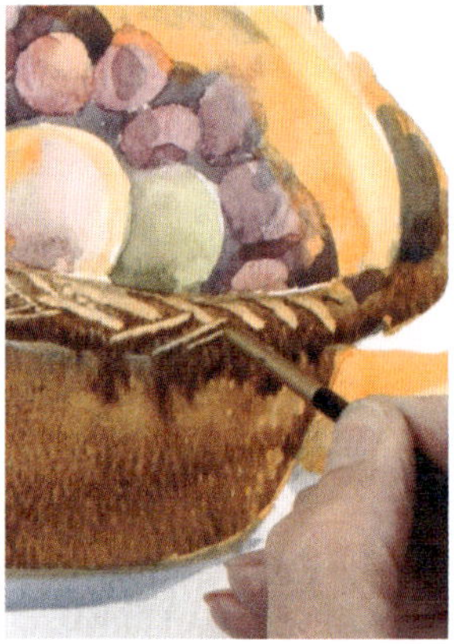

If the paint starts to dry before you finish the pattern of the weave, wet it on the paper with a little clean water. This will lift the paint enough for you to start working with the end of the brush again.

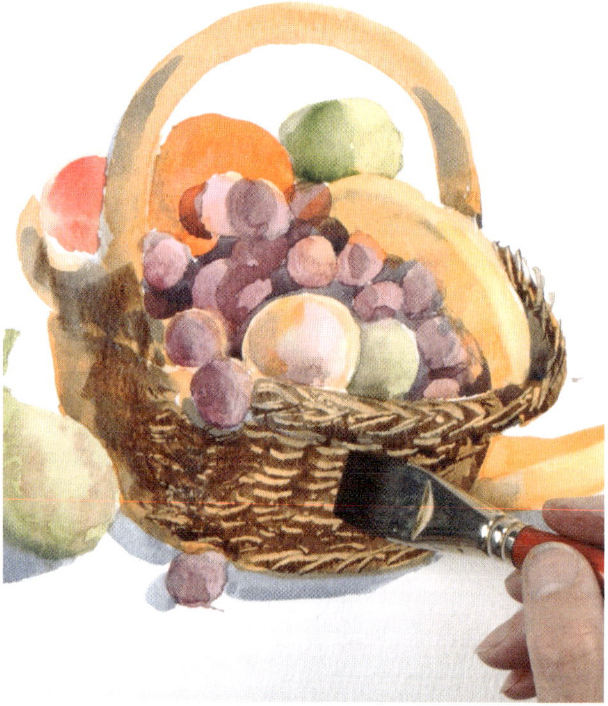

STEP 10

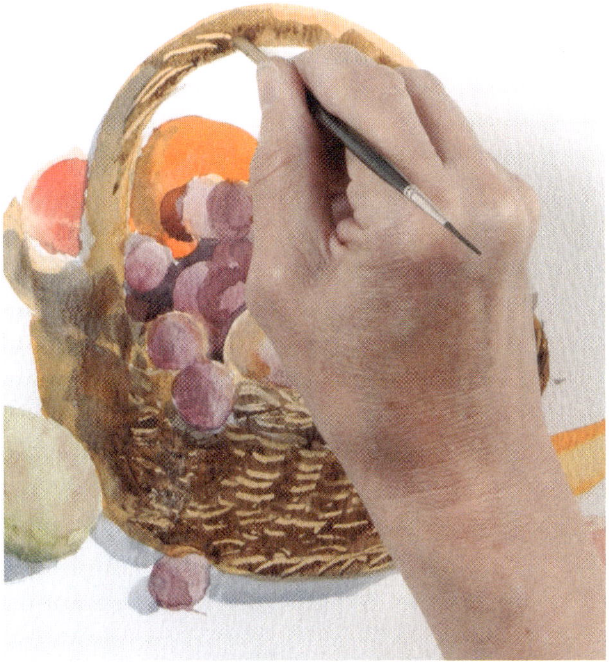

Apply the same mix over the top section of the handle. Because the handle is mostly in light, it doesn't need to be as dark as the rest of the basket and the weave is not as prominent.

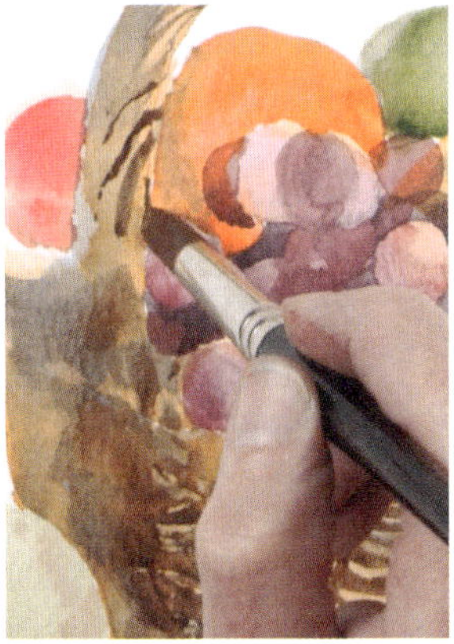

RIGHT As you work around the handle, the left-hand side gradually falls into shadow, and the weave becomes darker. Paint on the pattern of the weave with the round brush.

STEP 11

Take a step back from your work and check to see how strong the colour on the basket is. If it is too dark, you can lighten it. Let the existing paint dry, then add a wash of water over the top. As the paint starts to lift off, dab up the excess with some kitchen paper. You can then scratch the pattern of the weave back into the wet paint. Do this as necessary until you get the shade you need.

TRICK OF THE TRADE

Experiment with different kinds of water-resisting liquids to create accidental-looking textures. A few drops of washing up liquid or baby oil in a small amount of water will give a wide variety of streaks and spots, depending on how much you use. Combine these with touches of a wax candle or scratching off with a blade.

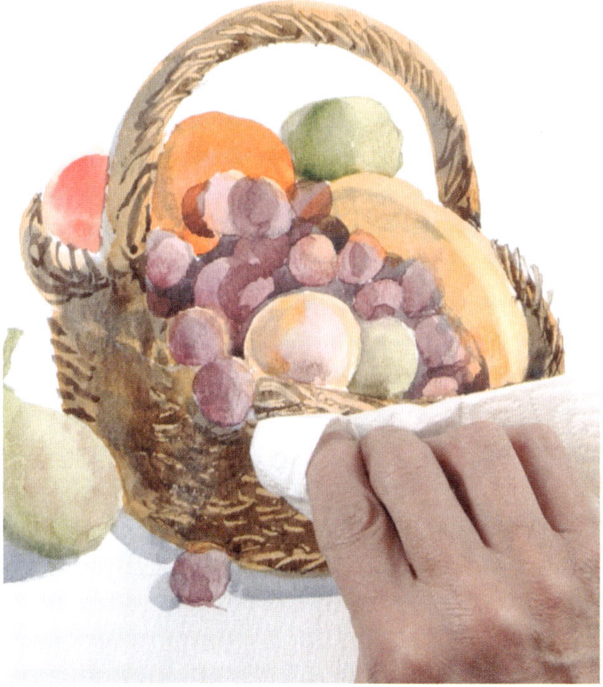

STEP 12

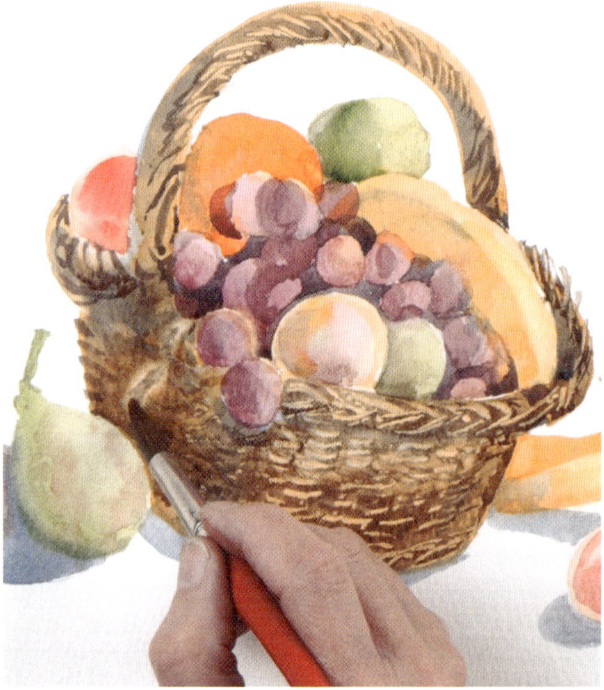

Add some small details to your work. First, lift off some of the dark mix on the side of the basket by applying water with the round brush to remove the paint. Add a faint line of the green mix you used earlier to indicate a small leaf.

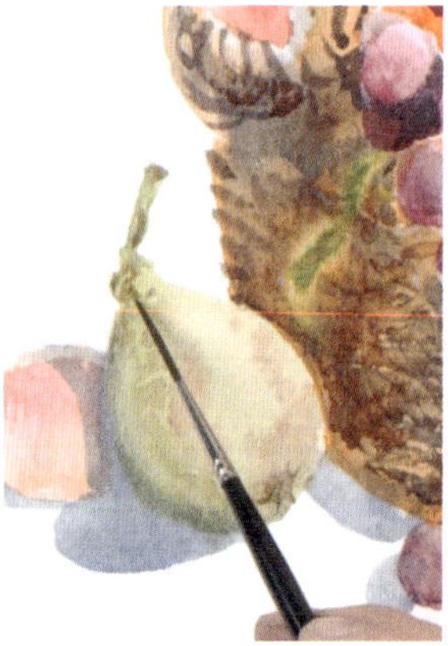

RIGHT Build up some detailed areas of shadow on the pear, just along the edge and the stalk, using the fine brush and the same colour mix as the leaf.

STEP 13

Repeat this detailed shading on the grapes, using the round brush. Use a strong mix of pure violet but use it sparingly – there is already a lot of subtle shading here that will be lost if you add too much dark colour. You can also paint in an extra grape or two just using the violet colour. This adds a little more depth to the image. Add some final touches to the peaches using the same colour.

TRICK OF THE TRADE

You can lift off colour on your entire painting, not just specific areas, by applying water right across the paper. You will lose some of the crispness of the original washes but many delicate shades will remain as a basis for recolouring. You can lift off as many times as you need to achieve a result that you are happy with.

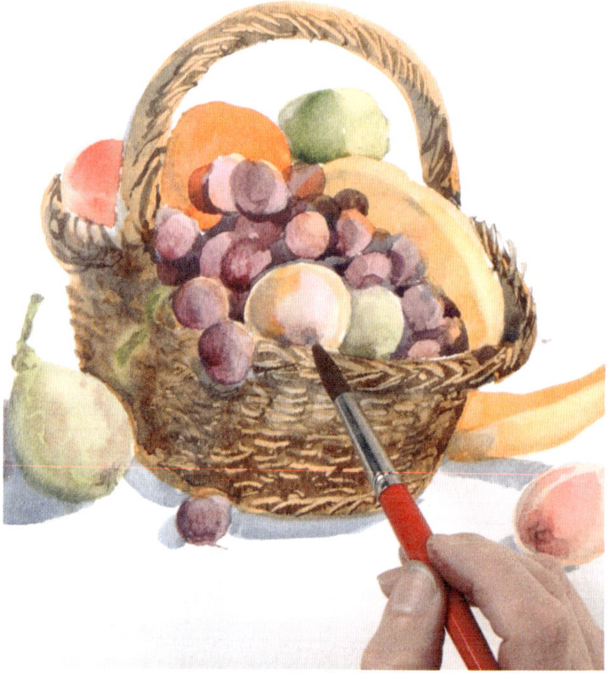

STEP 14

Take a look around your painting and see where the paint has strayed outside your pencil sketch. Clean up these areas and any other mistakes by scratching off the paint with the blade of a craft knife. The thick watercolour paper is capable of withstanding this but be careful not to scratch too hard.

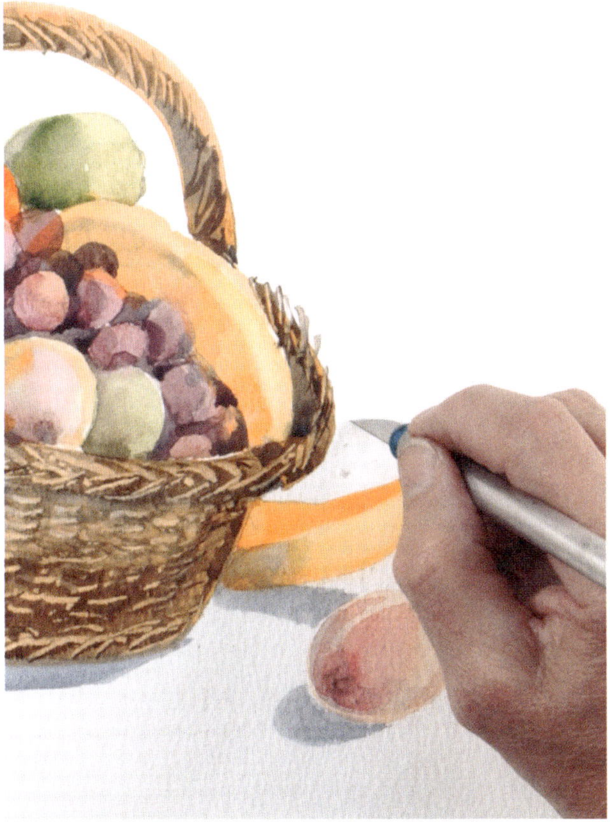

STEP 15

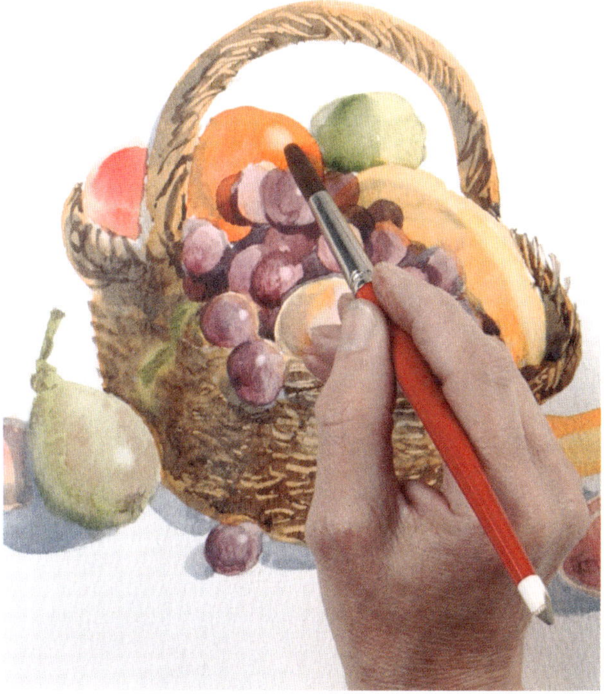

Add highlight areas to the fruit by lifting off some of the paint with water and a round brush, using a circular motion to create a round reflection. Make sure you rinse your brush thoroughly so as not to pull paint from one piece of fruit to the next. Also, don't add too many highlights or they will become too prominent.

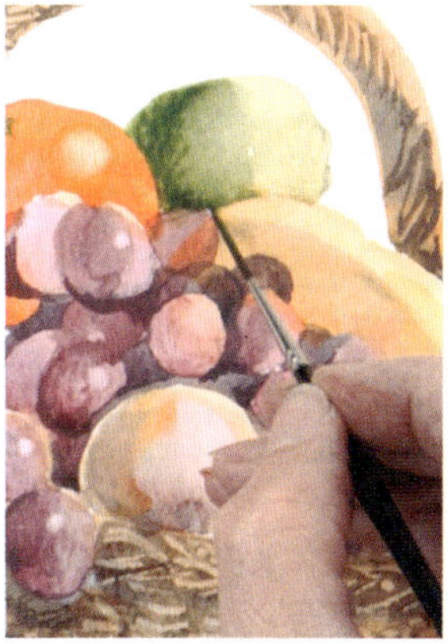

RIGHT Tidy up any last pieces of shading, such as the green around the edge of the apple, with the fine brush.

STEP 16

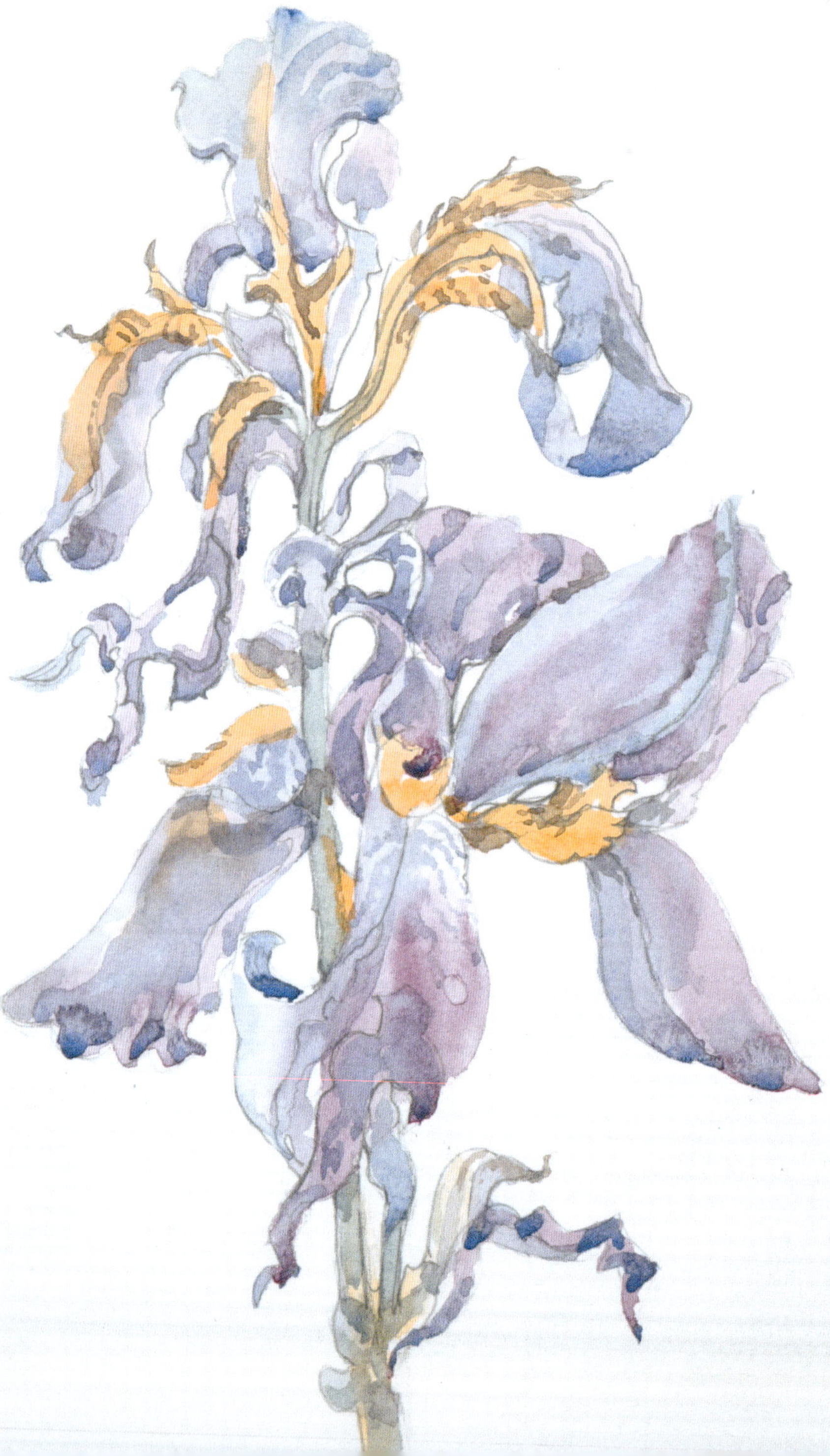

4
purple iris

john barber

500 x 330mm (20 x 13in)

Flowers are complex, delicate, and beautiful. They are also natural, living, and full of colour. These qualities combine to make them a challenge to paint – you need to balance the need to capture some detail with the need to preserve the rhythm of the lines, which can easily be lost by overworking the subject. To this end, a strong sketch is a good starting point for the purple iris in this project; it will also help you differentiate between the petals and the background when you start applying colour. Soften these lines by using only one main colour, with some sparing accent colours, to avoid overelaboration – too many colours will muddle your work and make you lose the delicacy you are trying to preserve.

TECHNIQUES FOR THE PROJECT

Working wet-in-wet

Laying a flat wash

Lifting off

WHAT YOU WILL NEED

Rough surface watercolour paper
Graphite pencils, 6B and 2B
Adhesive tack
Round brushes, no. 5 or 6, sable or synthetic
Rubber

COLOUR MIXES

3 Cobalt blue
4 Violet
8 Cadmium yellow
9 Cadmium lemon
10 Yellow ochre

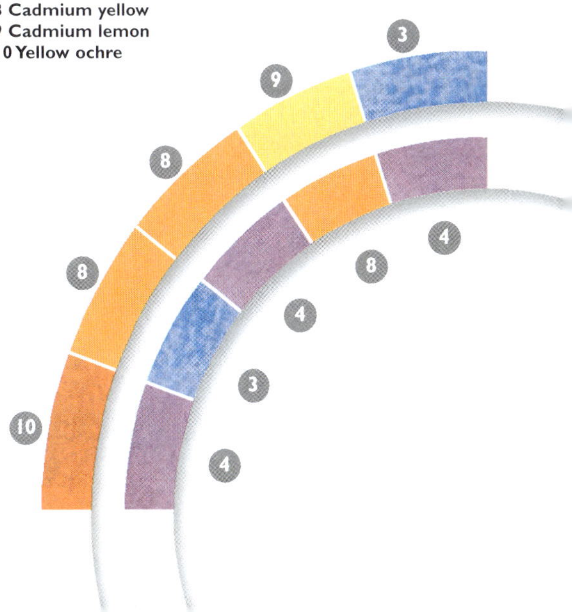

WORKING WET-IN-WET

Wet-in-wet means applying new wet paint on top of paint that has not yet dried. As well as adding one wet colour on top of another, wet-in-wet can also mean applying wet paint on top of a wet base of clean water. Both produce the same effect of allowing colours to run over the paper.

The great advantage of this technique is that when one colour is 'dropped' into another there are no hard edges, unlike the effect produced by wet-on-dry, where hard edges have to be softened. With wet-in-wet, the colours run together at the edges, but don't fully mix, making this a valuable technique when you don't need crisp edges.

This means that wet-in-wet is a classic technique to use when you can afford to let the paint run. This is particularly useful for subjects that have subtle variations in tone and texture that cannot effectively be captured by applying flat washes. Wet-in-wet is best used on flower petals, skies and clouds, and scenes involving water, where not only is it useful for colouring the water itself, but also for adding the colours of the river bed.

Practice wet-in-wet first on a piece of scrap paper, as it can be hard, but fun, to control. Also, use it sparingly – used too often, it can make your work look formless.

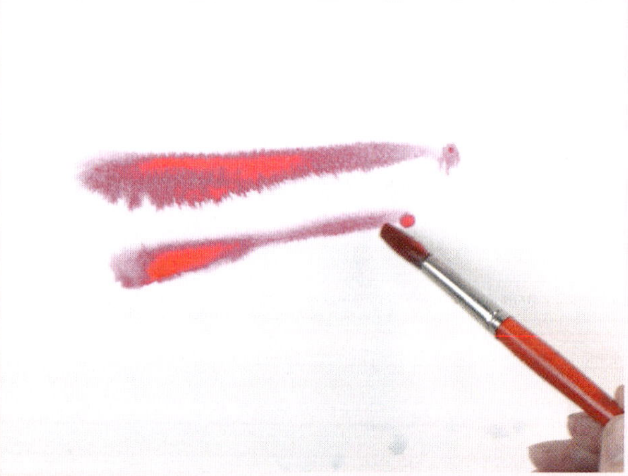

1 Mix two separate watercolour washes, in this case, violet and permanent rose. Lay down a couple of small lines of violet with a round brush. Load another round brush with permanent rose and dab it onto the wet violet paint.

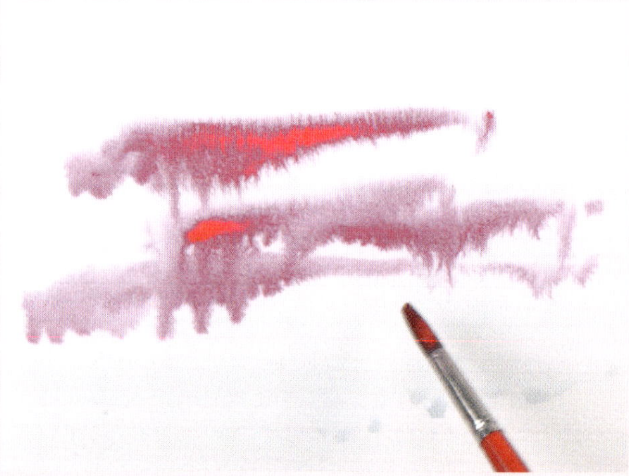

2 Both colours start to run down the paper. The permanent rose runs ('bleeds') into the wet violet and starts to spread and merge. Although the colours bleed into each other, they do not fully mix, leaving both colours still visible.

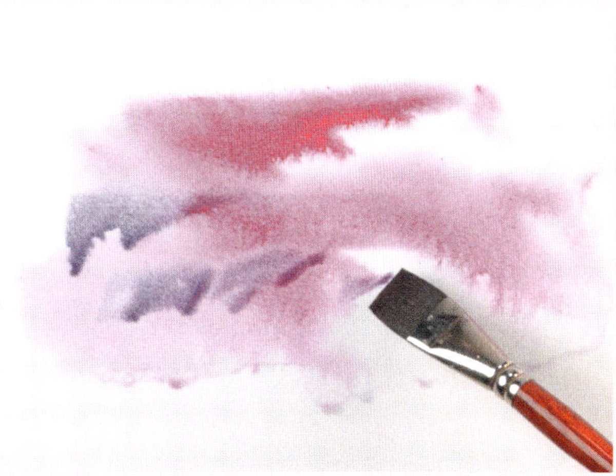

3 The violet has spread across the paper, with a hint of permanent rose in it. You can see how effective wet-in-wet is for creating areas of subtle tone and colour, from faint violet at the bottom left corner to a stronger pink colour at the top.

4 Allow the paint to dry, then add a layer of clean water over small areas of the dry paint with the flat brush. While the water is still wet, drop in a mix of violet and burnt sienna. The paint runs over the wet areas, further building up colour.

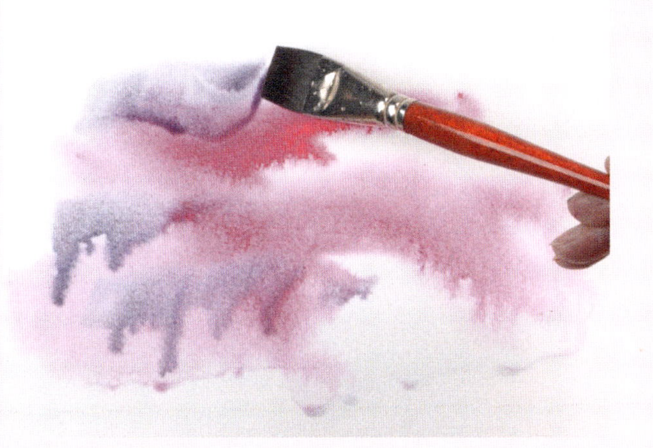

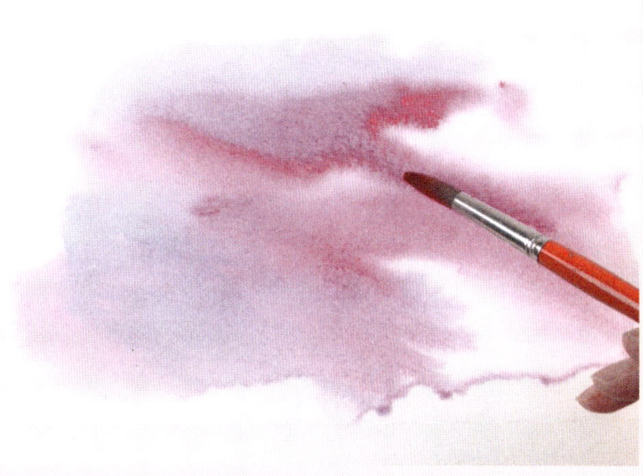

5 Add more small areas of water over the dry paint and drop in more of the violet and burnt sienna mix. You will see that the paint only runs over wet areas – it does not drip down the paper in the way that a flat wash does.

6 Last, you can gently manipulate and move the wet colour on the paper using the tip of a round brush. You can even blow gently on the paper to move the paint around. You can clearly see the graduations in colour from dark to light.

4 purple iris

Before you start sketching, study the way the lines of the flower interconnect and flow. Then start sketching using the 6B graphite pencil. The pencil lines are an integral part of the composition, so draw them firmly. Strongly outline the areas where the white paper will show through. This will help you tell the difference between the petals and the background when it is time to apply colour.

REMEMBER

Capturing the rhythm of the lines is more important than accurately recording every last detail. If you can manage to capture this rhythm, you will achieve a result that looks more like a flower than one produced by a fully accurate drawing – too much detail in a subject such as a flower creates a stilted composition.

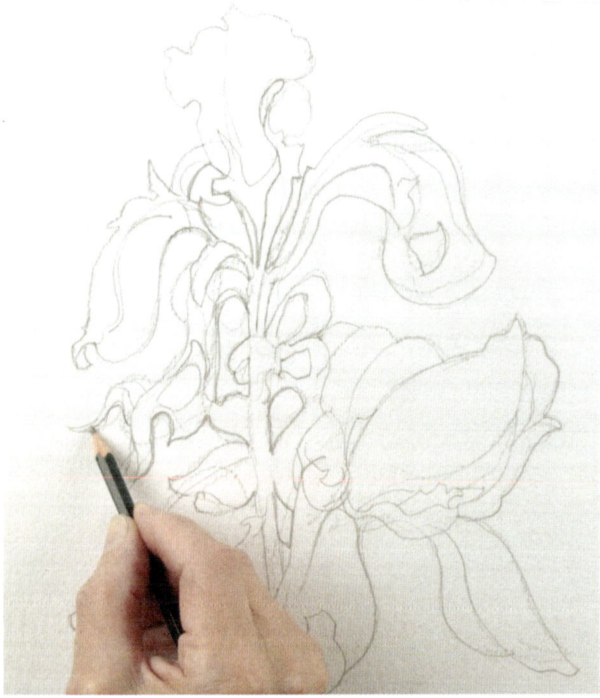

STEP 1

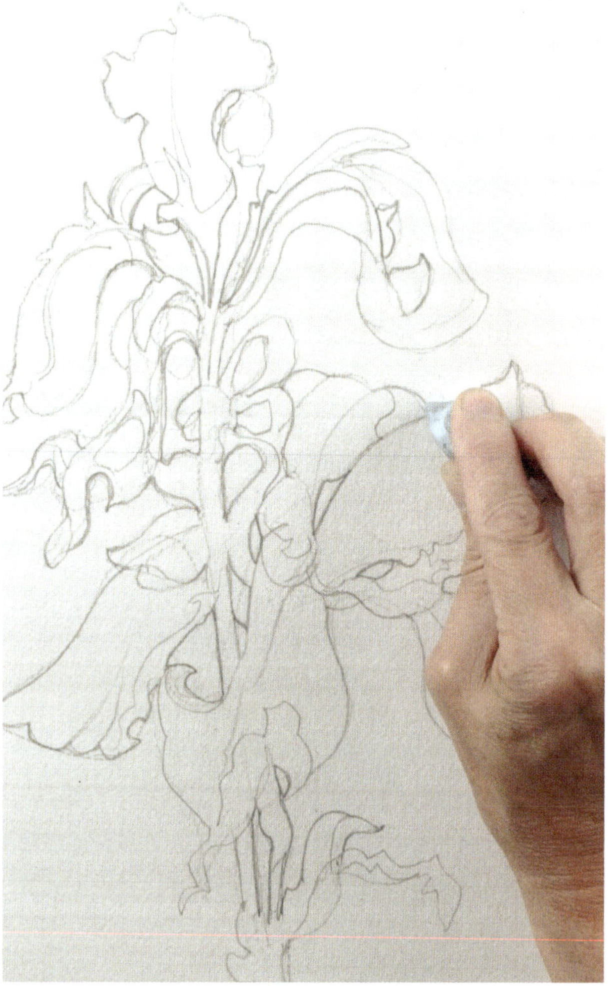

Your pencil lines may look heavy at first, but once you start applying paint, the colour will blend them into the background. Look around your sketch and see how it is coming together. Tidy up any areas where the pencil lines look confused or messy with some adhesive tack. This method of erasing leaves no marks.

STEP 2

Start applying colour to the petals using the wet-in-wet technique. First apply a wash of clean, clear water to one petal only. Remember to apply the water accurately within the pencil lines you have drawn for that one petal. Then, using the round brush, drop on a strong mix of pure violet to the wet paper.

TRICK OF THE TRADE

Colour will only run where the paper is wet, so do not worry that the paint will run outside your pencil lines. You can manipulate this characteristic to your advantage by leaving the top or edge of a petal dry. This will create an instant white highlight, since the paint will not stray into a dry area.

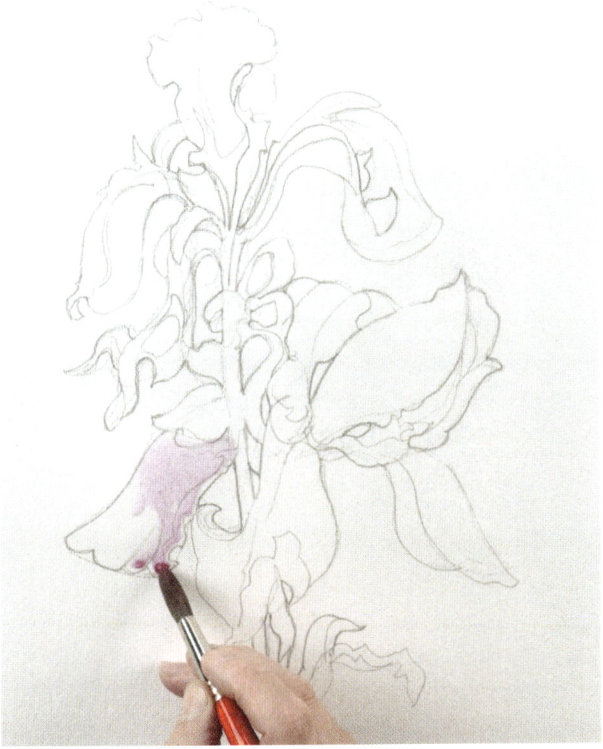

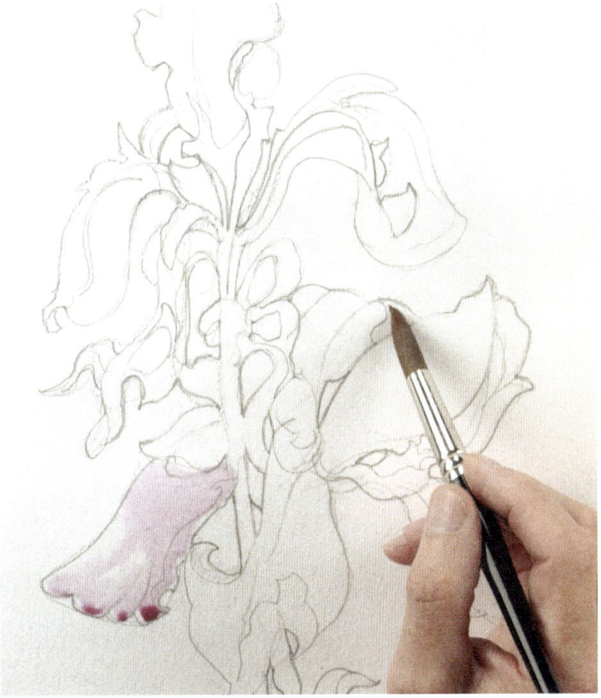

Work around different parts of the sketch, one petal at a time, applying colour as you go. This is better than concentrating on applying colour in one area only – you may find that you end up using too much and have to start over.

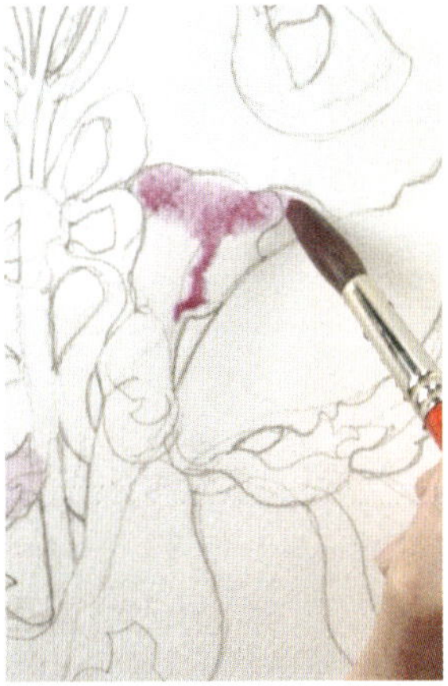

RIGHT Continue to apply a wash of water first, then drop in the violet paint. You will find that if you apply the water carefully you can create detailed areas of colour.

STEP 3 ▸▸

STEP 4 ▸▸

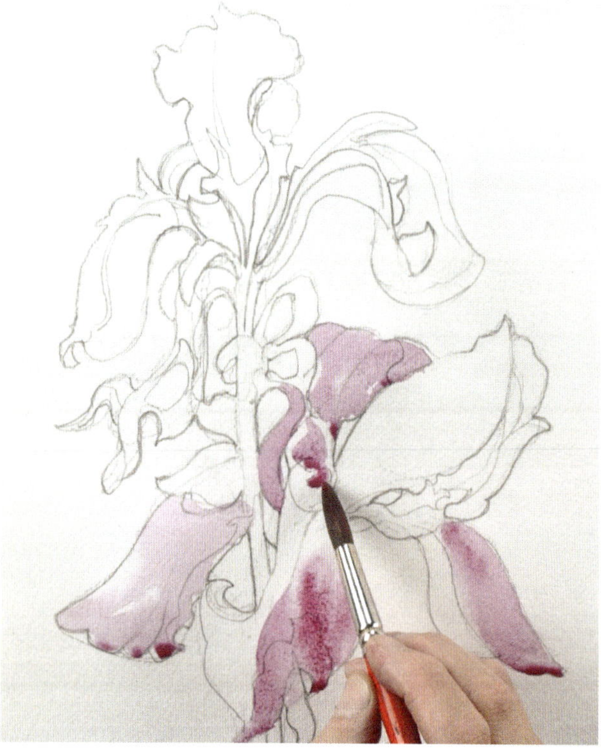

RIGHT Add a little cobalt blue to the violet mix to create a slightly cooler, more blue colour. Apply this wet-in-wet to the petals on the right of the flower.

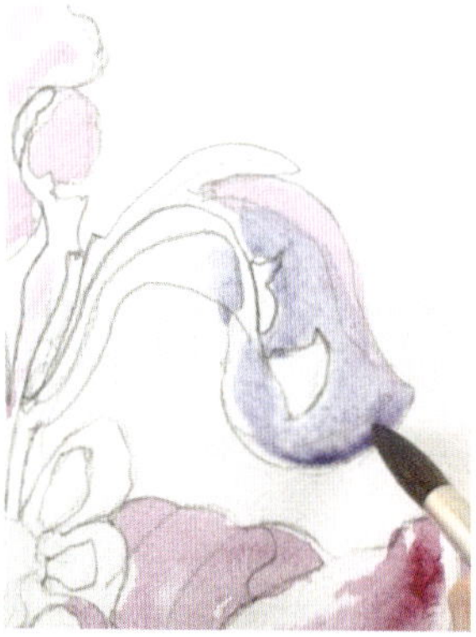

Thin down this cooler blue mix with a little water to produce a lighter blue colour and apply it wet-in-wet to the top petals, which are faint and delicate.

Not every petal has to be coloured using the wet-in-wet technique. To create some different textures and shades simply apply a flat wash of the same violet mix to some of the petals.

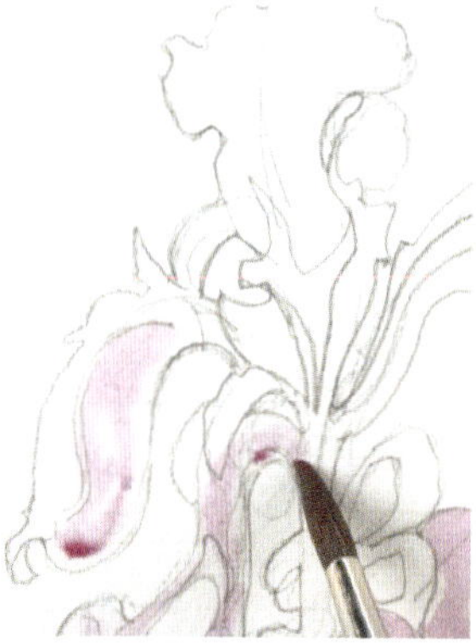

RIGHT Lighten the violet mix with a little water to create a pinker colour. Apply this colour wet-in-wet to create a different shade.

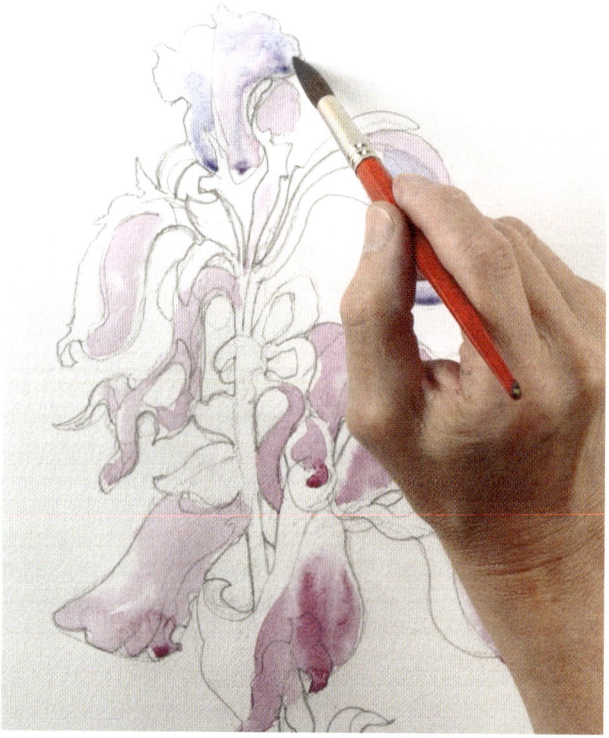

STEP 5

STEP 6

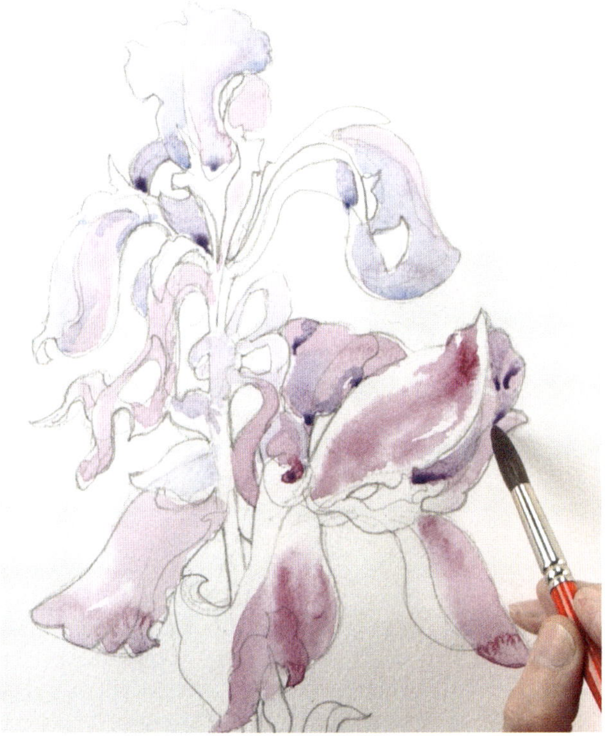

Work backward and forward between the violets and blues, applying a little at a time in specific areas, sometimes working wet-in-wet, at other times just applying small flat washes.

TRICK OF THE TRADE

Try to get some rhythm in your brushwork. Not every application of colour needs to be perfect, so don't labor each petal. Try to relax and hold the brush higher up the handle, gripping it less tightly. What you lose in control you will gain by making more attractive marks. As you practice, this will become clearer.

Work over the edges of the violet areas with this light blue mix and allow the two colours to blend together to build up deeper colours and more texture.

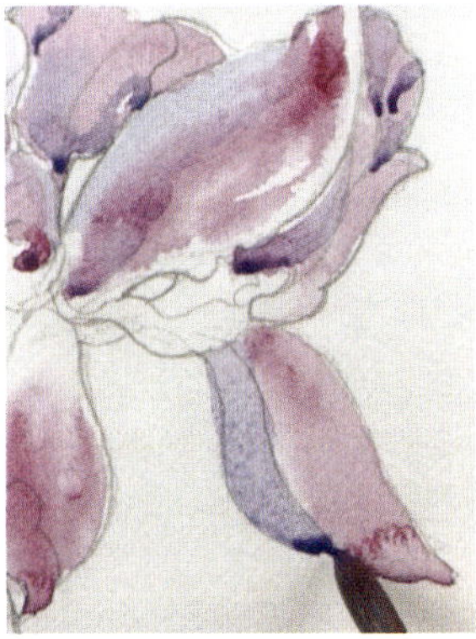

RIGHT In other areas, colour individual petals with the light blue mix on its own. Here, the blue is applied side-by-side with the violet to create an area of subtle contrast.

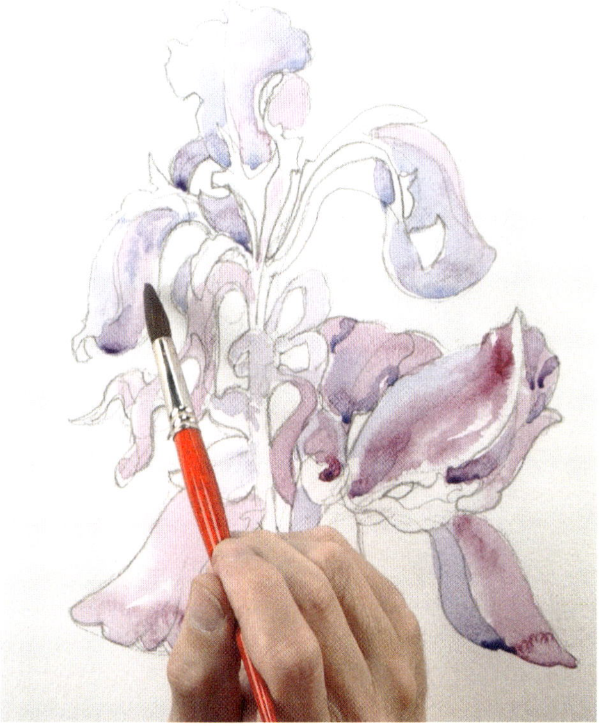

STEP 7

STEP 8

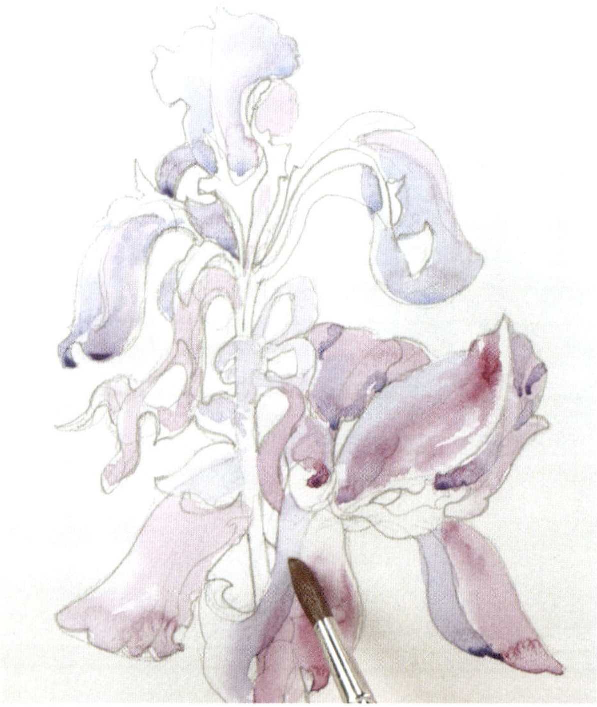

As you work, try to keep the darker tones nearer the bottom of the flower and the lighter tones nearer the top. This will make the iris look correctly weighted – warmer at the bottom, cooler at the top.

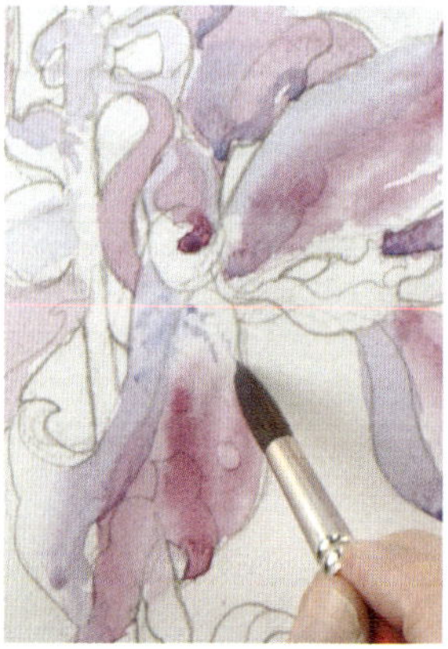

RIGHT Soften any hard edges between the colours by adding a little clean water to the edges with a round brush then blending the colours together.

STEP 9

RIGHT Mix two yellows – cadmium lemon and cadmium yellow – to form a bright accent colour. Start applying this at the base of the petals.

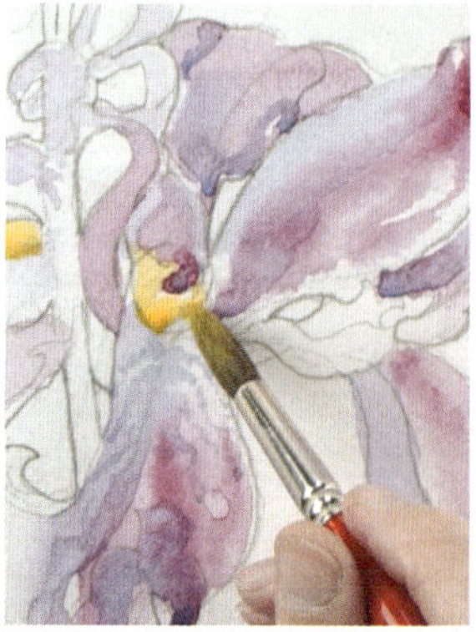

Work your way around the flower adding the yellow mix. Where yellow and violet meet, wet the edge of the violet colour with a round brush and clean water to lift the paint slightly. Dab a little of the yellow mix into the wet violet to blend the colours.

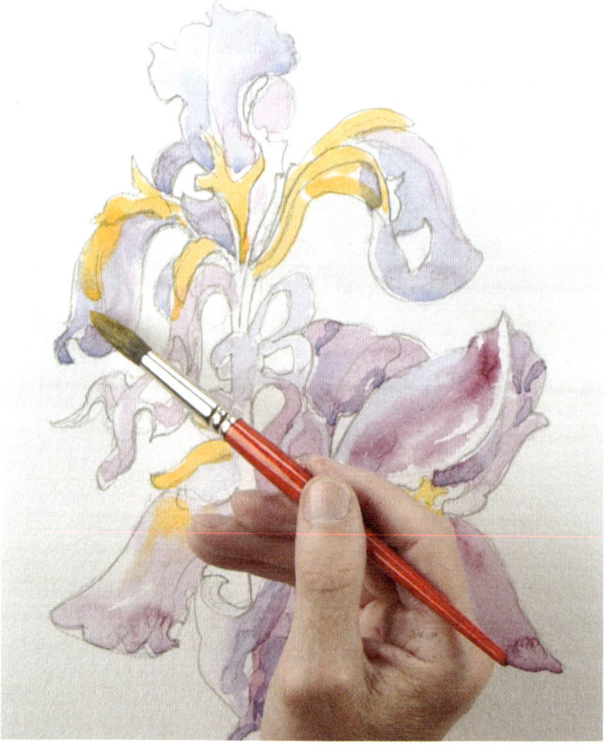

STEP 10

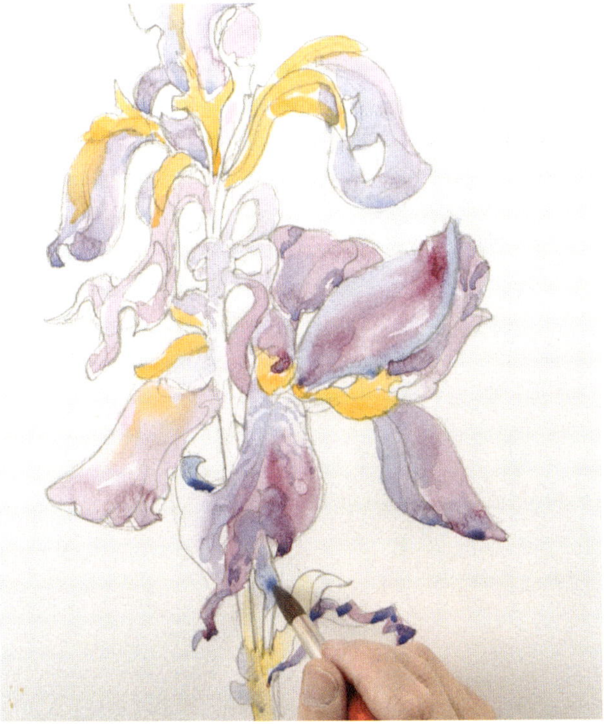

Make a strong mix of violet and cobalt blue. Start adding this darker tone sparingly to small sections of the bottom petals, where the colours are warmest.

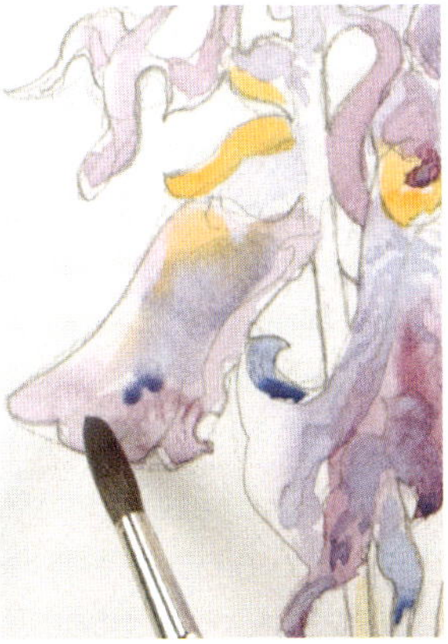

RIGHT Work some of this darker mix onto the petals using wet-in-wet. With a round brush, apply clean water over the top of the existing violet colour to lift the paint slightly, then drop on the darker mix.

STEP 11

RIGHT The middle section of the flower is the densest part of the painting and needs detailed modelling. Start by using the wet-in-wet technique for small areas of detail – these do not have to be extensive.

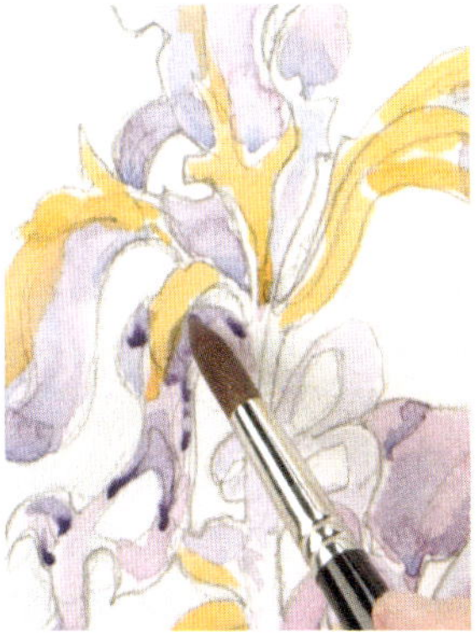

Build up further colour in the middle section by adding small flat washes of the darker mix as well as using wet-in-wet. Using flat washes helps build a variety of textures.

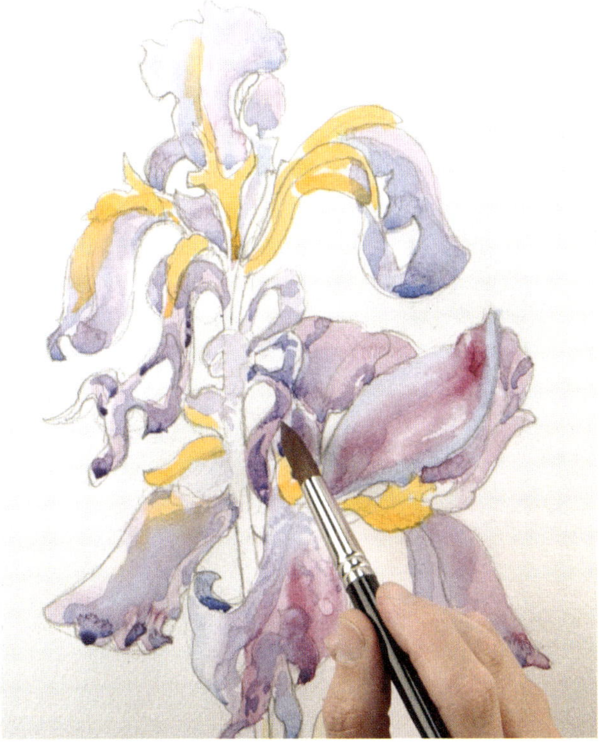

STEP 12

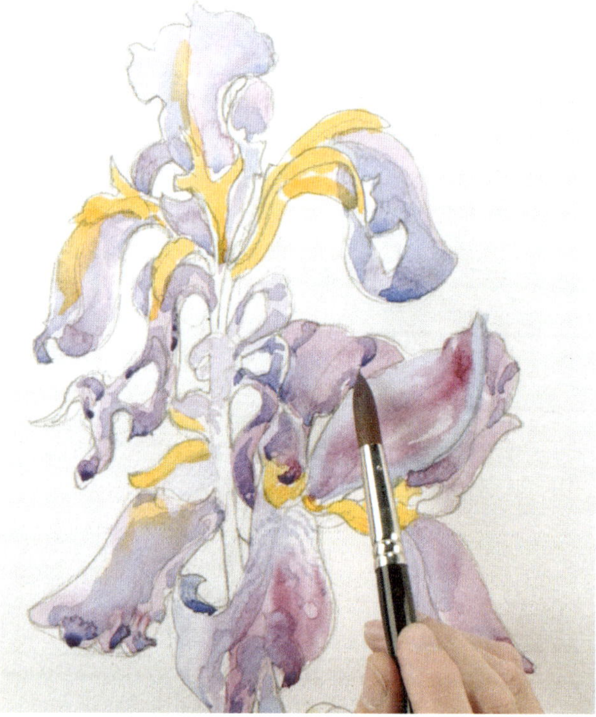

Mix some cadmium yellow and violet to create a light grey colour. Apply this to the underside of the yellow stems to create shadow areas. This gives the yellow areas some depth, to match the depth of the blue and violet petals.

TRICK OF THE TRADE

As you add more areas of colour using wet-in-wet, the brush you are applying the water with will start to pick up the blues and violets. Although you should usually be careful to use a clean brush, let this happen here – it will add a little extra variety to your colour scheme.

Continue to switch between flat washes and wet-in-wet, but be careful not to apply too much paint. The effect you are looking for is a subtle one, with lots of different shades and tones blending together to create an overall impression.

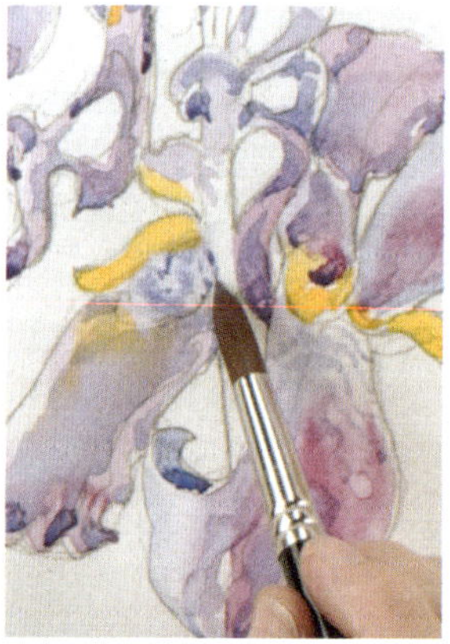

RIGHT Take a step back from your work to see what the overall effect of the colour scheme is. Finish off any small areas of detail, either working wet-in-wet or using a light wash.

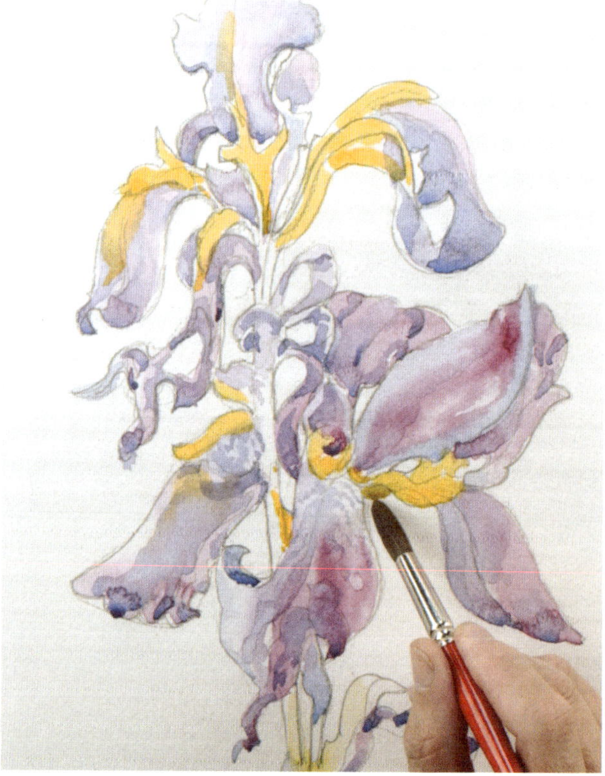

STEP 13

STEP 14

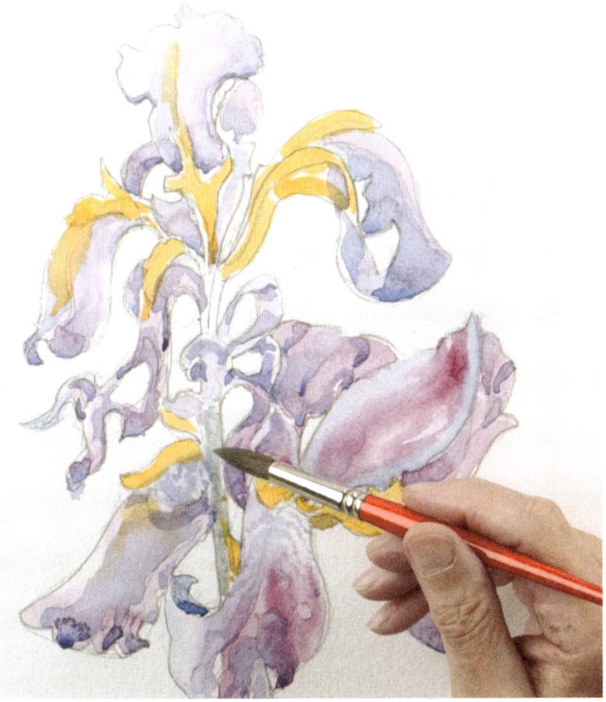

Mix some cadmium yellow and cobalt blue to create a soft green. Try not to use too much yellow – the green should look muted so it does not attract attention away from the violets, blues, and yellows. Fill in the central stem of the flower with this soft green colour.

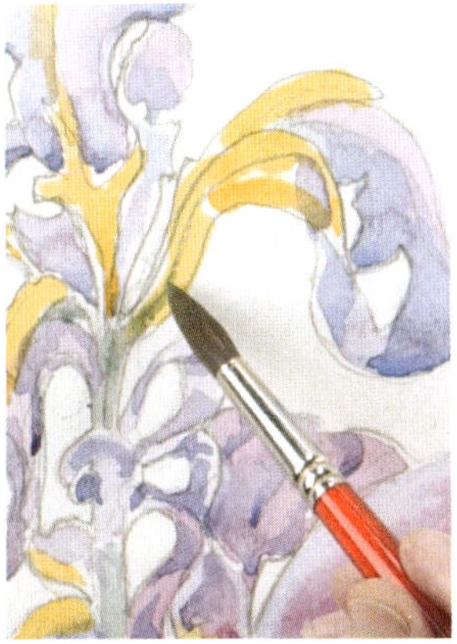

RIGHT Blend the green into the rest of the colour scheme by applying it over the yellow. This also helps build up a different green colour – olive green.

STEP 15

Clean up your painting by erasing all the pencil lines with a clean rubber. Work from the top down, gently erasing the lines as you go. Try not to rub too hard – you can scuff the surface of the paper.

TRICK OF THE TRADE

In a few places, soften the edges of the petals with clean water until they disappear and it is hard to see where the petal ends and the background begins. This is sometimes called 'lost and found,' and will give your work more depth and modelling. It is an important effect in all watercolour painting.

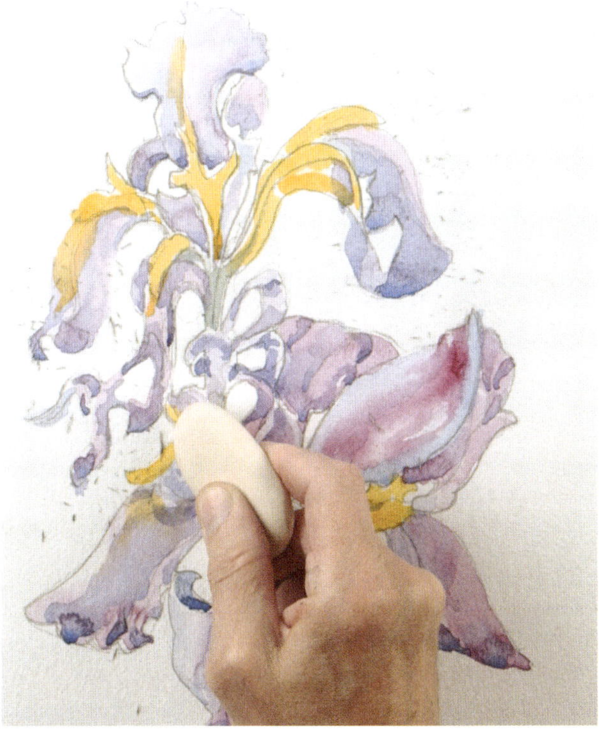

STEP 16

RIGHT Start the last round of modelling on the flower to add a professional-looking level of detail. Mix some yellow ochre and violet to create a brownish colour and add it to the yellow areas on the top left.

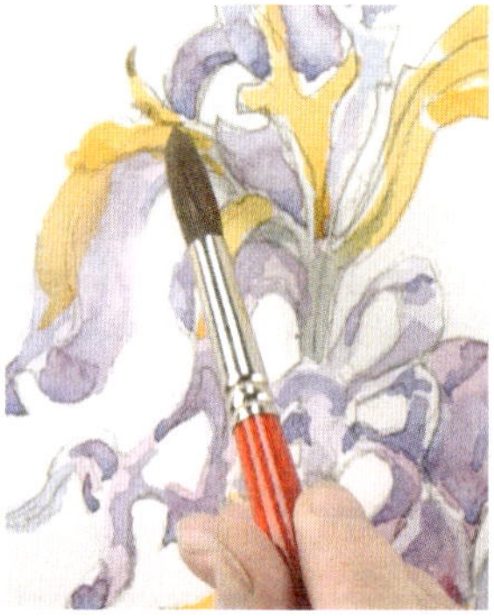

Work your way around to the right-hand side, then down to the bottom. Keep this shading to a minimum or you will lose the brightness of the original colour.

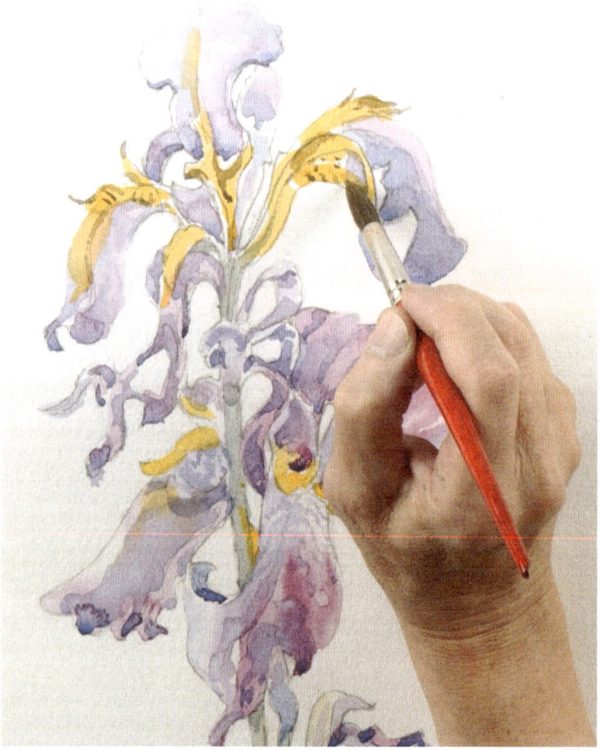

STEP 17

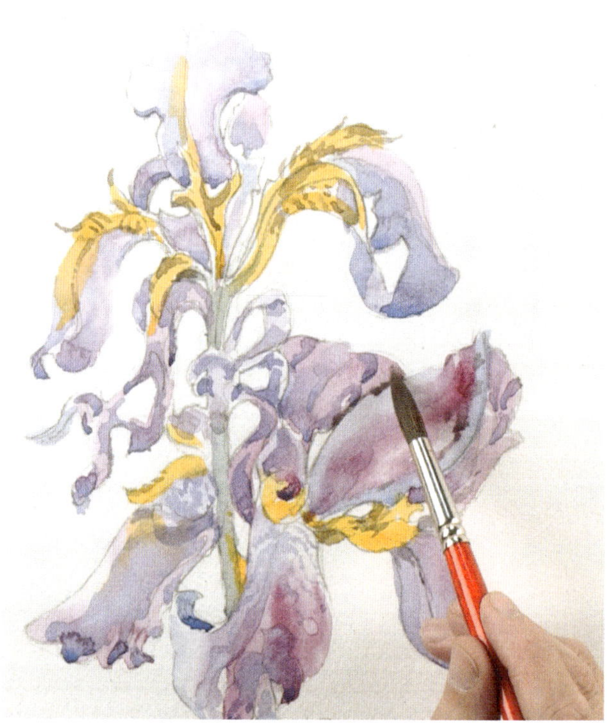

Add a final level of detail to the petal near the middle of the flower. The bottom of this petal is in shadow, so apply the same yellow mix sparingly just along its edge. This detail adds a little extra depth to the densest part of the flower.

TRICK OF THE TRADE

If your finished study looks too stark on the white paper, try dampening the background area and dropping in a few spots of a complementary colour. This will highlight your subject while removing the glaring whiteness of the paper. Practice this on a piece of scrap paper – you will soon learn which colours work together.

STEP 18

Make a light mix of pure cobalt blue and add this to the top of the right-hand petal. As before, this is another level of detail as well as a strengthening line – the violet colour is faint here and needs a little extra definition.

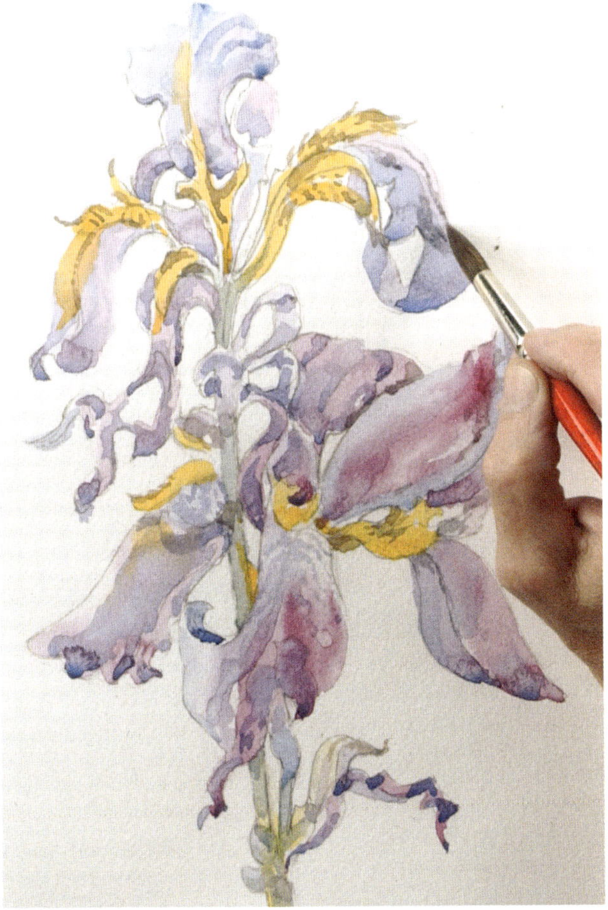

STEP 19

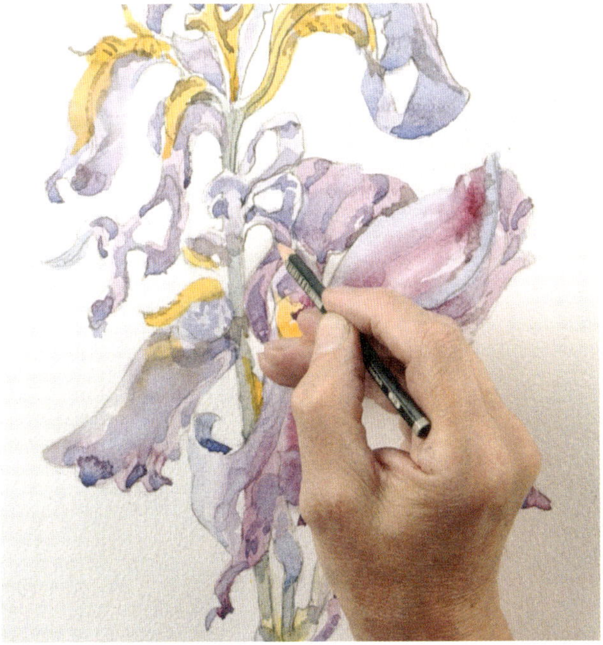

Let all the paint dry thoroughly. Then, using the 2B pencil, sketch around the most noteworthy outlines of the petals. Follow the edges accurately – the pencil lines are there to give the petals a hint of definition.

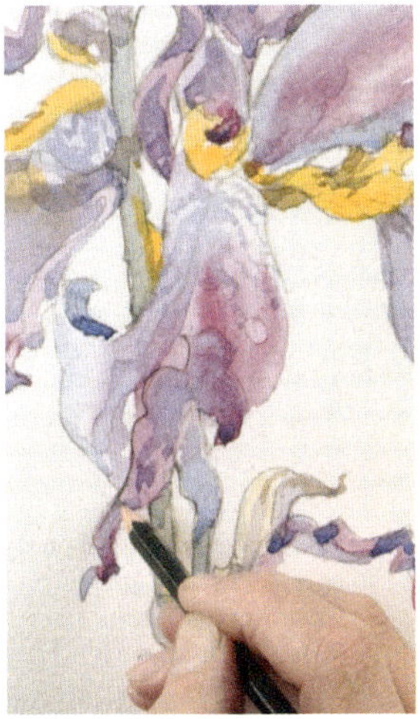

RIGHT You don't have to fill in every edge, especially where there is either strong colour, or conversely, a delicate edge. Also try including small areas of untouched white paper within the pencil lines to create an instant white highlight on the edge of a petal. Soften any heavy pencil lines with adhesive tack.

STEP 20

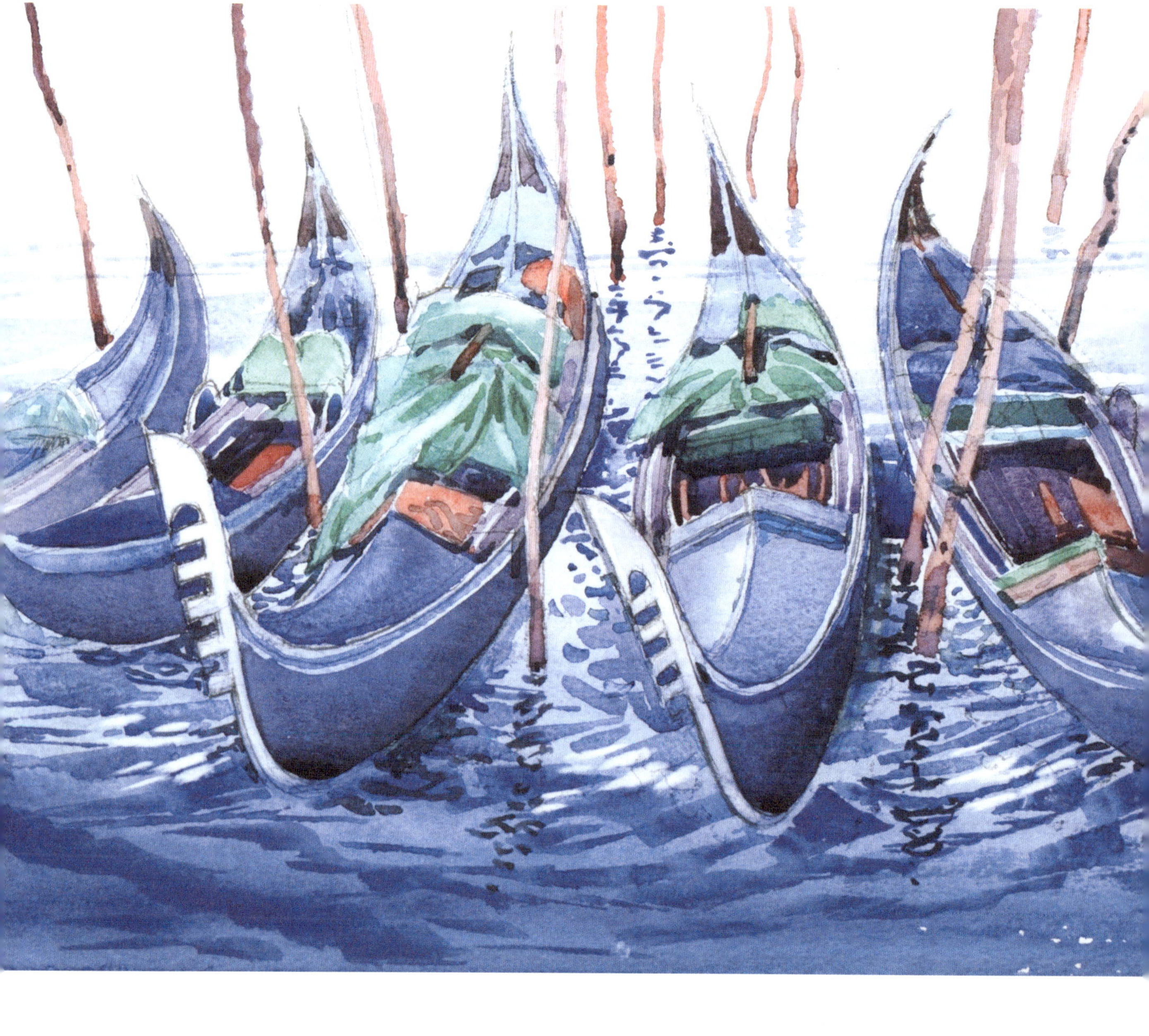

5
impressions of venice

john barber

290 x 400mm (11½ x 16in)

Watercolour painting essentially consists of building up a picture through laying a series of washes of paint diluted in various strengths with water. In this project, you will see how to paint two basic types of wash – the flat wash and the graduated wash. Flat washes are often used for backgrounds and artists often start with these to get some colour on the paper. These may then be overlaid with detail, as is the case here with the gondolas. Graduated washes, in which the wash gradually differs in strength across the paper, are useful for water and to suggest recession and distance. They are used in this project to show the reflection of the sky in the water and the movement in the water itself.

TECHNIQUES FOR THE PROJECT

Laying a flat wash

Laying a graduated wash

Working wet-on-dry

WHAT YOU WILL NEED

Rough surface watercolour paper
Soft graphite pencil, 6B, and adhesive tack
Round brush, no. 5 or 6, sable or synthetic
Flat brushes, 1.3cm (½in) and 2.5cm (1in), sable or synthetic

COLOUR MIXES

2 Prussian blue
3 Cobalt blue
4 Violet
5 Permanent rose
6 Cadmium red
8 Cadmium yellow
9 Cadmium lemon
11 Burnt sienna
12 Hooker's green

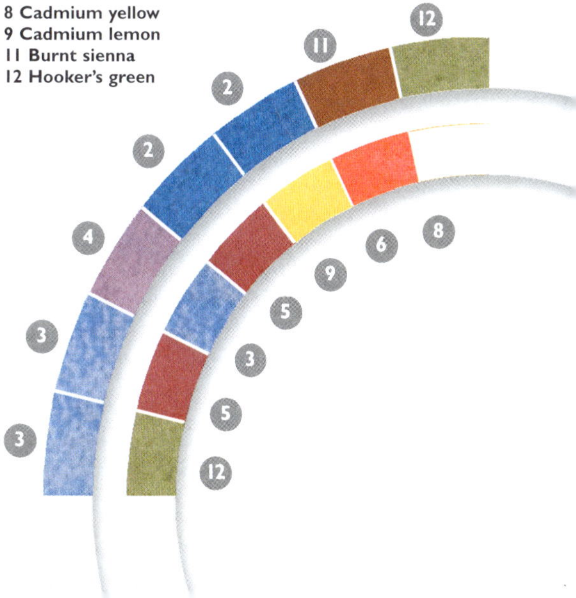

GRADUATED WASHES

The art of laying graduated washes is one of the most important skills you need to learn if you are to have a command over your painting. The aim is to make a smooth transition from dark to light, but the variations that occur in the actual flow of the paint are what makes the process so exciting and attractive. Eventually, you will develop your own ways of using the graduations to your advantage. In practice, you will need to learn the strength of your starting colour and the quantity of paint you need to cover a given area. You can lay a graduated wash onto white paper and this will give you clear colour. When you work over it, many different effects can be obtained. Even for experienced artists, the effects of laying one colour over another are constantly surprising and are one of the great joys of watercolour painting. Depending on the type of paper you are using, the first wash will either not be moved by working over it, or will begin to dissolve as you apply more paint. Try different papers and check their capacity to absorb and retain paint. Being aware of how your materials react is an essential aspect of painting. As in cookery, the right ingredients in the right quantities, added at the right time, bring good results.

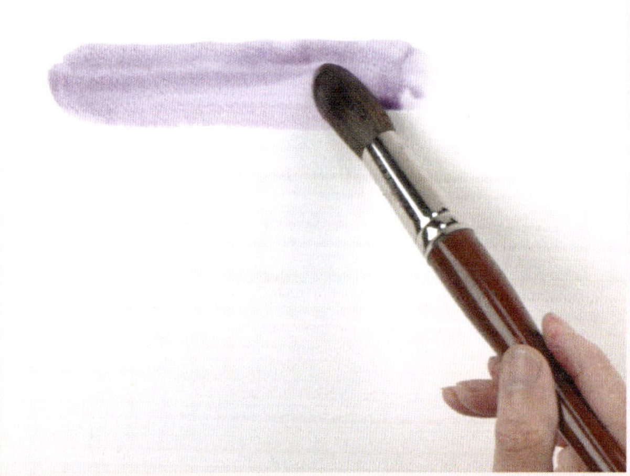

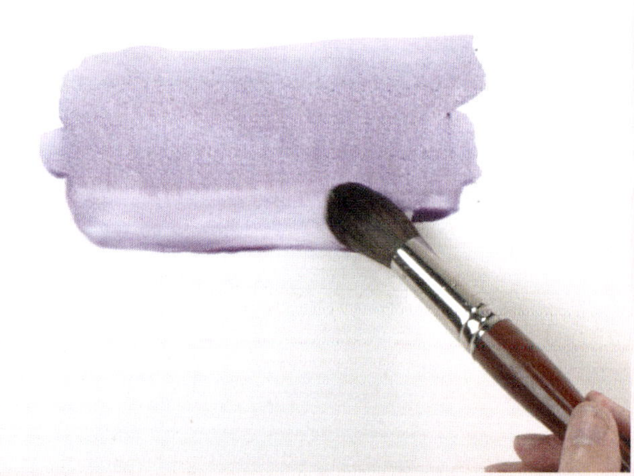

1 For graduated washes, mix a stronger colour than for most flat washes. Load your mop brush with colour and pull it across the paper from one side to the other, always working in the same direction – do not go backward and forward.

2 Now tilt your work slightly and begin to graduate your wash by dipping your brush in clean water and then into the paint mix you started with. Apply this to the bottom of the first horizontal band of colour before it is dry.

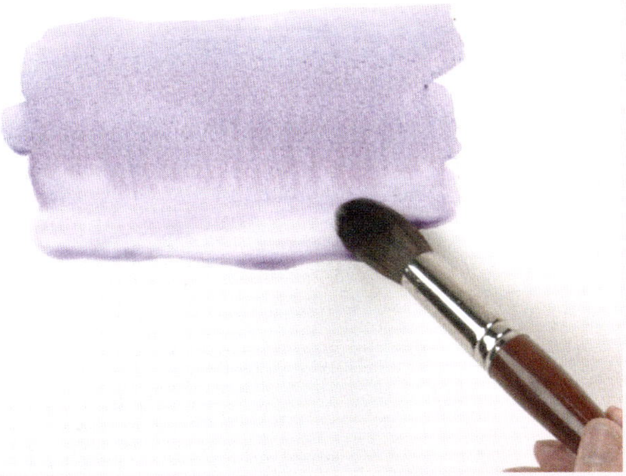

3 Repeat the process of dipping your brush in clean water each time before dipping it into the paint. By doing this, you gradually weaken the colour in your palette and the wash becomes lighter. Keep your wash wet and flowing at this stage.

4 As you add more water to your palette, the lightening effect will become clearer. Load your brush generously and work across the paper. Keep the paint flowing so that the drip along the bottom looks as if it will run down the paper.

5 As you cover the paper, you will notice the strong paint at the top of your wash starting to run down and blend with the lighter tones lower down. Do not worry if the graduation is not smooth – these washes take time and practice to achieve.

6 As you reach the bottom of your wash, stop dipping your brush in the paint – just put it in water and draw it across the paper. With each stroke, the colour will become fainter. When you are painting with clear water your wash is complete.

This is a fairly simple composition which owes its refinement to the lines of the gondolas rocking on the choppy waves. Sketch in the major lines using the graphite pencil, planning out the key elements of the composition and their relationship to each other. Soften any lines you are unhappy with using some adhesive tack. This is less harsh on the surface of the paper than using an rubber and does not remove the lines altogether, just knocks them back.

REMEMBER

You are in charge of your painting so do not be afraid to be bold. To help you with your confidence, plan where your washes are going to go before you apply them. Following through the stages in this project will also build your confidence but painting is also about trying things out for yourself, so move on to developing your own ideas.

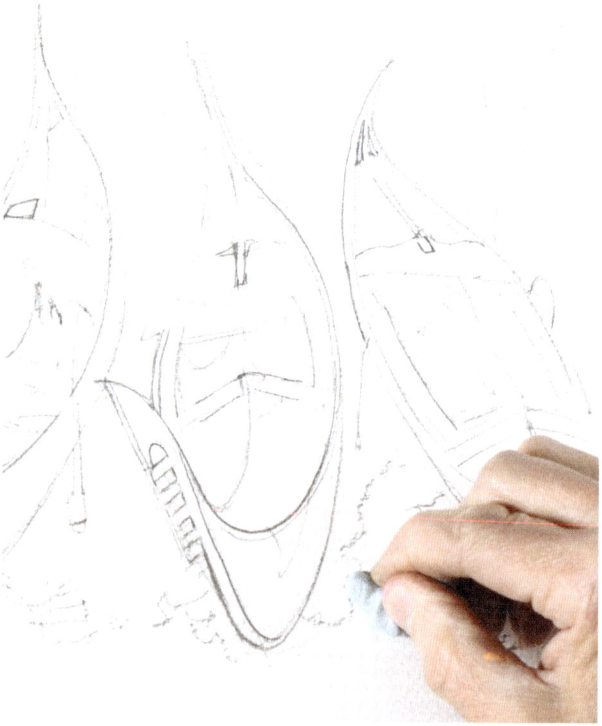

STEP 1

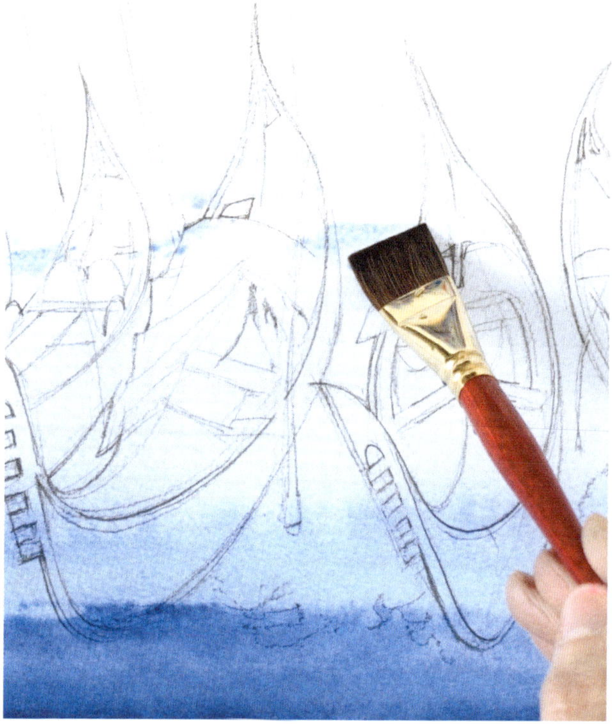

Turn your sketch upside down. Using the wide flat brush, apply a medium mix of Prussian blue in horizontal bands across the paper, adding more water for each band. Then turn the paper the right way up so the darkest colour is now at the bottom.

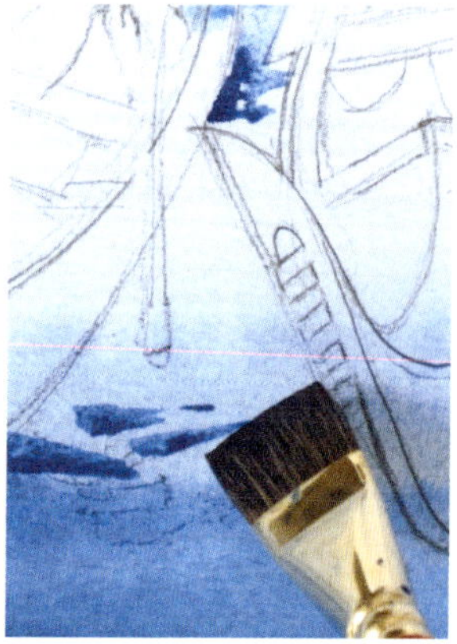

RIGHT Add dashes of stronger Prussian blue to suggest choppy waves in the foreground. Keep your strokes fluid to get a good sense of movement into the water.

STEP 2

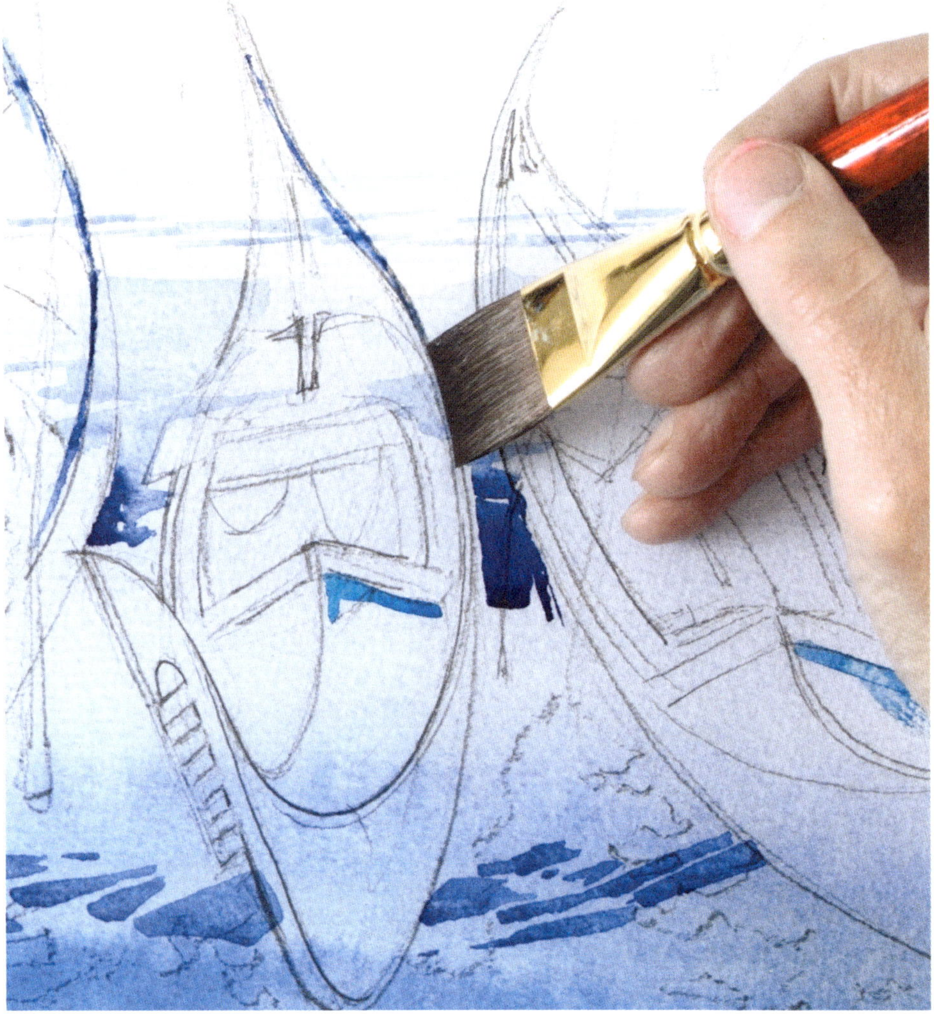

BE CONFIDENT

It is tempting to overwork watercolours but this results in muddy and obscured tones. The more you paint, the more you will appreciate how watercolours dry and how much paint to apply. Eventually you will become confident that your colours will dry as you want them to, although they may not look right while the paint is wet.

Define the edges of the gondolas with the same strong mix of Prussian blue. Instead of pulling the brush along the pencil line in one continuous stroke, place the edge of the brush on the line, one stroke at a time, to form a series of overlapping strokes. Work around the edges of all the gondolas in the same way.

STEP 3

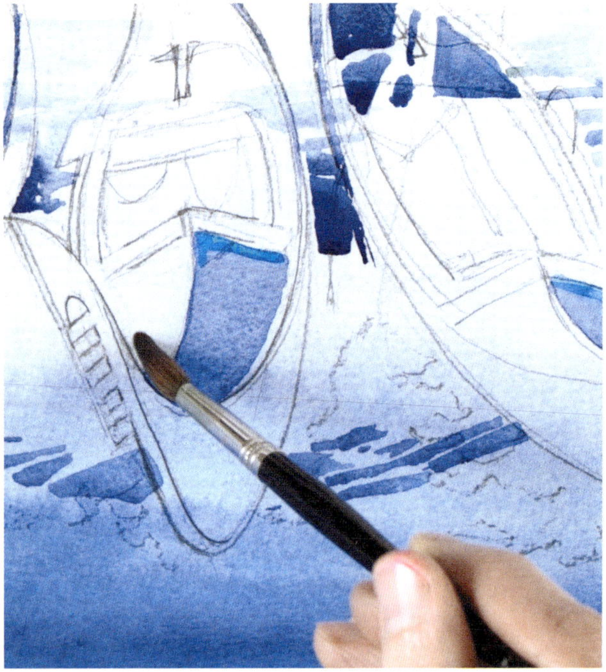

It is helpful to build up areas of the same colour wherever they occur in the painting. The darker areas of the prow of the gondola match the colour of the choppy waves in the lagoon, so use the same Prussian blue mix here, applied with the round brush.

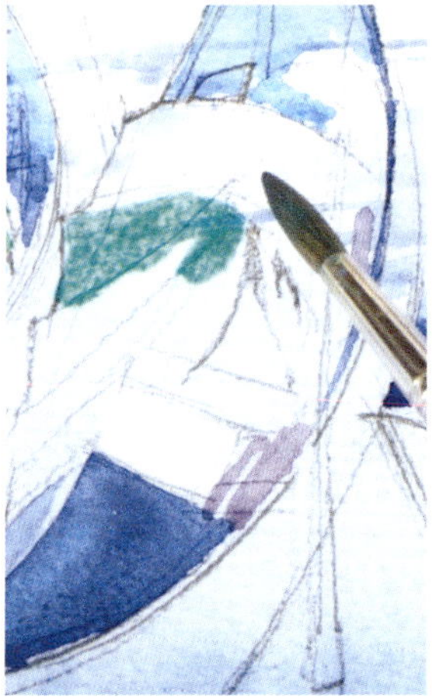

RIGHT When you have a good balance of different strength blues on your paper, move on to mixing colours for the green areas of the gondolas. The pale green here is a mix of Hooker's green and cadmium lemon.

STEP 4

Finish applying this pale green to the gondolas. Keep your work loose at this stage – if you attempt to make your work look too precise, your art will start to look wooden and stilted. Then darken your mix with a little more Hooker's green and add some slight shadow to the edges of the pale green. This gives your work some depth. The usual method of working with watercolours is to have the strongest tones nearest the foreground and the lightest ones farther in the distance.

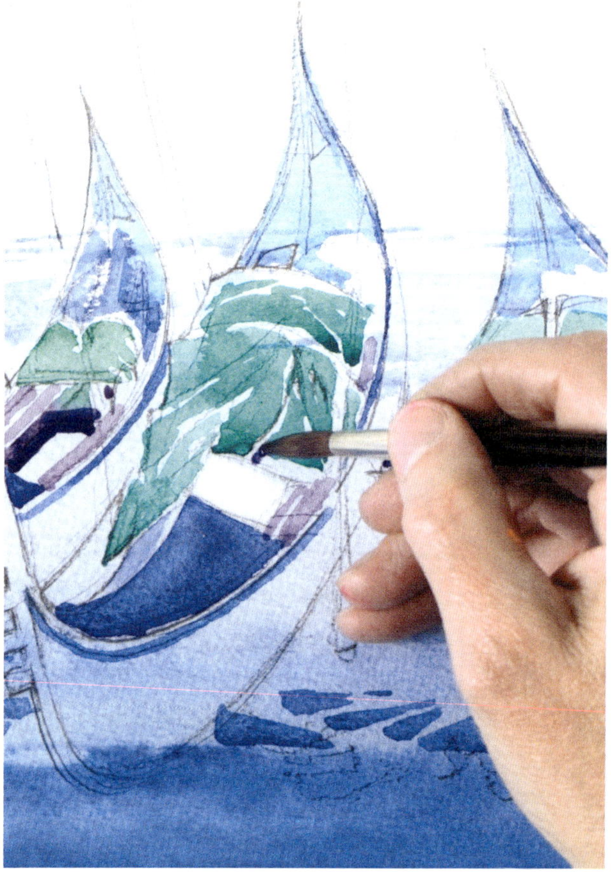

STEP 5

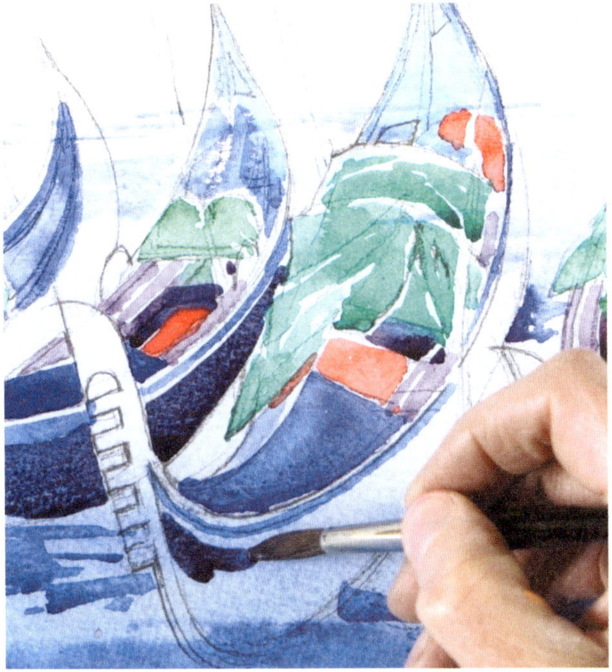

Add some accent colours to the boats with some red tones. First, mix burnt sienna and cadmium red and apply this to the interior detail on the gondolas. Add some Payne's gray and cobalt blue to the mix to create a deep red for the gondola on the left. Then use a strong mix of Prussian blue for the sides of the boats.

RIGHT Apply the Prussian blue down to the water line. Note that the edges of the sides of the gondolas are mostly white to separate the mid-blues from the darker ones.

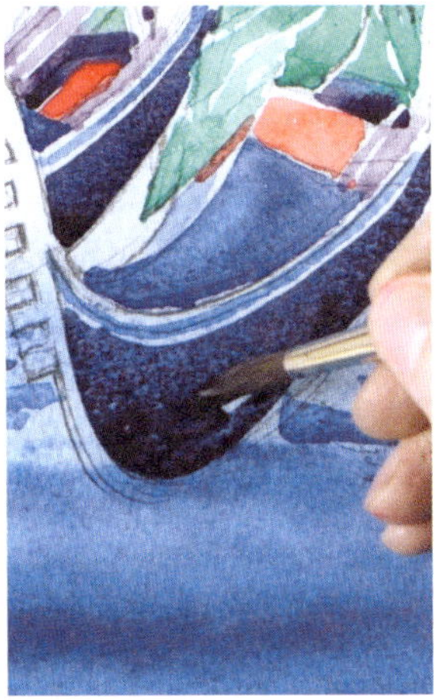

STEP 6

RIGHT Dab on small areas of the strong Prussian blue mix to the fretwork on the prows of the boats. These need to be applied fairly accurately, so don't let the paint run.

Build up the curved profiles of the gondolas using light mixes of cobalt blue. Don't worry if the lines are blurred in some places – this will add to the sense of movement. Use the medium flat brush here.

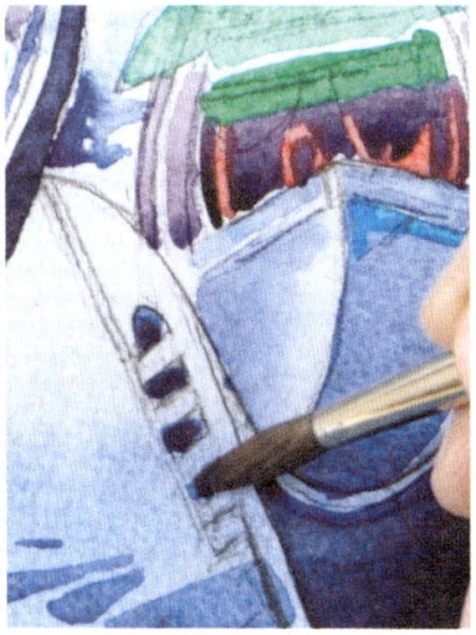

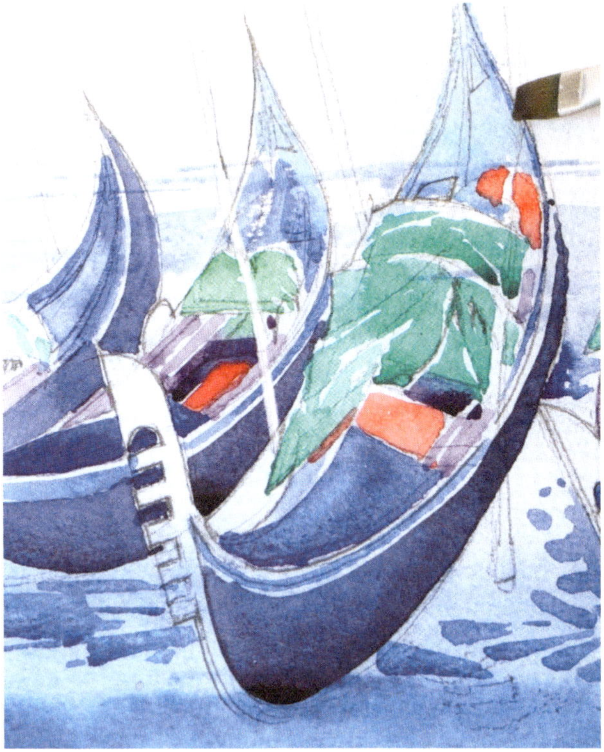

STEP 7

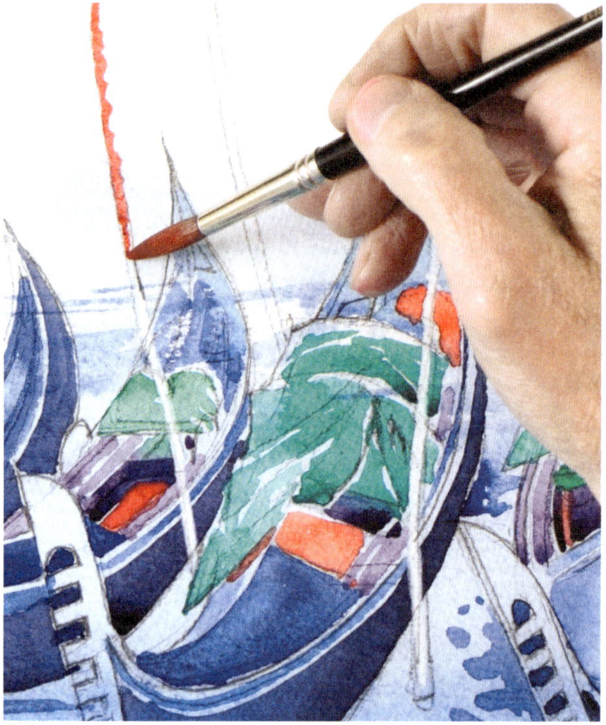

Build up some more colour in the interiors of the boats with touches of violet down the sides. Then start colouring the mooring posts with the mix of burnt sienna and cadmium red. Use the round brush here. Keep the lines fairly thin but don't be too concerned about keeping them straight – slightly crooked lines look more interesting than ones that are perfectly straight.

TRICK OF THE TRADE

Working with washes usually means working fairly fast, but that doesn't mean that there is no time to evaluate whether you are getting the effect you want. If you feel an area needs colour, don't be afraid to add another wash after the first one is dry. Alternatively, you can lift off the whole of the wash and recolour it.

STEP 8

RIGHT Build up some tone on the mooring posts with a little permanent rose. The posts are set at different angles to the water and to each other and these help the rhythm and recession in the composition.

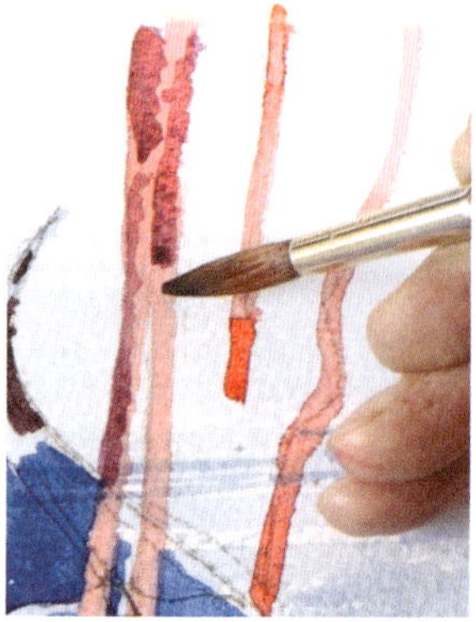

Add a second colour to the posts, such as the red you mixed for the interior of the gondola. Adding small amounts of colours that are tonally different creates depth and texture to your work.

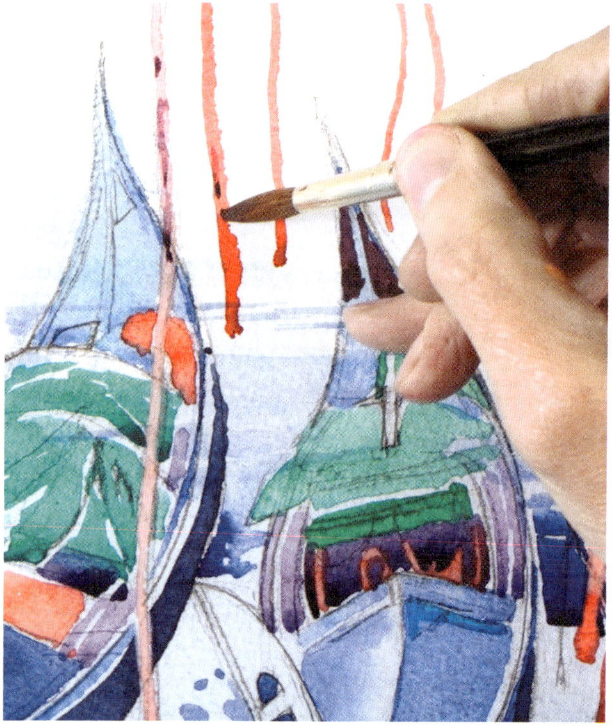

STEP 9

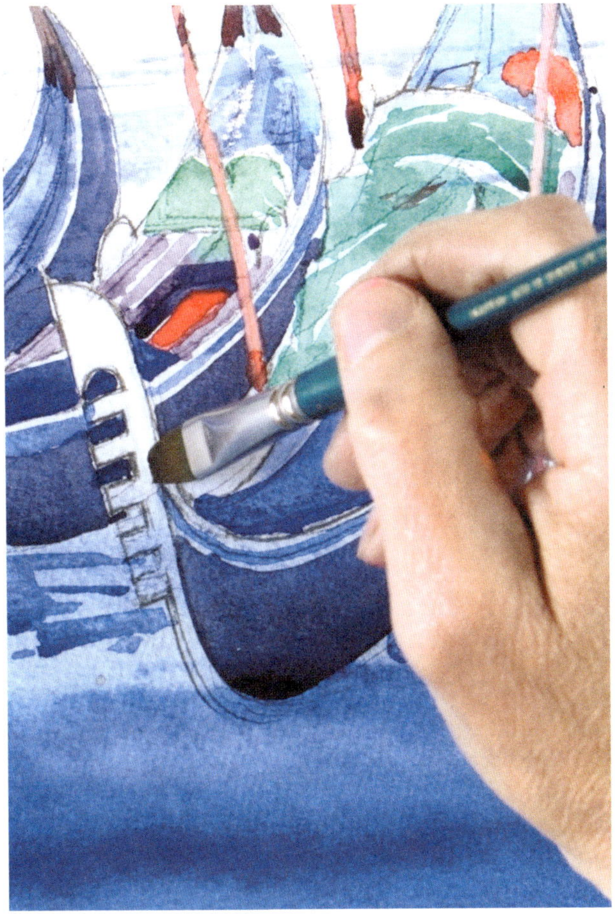

Using a pale cobalt blue wash, add colour to the prow with the medium flat brush. If it was left white, it would be too stark, but the wash you use should be subtle – you are trying to suggest that the prow is white, but is gently reflecting the blue of the water. Continue to add pale Prussian blue and cobalt blue washes to build up the water and the gondolas. The same colours are used for both, so you have to create areas of light and shadow through clever mixing of your colours.

STEP 10

Using the same brush, build up dark green shadows – mixed from Prussian blue and cadmium lemon – to the interiors. Although you have already shaded the green areas, you will have to build up more colour. Keep working around your painting and, as you build up shadow tones in one area, check that areas you have worked on previously still match up. Don't be afraid to go back and work further on earlier parts.

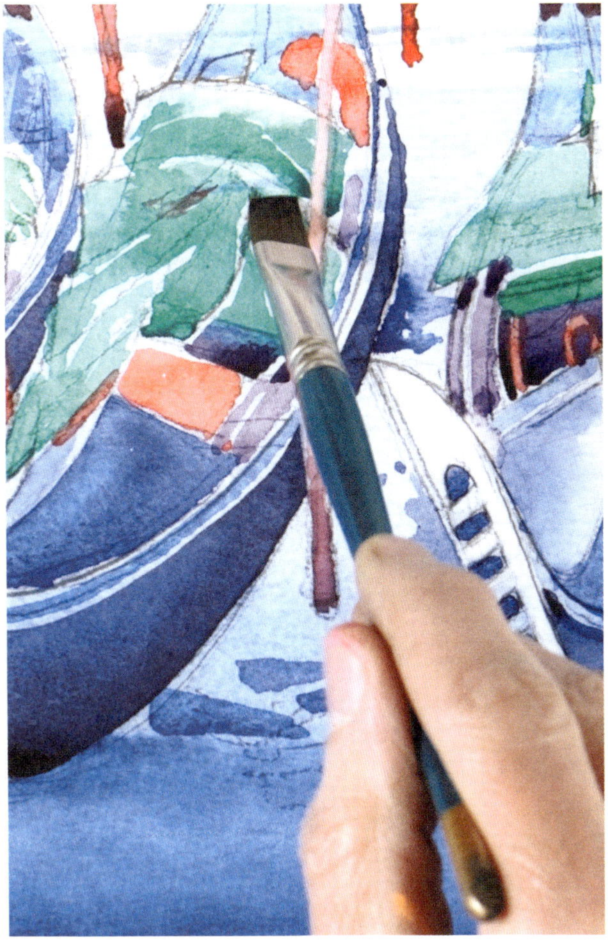

STEP 11

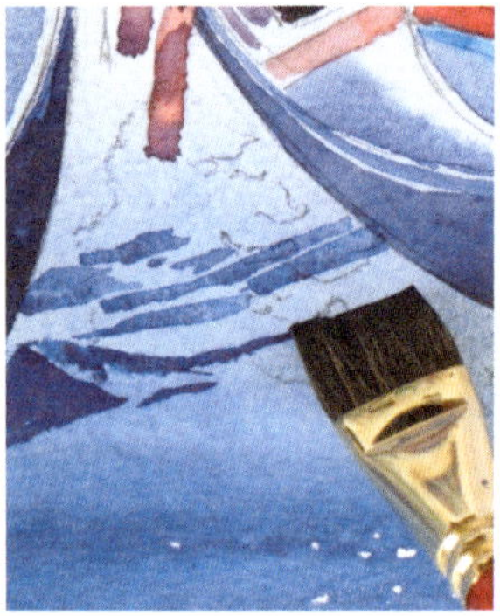

Start adding some fine detail. Using a mix of Prussian blue and permanent rose, start to add more waves with the corner of the wide flat brush. Keep these waves simple – they are really no more than straight lines.

RIGHT Work a light violet and cobalt blue mix onto the water under the edge of the boat. This suggests a little reflected light. These are small areas only so be careful not to overwork your painting at this stage.

TRICK OF THE TRADE

Constantly stop and evaluate how your work is looking as you go along. Remember that it is easier to add colour than it is to take it away. Also, too many shades in too many areas can be confusing on the viewer's eye and produces an overworked result. Simple flat shapes are best.

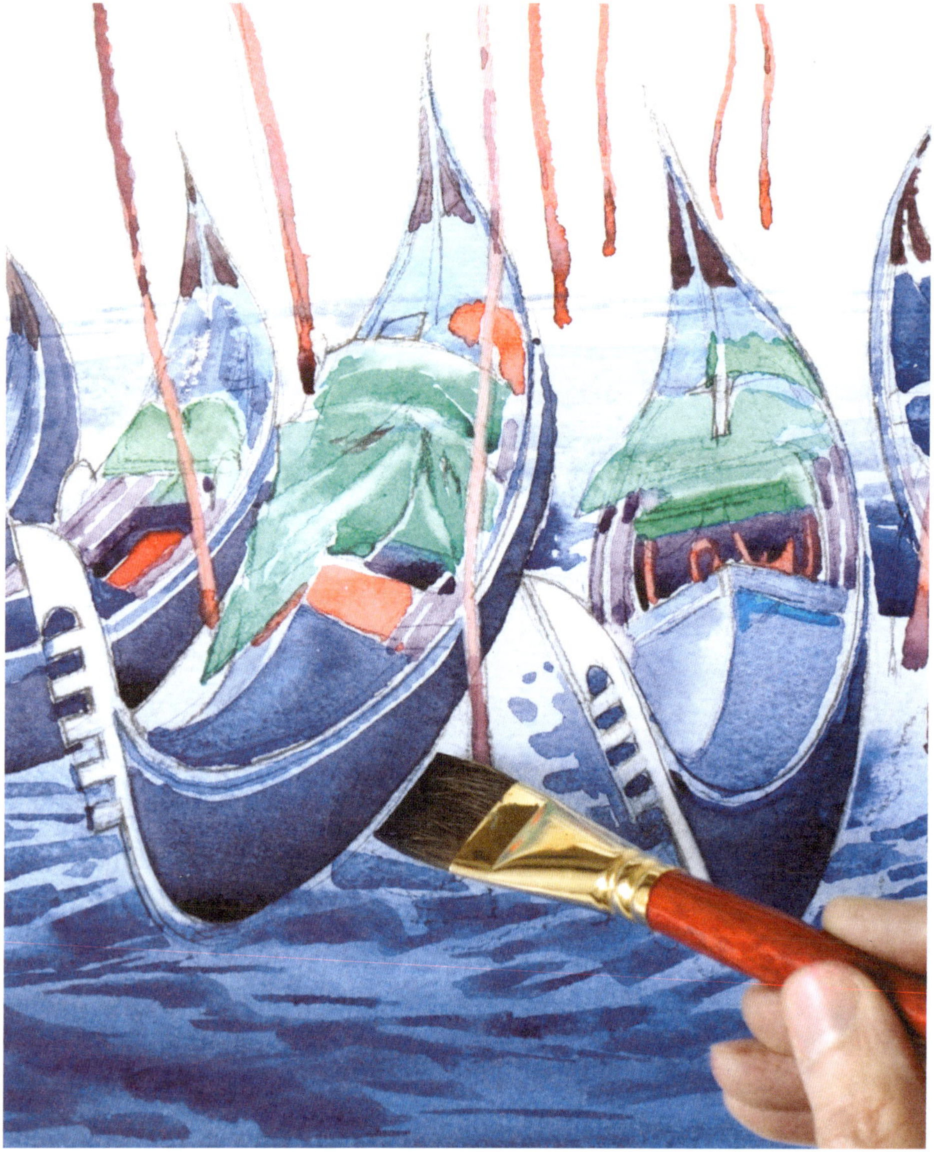

STEP 12

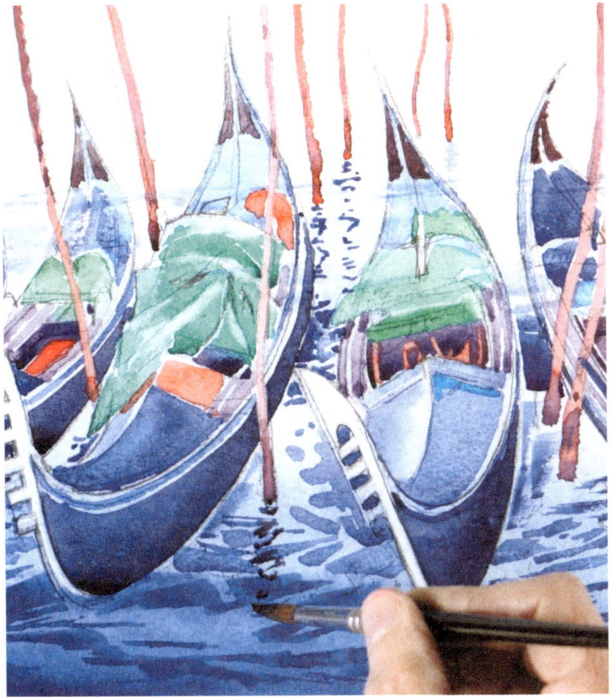

Darken the bottom ends of the mooring posts using a mix of cobalt blue and permanent rose. This colour ties the posts to the blue of the water and follows the principle that the nearer the posts are to the water, the stronger the colour mix needs to be. Conversely, the top ends of the posts are paler. Then, with the same mix, add small irregular dashes to the water to suggest the reflection of the poles. Make each mark freely and do not go back over them. Use the round brush here.

BE CONFIDENT

Consider whether you are getting the sense of light and movement that you want into the water. If you are struggling, look at a photograph of the sea and examine where the areas of light and shade are and try to replicate this. This will help you to judge the precise shades you need and, equally importantly, where to place them for maximum effect.

STEP 13

RIGHT Go back to the mix of permanent rose and cobalt blue and pick out small details on the prows of the gondolas. Keep the brush lightly loaded so as not to flood your work.

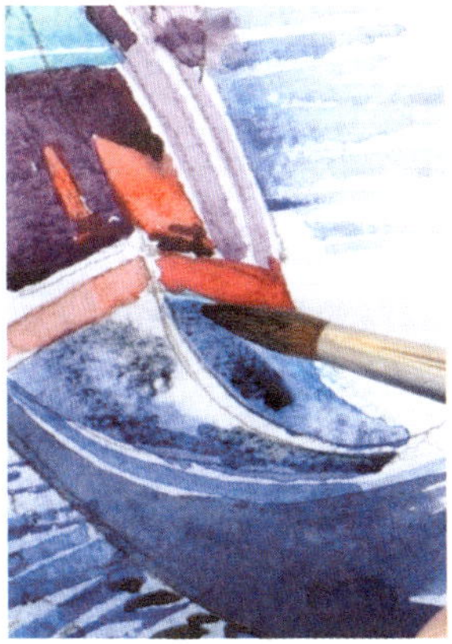

Build up any last areas of shading on the prows. There are now several different shades of blue used here, ranging from dark blue to almost white. Notice how this is achieved using very small amounts of paint.

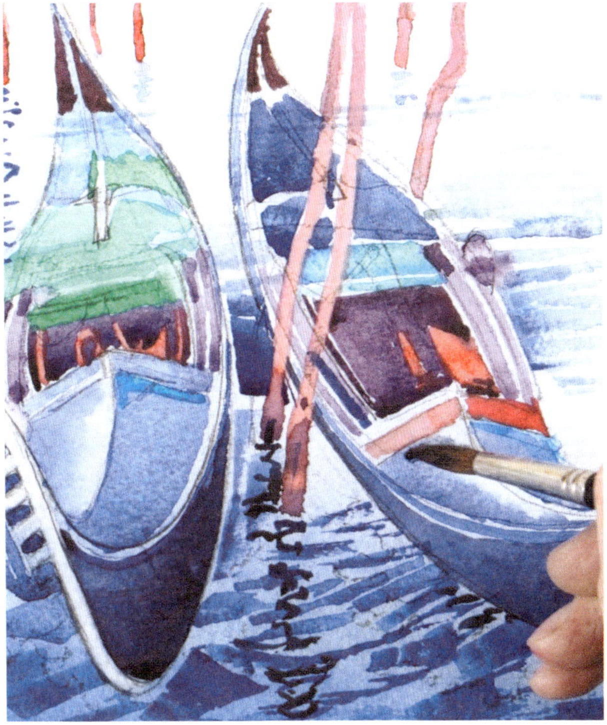

STEP 14

RIGHT Mix cobalt blue and Hooker's green to make a blue-green to pick out more shadows on the interiors of the gondolas.

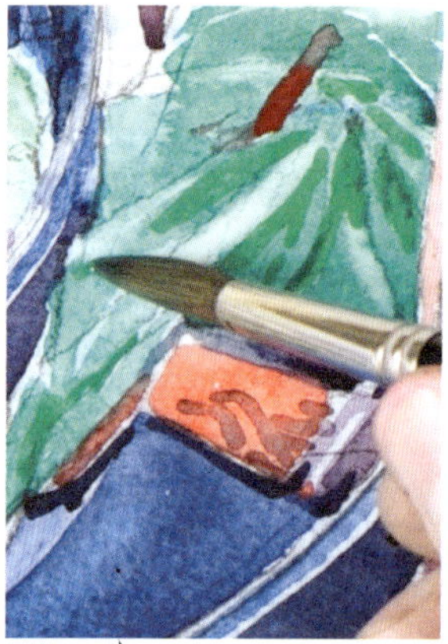

Mix Prussian blue and permanent rose for the high points of the stern. These, along with the underside of the prow in the foreground, are the areas of the composition that are in the greatest shadow.

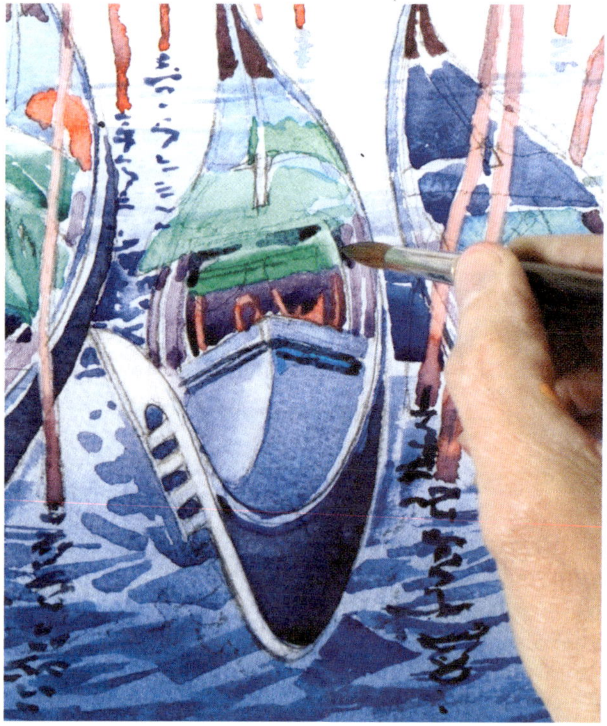

STEP 15

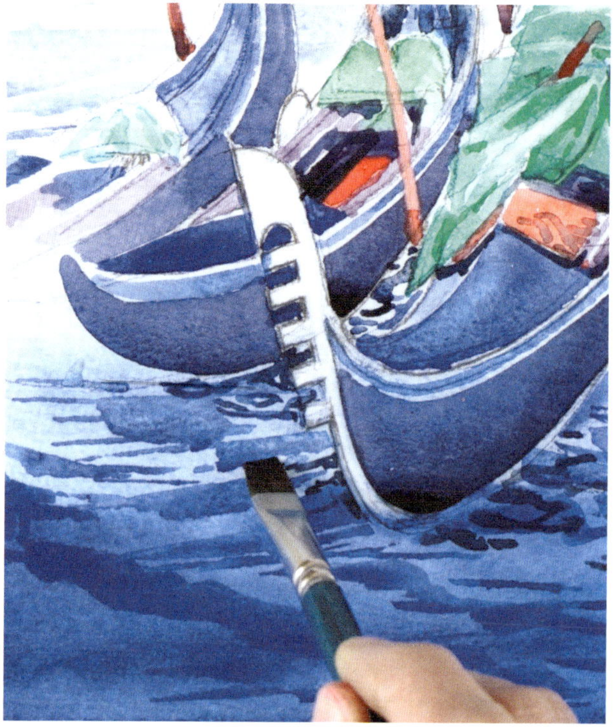

Using the same dark mix of Prussian blue and permanent rose and the medium flat brush, add the finishing touches to the waves in the foreground. These come just under the prows of the boats, where there is least light. Because they are so dark, use them sparingly – you do not want them to attract the viewer's attention too strongly.

TRICK OF THE TRADE

Don't be tempted to be frugal with your pigments. While it is true that good-quality paints can be expensive, there is nothing worse than running out of a colour mix simply because you underestimated how much you would need. It is often the case that you want more of a shade as a painting progresses, so mix plenty of colour.

STEP 16

Now dip your medium flat brush in clean water and apply it to the paper, moving it gently from side to side to lift out some of the colour in between the boats. This creates sparkling highlights. As with applying dark shadow tones, do not overdo the highlight effect – a few light areas here and there will be enough. Also note how the water has been created by using only a few shades and strengths of colour, and yet the overall effect is one of waves and movement. A restricted palette can often be a bonus in watercolour work as you resist the temptation to overmix, which can cause colour to lose its vibrancy.

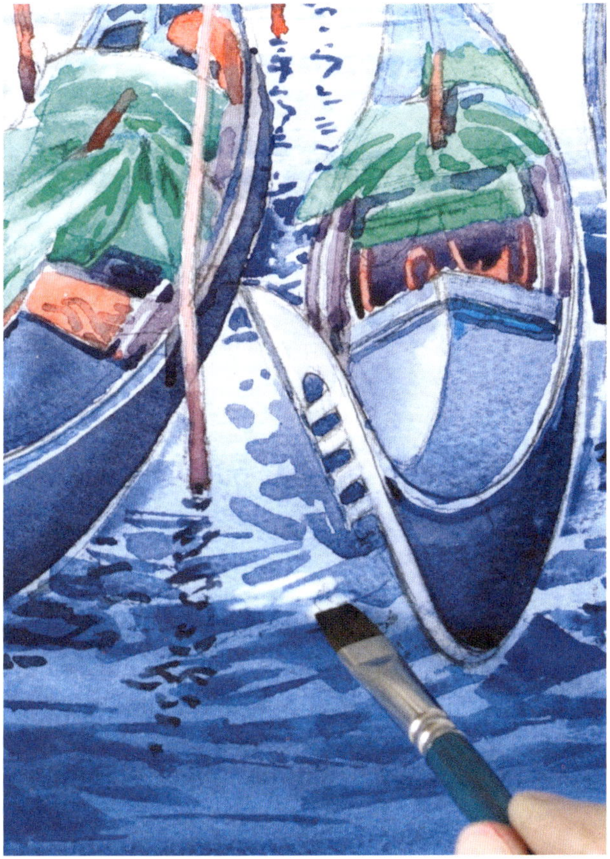

STEP 17

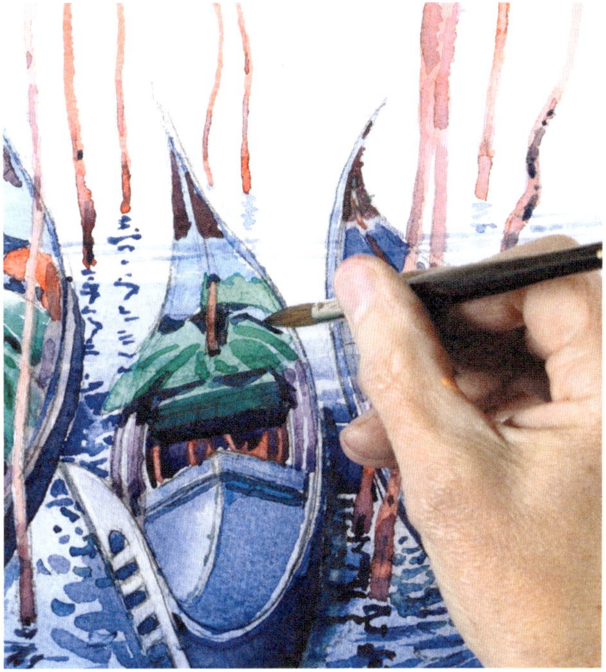

Use the round brush and a mix of Prussian blue and permanent rose to add the last details of the interiors. Don't add the same details to every boat – they should all have some individual characteristics.

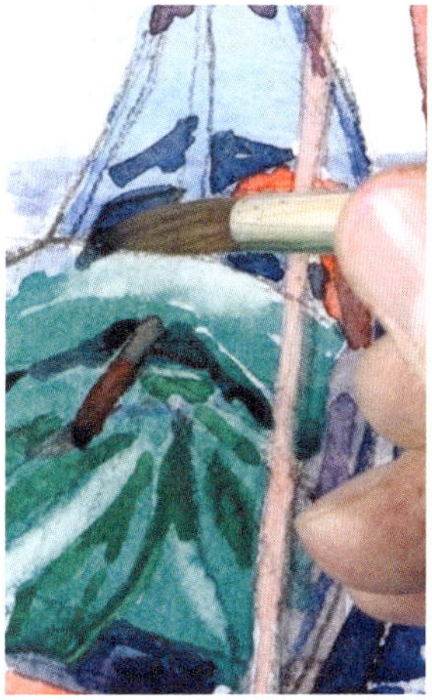

RIGHT Take a final look at your finished work and make any final adjustments, then leave to dry. Do not consider making any changes, however minor, until your work has dried evenly.

STEP 18

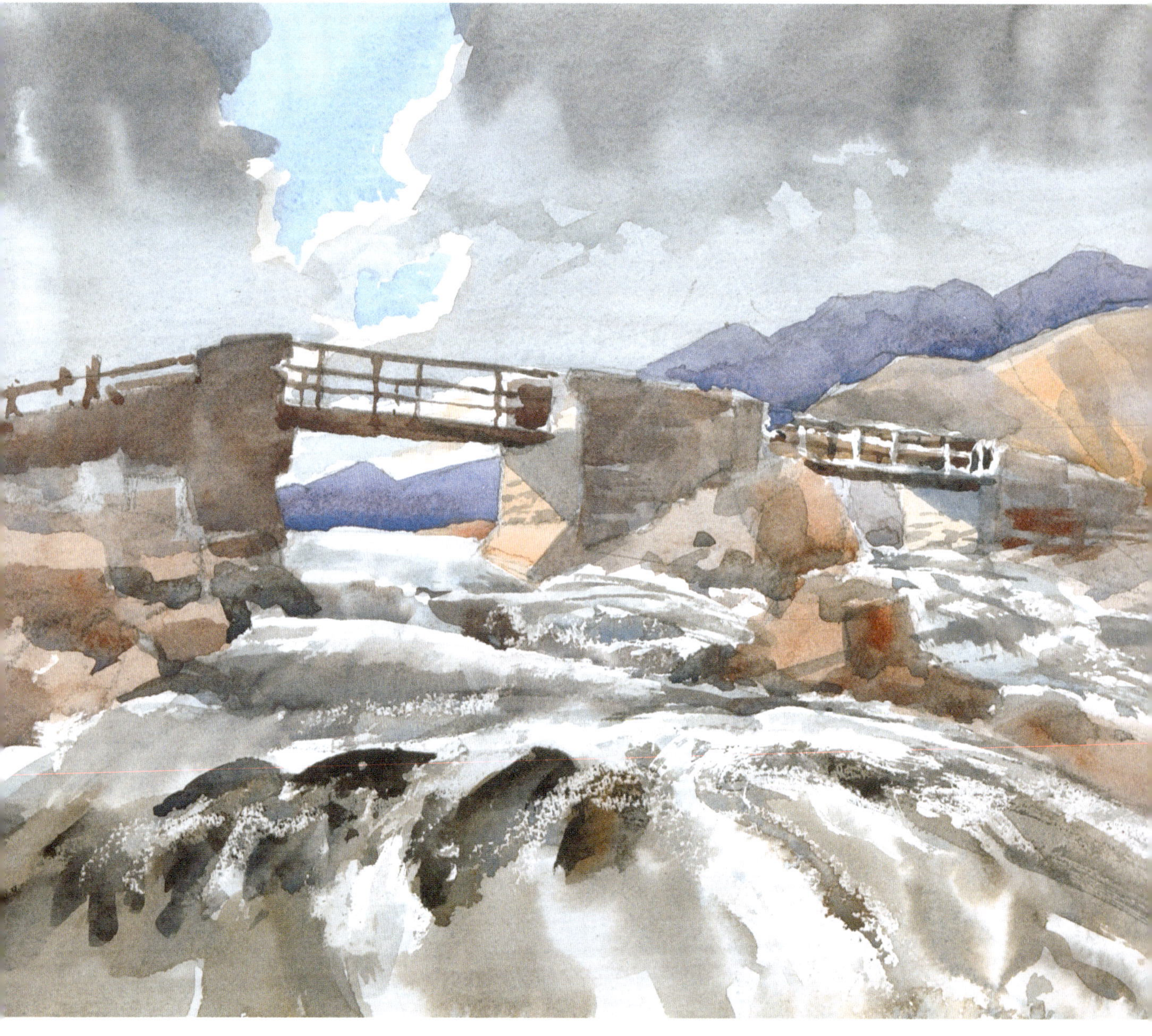

6

bridge at pont-y-garth

john barber

400 x 500mm (16 x 20in)

This project is an great exercise in painting that most fleeting of subjects – moving water. First, you will see how to mask out areas of paper to create the sparkling reflections that makes water so fascinating, as it picks up light from the sky and the colour of the dark tones of the river bed. You will also learn how to create a brooding, dramatic sky. Working wet-in-wet is the best way to get high-quality results for both water and sky, since the paint is allowed to run (in a controlled way) in a variety of directions. However, as you will see, it is best not to overuse this technique, since capturing the impression of what you are looking at is more important than replicating every detail.

TECHNIQUES FOR THE PROJECT

Masking out with masking fluid and wax

Working wet-in-wet

Working wet-on-dry

WHAT YOU WILL NEED

Rough surface watercolour paper
Graphite pencil, 6B
Masking fluid and wax candle
Old, small round brush, synthetic
Flat brush, 2.5cm (1in), sable or synthetic
Round brushes, no. 5 or 6, sable or synthetic
Kitchen paper and rubber

COLOUR MIXES

1 Payne's gray
3 Cobalt blue
4 Violet
10 Yellow ochre
11 Burnt sienna

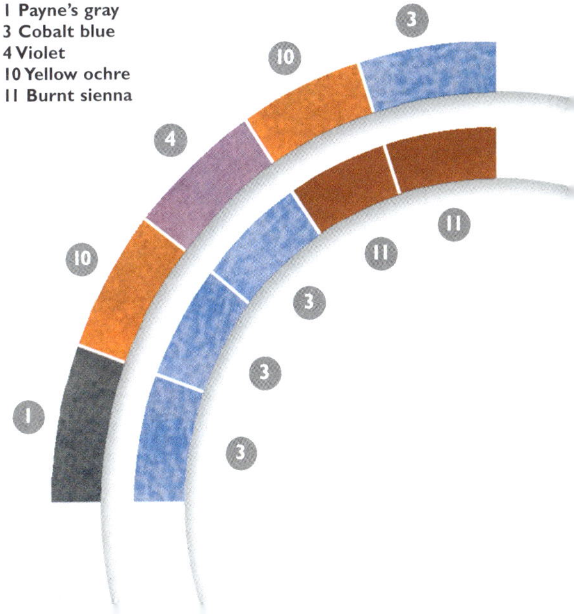

MASKING OUT USING MASKING FLUID

Masking out is based on the idea that oil and water don't mix. This means that you can deliberately create a 'mask' (also called a 'resist') on specific areas of paper to cover it up from the paint you are applying on top of it – the paint is repelled and the paper underneath remains untouched.

Masking out can be done in two ways: Using masking fluid, or by using a wax candle. Masking fluid, featured here, comes in a bottle and is painted on with a brush. Once you allow it to dry, it completely seals off the paper underneath and dries to a rubbery consistency that can be simply rubbed off later using your fingers. Because masking fluid is painted on, it produces a type of watercolour negative – you are creating areas of non-colour, rather than areas of colour. Also, because it is a painted medium you can mask out any area or any shape you like.

Masking out is ideal for creating highlights on your work, allowing you to capture the reflected light coming off leaves in a woodland scene or the sparkle seen on water in bright sunlight. It also has a more pragmatic use – you can use it to protect areas of your work where you do not want paint to run, which can then be worked on later.

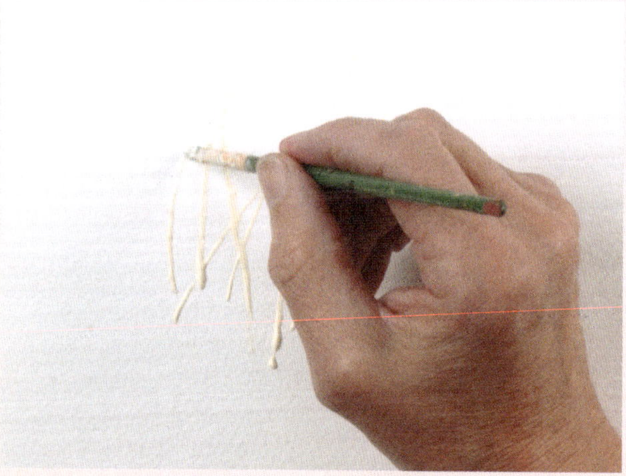

1 Paint on the masking fluid using a brush. Use an old or inexpensive brush to do this – the fluid tends to stick to the bristles and will eventually ruin a good brush. Paint on any shapes you like but try to stick to your original design.

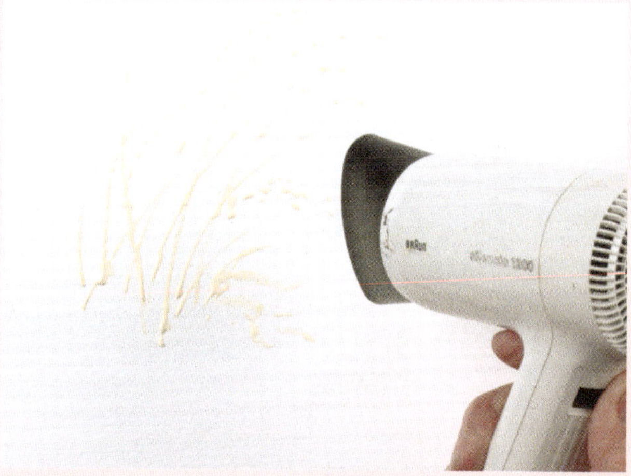

2 To speed up the drying process, use a hairdryer. The fluid will dry to leave a yellow-coloured residue. It does not matter that the residue is thicker in some areas than others as long as it covering the required areas of paper.

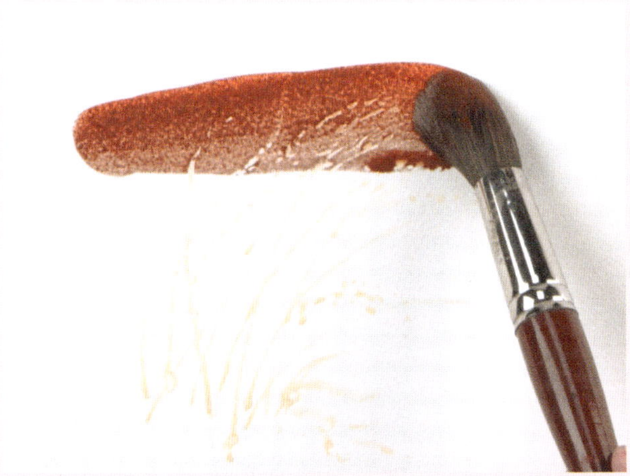

3 Mix some paint, in this case a deep red, and apply it over the masked-out area with a mop brush. You will quickly see that the paint covers the paper, but is repelled by the fluid, no matter how small the quantities of masking fluid are.

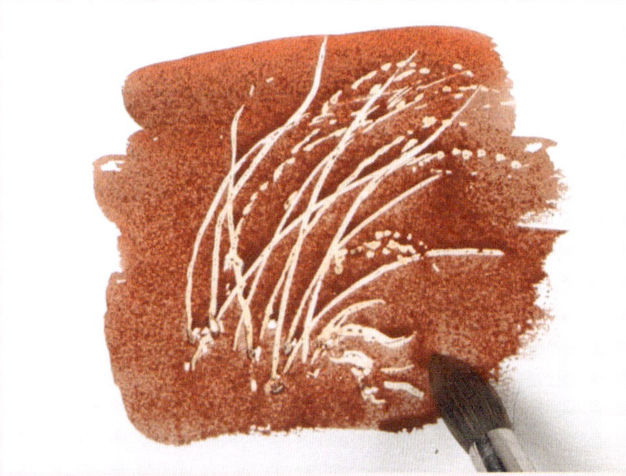

4 Finish applying the colour to reveal the design you painted on with the masking fluid. In this case, the 'negative' is a patch of reeds blowing in the wind. You can see how detailed the effects can become, down to the very small dots.

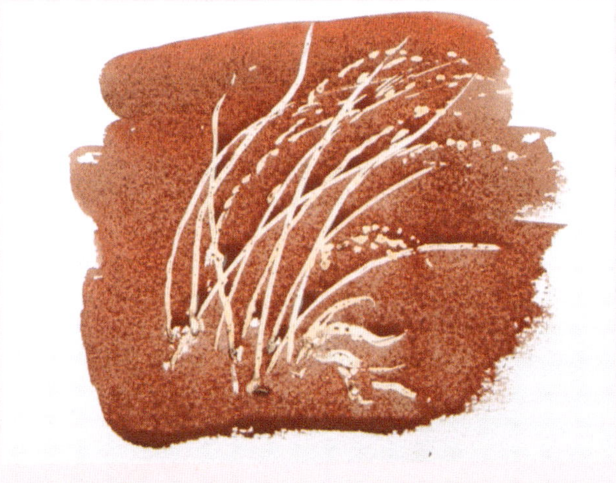

5 Take a step back to check the effect. One added feature of masking fluid is that the paint dries darker in the areas between the fluid because the mask stops the paint running down the paper. This creates a series of little graduated washes.

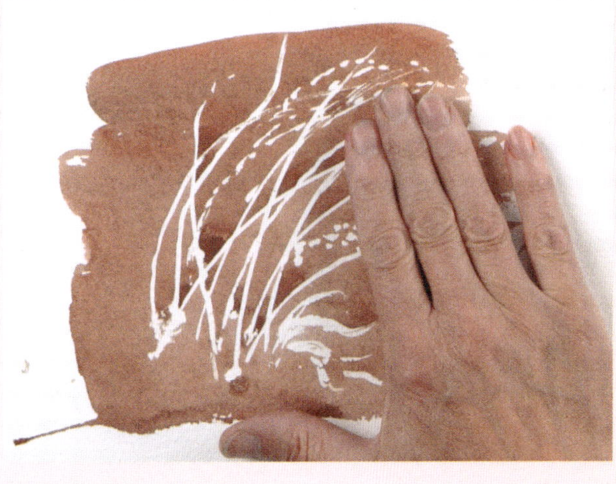

6 Leave the paint to dry thoroughly, including the drips of paint on the fluid. Then with clean hands, rub your fingers over the dry fluid to remove it. You may have to rub quite firmly – eventually the fluid with roll up into a ball.

6
bridge at pont-y-garth

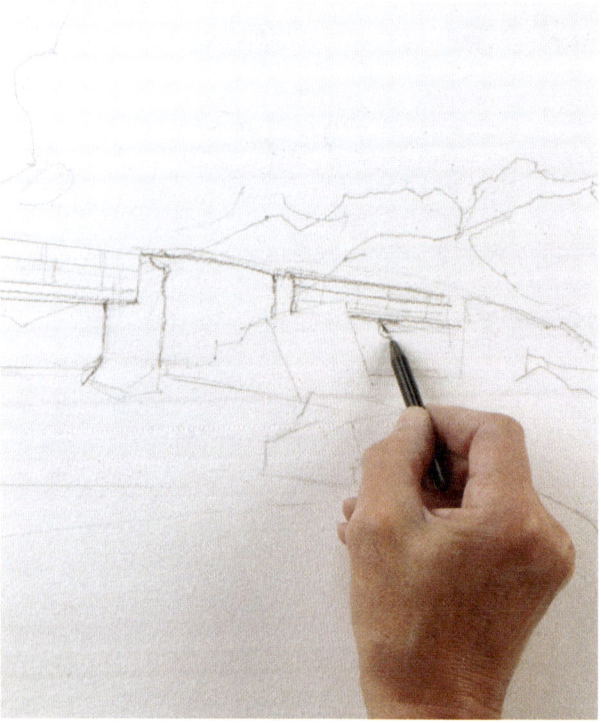

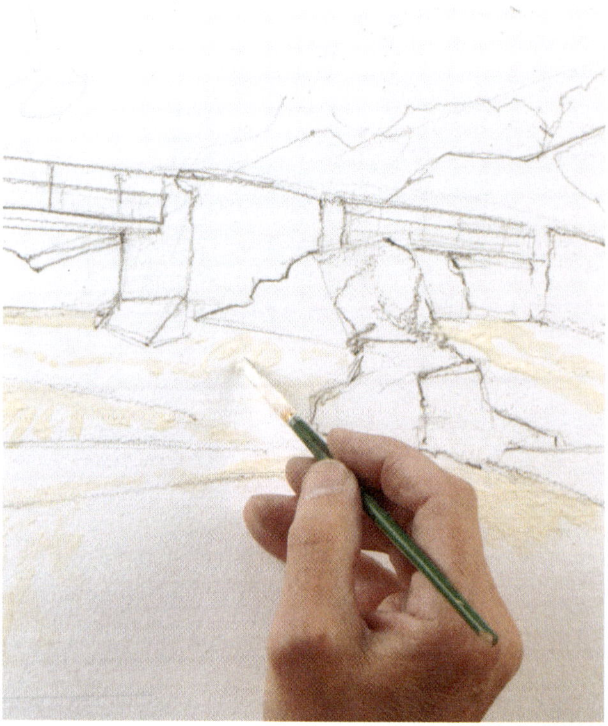

Sketch the details of your composition first, using the graphite pencil. The composition is roughly based on a diagonal cross, with the bridge, which is the focal point, at the center. This makes the eye level low, so the viewer is looking upward, an aspect that creates some drama in the image. Lightly sketch the lines first, then strengthen the most important ones, such as those marking out the bridge.

REMEMBER

Notice how to hold the pencil – grip it up the shaft. Your sketch should be made up of lightly drawn lines that give a clear outline of the scene but it does not have to be completely accurate. Holding the pencil in this way allows you to see exactly what you are doing without your own hand obscuring your view.

Apply the masking fluid to the foreground areas using the old brush. The fluid will create white areas that suggest the reflection of light coming off the water. Don't work too precisely – reflections tend to be random.

RIGHT Also use the wax candle for masking. The wax resists the paint on the 'mounds' of the paper but allows it to flow into the 'pits' in between – a very effective way of creating a sparkle effect on the water.

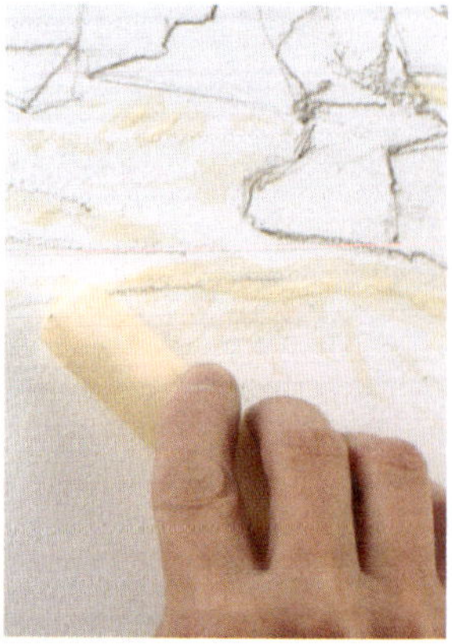

STEP 1

STEP 2

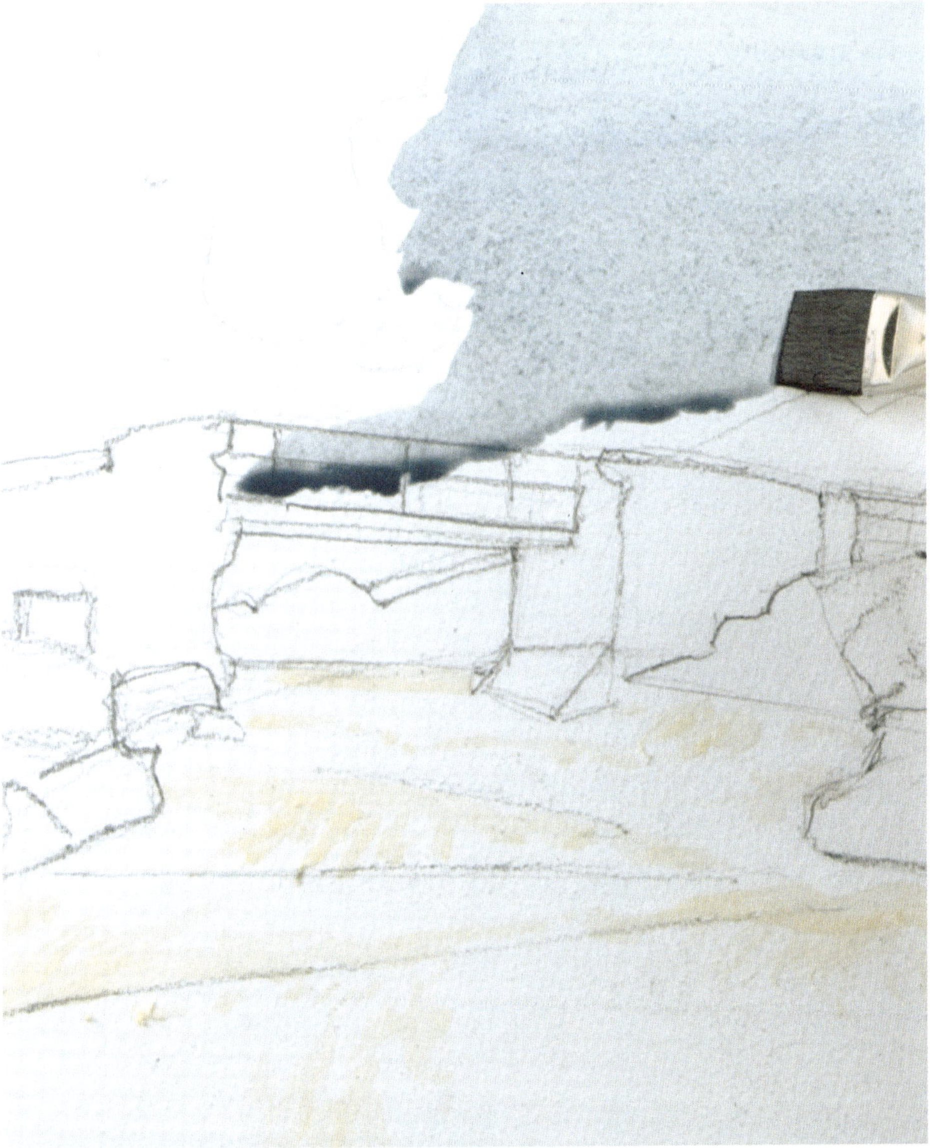

BE CONFIDENT

It can be tempting to be too timid when applying a flat wash – so much colour is applied so quickly to the paper, and some it drips down. To help overcome any anxiety, make sure you know where you are going to apply the paint before you start. This will give you the confidence to paint freely, knowing that you are less likely to make a mistake.

Apply a flat wash to the cloud on the right using the flat brush. The clouds are deliberately designed to look dark and dramatic, so use a mix of cobalt blue, burnt sienna, and Payne's gray. Work from the top down, leaving a white gap between your wash and the pencil lines that mark the edge of the cloud. Take the wash down past the horizon to make sure that all the white areas are covered. Then repeat on the left-hand cloud.

STEP 3

bridge at pont-y-garth

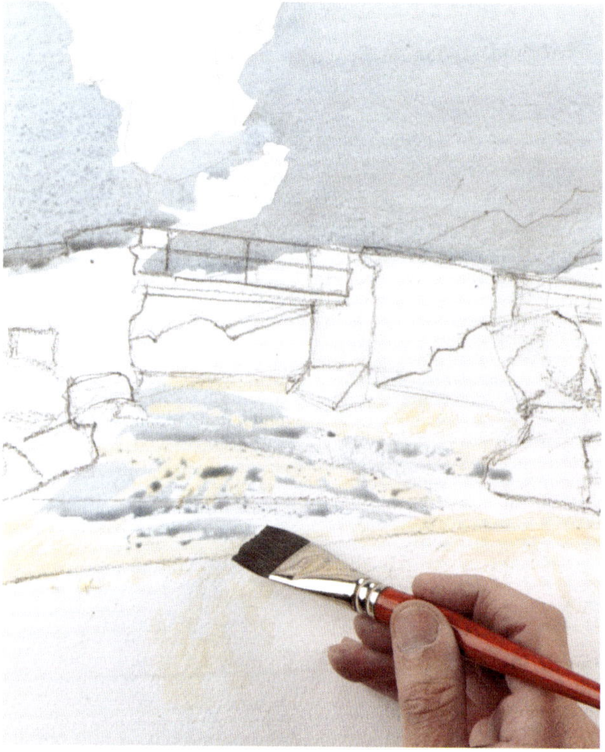

Because the water reflects the sky, apply the colour you used on the clouds to the river, painting over the masked out area. Again, work from the top down. As you reach the bottom, add a little more water to the wash to lighten it.

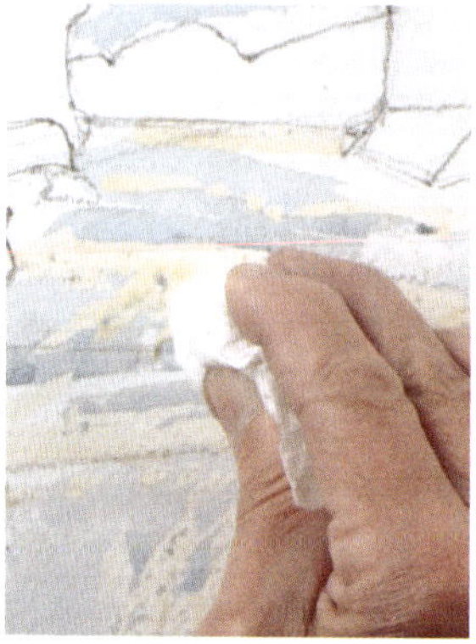

RIGHT Allow the colour to dry thoroughly, then mop off any excess paint from the mask with a little kitchen paper.

STEP 4

RIGHT Start to colour the bridge, using a warmer grey created by adding a little more burnt sienna to the mix you used on the clouds. Don't be afraid to let the paint drip down a little – it will add extra texture to the next colour to be applied.

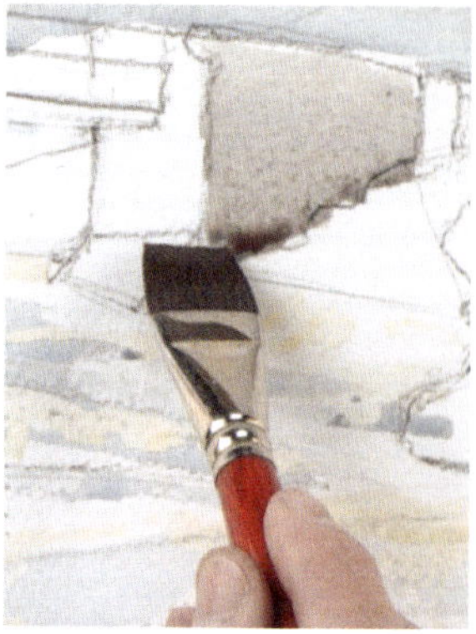

Add more burnt sienna to the mix to colour the rocks. This warmer, redder colour brings the rocks closer to the viewer's eye.

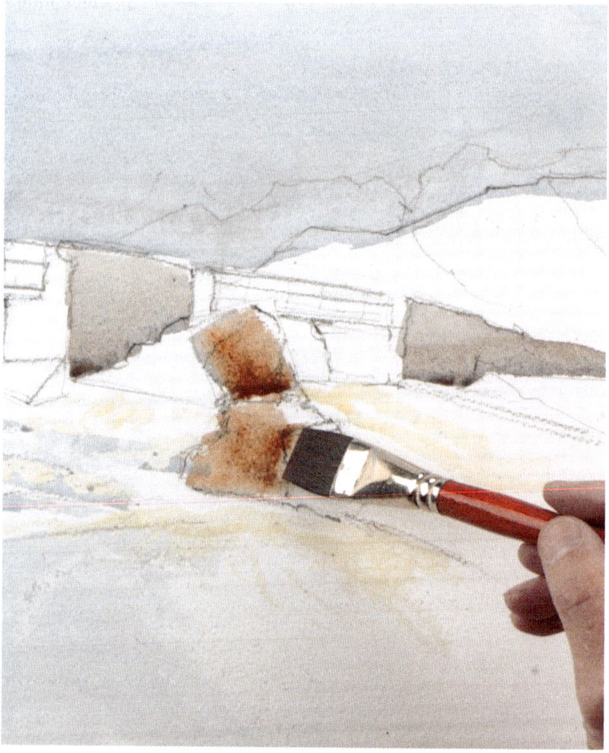

STEP 5

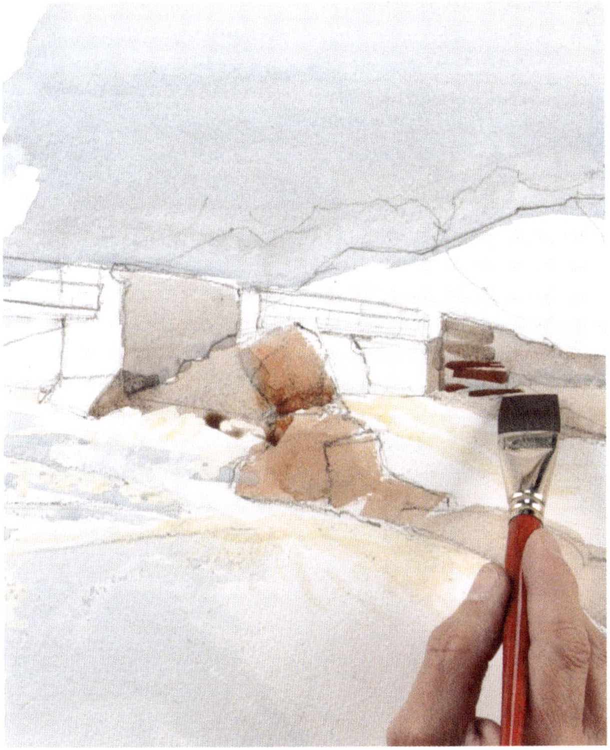

Build up shadow on the rocks by again adding a little more burnt sienna to the mix. Then build up shadow on the stonework on the bridge by adding yet more burnt sienna, with some cobalt blue, to create a really strong colour. Use horizontal strokes to hint at rough stonework.

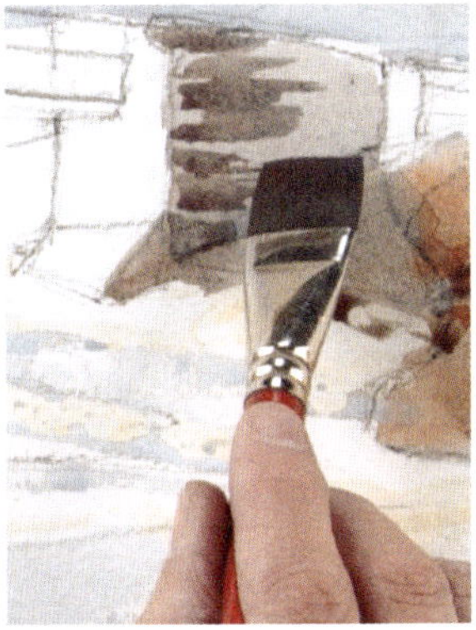

RIGHT Repeat, using the same colour and brush strokes, on the stonework that forms the mid-section of the bridge.

STEP 6

Apply most colour to the stonework on the left-hand side of the bridge. This part of the stonework is most prominent and so carries the most colour. This time, apply solid colour using the full width of the brush, rather than small horizontal strokes.

TRICK OF THE TRADE

All your watercolour work follows the same basic principle – working from light to dark. This means that you should not be afraid to work around different parts of your painting applying light colours first before building up shade and shadow with darker tones. This produces better results than attempting to finish one part of your work first before moving onto the next.

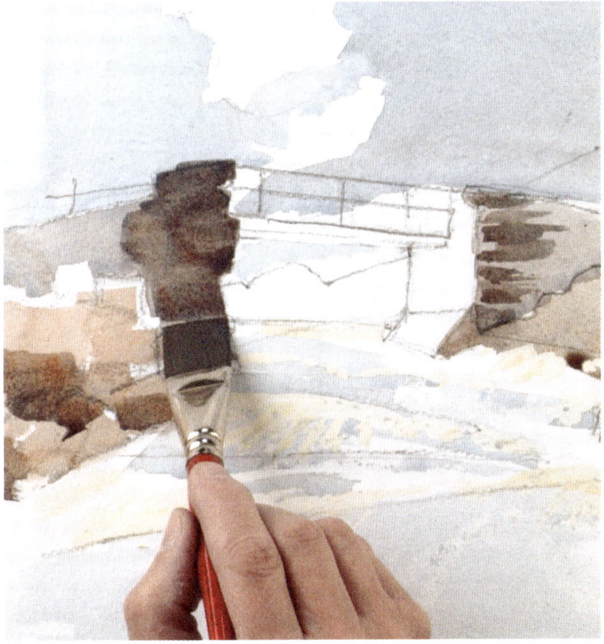

STEP 7

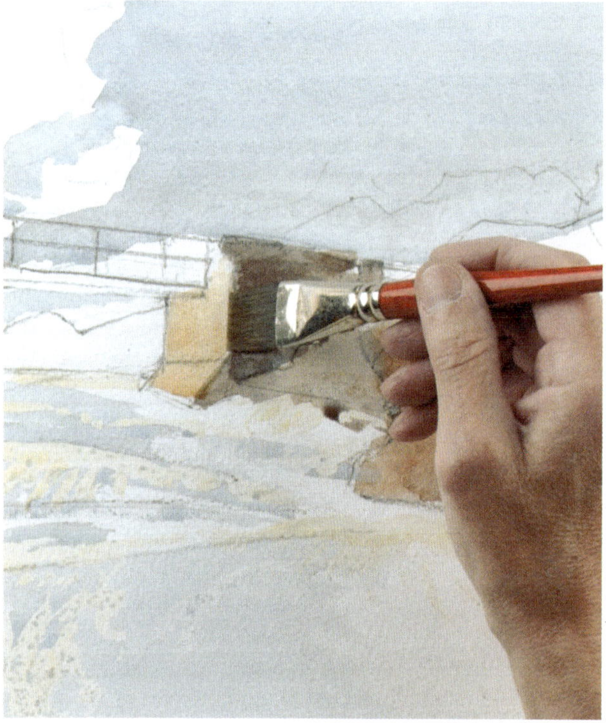

RIGHT Build up further colour on the rocks closest to the viewer with strong red mix, containing more burnt sienna.

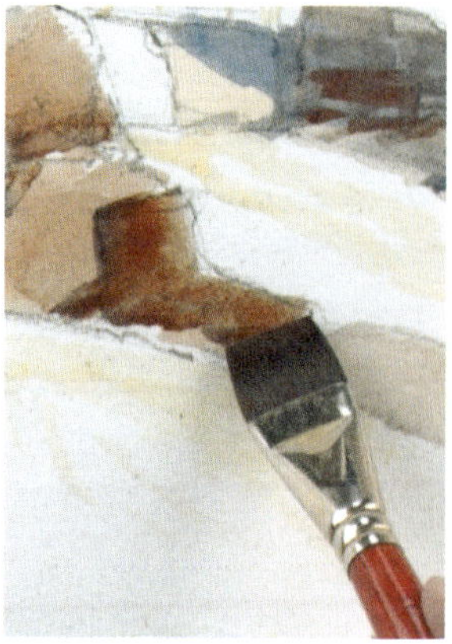

Finish off the shadow on the stonework using the colour mix you used for the cloud. Notice how a little extra shadow detail is created at the foot of the stonework by adding this mix over the colour of the stone.

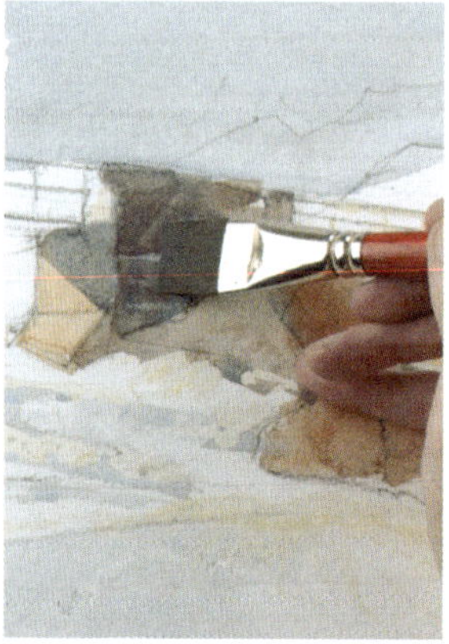

The light source is at the top left, highlighting the stonework under the bridge. Colour this using yellow ochre, burnt sienna, and a little cobalt blue, creating a light, warm colour.

RIGHT Fill in a sharp shadow on the stonework under the bridge, using the mix you used for the clouds and water. This shadow needs to be painted accurately. Also take the wash onto the adjacent dark stonework to further build up colour there.

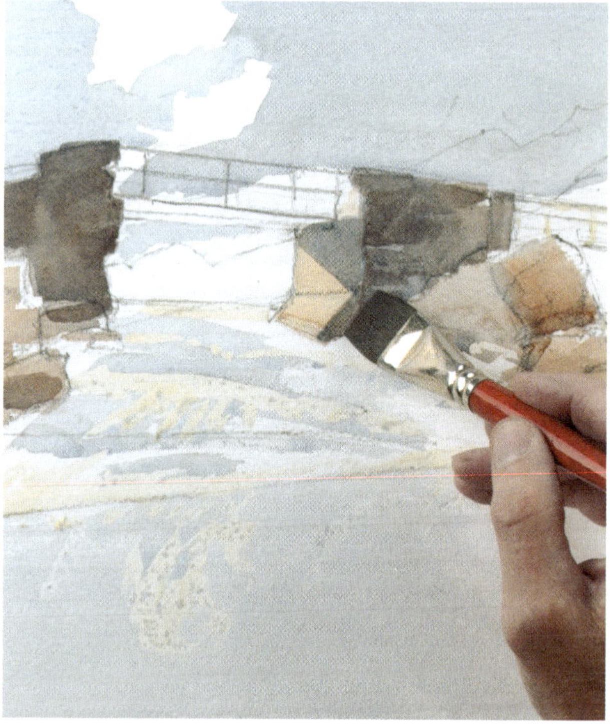

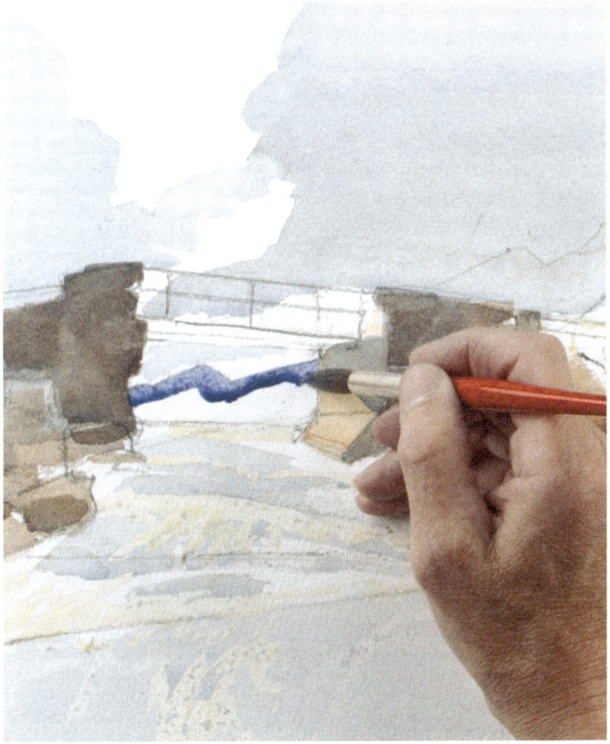

Rub out any visible pencil lines on the clouds, then add in the blue mountains in the distance. Use the round brush here to apply a strong mix of violet and cobalt blue.

RIGHT The colour mix gets darker around the bottom edge. To create this extra colour, dab more paint into the first wash while it is still wet and let it diffuse. This is a variation on the wet-in-wet technique.

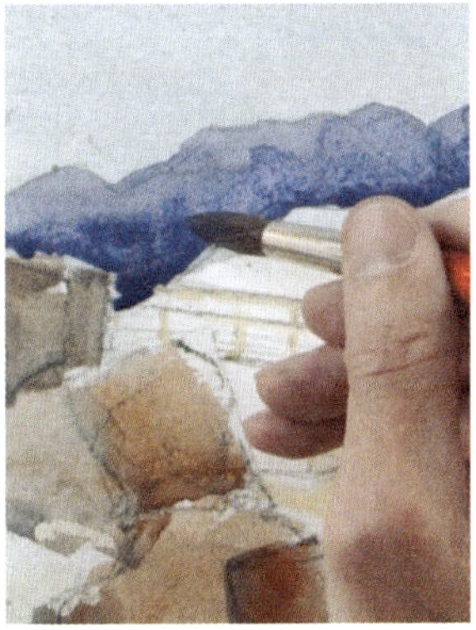

STEP 10

RIGHT Use pure cobalt blue to create the blue sky breaking out between the dark clouds. The outline of the blue sky should roughly mirror the shape of the edge of the clouds, with a white gap in between the two.

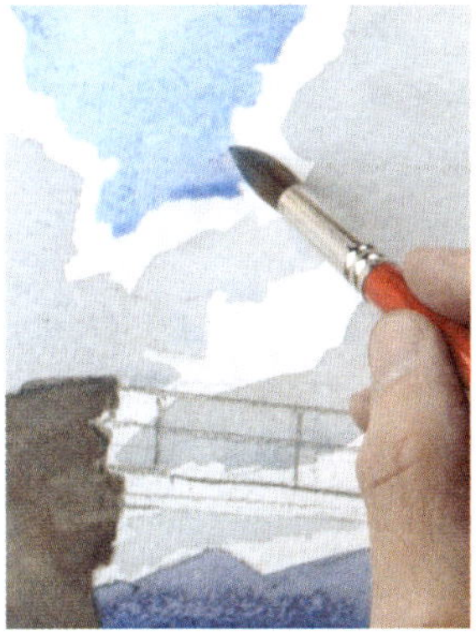

Apply a flat wash of faint yellow ochre on the white of the sky. This indicates that sunlight is creeping around the edge of the dark clouds.

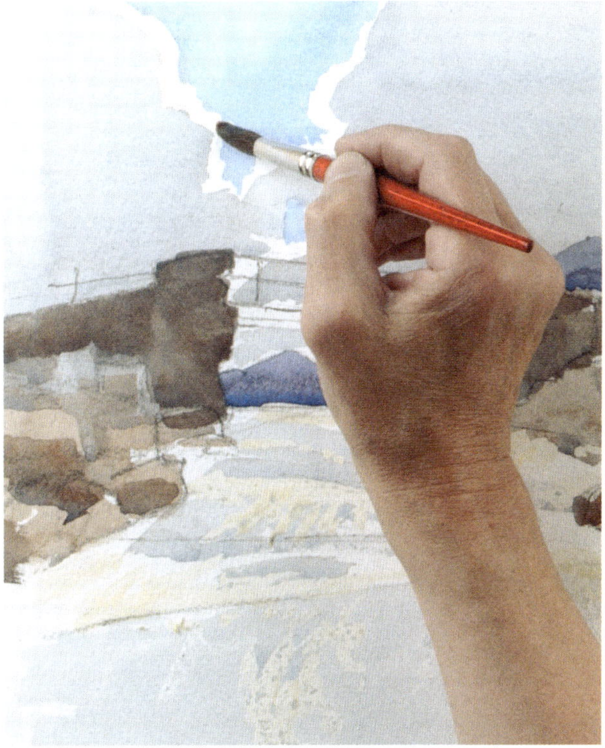

STEP 11

6 bridge at pont-y-garth

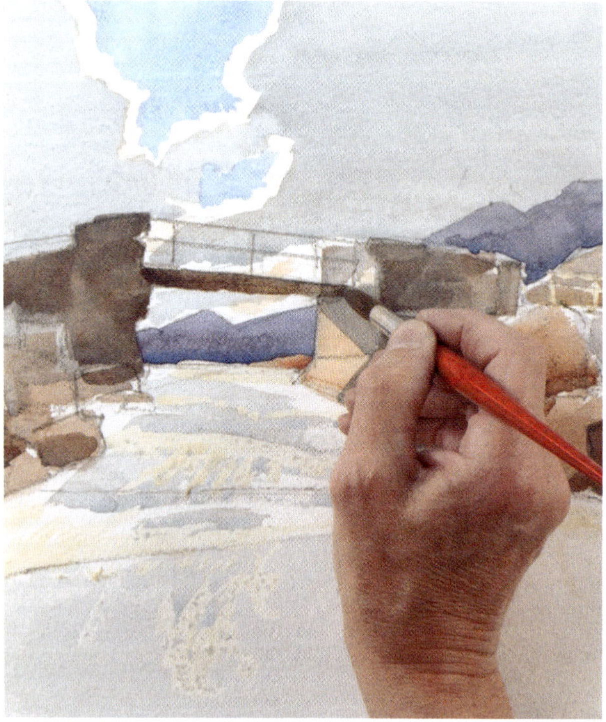

Apply colour to the underside of the bridge. Because the bridge is the focal point of the picture and is silhouetted against the sky, use a strong mix of dark colours – cobalt blue and burnt sienna.

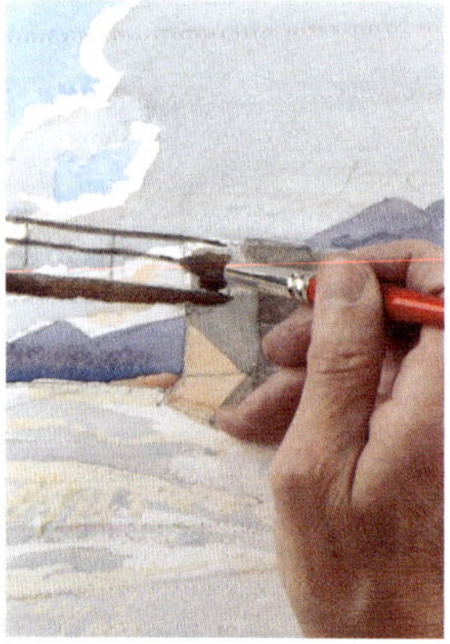

RIGHT Paint the handrails using the same colour, using the tip of the brush. Make the handrails appear asymmetrical – this gives them more visual interest than creating accurate, symmetrical lines.

STEP 12

Using wet-in-wet, create the shapes for the rocks in the river. Apply a wash of clean water to a small area then immediately drop in a mix of yellow ochre and cobalt blue. Make the mix strong as it will dissolve quickly on the wet paper. Repeat on all the river areas.

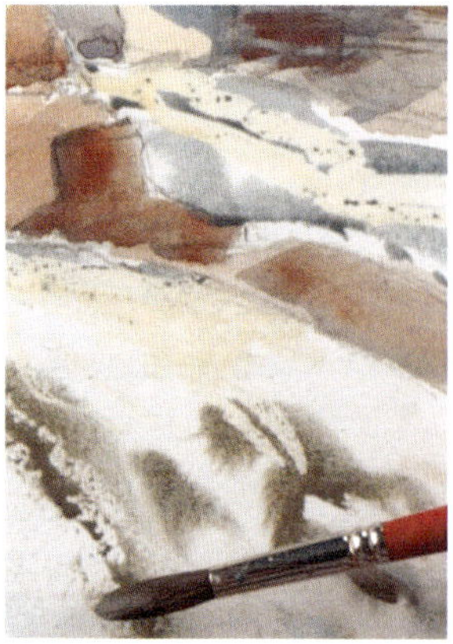

RIGHT Work in quick strokes, letting the colour run. This produces the many colours you see when water runs over dark rocks. Pick up any excess with the flat brush.

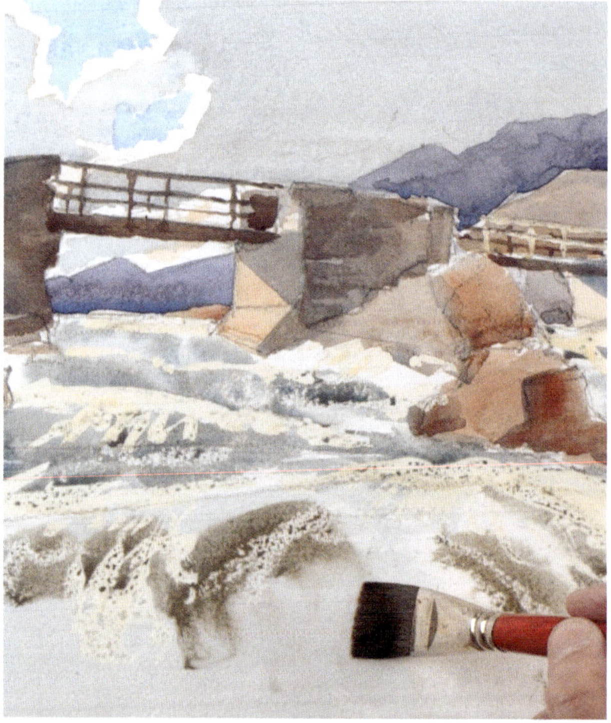

STEP 13

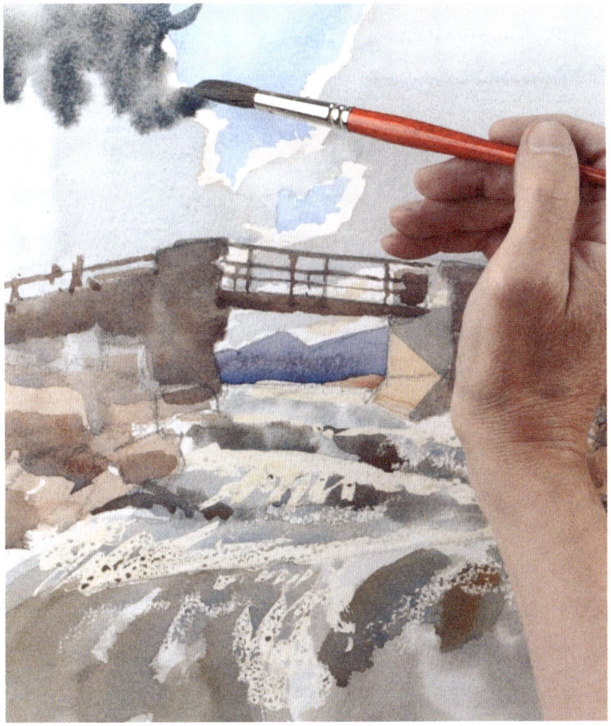

Repeat the wet-in-wet process on the dark clouds to build up a dramatic stormy look. Apply clean water on the top half of the cloud area then add Payne's gray with the round brush. The colour will not run beyond the edge of the wet area.

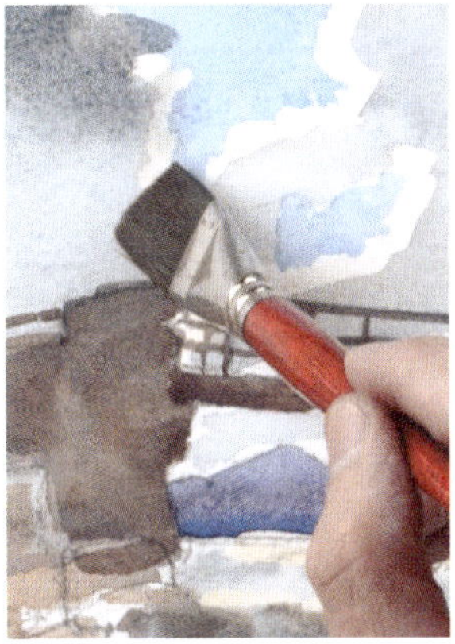

RIGHT Again, pick up any excess paint and water by gently dabbing it with the flat brush, but don't be too fussy.

STEP 14

RIGHT Repeat the wet-in-wet process on the right-hand cloud using the round brush. Letting the paint spread where it will creates great depth and texture – perfect for a dramatic stormy sky.

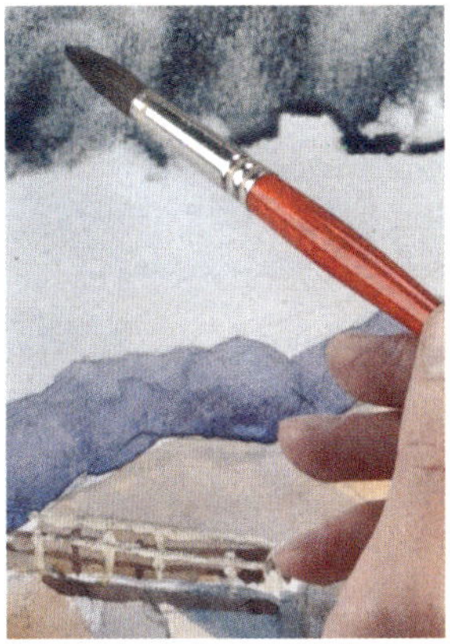

Let all the paint dry thoroughly. Then rub the tips of your fingers over the masking fluid to remove it. It will roll up into a ball, leaving bright white paper underneath, ready to work on.

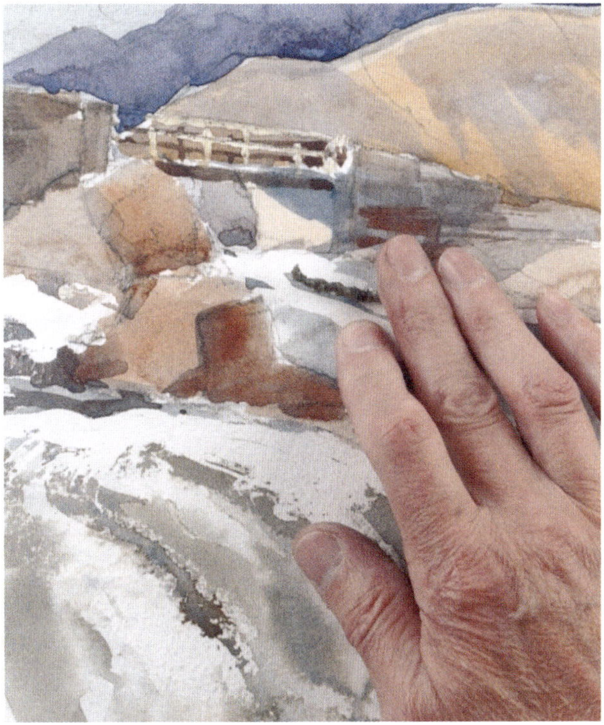

STEP 15

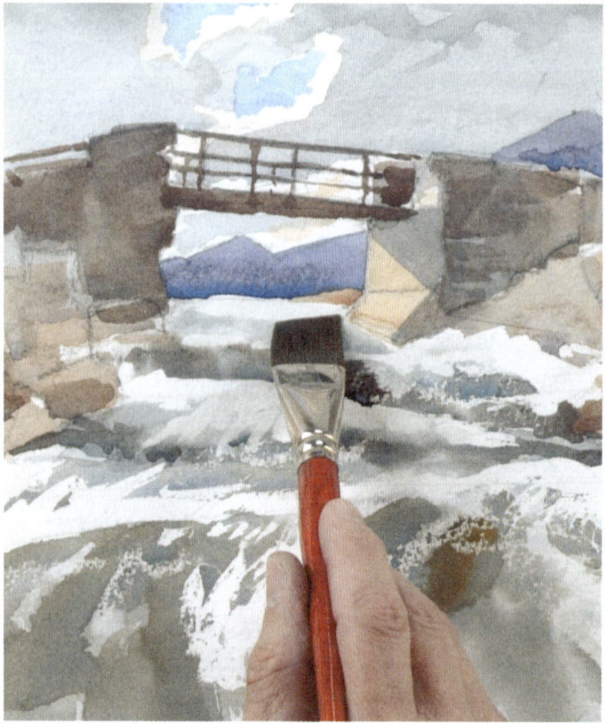

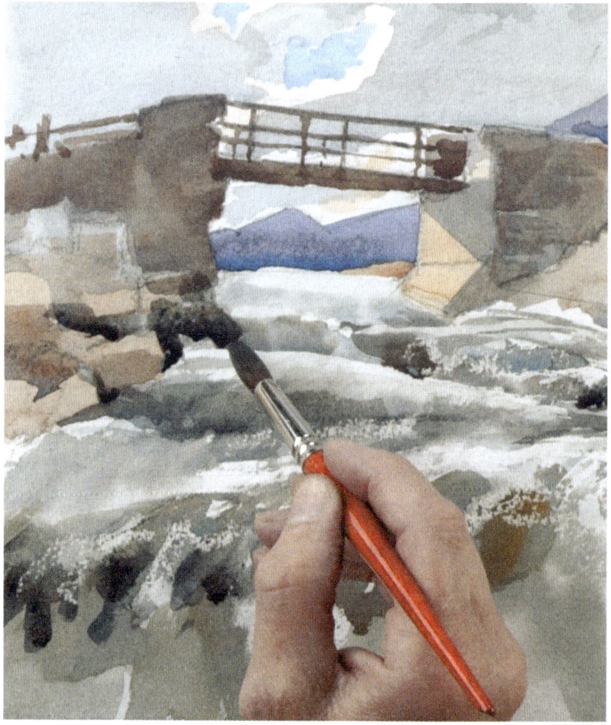

Start to work more colour into the river. First, apply clean water over the hard edges of paint created by the masking fluid using the flat brush. Doing this softens the edges and adds to the feeling of moving water. This technique is called working wet-on-dry.

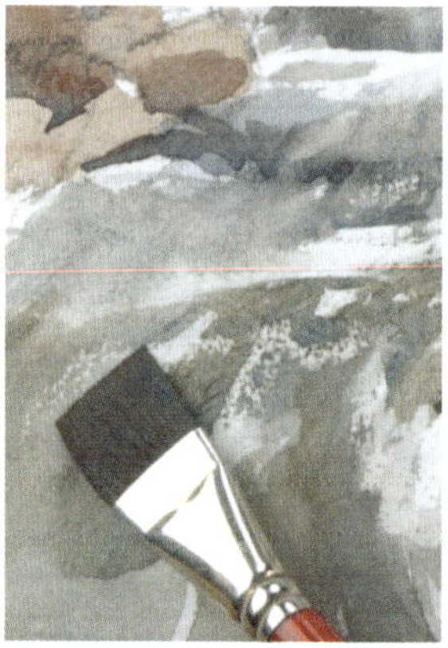

RIGHT Build up colour by adding a light wash of Payne's gray. This brings all the colours together while still reflecting the colour of the sky.

Work colour into the river near the bridge using a strong mix of pure Payne's gray. This creates extra areas of shadow and contrasts with the lighter grey washes. Work fairly accurately with the round brush – your colour build-up should be subtle, or else the dark colours will be the first things the viewer will see.

TRICK OF THE TRADE

As you build up your colours, no matter what technique you are using, take a step back from your painting to see how you are progressing. It is easy to get caught up in the fine detail and to forget to check how well you are capturing the essence of the overall scene. Too much detail will also detract from the focal point.

STEP 16

STEP 17

In the same way, work around the river adding the same dark colour to the rocks. Be careful not to add too much. As before, the colour is intended to be an accent shade only, to indicate dark rocks sticking up above the level of the water.

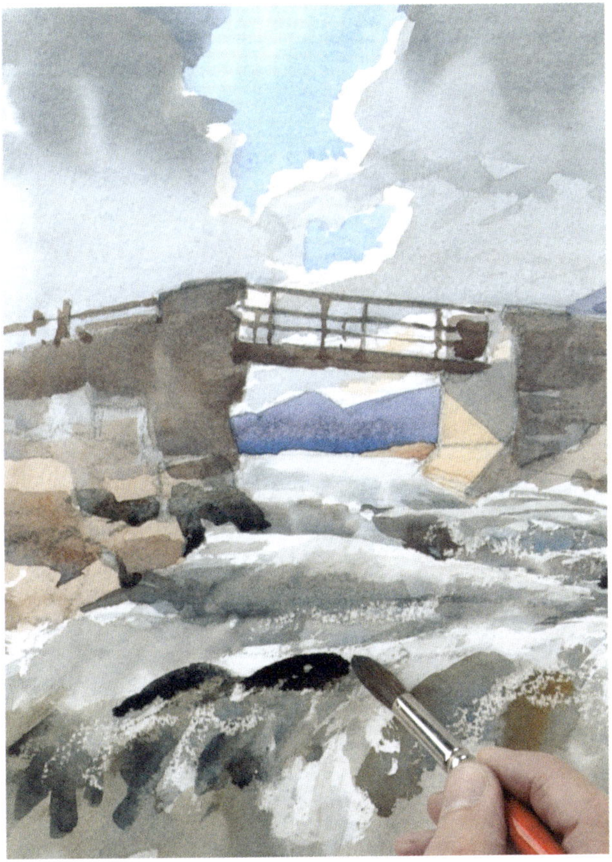

STEP 18

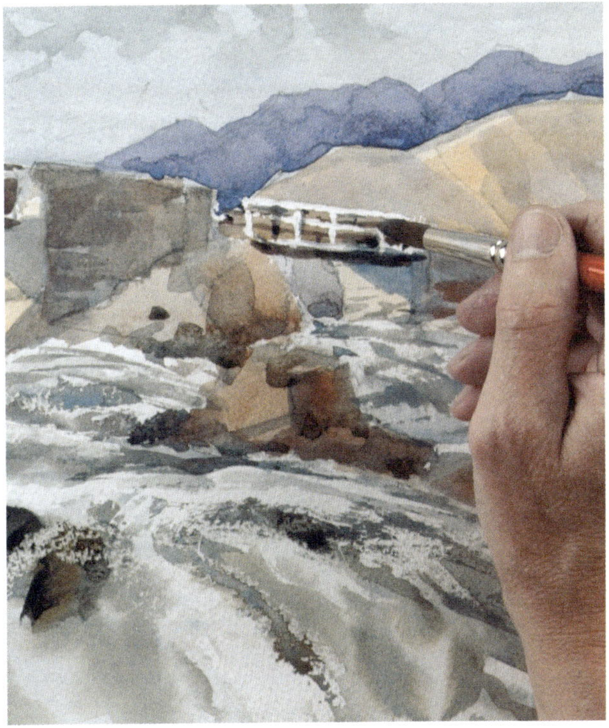

Clean up any detail around the handrail with the mix you used previously on this detail. Also use the same colour to add small areas of detail to the brickwork behind the railing.

RIGHT Finish off the composition by adding a cool blue reflection to the stonework on the underside of the bridge. Use a light mix of Payne's gray and cobalt blue for this – a perfect colour for a reflection cast by water.

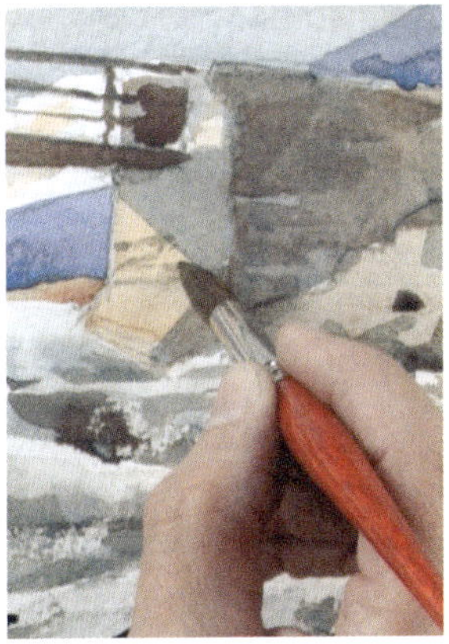

STEP 19

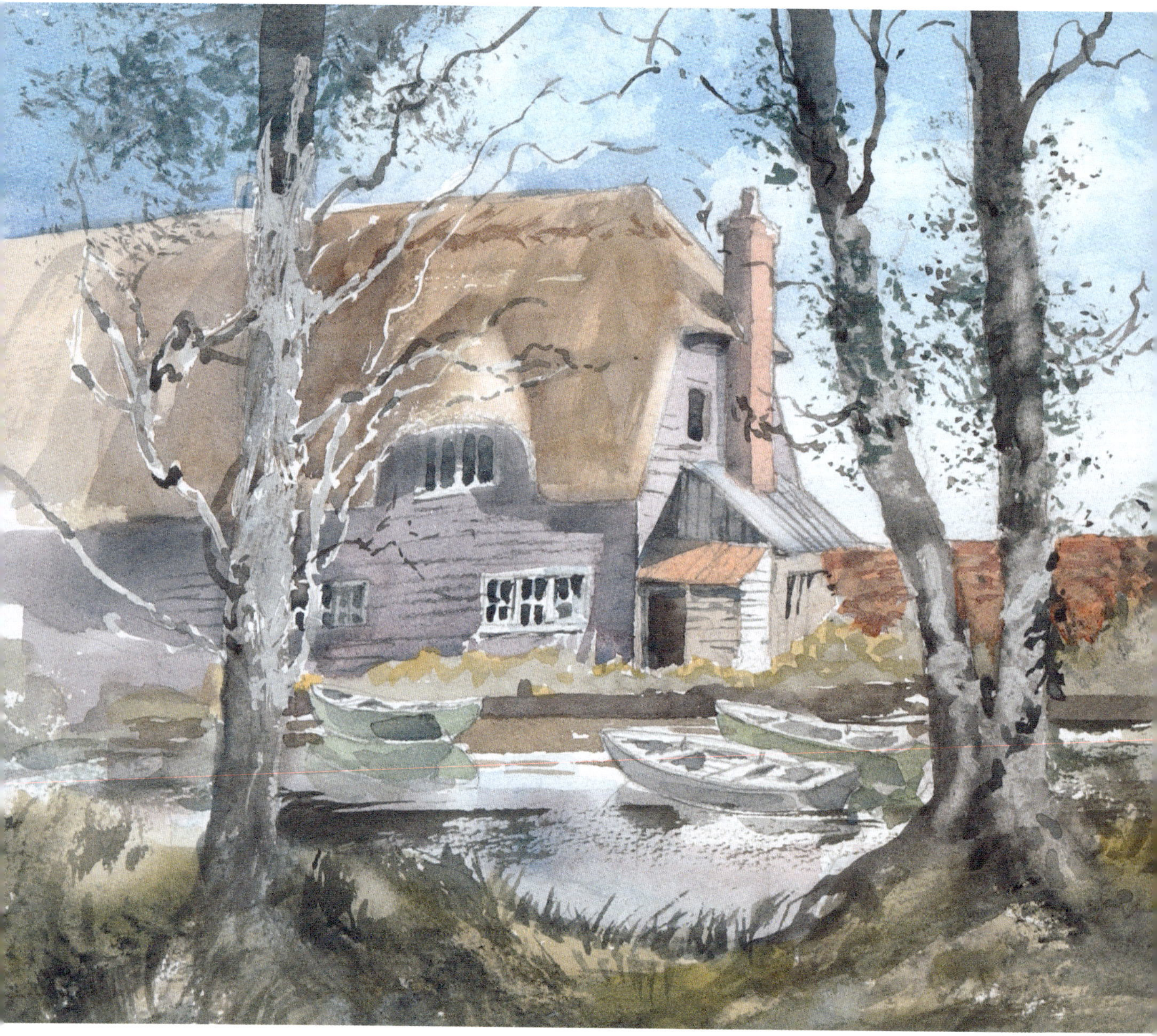

7
constable's granary

john barber
400 x 500mm (16 x 20in)

Old buildings often look as though they have grown out of the same ground as the trees and fields that surround them, and the granary in this project is an exercise in recreating this idea. First, you will see how to develop a visually interesting scene, with a view point that leads the eye through the trees to the building beyond. Buildings are brought to life by detail, so practice working accurately with your brush. It is also important that man-made objects blend with their natural environment, so try to achieve consistent tones with your colours. Lastly, the varied brushwork and techniques in this project create lots of textures and depth, to further breathe life into your work.

TECHNIQUES FOR THE PROJECT

Laying a graduated wash

Working with a dry brush and lifting off

Sponging

WHAT YOU WILL NEED

Rough surface watercolour paper
Graphite pencil, 6B
Masking fluid
Old, small round brush, synthetic
Flat brush, 2.5cm (1in), sable or synthetic
Hog hair brush
Round brush, no. 5 or 6, sable or synthetic
Kitchen paper and natural sponge

COLOUR MIXES

1 Payne's gray
2 Prussian blue
3 Cobalt blue
5 Permanent rose
8 Cadmium yellow
10 Yellow ochre
11 Burnt sienna

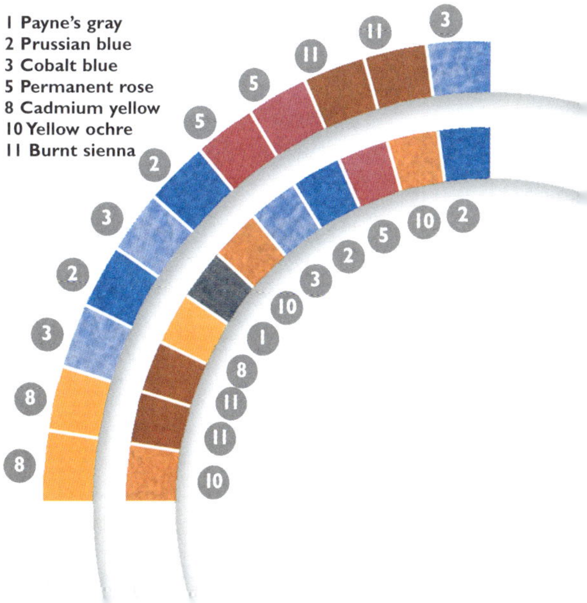

SPONGING WITH NATURAL SPONGE

A natural sponge is a great tool for any painter. Buy the largest one you can afford and treat it carefully: It will serve you for a lifetime. When you touch the painting with different parts of the sponge, you will get a great variety of small marks. By turning the sponge each time before putting it on the paper you will avoid any impression of 'printing' or repetition of marks. The surface of the sponge is formed from many small cone-shaped points, each of which acts as an individual brush. When using a sponge mix up plenty of paint and make it stronger than you would for brush painting. Do not wet the sponge before putting it into the paint as this will dilute the crispness of the marks it makes. You will soon learn what sort of marks you get from different parts of your sponge and see where they can be applied to your picture. Sponge textures are useful on walls, trees, rocks, broken earth, paths, and many other features in your painting. Test it on scrap paper first to see what marks appear.

A wet sponge is ideal for removing paint or even wiping over a whole picture and leaving a pale trace of colour for you to start working on again. When you have finished, wash your sponge under a tap.

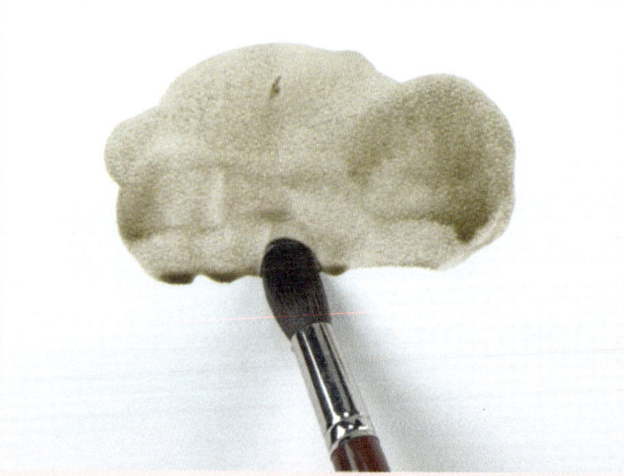

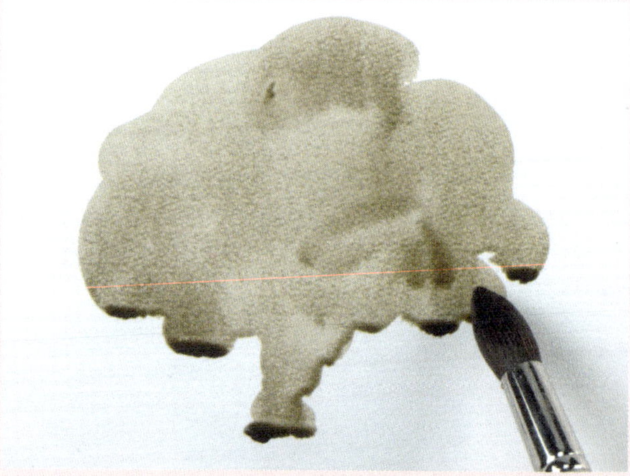

1 Before using the sponge on a painting, try using it on various shapes that you have drawn as flat washes. Take a large mop brush and paint the shape of a tree, for example. This does not have to be a perfect flat wash.

2 It is good to let some drips dry along the bottom edge to give some modeling to your tree shape. There is no need to pencil the tree first or to copy the example closely. Even with a simple exercise like this it is better if you draw from nature.

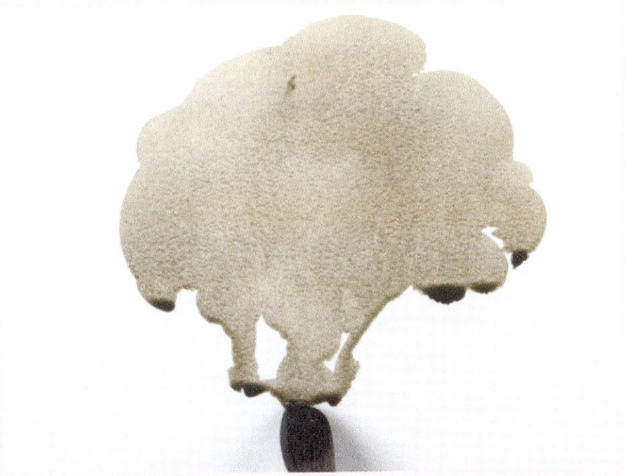

3 Once you have decided on your tree shape, let it dry completely. This basic wash should not be too dark otherwise the sponge marks will not show clearly on it. Add more paint to your mix, ready to start sponging.

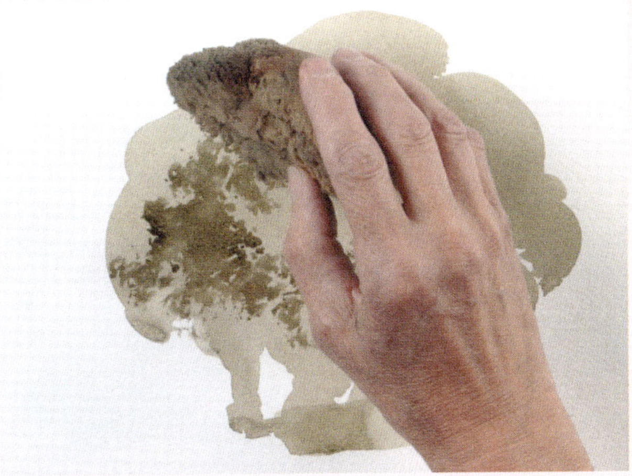

4 Dab the sponge into the stiff paint and test on scrap paper. If you like what you see, dab lightly on your painting. Hold the sponge so that it just touches the paper. Repeat with a bouncing movement. Do not press or you will get one large blot.

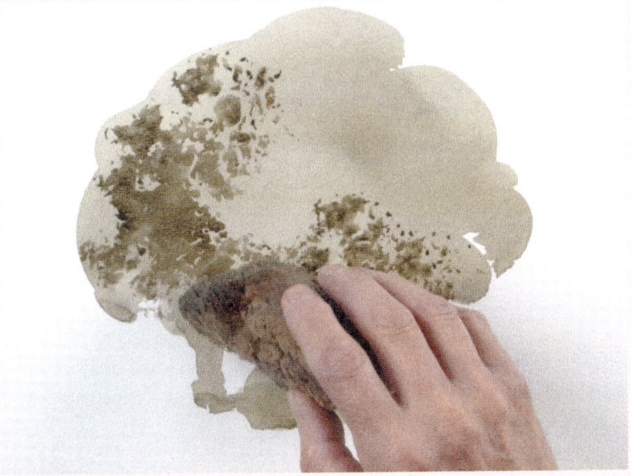

5 At first, keep your sponging to the dark side of the tree. Look at your first marks and judge whether you need more texture. As the paint dries on the sponge, it will make more delicate marks. Use this to add texture to the lighter side too.

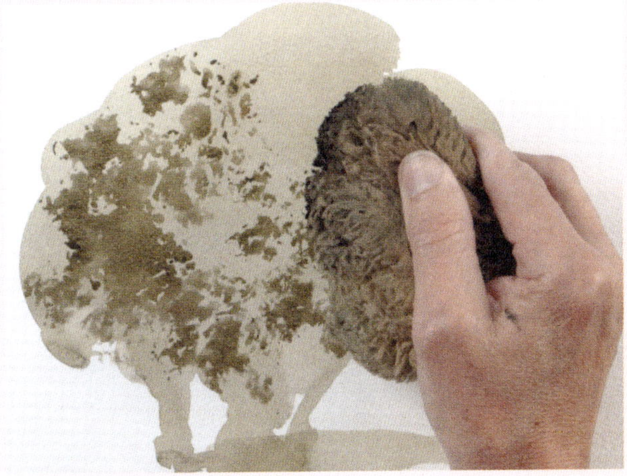

6 Continue dabbing and rolling the sponge. Experiment until the sponge makes no more marks, or stop when the work is dry, then load your sponge and continue. Try dabbing on a wet wash with the sponge to make your textures fade and soften.

7 constable's granary

Using the soft graphite pencil, lightly sketch in the lines for your composition, keeping your grip on the pencil relaxed. Some of the lines need to be fairly accurate, such as the lines for the granary, while others can be looser, such as the branches of the trees. Then work back over the most important lines, such as the roof line and the chimney of the granary.

REMEMBER

Masking out is a valuable tool to use here. Apply it to the tree on the left-hand side. This is because you do not want the colour applied to the granary to get caught up with the colour of the tree. So masking out can also be used as a method for keeping two sets of colours separate so they can be worked on at different times.

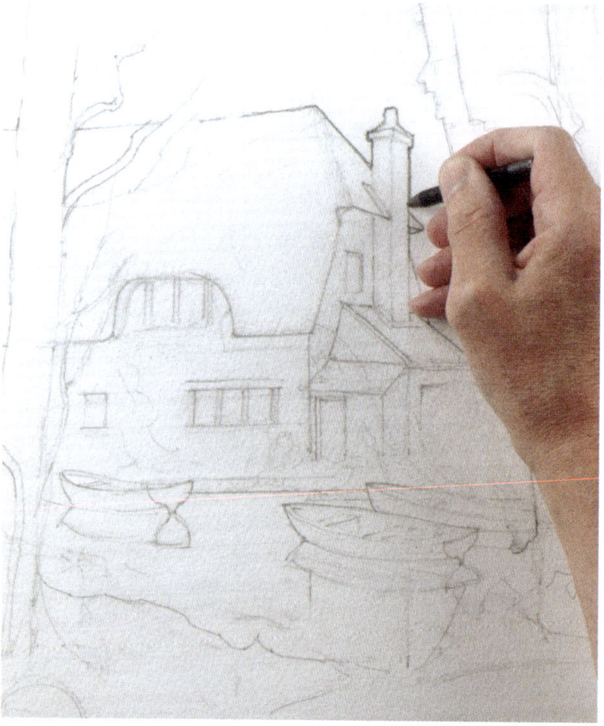

STEP 1

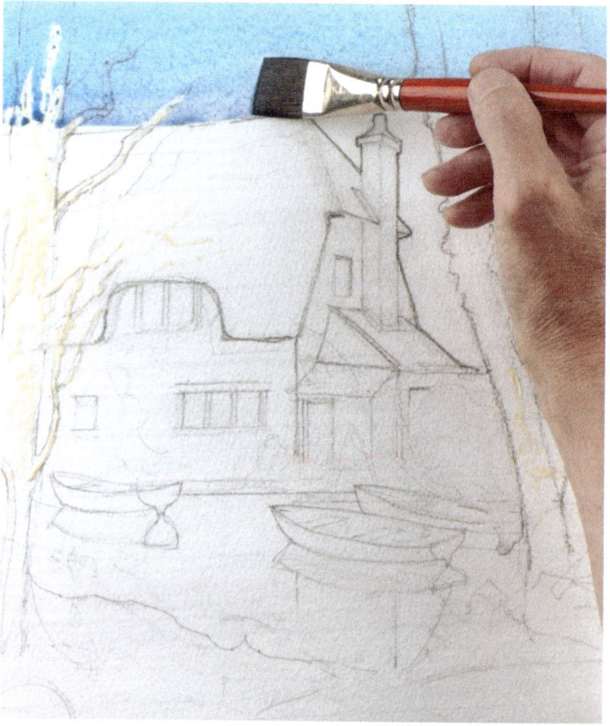

Apply the masking fluid with an old brush, then apply a flat wash of cobalt blue and Prussian blue to the sky using the flat brush, working in horizontal bands from the top down. As you get closer to the horizon, dilute the colour with more water. This creates a graduated wash.

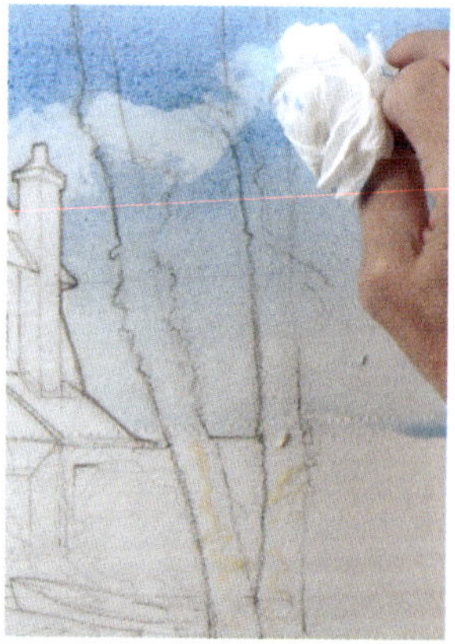

RIGHT Dab away some of the wet paint with kitchen paper. This is called lifting off, and here, it is perfect for creating the uneven textures of white clouds.

STEP 2

Lifting off the paint will, however, produce some hard edges on the clouds. To blend the sky and the clouds together, wet the hog hair brush with water and scrub it over the hard edges, soaking up the excess water with kitchen paper. The clouds should now have plenty of texture and depth.

BE CONFIDENT

Use the biggest brushes you can manage on a subject like this and live with the marks that they make. This will make your work lively and help you to be more confident in the way you handle the paint. A few dribbles of paint that you did not intend may give your art just the texture it needs.

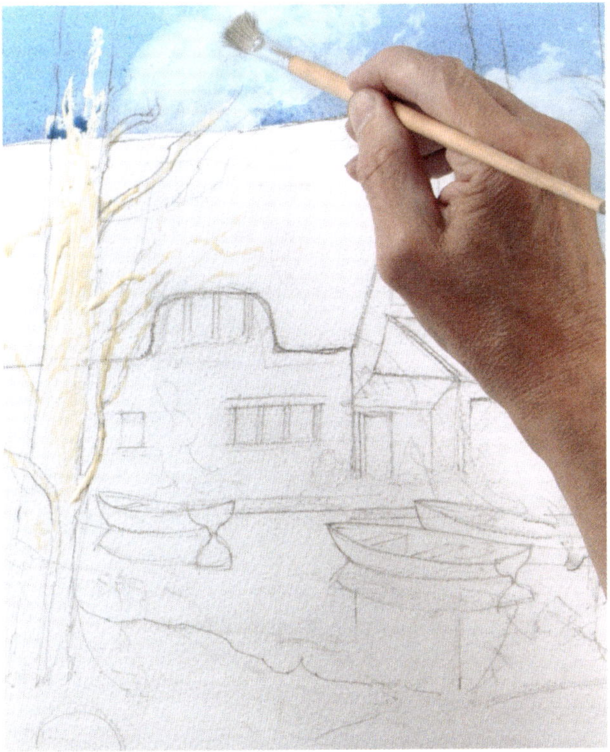

STEP 3

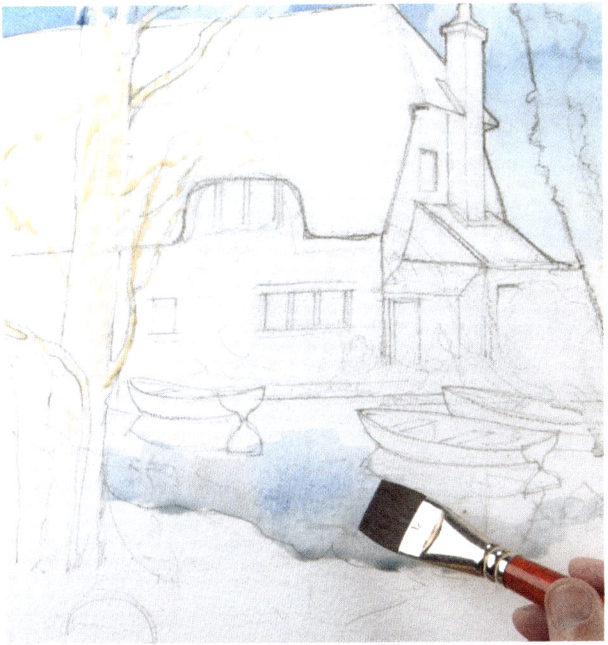

Since any expanse of water will partly reflect the colour of the sky, apply the same blue mix that you used on the sky to the river, using the wet-in-wet technique. With the flat brush, apply a layer of clean water to the bottom section of the river area, then drop in the blue mix.

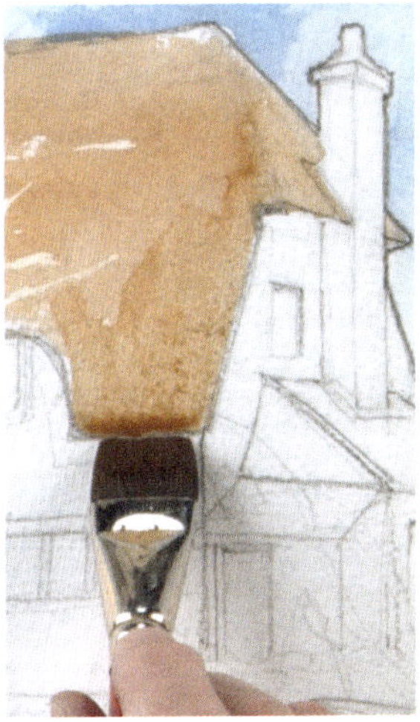

RIGHT Apply a flat wash of burnt sienna, yellow ochre, and a touch of Prussian blue to the roof of the house. The masking fluid will stop some of the paint reaching the paper underneath. Do not let the paint cross the pencil lines.

STEP 4

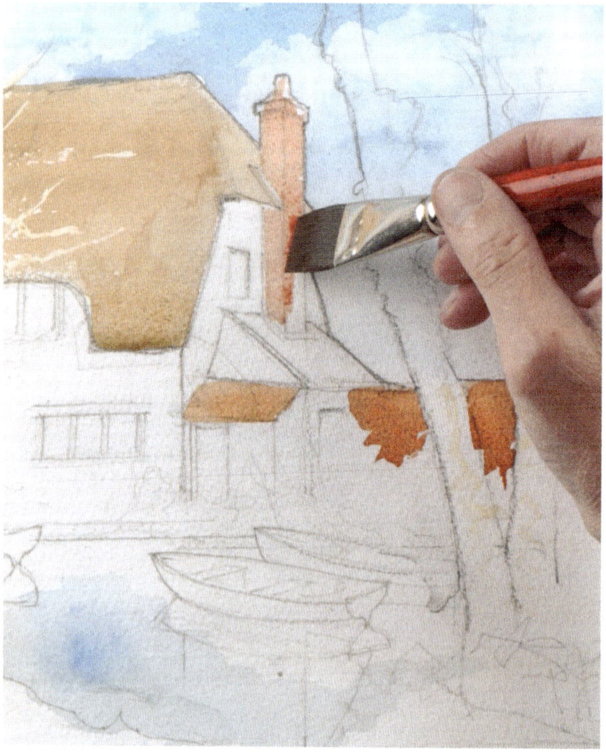

Start building up colours on the granary. Apply burnt sienna to the small roof and wall to the right of the building, using a slightly more dilute mix for the roof. Then add permanent rose to the burnt sienna and apply this pinker colour to the chimney.

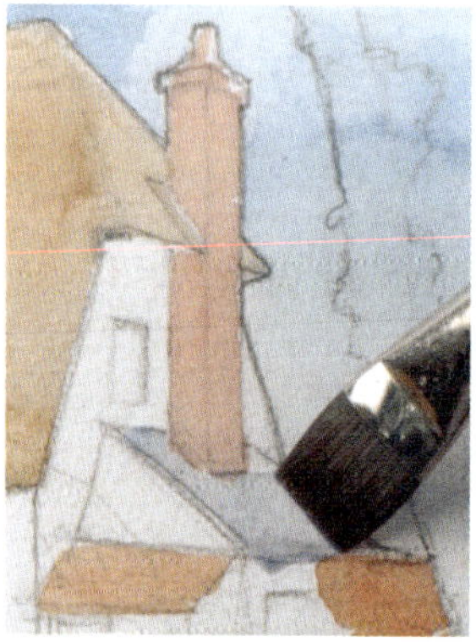

RIGHT Use permanent rose and Prussian blue for the roof under the chimney. This creates a good contrasting colour.

STEP 5

RIGHT Colour the front wall of the granary using a mix of permanent rose and cobalt blue to create a warm violet colour.

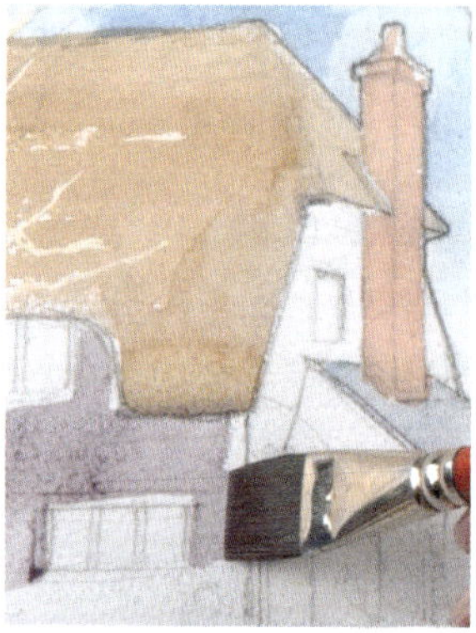

Lighten this mix with a little more water and apply it to the end wall, which is in light. Then add shadow under the eaves and to the edges of the building using Payne's gray. Notice how the tonal values of all the colours used on the granary are the same strength.

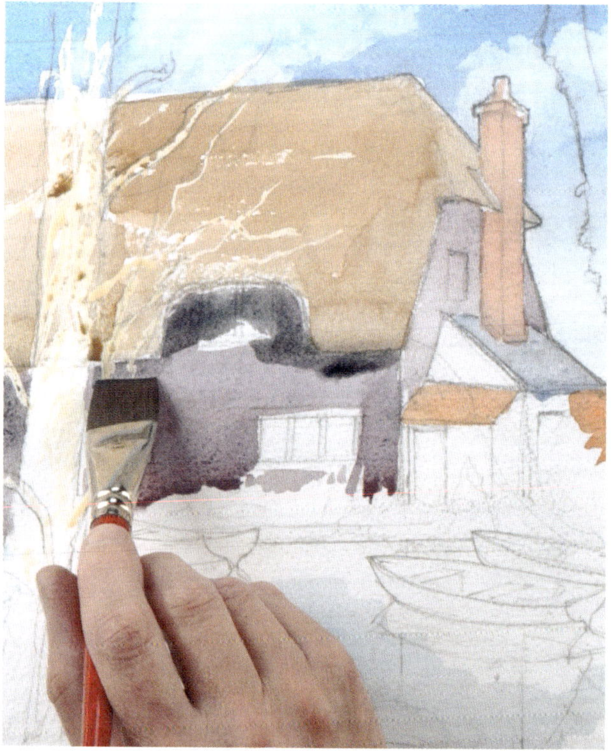

STEP 6

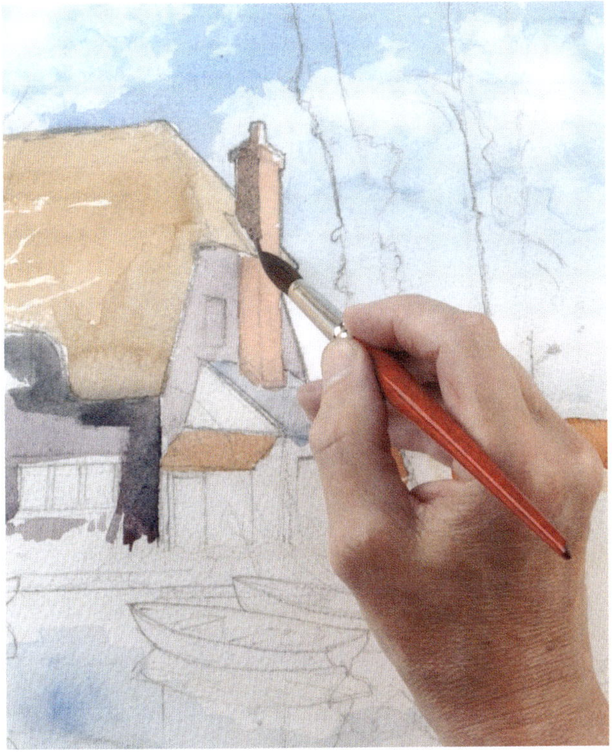

Continue to build up shadow on the house using the round brush for more accurate work. Keep your shadow areas consistent throughout. Here, we have used a mix of permanent rose, cobalt blue and Payne's gray to shade the front edge of the chimney.

RIGHT Continue the colouring process, working around the front of the granary. Use yellow ochre on the front of the small shed and gate.

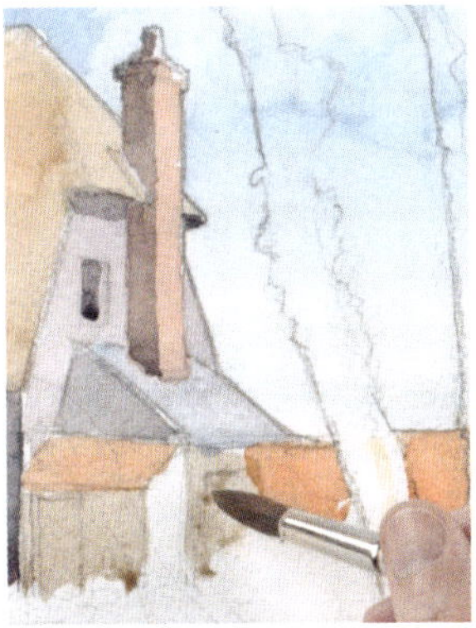

STEP 7

RIGHT The rooms inside the granary are unlit and so appear very dark. Use Payne's gray for these areas.

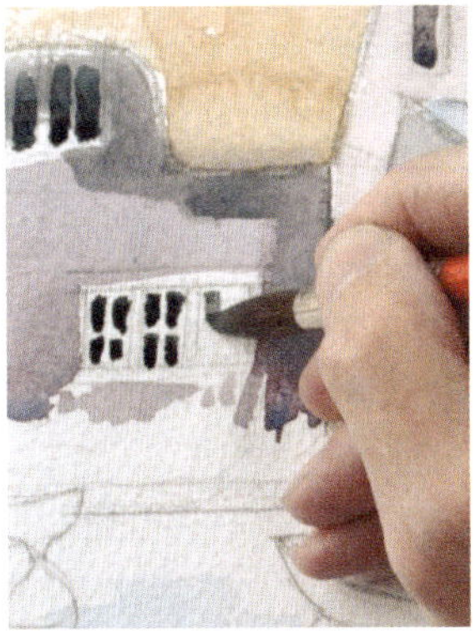

Using wet-in-wet, apply the wash you used on the walls of the house on the river – the water reflects the colour of the building. Do this by applying a wash of clean water and dropping the violet-coloured mix into it. Then mix Prussian blue and yellow ochre for the grass and bushes.

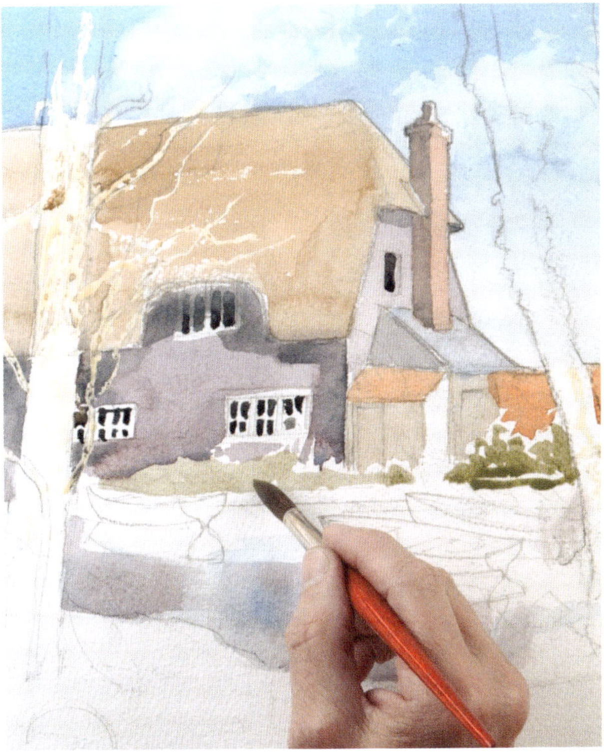

STEP 8

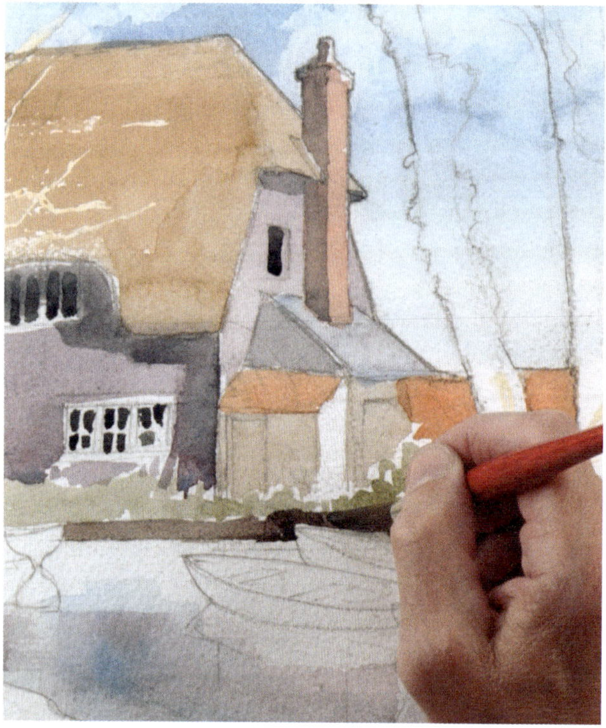

RIGHT The building is the focal point of the painting, so keep the colour of the boats paler. Use a light mix of cobalt blue and Payne's gray for the sides of the first boat.

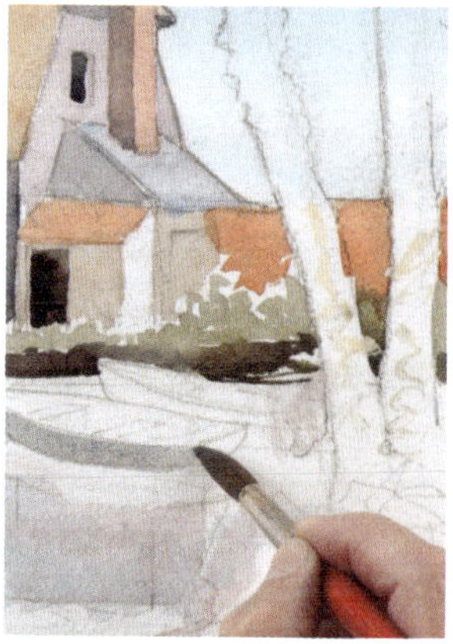

Use a darker mix of the same colours for a touch of shading on the sides of the boat as well as some internal detail. Note how much of the boat is left uncoloured to maintain the muted look.

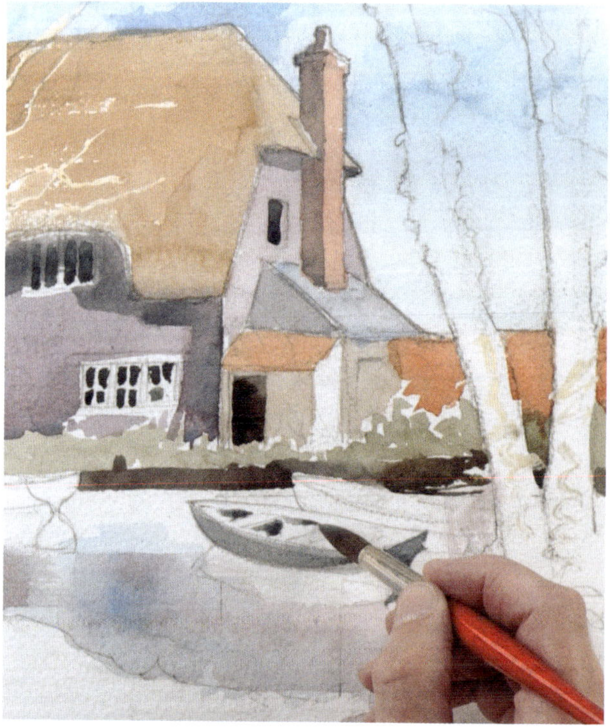

Now you can start adding areas of detailed colour. The dark wooden boards along the edge of the river are coloured with a mix of the green you used on the grass and bush, and permanent rose.

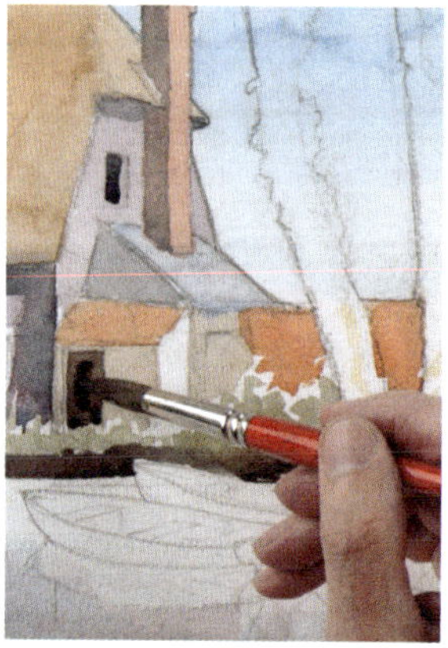

RIGHT Also use this colour for the small door. Make sure your painting is very accurate in these areas – the mix should not run into other areas of colour.

STEP 9

STEP 10

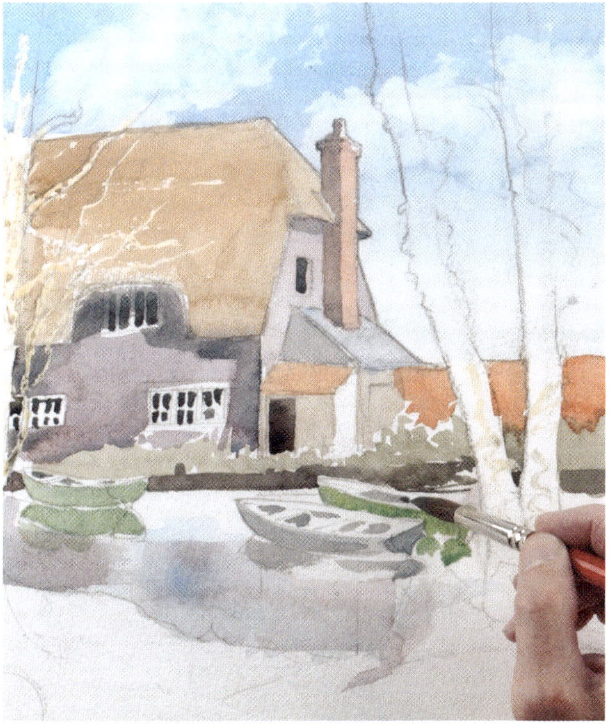

Build up reflections in the water by adding a little of the same grey mix to the river, just alongside the boat. Then, for variety, colour the other boats, using a light mix of Prussian blue and cadmium yellow.

RIGHT Continue with the reflections by adding the green mix you used on the grass to the river using the dry brush technique. Load the brush with only a little paint and rub it across the surface of the paper.

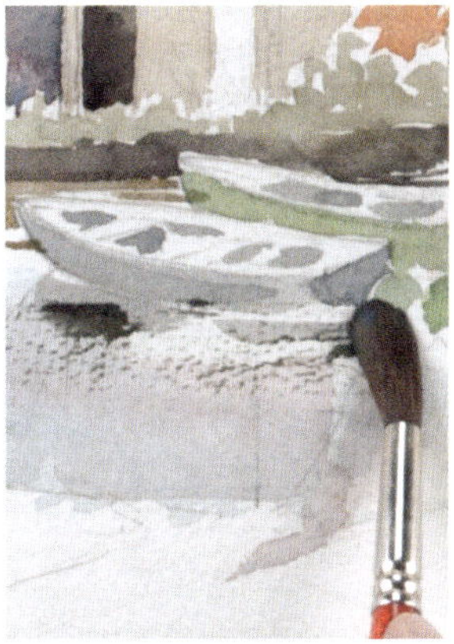

STEP 11

RIGHT For speed, try blowdrying your work to dry the paint quickly. Be careful not to blow any drips of paint around, however, as you may end up with unwanted paint in some areas.

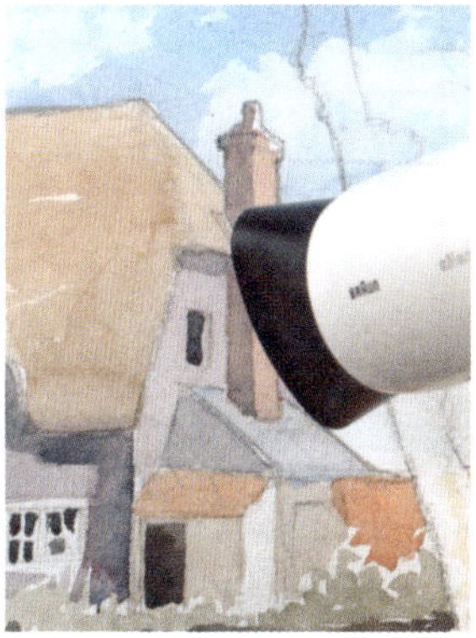

Use the dry brush technique again on the thatch, using a slightly greyer mix of cobalt blue and burnt sienna. This will give extra texture to the thatch and emphasize any curved areas, such as those over the top windows.

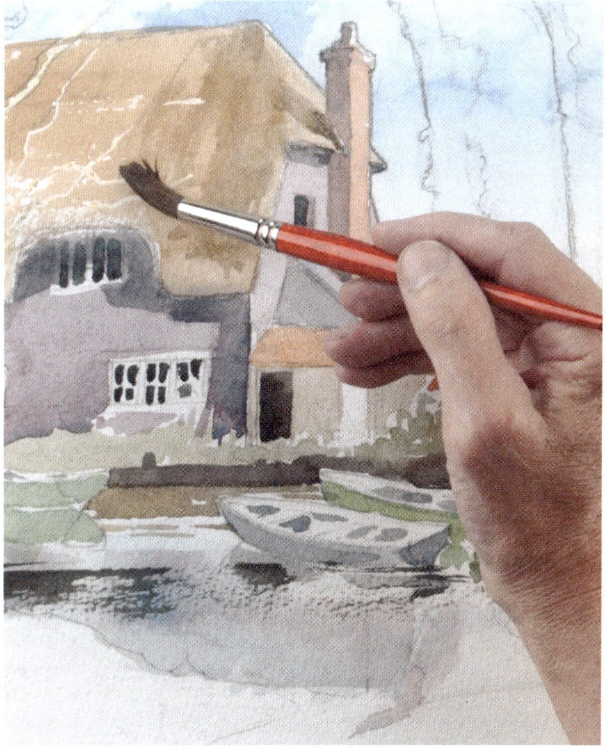

STEP 12

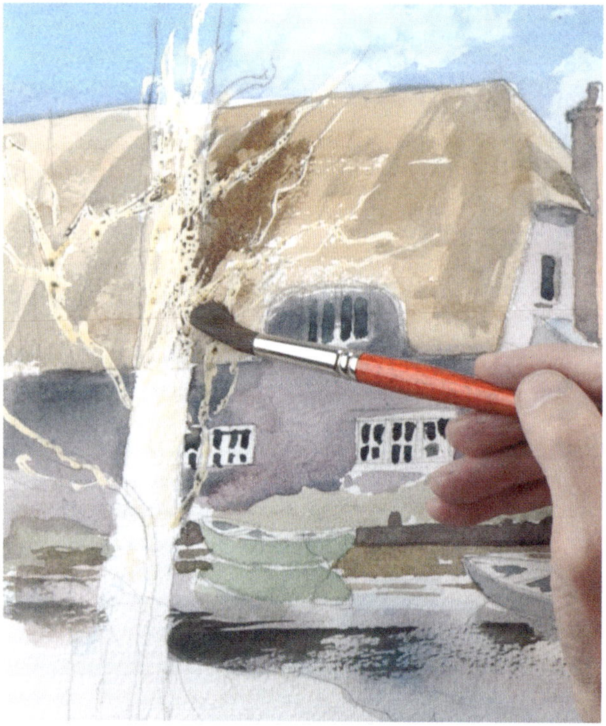

Add a little more Payne's gray to your mix, then apply the colour to the tree on the right of the painting. Lift off some of the excess paint with a piece of kitchen paper but don't do this along the entire length of the trunk. This way you will get lots of different textures – perfect for an old tree.

TRICK OF THE TRADE

When sponging paint onto the paper, create plenty of strong colour by mixing less water with more colour than usual. Apply the colour with a dry sponge, rotating it slightly in your hand before each dab. This will ensure a variety of marks and avoids a repetitive 'printing' effect.

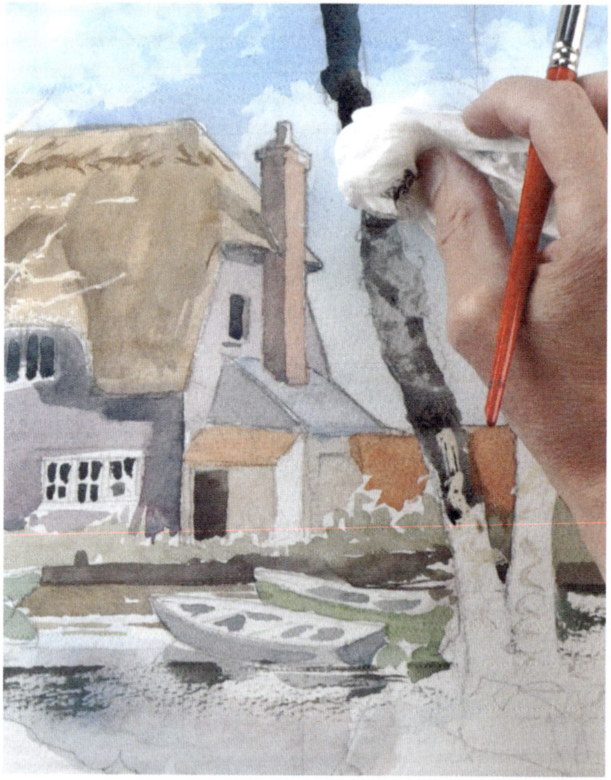

Finish the thatch on the roof with a darker mix of burnt sienna and cobalt blue around the tree. Add some small touches of detail to the roofline.

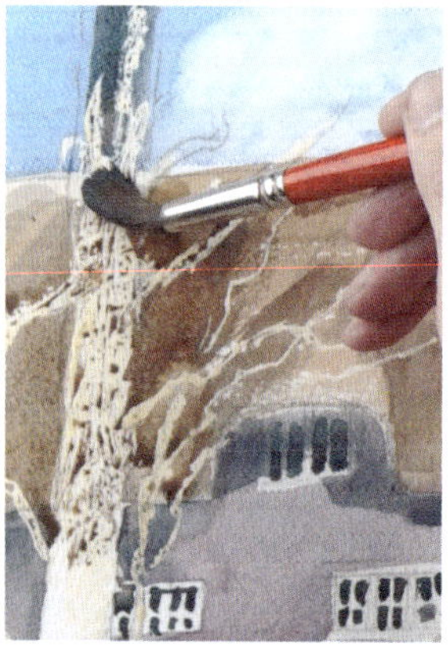

RIGHT Start colouring the trees. Here, we have used a mix of Payne's gray, cobalt blue, and burnt sienna on the tree trunk. Work the brush down from top to bottom, over the masking fluid, using the dry brush technique.

STEP 13

STEP 14

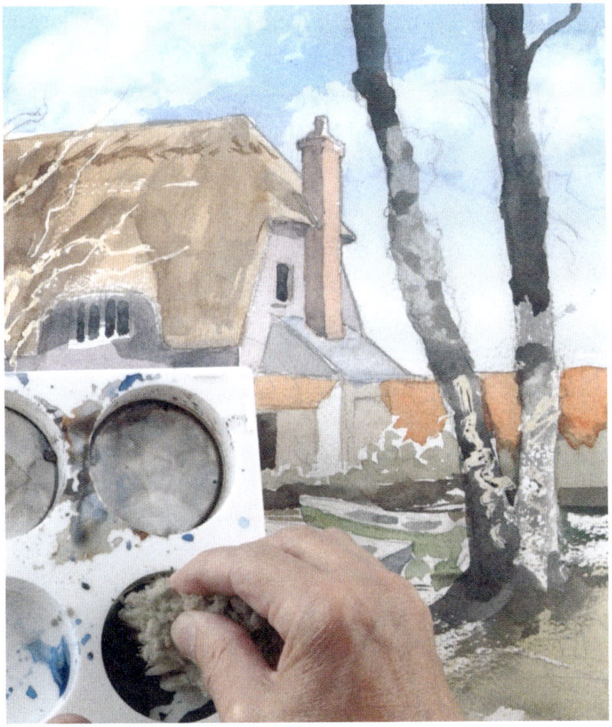

Create a muted foreground under the trees with cadmium yellow, burnt sienna, and cobalt blue, applied with a dry brush. Then mix Prussian blue, yellow ochre, and cadmium lemon to create a strong dark green for the foliage. Dip a natural sponge into the mix for the sponging technique.

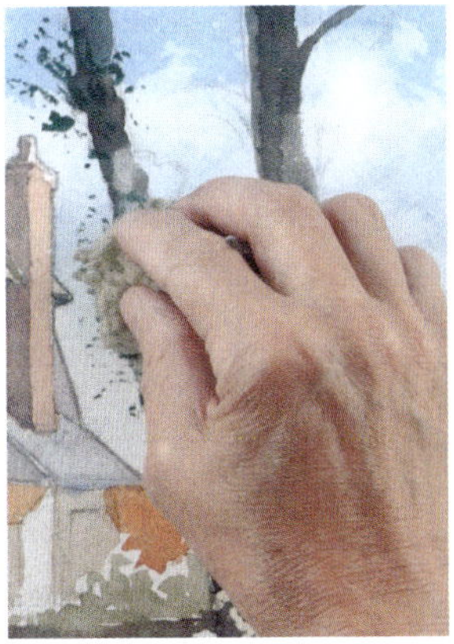

RIGHT Press the sponge onto the paper, working along the length of the tree trunks. This hints at the foliage growing on the trees.

STEP 15

Let the paint dry thoroughly (use the hairdryer if necessary) then remove the masking fluid from the tree trunks. Make sure your hands are clean, then rub the pads of your fingers over the dry fluid. It will start to come off, balling up as it does so. The paper underneath should be white.

TRICK OF THE TRADE

Try using the sponge on both dry and wet washes. The sponged texture will stay crisp and dark on a dry surface but will spread softly and grow paler on a wet one. Wet the sky slightly then lightly sponge some green colour onto the wet surface. Allow it to dry, then dab on the same colour again. The result will be a fine variety of small leaves.

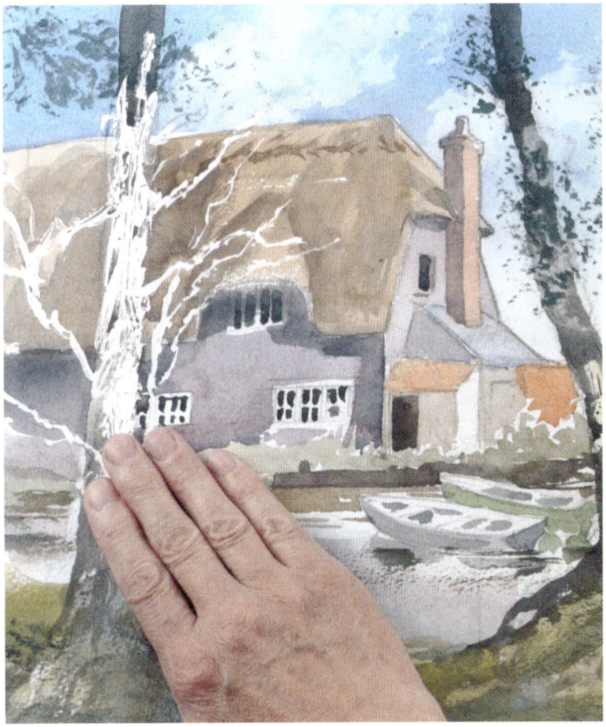

STEP 16

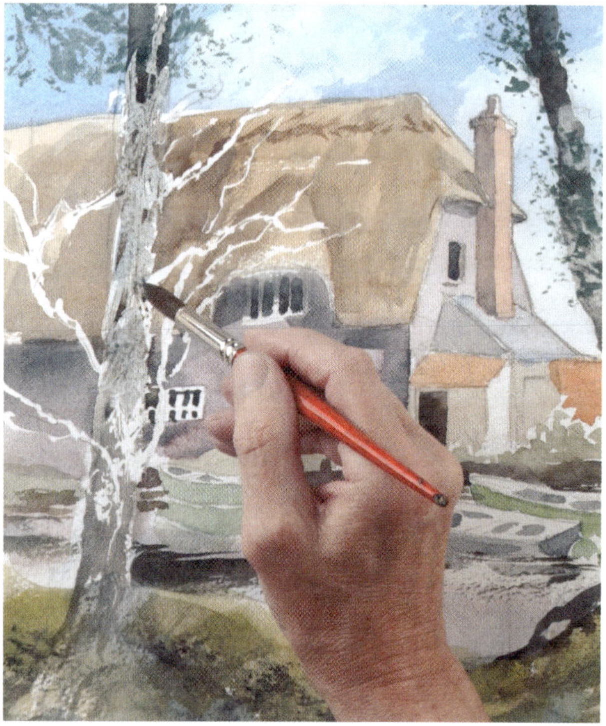

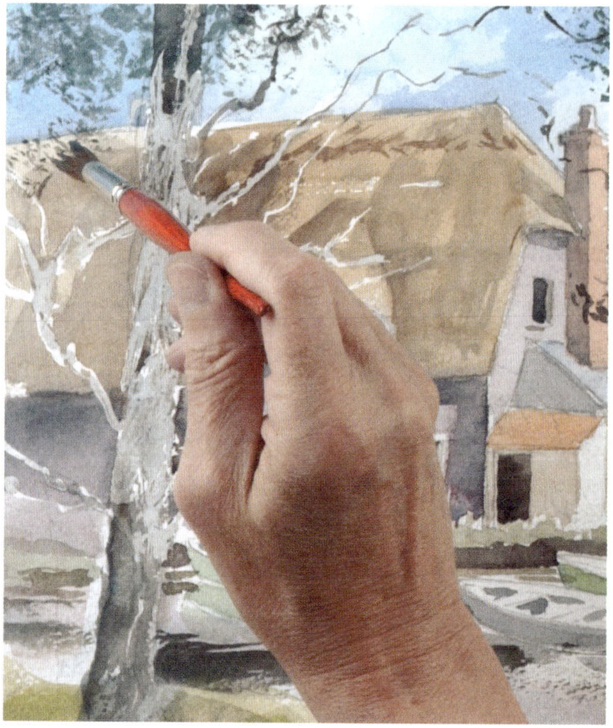

Start working on the white areas left by the fluid to create new shades and textures. Use a light mix of cobalt blue and burnt sienna. Notice how the light area on the trunk deliberately falls in front of the building, so the building always remains the focal point. Use the round brush here.

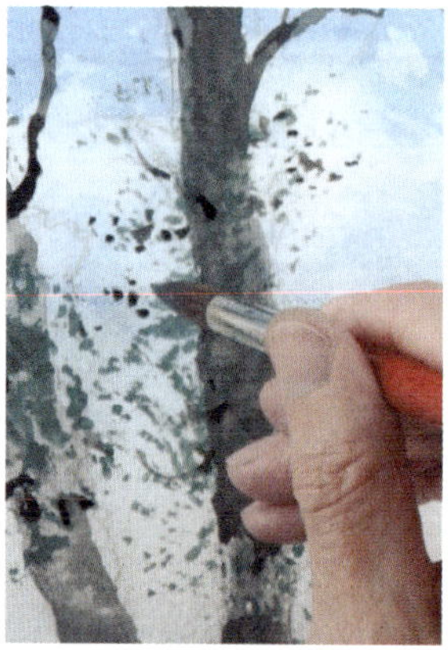

RIGHT Add extra spots of colour to the foliage by adding Payne's gray to the mix. Don't add too many extra leaves or the overall look will be too dark.

Add a final touch to the foliage on the trees with the dry brush technique. This time, however, instead of rubbing the brush over the paper, dab it tip first onto the paper so the hairs spread out. The small, random shapes this creates gives a good impression of foliage.

TRICK OF THE TRADE

If you feel unhappy with any part of your picture, sponge off the colour with clean water. Your work will not disappear but will remain as a paler version of what was there before, enabling you to work it up again to harmonise it with the rest of the picture. Many of J.M.W. Turner's great watercolours were created in this way.

STEP 17

STEP 18

RIGHT Finish the granary with some fine, textured detail. Apply very thin lines of Payne's gray across the exterior of the building.

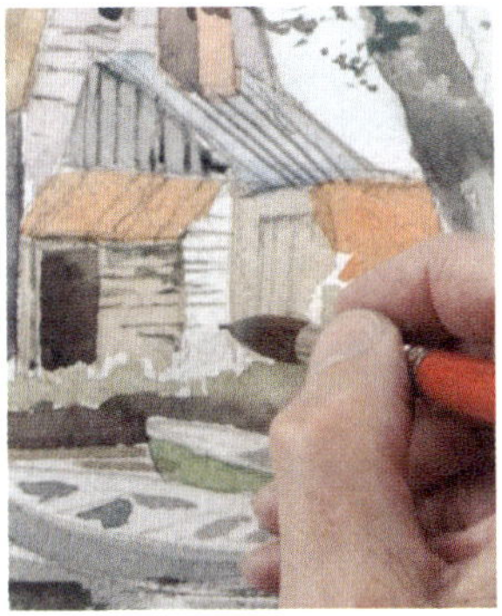

Build up colour and detail on the foreground using the flat brush and a dark mix of cadmium yellow, yellow ochre, and Prussian blue. This is a good colour for the dark grass around the base of the trees and at the edge of the water.

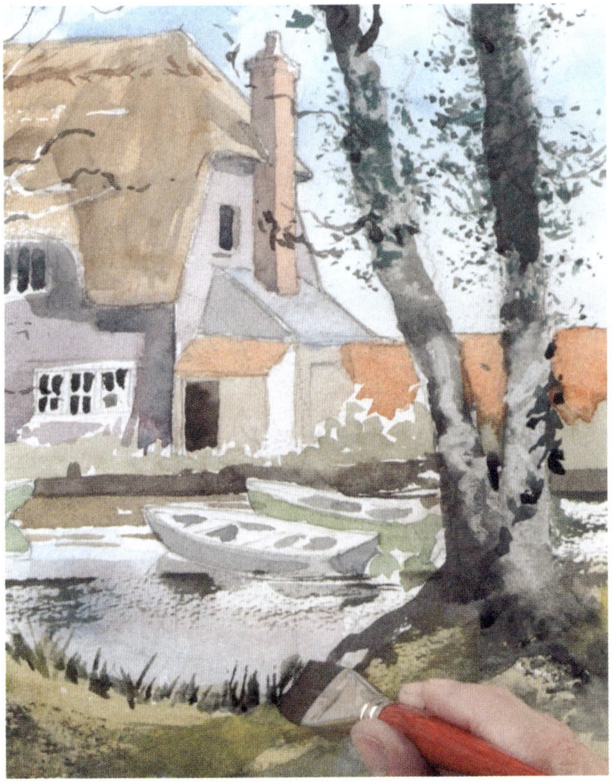

STEP 19

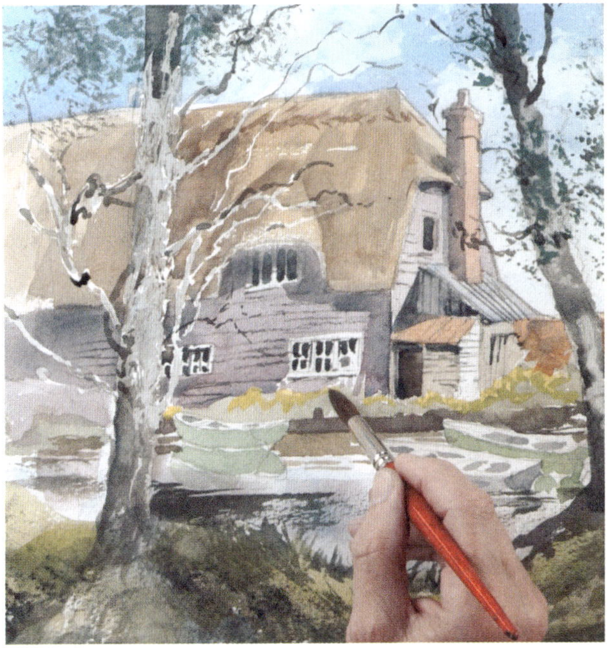

Add a thin line of cadmium yellow with the round brush to brighten the foliage next to the granary. This is an effective accent colour that creates a break between the building and the river.

RIGHT Lastly, lift off some of the dark foreground paint to create a stronger contrast between light and shade. Dip the hog brush in some water and scrub it over the darkest areas, such as at the base of the trees. Lift off the excess paint and water with some kitchen paper.

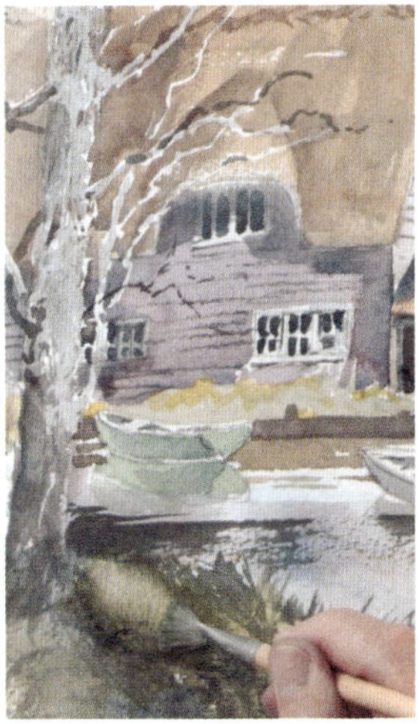

STEP 20

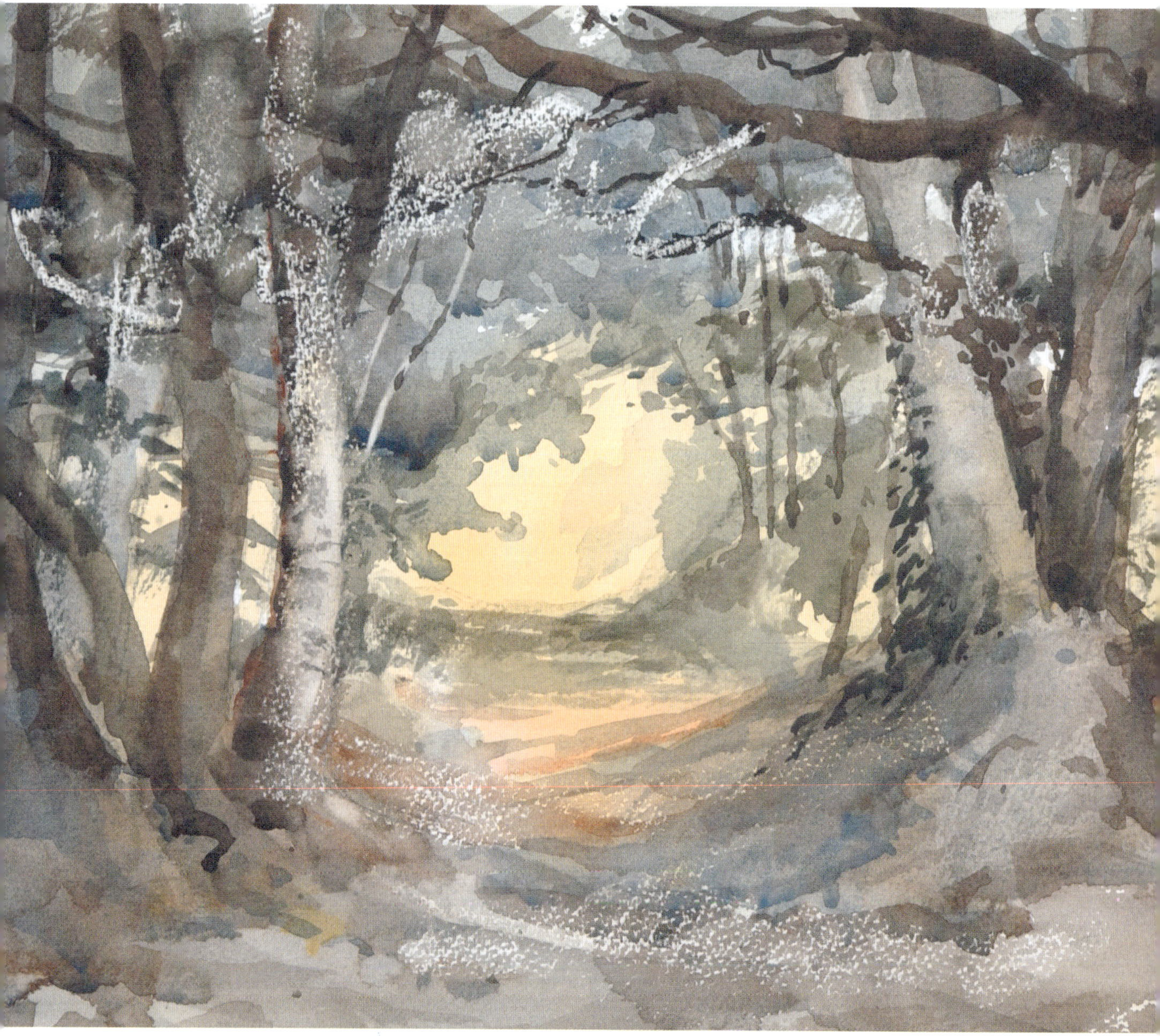

8

woodland glade

john barber

400 x 500mm (16 x 20in)

Trees and foliage are one of the most popular subjects for watercolour painting, yet are among the hardest to get right. The myriad numbers of leaves and branches all reflect different intensities of light and their shapes merge into one another in countless ways. This project shows you how to get the best from woodland scenes by demonstrating how to construct the basic shapes that characterize the natural environment. It then shows you how to build up the large number of tones that, added together, create the broad areas of colour you see when you look at woodland. Last, it shows ways of picking out highlights and creating areas of contrast to add visual interest to your work.

TECHNIQUES FOR THE PROJECT

Masking out with wax

Working wet-in-wet

Working with a dry brush

WHAT YOU WILL NEED

Rough surface watercolour paper
Soft graphite pencils, 6B and 4B
Wax candle
Mop brush, sable or synthetic
Flat brush, 2.5cm (1in), sable or synthetic
Round brushes, no. 5 or 6, sable or synthetic
Hog hair brush
Kitchen paper, natural sponge, and craft knife

COLOUR MIXES

1 Payne's gray
3 Cobalt blue
8 Cadmium yellow
11 Burnt sienna

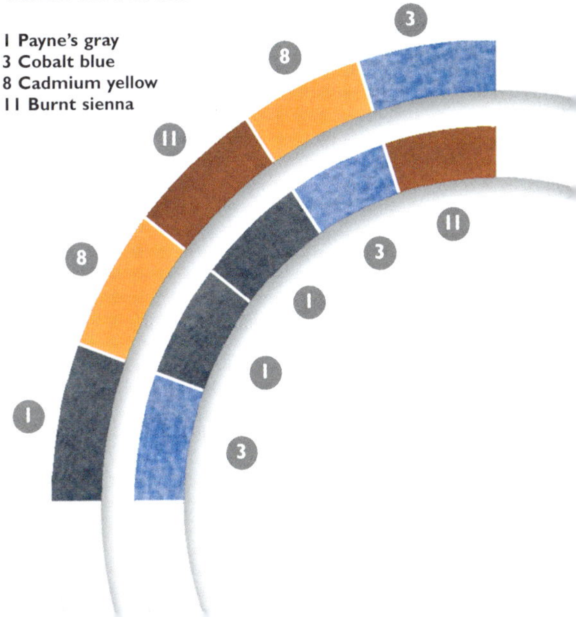

WORKING WITH A DRY BRUSH

By applying an almost dry brush to a dry flat wash, the brush hairs and the surface of the paper will give broken lines or spots of colour. These can be used to create interest in flat areas, to model forms to give the impression of solidity, or indicate a third dimension. Old brushes are often useful in this technique as the hairs spread and deliver many fine dots. Wipe the side of the brush on your scrap paper until the hairs fan out so each hair can make a separate mark. You can also buy a fan brush, which has the hairs permanently spread out by a flat metal ferrule. These are very useful for depicting fur or foliage. Experiment with swift strokes, barely touching the paper, or hit straight down on the paper, which makes marks with the sides of the hairs. In this technique you can work up fine detail and control tone accurately. If you overwork an area, you can dampen it and start again. Albrecht Durer (1471–1528) was a great master of dry brush detail but the American, Andrew Wyeth, has taken the technique even farther in our own time. As with all the techniques of painting, much can be learned by copying and from this you will learn what you need for your own personal style.

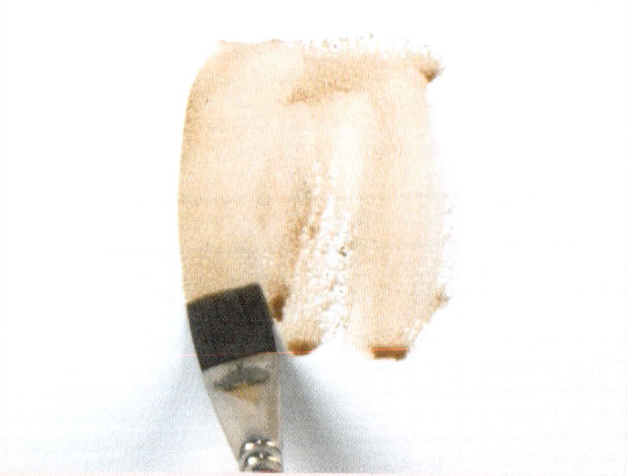

1 Apply a fairly pale wash to rough paper using a flat brush. You are not aiming to lay a smooth wash, just a background tone. You will notice that if you use a quick brush stroke, small amounts of air are trapped under the brush.

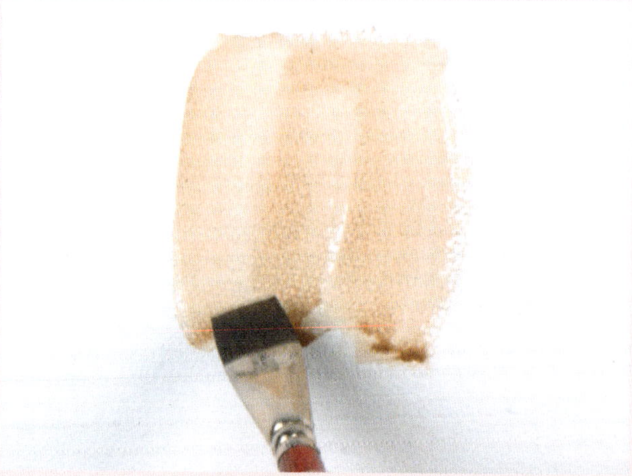

2 The edges of the paint break up on the texture of the rough watercolour paper. This is already painting in the dry brush manner, distinctly different from the crisp edge of flat washes. This can be clearly seen on the right of the illustration.

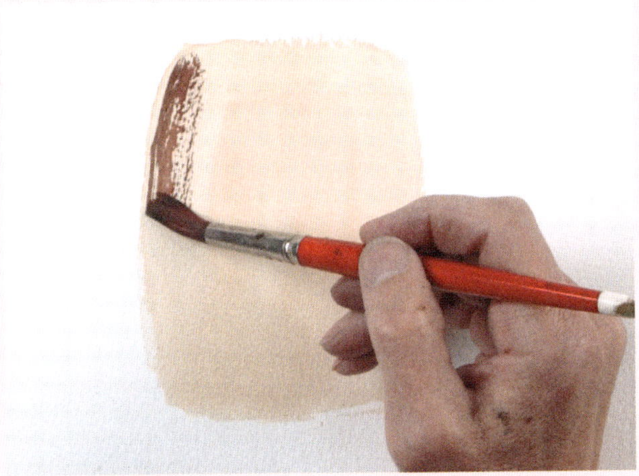

3 Make sure your background patch is dry before you begin overlaying dry brush marks. Dip a round brush in a darker wash and partly dry it on some kitchen paper. Using the side of the brush, pull it swiftly down the paper, without pressing hard.

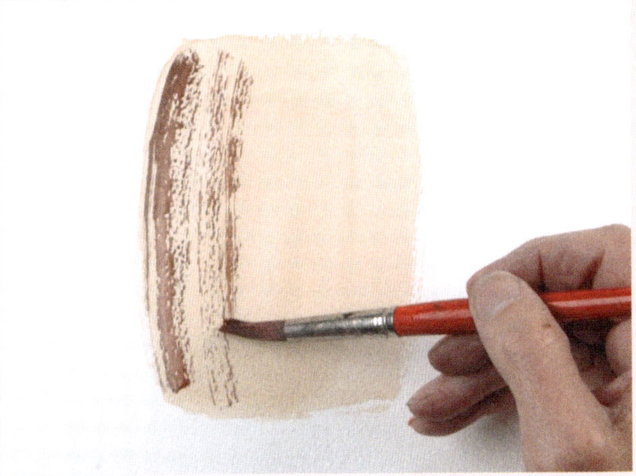

4 Repeat this stroke many times until you get control over three things: The dryness of the brush, the pressure on the brush, and the speed of the brush movement. Practice will give you confidence in your work.

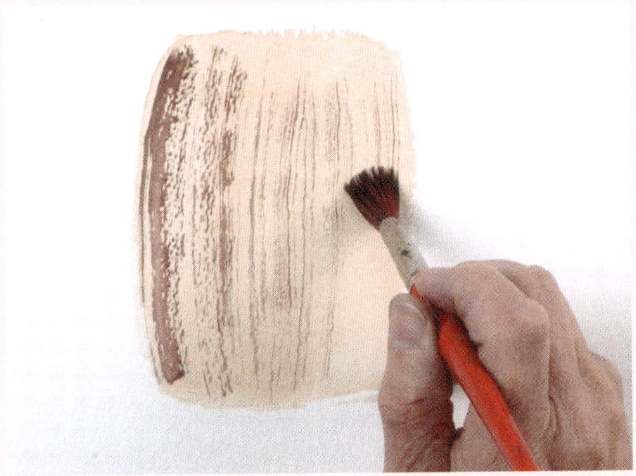

5 In this illustration, you will see how the brush is flattened to a fan shape so that each hair acts as a separate tiny brush. On smooth paper, this will produce fine continuous lines but here they are broken by the surface of the paper.

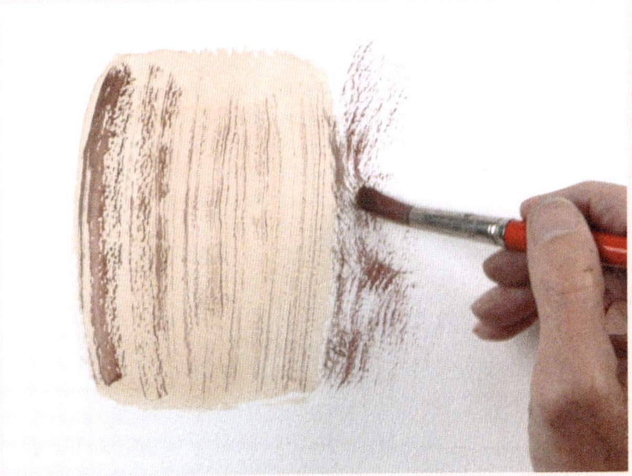

6 Begin to work toward the right, onto the white paper. Note the kind of textures your brush is making. Use the point of the brush as well as scrubbing with the side. Continue making marks until no more paint comes off the brush.

8

woodland glade

Sketch your scene with the soft graphite pencil. Keep your lines loose and relaxed for this sketch, only capturing the outlines of the main trees and loosely marking out areas of dense foliage. It is best not to try to sketch every leaf and branch – you are trying to capture an impression of what you are seeing, rather than record every detail.

REMEMBER

Because of the changing nature of dense woodland, no two artists will ever paint it in the same way. So it is best to regard this project as a way of working rather than something to be copied. This is exactly what will make your painting more personal and, with practice, will form the basis for your own unique style.

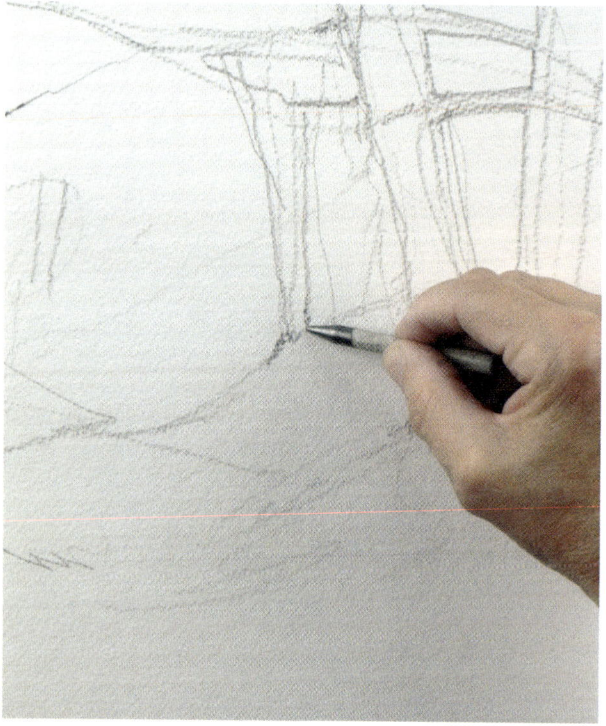

STEP 1

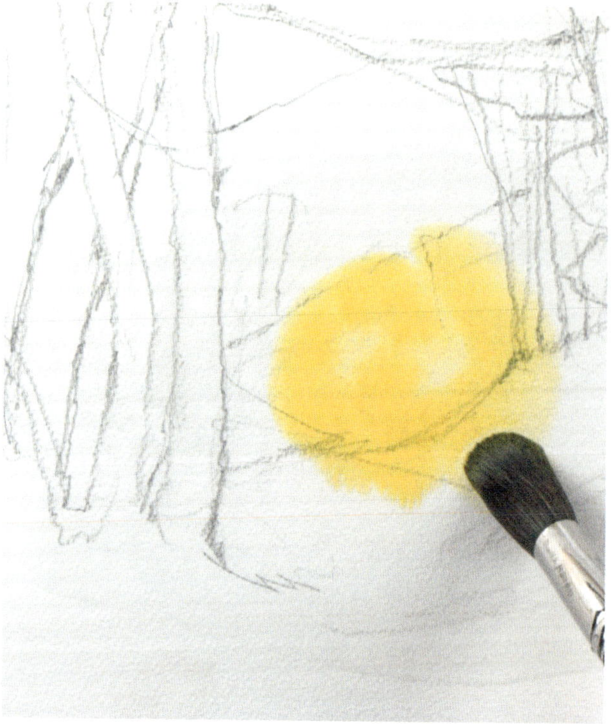

Start painting the central area of your sketch – the focal point – with the mop brush. Lay down an area of clean water, then drop in some cadmium yellow, wet-in-wet.

RIGHT Mask out areas on the upper part of the foliage with the wax candle. Rub the candle over the paper in various random lines. This gives a deliberate 'accidental' coverage rather than precise lines.

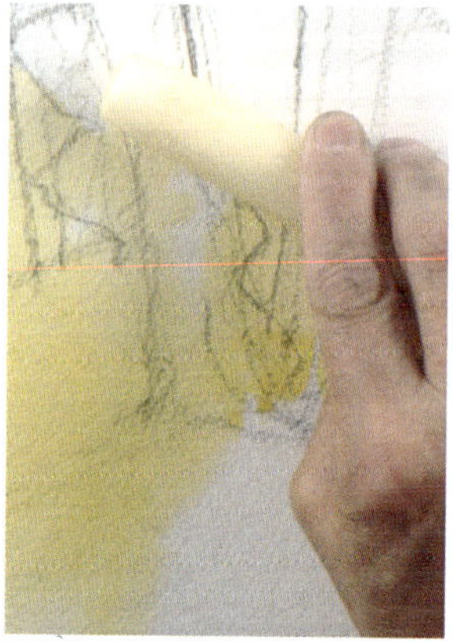

STEP 2

Paint over the top part of the sketch with a mix of cobalt blue and burnt sienna. This produces a grey-green colour, darker than the lighter yellow in the centre. Apply darker colours closer to the edge of the painting to lead the viewer's eye into the middle of the image.

BE CONFIDENT

In a scene like this where the slightest breeze or change of light can alter everything you see, use the brush freely to capture a quick impression. Try loading the brush and using the curved side instead of the point, letting it roll on the paper. Relax your grip on the handle and be surprised by the results.

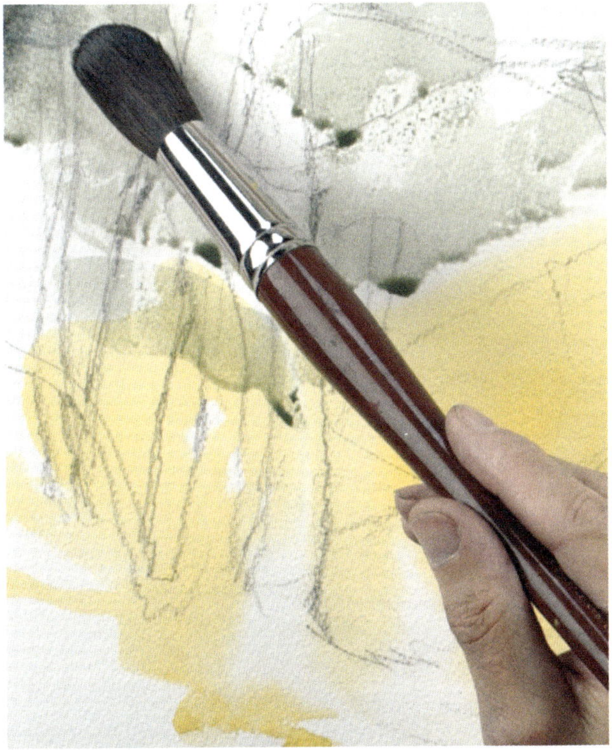

STEP 3

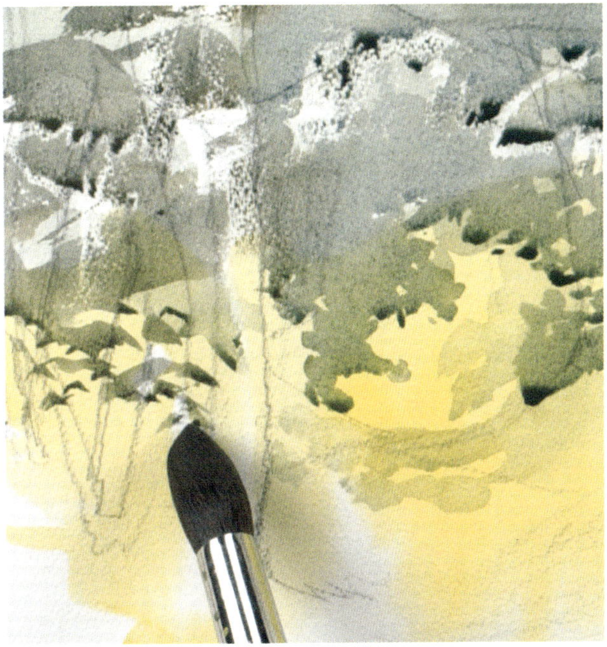

With the tip of the brush, add dabs of the grey-green mix over the top of the cadmium yellow to create a further green shade. This can be done fairly randomly, but don't overdo it. It is also a good way of practicing creating small areas of detail with a big brush.

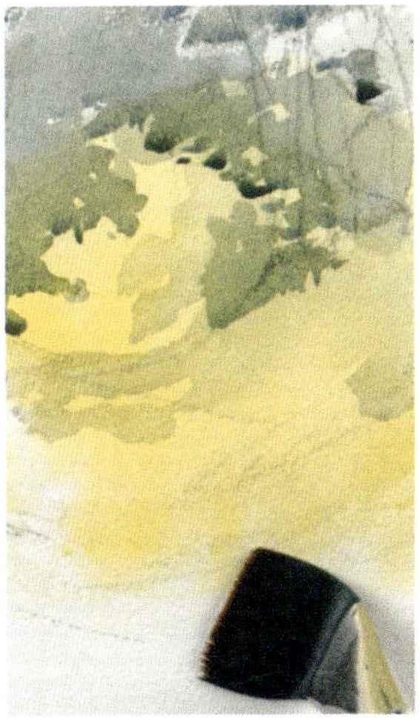

RIGHT Build up colour over the yellow by diluting the grey-green mix and applying it loosely with the flat brush.

STEP 4

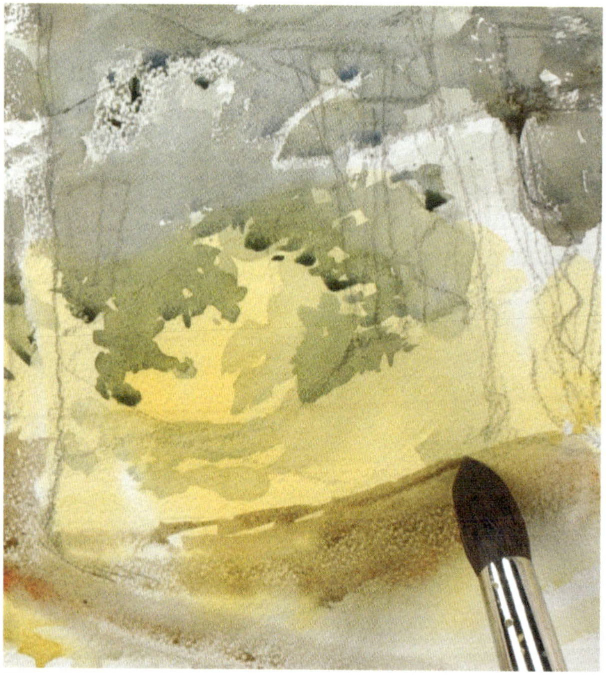

RIGHT Apply different strengths of the same warm mix to the left-hand tree trunks, sometimes covering the whole of the trunk, sometimes just covering one edge. The mix on this trunk has more burnt sienna added for a redder look.

Dilute the red wash to create a different tone and apply this to the right-hand trunks. Overall, aim for a uniform colour scheme that has interesting variations in tone.

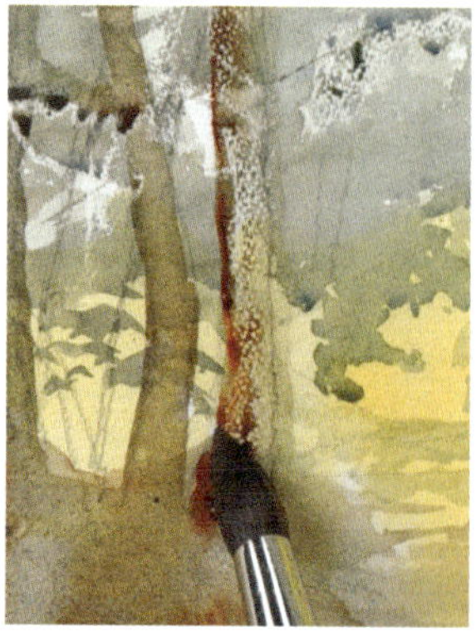

Add more burnt sienna to the grey-green mix to create a warmer shade and apply this to the bottom of the scene, wet-in-wet. Lay down a wash of clean water over the bottom of the painting and drop the warmer colour into it using the mop brush.

RIGHT Notice how a variety of colours are created by the wet-in-wet technique, depending on where the paint runs over the different base colours. These variations create the vast range of tones you see when you look at woodland.

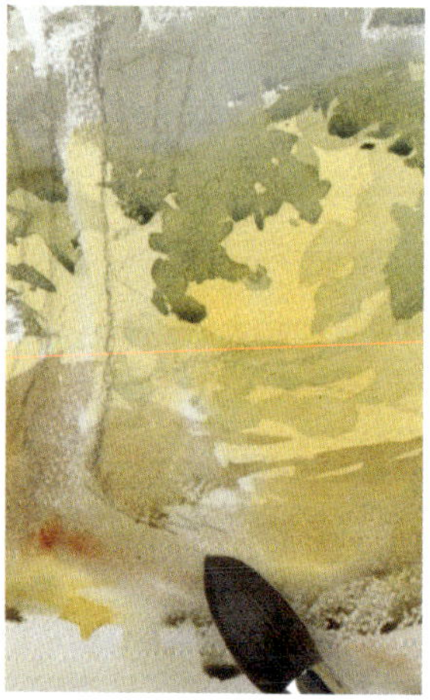

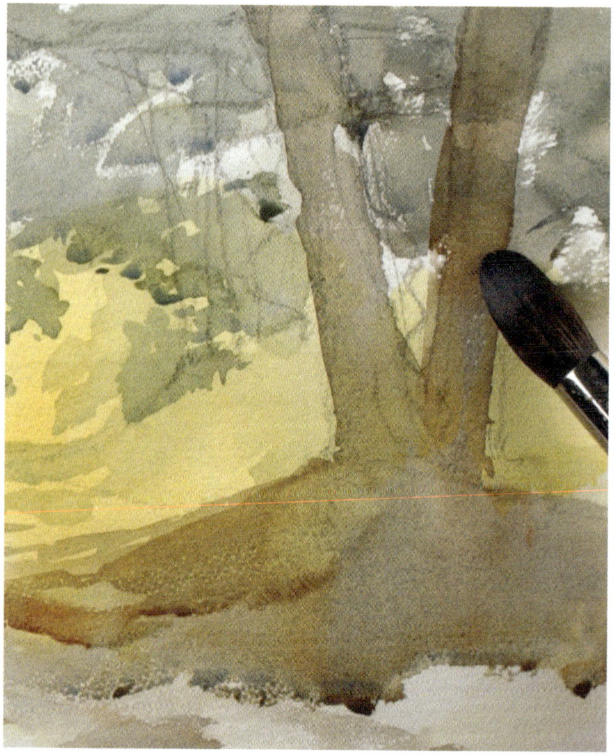

STEP 5

STEP 6

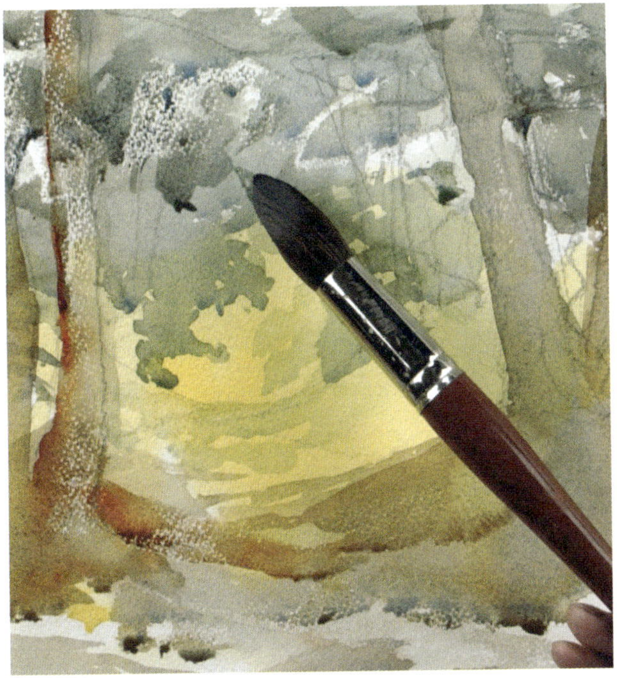

Build up colour over the top foliage with the grey-green colour you mixed earlier, but instead of applying another wash, use the dry brush technique. To do this, load the brush with only a little paint and drag the side of it over the paper. The rough surface will pick up the paint.

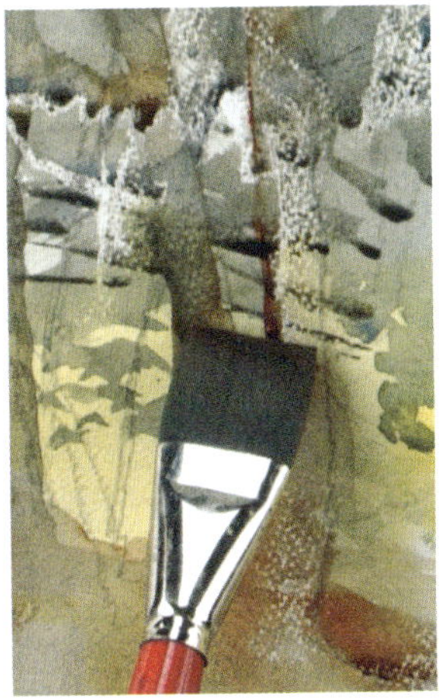

RIGHT Add more cobalt blue to the mix and dip the edge of the flat brush into it. Edge paint onto the paper to form a series of short horizontal lines. These lines break up the more rounded vertical shapes.

STEP 7

RIGHT Another way to create new colours is to mix together paint that is still wet on the paper. If you use the point of the round brush, you can also use this opportunity to create new shapes on the paper.

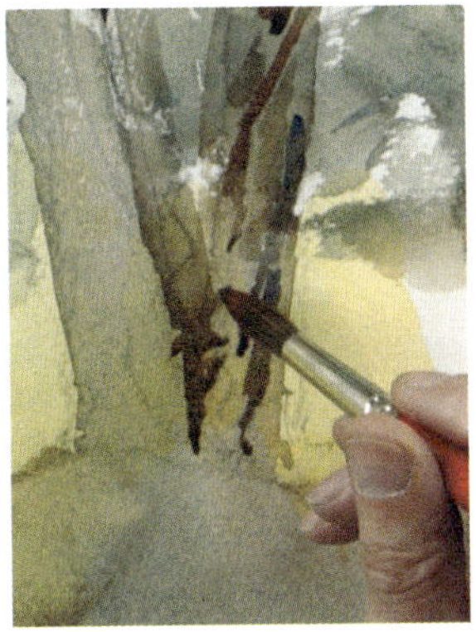

Take a step back from your work and see which areas need more work. Here, we have worked more colour into the foliage at the bottom of the painting with the flat brush.

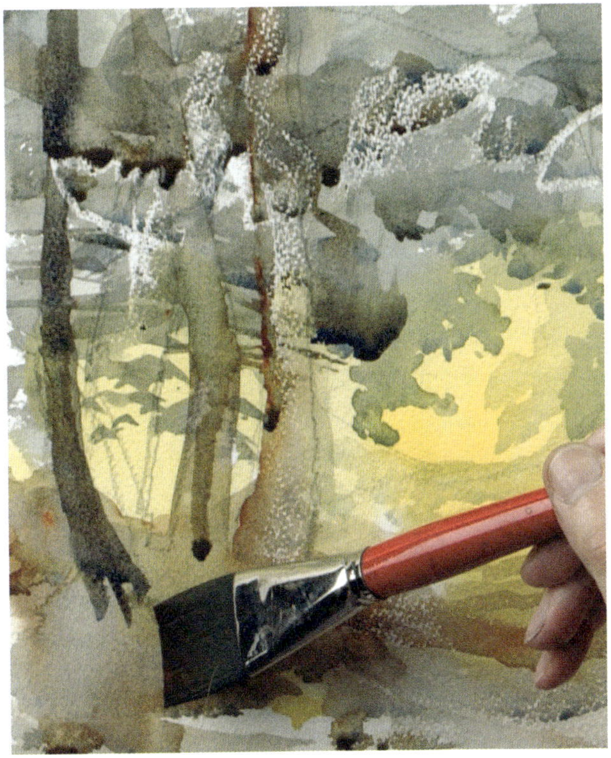

STEP 8

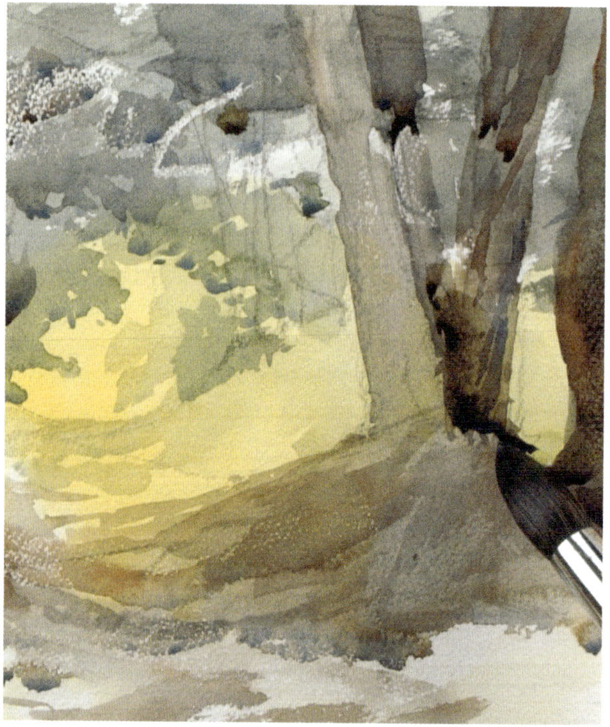

Darken the grey-green mix with Payne's gray and add this shadow colour to selected parts of the painting, such as the base of the tree trunk, using the mop brush. These are the first of the dark shadows so use them sparingly – you can always add more later.

RIGHT Dilute this dark colour slightly and use it to work up more shadows and to graduate any hard edges onto the tree trunks on the left-hand side of the image.

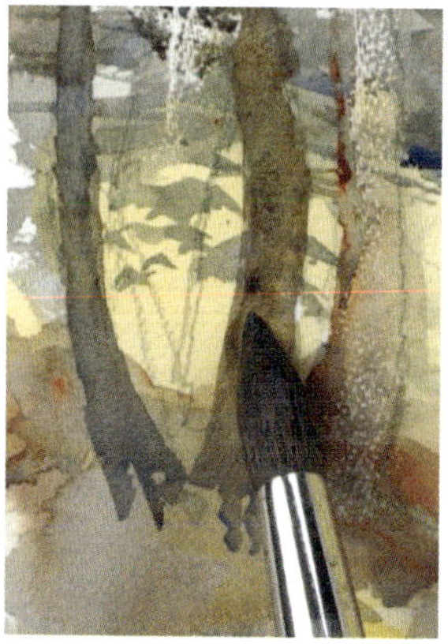

STEP 9

RIGHT With the round brush, build up colour in the middle of the painting using a light mix of cobalt blue, burnt sienna, and a touch of cadmium yellow. Again, graduate any hard edges in this part of your work and add some more detailed foliage with the point of the brush.

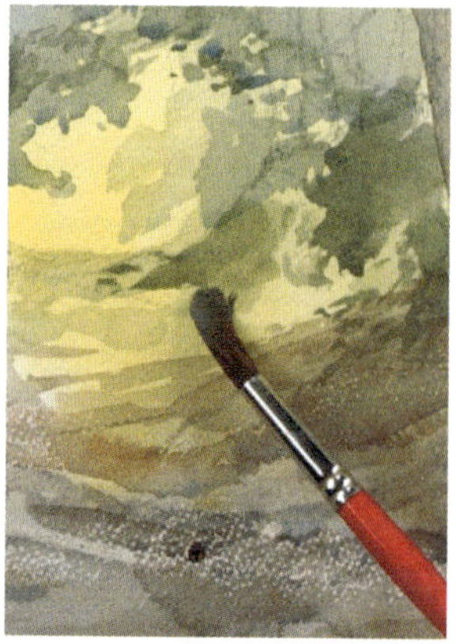

Add a little more burnt sienna to the mix and, using the dry brush technique, work more colour into the base of the trees, again using the round brush.

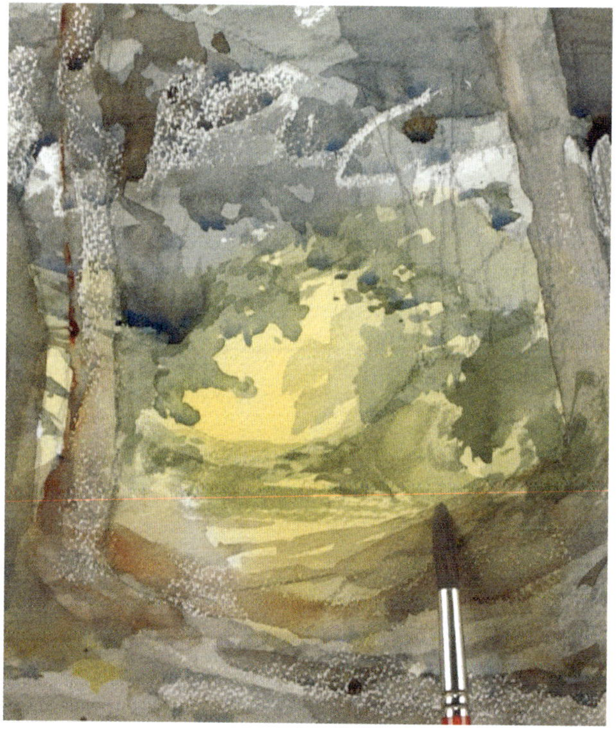

STEP 10

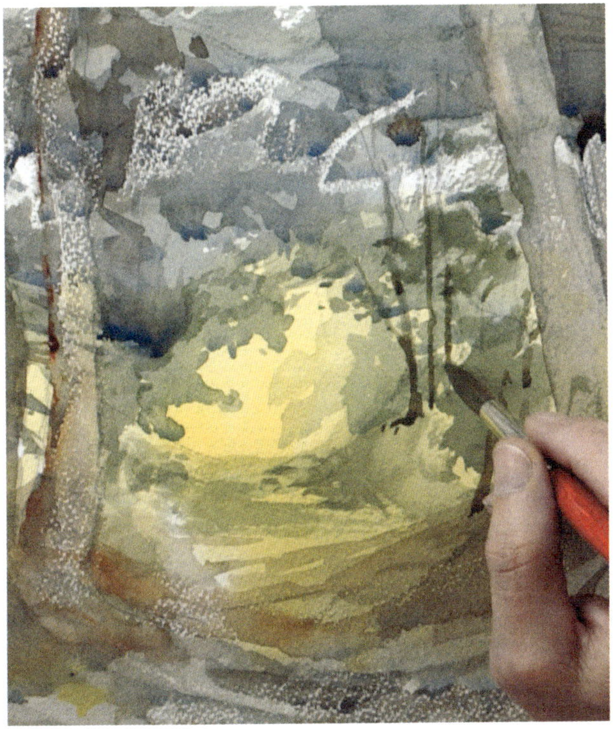

As well as constantly building up shades and colours, you can start adding small areas of detail. Add a little more cobalt blue, burnt sienna, and water to the same mix and paint on some thin vertical lines to indicate background trees. Hold the brush like a pen for accuracy.

RIGHT Work the paint down into the swirl of colour in the middle of the image. This ties the bases of the trees neatly to the rest of the composition.

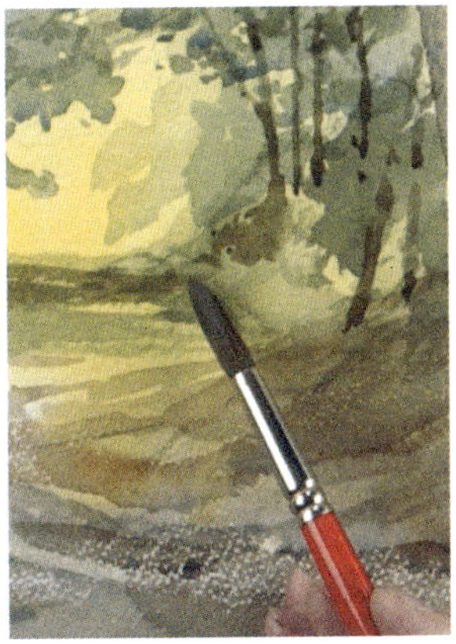

STEP 11

RIGHT Again, take a step back and decide where colour needs to be built up further. Here, we have added more Payne's gray to the same mix, creating a dark colour for the tree trunk on the left.

Touch up other areas around the tree trunks with this colour. Notice how many colours are overlaid on top of each other and how this process creates the vast number of tones you need for a convincing painting.

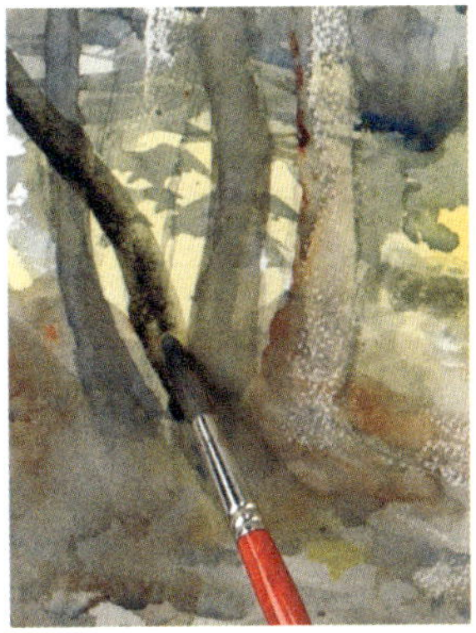

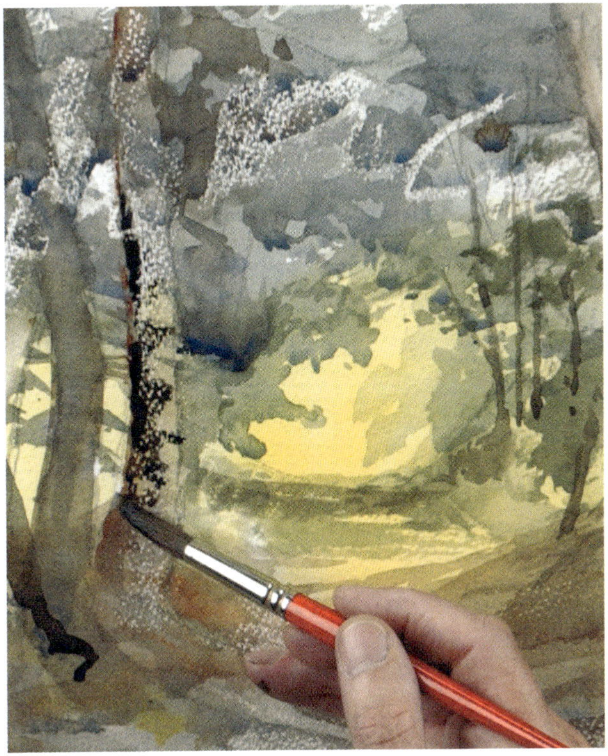

STEP 12

8 woodland glade

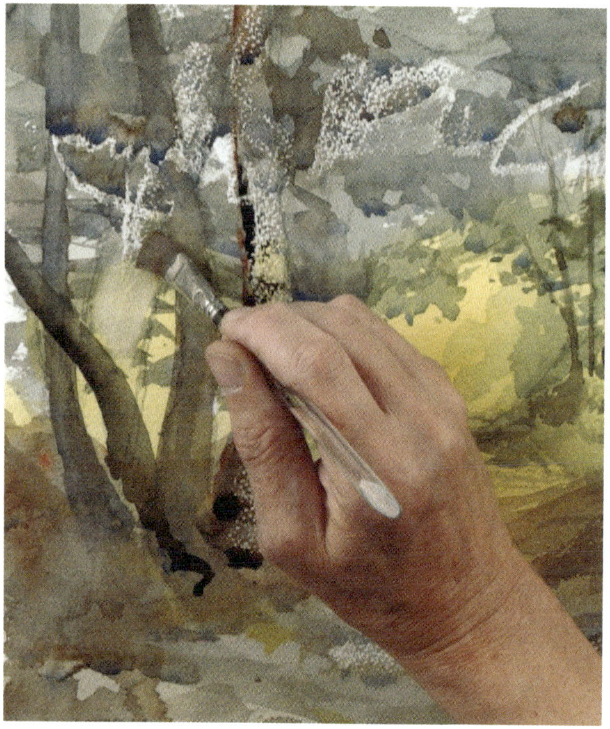

Add some more texture to the trunks using a little Payne's gray. Then work your way around your artwork adding any extra areas of detail with the round brush.

TRICK OF THE TRADE

If you need to lighten an area of paint, like a tree-trunk, use a flat, short-haired hog or bristle brush (as used in oil painting) on wet paper. Work the brush backward and forward using the narrow edge like a small scrubbing brush. You may have to repeat this several times.

Create some lighter accent areas on the background. To do this, dip the hog hair brush in clean water and rub it over the paint. This will lift off the paint.

RIGHT Dab away areas of excess water with some kitchen paper. Work your way up the tree trunk, lifting off as you go. This creates the idea that a shaft of light has fallen between the branches of the trees and is highlighting one of the trunks.

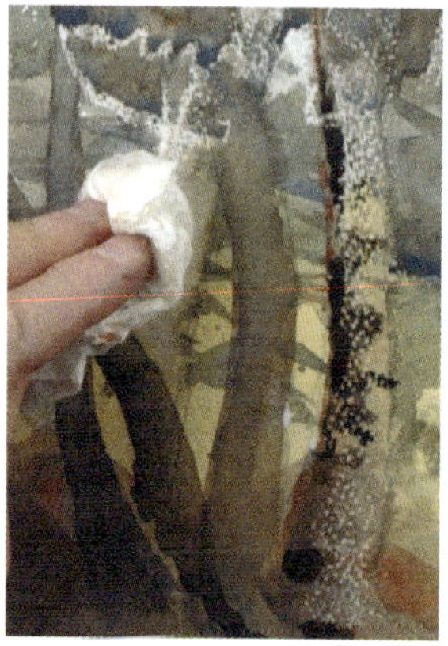

STEP 13

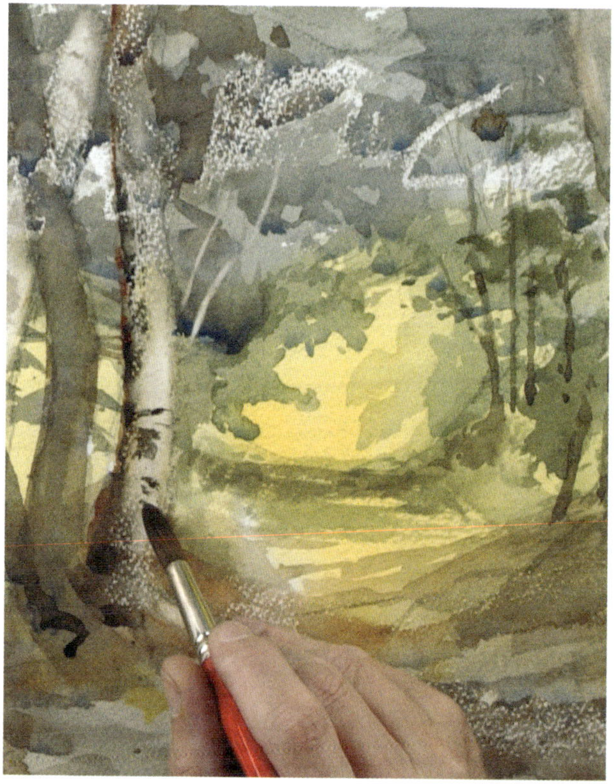

STEP 14

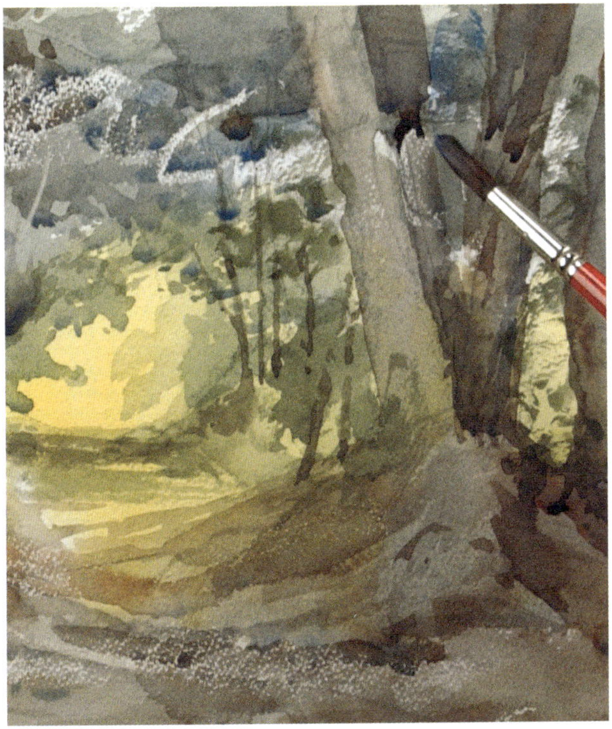

Woodland scenes such as this build up bit by bit, so add shading and detail as you go. Here we have added a little more detail to the shadow area between the trees with a light mix of cobalt blue.

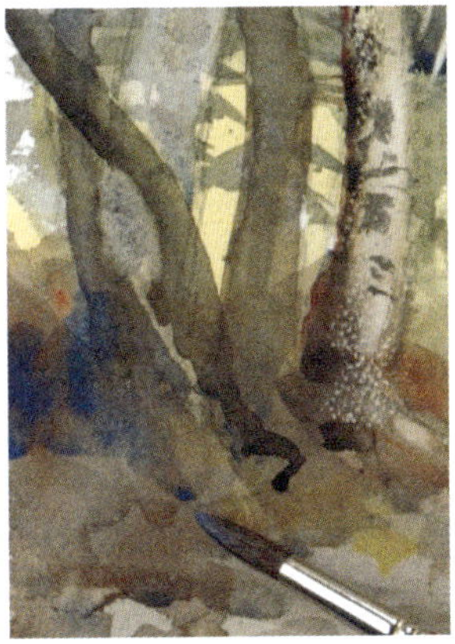

RIGHT Add some more accent colours to the scene using a stronger mix of cobalt blue. Apply this to the woodland floor and to the base of the tree trunks on the left-hand side.

STEP 15

Warm the scene with a light mix of burnt sienna, adding it to the bottom edge of the middle area. Putting this warmer colour here helps lead the viewer's eye to the centre of the scene.

TRICK OF THE TRADE

Dip an old toothbrush in paint and pull a brush handle across the bristles to spatter spots of paint onto your work. Mask all other areas to prevent the paint ending up in unwanted places. This technique is ideal for foliage and small flowers, with dozens of leaves and petals created in barely a few seconds.

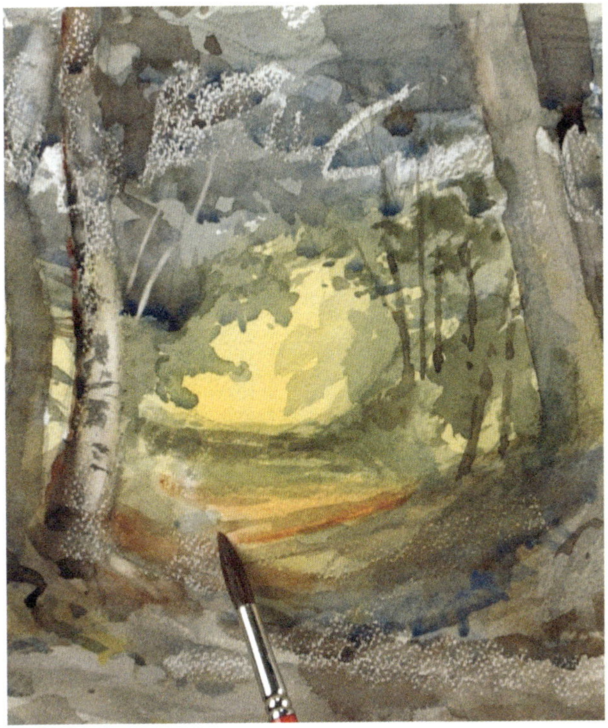

STEP 16

8

woodland glade

RIGHT Mix some burnt sienna, cobalt blue, and Payne's gray. This creates a strong, dark colour, perfect for creating foreground branches. Start by adding these in the top left of the painting.

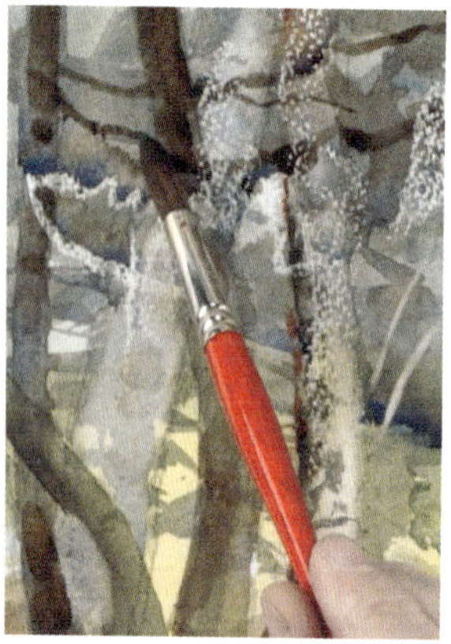

Add more branches across the top right of your work. Paint them on in a variety of shapes and sizes. Add a little Payne's gray to the mix as you work to increase the variety of colours in this part of the image.

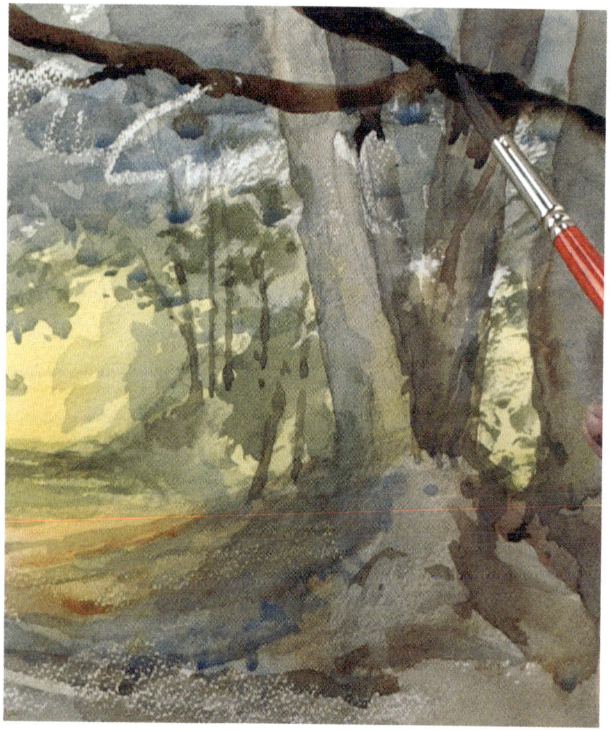

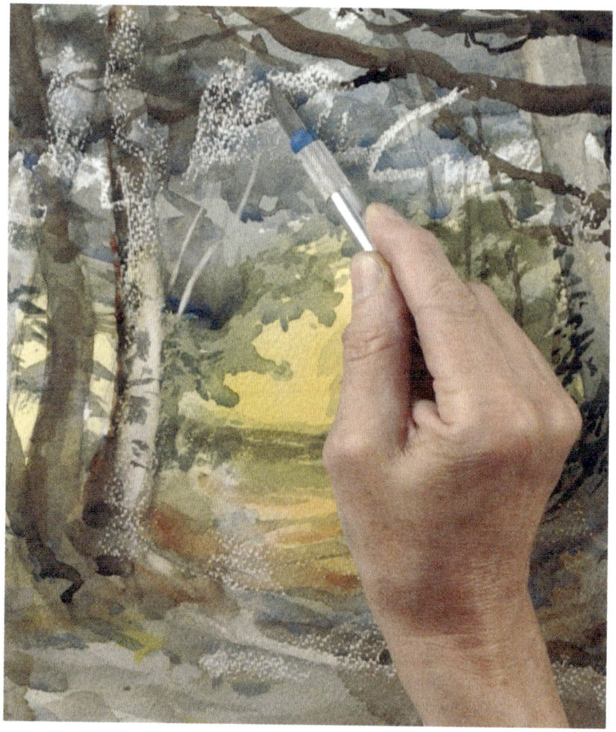

Add some dashes of Payne's gray and cobalt blue to the tree trunks to indicate ivy, then scratch off small areas of paint with a craft knife. This is another technique for clearing an area of paper that is covered by several washes so you can build up finer detail with a smaller brush. Here, we have scratched off some small lines that can be worked up into branches.

TRICK OF THE TRADE

Try gently rubbing the paint on areas that have been overworked with a piece of fine sandpaper. This will bring up little specks of sparkling white paper, ideal for creating lots of areas of reflected light in one go. You can add a colour wash over this if the effect is too obvious – the scratched spots will absorb the paint again.

RIGHT Fill in the scratched off areas you have just created with a mix of Payne's gray, burnt sienna, and cobalt blue. Use the tip of the brush to carefully add in the new branches.

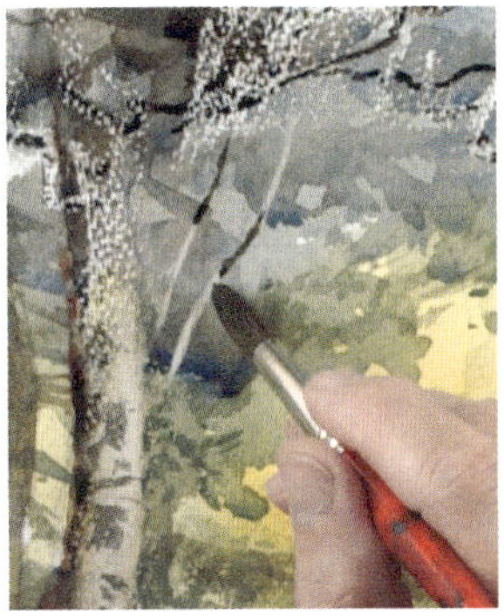

You don't always have to build up colour with paint and a brush – a 4B pencil works well for creating defined areas of detail, especially over the masked-out wax areas.

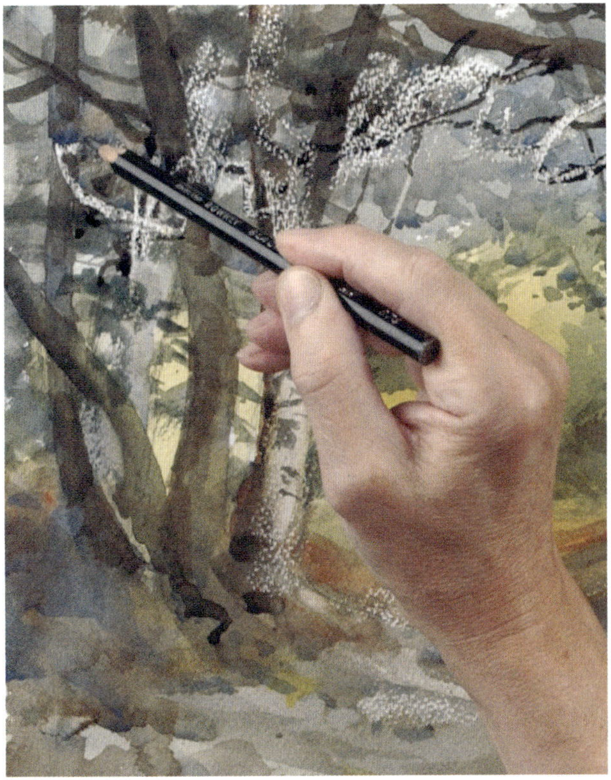

STEP 19

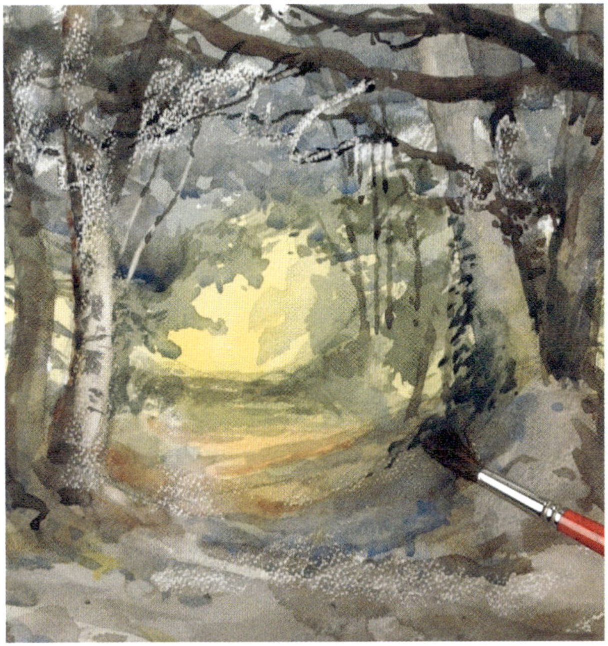

Because the painting is constructed of so many applications of colour, you are bound to end up with some hard edges. Soften these with the edge of a round brush and a little water.

RIGHT Take a final look at your finished work and see where any areas of small detail can be added. Here, we have used the scratching off technique to create extra areas of highlight on the left-hand side of the woodland floor.

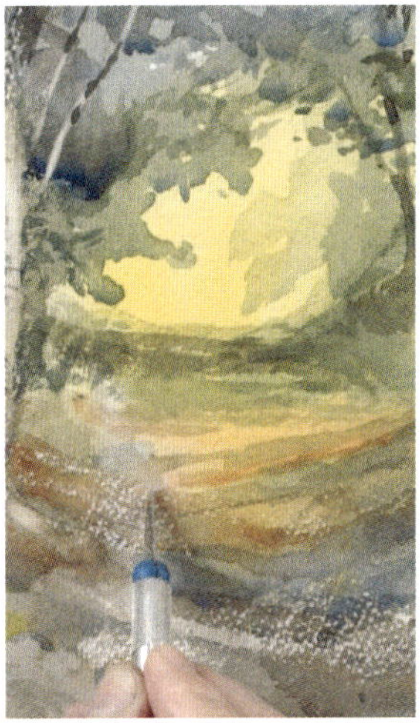

STEP 20

index

index

Picture credits

All artworks by John Barber except: p. 10 (right) © Margaret Dinkeldein; p. 11 © Roger Hutchins; and pp. 40–49 © as credited to individual artists.

Author's acknowledgments

I would like to thank my wife, Theresa, for her loving support during the countless hours I spent in the studio preparing this book. And many thanks to John Broad of the Honor Oak Gallery for his friendship and help with the paintings in the gallery section.